D1366431

Future Bright

FUTURE BRIGHT
A Transforming Vision of Human Intelligence

Michael E. Martinez

3874 9715

OXFORD
UNIVERSITY PRESS

East Baton Rouge Parish Library
Baton Rouge, Louisiana

OXFORD
UNIVERSITY PRESS

Oxford University Press is a department of the University of Oxford.
It furthers the University's objective of excellence in research, scholarship,
and education by publishing worldwide.

Oxford   New York
Auckland   Cape Town   Dar es Salaam   Hong Kong   Karachi
Kuala Lumpur   Madrid   Melbourne   Mexico City   Nairobi
New Delhi   Shanghai   Taipei   Toronto

With offices in
Argentina   Austria   Brazil   Chile   Czech Republic   France   Greece
Guatemala   Hungary   Italy   Japan   Poland   Portugal   Singapore
South Korea   Switzerland   Thailand   Turkey   Ukraine   Vietnam

Oxford is a registered trademark of Oxford University Press in the UK and certain other
countries.

Published in the United States of America by
Oxford University Press
198 Madison Avenue, New York, NY 10016

© Oxford University Press 2013

All rights reserved. No part of this publication may be reproduced, stored in a
retrieval system, or transmitted, in any form or by any means, without the prior
permission in writing of Oxford University Press, or as expressly permitted by law,
by license, or under terms agreed with the appropriate reproduction rights organization.
Inquiries concerning reproduction outside the scope of the above should be sent to the
Rights Department, Oxford University Press, at the address above.

You must not circulate this work in any other form
and you must impose this same condition on any acquirer.

Library of Congress Cataloging-in-Publication Data
Martinez, Michael E.
Future bright : a transforming vision of human intelligence / Michael E. Martinez.
    pages cm
ISBN 978–0–19–978184–3
1. Intellect.   I. Title.
BF431.M38367 2013
153.9—dc23
2012042790

9 8 7 6 5 4 3 2 1
Printed in the United States of America
on acid-free paper

Dedicated to Lindy, Kiely, Amy, and Hillary

CONTENTS

FOREWORD

Over the last 50 years, the United States and many other developed countries have transitioned from an industrial economy based on manual labor in factories to a postindustrial economy based on cognitively challenging use of new information and communication technologies. Whereas previously one's livelihood typically depended on securing a permanent unionized factory job, today those jobs are much rarer, and success largely depends on the ability to read critically, write cogently, analyze complex data, solve problems, and communicate effectively in multiple media with people around the world. In other words, the age of intelligence is upon us.

Michael Martinez has done more than perhaps anyone else to elucidate the significance of this age. *Future Bright* distills his 30 years of research on what intelligence is, why and how it varies, the relationship of intelligence to the mind and brain, the nature–nurture dilemma, and how experience can cultivate intelligence. He proposes and eloquently explains his vision of the structure of human intelligence, which, in his view, is rooted in *fluid intelligence* (the ability to solve problems), *crystallized intelligence* (accumulated knowledge), and *effective character* (a "smart heart"). And perhaps most important, he presents proven strategies that individuals, parents, and schools can put in place to foster the development of intelligence.

Sadly, Professor Martinez passed away on April 5, 2012, at the age of 55 after nearly a decade-long battle with cancer. I had the good fortune of working closely with Michael during the last 12 years of his life. Michael was the epitome of everything he has written about, radiating the kind of problem-solving ability, accumulated wisdom, and effective character that he discusses in his book. He pursued intellectual problems vigorously for decades, always with a deeply critical spirit and a complete open mind. He touched the lives of dozens of graduate students and thousands of undergraduates with his compelling and democratic vision of how the mind works. He involved scores of these students in his own research projects, and especially in his most recent "Brain Boost" project, which put his ideas into practice through practical hands-on programs to raise the intelligence of children in local public schools. He lived a rich and stimulating life through his faith and family, his deep and long-lasting friendships, his lifetime commitment to good health and exercise, and his passion for adventure.

The world will miss Michael Martinez, but fortunately he has left something of great value behind. *Future Bright* shows how all of us can strive to live as intelligently as Michael did, and help our children do so as well. It is Michael's legacy.

Mark Warschauer

ACKNOWLEDGMENTS

I would like to acknowledge the people who helped bring this book to completion. A number of people read and commented on the manuscript at earlier stages, including Doug Piper, Scott Wood, Michael's wife, Stephanie Martinez, and his four daughters, Lindy Stice, Kiely James, Amy Lajiness, and Hillary Martinez. After Michael's untimely death, Lindsey Richland, Jeneen Graham, and Robert Calfee all provided input during the publishing process. And I am especially grateful to the editorial, production, and marketing staff at Oxford University Press for their unwavering and expert commitment to this book every step along the way.

Finally, I would like to give special recognition to Janice Hansen, a former PhD student and collaborator of Michael's. Janice was heavily involved in supporting this book's publication both before and after Michael's death. She read and provided very thoughtful feedback on multiple versions of the manuscript, carefully read the copyedited versions provided by OUP, and responded to the editors' inquiries. She also helped gather information for marketing materials, catalogue copy, and other documents vital for the book's success. The Martinez family and I are deeply indebted to Janice for the dedicated support that she provided.

—Mark Warschauer
Professor and Associate Dean
School of Education
University of California, Irvine

INTRODUCTION

You've been thinking about intelligence in the wrong way. Almost every-one assumes that intelligence is a genetically programmed trait like eye color—set from birth and unalterable. Yet the extensive body of research on human intelligence demonstrates that this assumption is false. Our best data show that IQ, the most common measure of intelligence, fluctuates within a person's lifetime as well as from generation to generation. This is our conceptual starting point: IQ scores are changeable. This central fact raises the all-important question of what causes IQ scores to shift up or down. The question is interesting, certainly, but it is also tremendously important, because it implies that with the right environment intelligence levels can be increased intentionally. This possibility holds implications for you and for the world around you. It is the conceptual centerpiece of *Future Bright*.

For a moment, imagine a world in which the average person's intelligence is much higher than it is currently. Would such a world be different than the present one? Now consider what it would be like if your own intelligence became significantly higher. At a minimum, the prospect is intriguing, perhaps so much so that you might feel compelled to learn more about it and, if possible, to put some of the presented ideas to the test. All these possibilities engage our imagination because intelligence is not a trivial quality with marginal importance to the world. Intuitively, we know it's crucial. More than ever, in fact, intelligence is essential to living an effective life. The skilled use of the human mind has always been important, but in the 21st century intelligence has moved to center stage as the key resource of effective human activity. To be optimally effective, people in every walk of life must be equipped to think, work, and live intelligently. Intelligence is therefore pivotal to individual and collective survival and success, and to prosperity.

Future Bright advances a powerful idea: Human intelligence is modifiable. This idea clashes with the outdated but still widely held assumption that intelligence is determined at birth and fixed for life. This book shows, instead, that intelligence can shift from generation to generation, a fact proven by the discovery of rising IQs in the 20th century. As the work and life experience of the human population morphed radically, so did intelligence. IQs rose steadily around the world. The power of life experience to raise intelligence also holds for individuals. Research tells us that, with the right kinds of experience, intelligence can be learned and IQ scores will rise in parallel.

Learnable intelligence is more than an interesting fact; it's vital to everyday life. That's because intelligence is foundational to success in every major arena—in schools, on the job, and in the broader contexts of life. More than that, learnable intelligence is essential for the survival and prosperity of organizations, economies, and nations—and indeed the entire planet. These startling ideas form the core of *Future Bright*. Together, they present a vision of human potential for the individual person as well as the collective good.

Future Bright

CHAPTER 1

The Sine Qua Non of Success

What makes for success in today's world? One thing is sure: It's not what it used to be. That's because the nature of human enterprise has shifted radically from prior decades. During the 20th century, three broad segments could be identified—white-collar professionals, blue-collar laborers, and clerical workers. This segmentation of the labor force has long been considered outmoded.[1] The key emergent sector of labor is composed of workers whose primary activity is to work not with their hands, but with their minds. Increasingly, the workplace demands people who know how to gather, interpret, and act on information, not assembly line parts or raw materials. Former secretary of labor Robert Reich called these workers *symbolic analysts*.[2] They constitute the most highly sought-after workers in every field, and they are the best rewarded monetarily. Human intelligence is now the unrivaled capital resource of the 21st century workforce.

The economic value of intelligent minds is supported by data showing that more education usually translates to better pay. This is not too surprising—we expect that, on average, a college graduate will be paid more than a worker with a high school education. This pay gap, commonly known as the wage premium or earnings differential, is well established. More interesting is that wage premiums have been growing over time. Gaps in wages have increased among workers with varying levels of education—those holding advanced degrees, college graduates, high school graduates, and workers with less than a high school education. Over the past three decades, pay rates have been drifting upward for workers with bachelor's or advanced degrees. For high school graduates, hourly wages have remained flat or trended slightly down, and workers with less than a high school diploma earned significantly less each year.[3]

What is responsible for the growing wage premium? It seems as though supply and demand ought to figure into the rising economic value of a highly educated workforce. If so, this presents a puzzle because a growing proportion of the labor force is highly educated. By itself, a greater supply of highly educated workers ought to drive down wages. The obvious conclusion is that the rising wage premium is associated with increasing demand. As never before, the labor market needs highly educated workers and rewards with them with wages that reflect their economic value. That value reflects not only a more knowledgeable worker, but also a more intelligent one—a college degree translates into a 10- to 15-point IQ advantage.[4] A university degree is therefore a proxy for a more intelligent mind.

Mental proficiency is demanded by the world economy partly because of the massive infusion of computers into the workplace and every corner of human endeavor. Until the invention of the computer, mental work was the province of the human mind. The succession of technologies through the ages, accelerating in the Industrial Revolution of the 1800s, greatly leveraged muscle power. Labor-saving inventions resulted in economic efficiencies that led to greater democratization of wealth and a growing middle class. There were downsides as well, including risks of a ravaged environment and a dehumanized worker.

As late as 1970, blue-collar and clerical workers could realistically pursue the American Dream. This is no longer the case. Skilled labor, though not completely outmoded, has for years been at risk for replacement by robotic technologies or outsourcing to whatever nation can supply the cheapest labor. Long gone are the days when skilled labor promised a pathway to the middle class. Physical labor and routine clerical work have been downgraded in their value to the economy as evidenced by declining pay rates and by the disturbing term "the working poor." The rise of symbolic analysts signals an irrevocable shift in the nature of work. Over the past few decades, intellectual ability has moved to center stage. Mental work, not physical labor, is the engine of economic growth and prosperity.

For all the profound effects of technology on life and work, what was protected until recently was the human mind's monopoly over information processing. With the advent of digital computing, machines began to encroach on this domain with rising insistence. Never before had civilizations faced this most remarkable of human inventions—machines that could think. Labor adapted by trying to understand what indispensable roles the human mind could play as computers took over many functions of processing and storing information. Over time, machines became more than complements; now they were competitors. Consequently, the human mind is forced to concentrate on the things it does best. The question we must ask is: What functions of the human mind cannot be imitated by any machine, no matter how sophisticated?

Intelligence, the hub of human intellectual capability, is the most empowering technology of all. But to capitalize on this potential, we must try to understand specific expressions of intelligence on which the human mind has a monopoly—the things it can do better than any machine. We can begin by noting that computers excel at any task that can be reduced to a set of logical rules. Even this simple fact has consequences. Clerical workers once identified as secretaries no longer function simply as conveyers of information—taking notes, retrieving files, and composing memos. Administrative assistants must perform a range of tasks from managing large databases to coordinating complex schedules and timelines, as well as tracking priorities and deadlines. In this way clerical workers adapted by drawing more fully on skills best identified with the human intellect. Computers have transformed blue-collar labor as well. Machines that are computer-controlled help explain declines of blue-collar workers. Routine work, whether cognitive or manual, is increasingly consigned to computers or computer-controlled machinery.

What, then, is the province of the mind? The human intellect seems to be unrivaled in at least two ways. First, it is the world's best problem solver. Whereas computers deal nimbly with routines, the mind is fantastically good at making sense of complex information and using that information to solve problems. Through its capacity for creative insight, the human intellect can detect patterns and pathways that often remain opaque to even the most advanced computational devices. When ambiguity complicates the picture of any worthwhile endeavor or enterprise, computers operate best as helpful complements. The human mind must lead the way.

The second signature strength of the human intellect is in coordinating work that requires facile social interaction. To be productive in such situations, fluid communication must be combined with sensitivity to the emotional tone of interactions. This means the effective worker must take into account the myriad ways in which people differ—in personality, drive, work habits, acumen, experience, and cultural norms. Sensitivity to human differences underlies the ability to achieve functional collaboration to reach important goals. Workers must increasingly work in varied teams and across international and cultural boundaries. On these two key aspects of modern work—expert problem solving and complex communication—the human mind still reigns supreme.[5]

As the nature of work has shifted from physical labor in factories to mental production of inventive ideas, computers have forced the question of what only human beings can do well.[6] We now know the answer: The key human resource is intelligence—especially those forms of intelligent expression performed exclusively by capable minds. Intelligence in its various manifestations is the invisible dynamo of the global economy. It's also essential to solving complex social and environmental issues. Communities and nations alike face seemingly intractable problems of environmental threat, depletion of nonrenewable energy sources, ethnic tension, and political strife. The real world presents a tangle of troubles so complex that it's easy to despair. Indeed, there is little hope of solving our most recalcitrant problems apart from a tremendous reserve of human intelligence, allied with wisdom and goodwill.

In this book we will explore why intelligence is vital to human effectiveness in school, in the workplace, and in everyday life. We will probe the meaning of the word *intelligence*, how conceptions of intelligence have changed over time, and what the best current research on intelligence says about its nature. Most important, we will pose the question, "Can intelligence be increased?" We will find that the answer to that question opens wide vistas of hope and possibility for individuals and communities—and, indeed, for the entire human race.

MEASURING THE MIND

The scientific study of intelligence can be traced back to the mid-19th century. In 1869, the British scholar Francis Galton published a book entitled *Hereditary Genius* in which he declared that people differ greatly in their intellectual gifts, and that those differences are inborn. In his book, Galton asserted these assumptions plainly:

> I have no patience with the hypothesis...that babies are born pretty much alike....I object to pretensions of natural equality. The experiences of the nursery, the school, the University, and of professional careers, are chains of proof to the contrary.[7]

Yet Galton was no mere ideologue. He was prepared to put his ideas to the test using both biographical and scientific data. In his biographical analysis, Galton identified 1,000 men whom he regarded as "geniuses." These were men whose intellectual and creative leadership left an enduring mark on society and culture. Galton assumed that eminence was rare, occurring about once in every thousand men. The question was whether this rare quality, genius, was randomly scattered or whether eminence ran in families. Galton's assumptions seemed to be confirmed: Men who were famous for their enduring accomplishments were more likely than their more common peers to have eminent sons and grandsons. Galton had a ready explanation: The cause of familial eminence was that highly accomplished relatives shared a common pool of superior genes (thus the title of his book, *Hereditary Genius*). Notice that Galton's hypothesis hints strongly at a similar concept from the theory of evolution, biological fitness. The connection is no accident: Galton's cousin was the famous proponent of evolution by natural selection, Charles Darwin.

Galton emphasized genetics and downplayed the environment as the basis for eminence.[8] One reason for doing so is that many of the eminent men Galton studied grew up in poor families.[9] Galton thought that if genius could arise from poverty, then its source must be genetic inevitability. But this tendency to favor nature rather than nurture may not have been a purely scientific deduction. As a member of the British social elite, Galton may have wanted to justify the social position of the wealthy British class by proving that their (and his) high station was a natural consequence of superior biology. If Galton's hypothesis could be proven correct, then social stratification was as expectable as any other fact of nature. Though Galton's motives can be questioned, his zeal for measurable data to test his hypothesis was genuine. He knew that sweeping claims about human nature must be backed by evidence, and he launched an ambitious program of research to explore these claims.

By virtue of his quirky personality, Galton was perfectly suited to test his ideas. He collected mountains of data bearing on his research questions. Galton was particularly enamored with quantifying human characteristics, sometimes to the point of obsession. Galton was even reputed to rank the beauty of women he observed in various cities of Britain by surreptitiously recording his ratings of female passersby on paper tucked into his pocket. His serious work, though, concentrated not on superficial qualities, but on low-level biological capabilities, such as the ability to distinguish between fine differences in colors, tones, and weights. Here we see Galton's assumptions asserted: If people differ in their fundamental biology, then those differences will eventually give rise to variability in their achievements in the world. To understand giftedness at the level of basic biology, Galton studied the activities of wool sorters, tea tasters, and piano tuners, believing that their honed skills were based on their abilities to sense fine distinctions through their senses.[10]

Galton was enterprising in his data collection. At the International Health Exhibition held in London in 1884, he charged participants a fee to take measurements of their sensory acuity, reaction time, and the like. With data in hand, Galton compared the biological characteristics of common Londoners with Fellows of the Royal Society.[11] The result? Galton's hypothesis was not confirmed: Wealthy British men exhibited no obvious biological superiority on Galton's measurements.[12] Francis Galton's grand hypothesis—that higher social echelons were distinguished by measurable biological superiority—was not backed by evidence. Yet Galton's place in the history had already been established: His obsession, the quantification of human characteristics, became foundational to the branch of psychology known as psychometrics. Anyone who has taken a standardized test has experienced the practical consequences of Galton's legacy, because the science of psychometrics underlies the construction, analysis, and interpretation of test results. For this profound contribution to science, Galton is recognized as the father of mental measurement.

Galton made additional contributions to the science of human traits. For example, he identified connections between psychological characteristics and genetic heritability, echoing the theory of his cousin Charles Darwin in *The Origin of Species*. Galton also distinguished between identical and fraternal twins, noting that identical twins were more likely to share psychological traits. The identical/fraternal distinction later proved to be profoundly important to modern studies on the heritability of traits. Collectively, Galton's insights became foundational to the modern field of behavioral genetics, which quantifies the contribution of genes to human variation in disease, mental illness, personality, intelligence, and other traits. Although Francis Galton was mistaken in many of his beliefs and assumptions, equally often he was tremendously insightful. His legacy of ideas, insights, and methods extends to this very day, illuminating the biological basis of human characteristics in their panoramic diversity.

THE FIRST INTELLIGENCE TESTS

In Victorian England, Francis Galton launched a new paradigm of scientific inquiry by quantifying human traits, and by using precise measurements to test his theories with a degree of objectivity. Galton focused on such low-level biological traits as reaction time, by implication neglecting higher-level thinking. But if low-level traits could be quantified, why not higher-level expressions of memory, comprehension, and problem solving—the kinds of mental activity that we readily associate with the word *intelligence*? Although Galton himself did not pursue this possibility, it wasn't long before other scholars extended the new field of mental measurement to include high-order cognition. In the late 1890s, the French psychologist Alfred Binet took measurement exactly in this crucial new direction, with profound results.

Just before the turn of the century, administrators of the Paris school system presented Alfred Binet, already a famous psychologist, with a challenging problem. The administrators wanted to understand why some children were experiencing difficulty learning in school. Their concerns were practical. They wanted to separate students into two categories: children whose learning problems were caused by low intellectual ability and those who had the mental capability to succeed but failed for other reasons, such as poor motivation.[13] The school system commissioned Binet to solve this puzzle, namely, to find a way to distinguish between the two categories of students. In response, Binet constructed what we now recognize as the world's first true test of intelligence. It included puzzles, memory games, and questions about general knowledge. It was a grab bag of intellectual probes, not a coherent set of questions, yet it got the job done. Binet's test was surprisingly accurate at predicting children's school success. The test identified children unlikely to thrive in normal school settings—those who required adaptations if they were to succeed.

In devising his test, Alfred Binet shifted the focus of attention to higher-level mental activity—a huge change from Galton's method. Importantly, Binet also found a way to place these measurements on a common scale. Binet's innovation was "mental age." The concept is straightforward. If child's mental ability matches the average of peers of the same chronological age, then his mental age and chronological age are identical. More typically, though, his mental age will be somewhat lower or higher than the average of his peers. For this reason, it's not only possible but important to separate chronological age from mental age. For example, a precocious six-year-old child might exhibit mental qualities more typical of a seven-year-old. In this case, the child's chronological age is six, but his mental age is seven. To make this distinction, Binet established baselines of performance for children of different ages; he had to determine in fairly exact terms what level of performance was average for children at each age. In the language of testing, Binet needed to establish *norms* for each age group. Once those norms were established, Binet could designate a mental age to each child based on that child's test performance.

The separation of mental age from chronological age was critical in the budding theory of human intelligence, but one additional innovation was needed. The trick was to compute a ratio between the two. This was not Binet's invention, but rather the contribution of the German psychologist Wilhelm Stern.[14] Stern's formula was simple:

$$\text{Intelligence quotient (IQ)} = \text{Mental age/Chronological age} \times 100$$

The formula shows why IQ is a *quotient*—it's the answer to a division problem. When mental age is divided by chronological age, it yields a fraction. In the simplest case, a child's performance is exactly average for his peer group. If so, then mental age and chronological age are identical, and their ratio is 1. Multiplied by a 100, this gives an IQ of 100, which is the critical number on the IQ scale. Using Stern's formula, IQs of less than 100 are below average because they indicate that a child's mental age falls below his chronological age. When IQ is greater than 100, then the child is above average: His mental age is higher than his chronological age.

Although a remarkable advance, the IQ formula has a few serious limitations. By itself, it says nothing about what a child can actually do. It quantifies intelligence without "qualifying" it. The IQ scale is completely relative because it is computed only by comparisons with other people. This relativistic orientation—the anchoring of IQ to comparisons with others—has continued to the present, but with one important change. The original method of dividing mental age by chronological age is now considered obsolete. To understand why, consider how the original IQ formula would apply to adults. The concept of mental age works fairly well for children, but is quite meaningless for adults. An eight-year-old girl might be pleased to know that her mental age is 16, which is double her chronological age. Would she be pleased if, at age 20, she were told that she had the mental age of a 40-year-old woman? Clearly, the meaning of mental age breaks down in adult populations, and so the calculation of an intelligence quotient—mental age divided by chronological age—is not serviceable. Another method for the quantification of intelligence was needed.

The now common method for computing IQ is based on the famous, or perhaps infamous, bell curve. The bell curve, also called the normal distribution, is used not only to measure intelligence. It also depicts the typical variation in many other human qualities. Height, for example, varies greatly but not evenly. Very tall and very short people are rare; people of medium height are commonplace. When population height is depicted on a graph, the expected pattern is a bulge in the middle with symmetrical tapering on both ends. The normal distribution was not derived from the study of height or intelligence. Rather, it is a mathematical pattern that approximates many qualities found in nature. Human intelligence, it turns out, has qualities that make the normal distribution a reasonable approximation: Like height, measured intelligence clusters around medium values, and extreme values are somewhat rare. But the normal distribution is an approximation rather than a conclusion about intelligence. In reality, the human population has too many extreme scores—both high and low IQ—to make the normal distribution 100% accurate.[15]

One handy feature of the bell curve is that any measurement, say your own height, does not need to be expressed in particular units, such as feet or meters. Instead, all measurements can be converted to a common scale. This little feat of magic is accomplished by expressing your height only in terms of how it compares to the entire population. Is your height exactly average? Above? Below? The normal distribution allows you to say exactly how much any measurement—height, IQ, or whatever—differs from the population average. The departure from average is measured in units called standard deviations, symbolized *s*, which function as the common denominator. The height of a six-foot man, for example, might translate to half a standard deviation above average, or above the mean, for men. A woman whose stature is six feet would be *far* above average. To present this fact fairly, the proper comparison group would be other women. Such a comparison might show that her height translates to two standard deviations above the mean for women. The convenience of translating heights to means and standard deviations is that it places the heights of men and women on a common scale. It shows how much a six-foot-tall man exceeds the average for men, and how much a six-foot-tall woman exceeds her comparison group, other women.

Other traits, such as weight, work in just the same way. Although height and weight are different measurements, both can be expressed in standard deviation units. Quantities that are even more unlike can be placed on a common metric. This can lead to informative comparisons. Knowing that a man's height is half a standard deviation above the mean and his weight is half a standard deviation below tells you something about the man's body type—he's extremely lean. And here's the amazing part: Vastly different qualities of the same man—blood pressure, shoe size, visual acuity, grip strength, reaction time, and IQ—can also be placed on the bell curve and expressed in standard deviation units.

When IQ is measured in standard deviation units, different IQ tests can be translated to a common scale. This means that IQ measured on a Stanford-Binet scale can be compared to the Wechsler Intelligence Scale for Children (WISC), or to any other intelligence test. Through the convenience of translation to a common scale, possibilities open for developing innovative tests of intelligence without losing the benefits of translation to the familiar IQ score. By emphasizing comparison, the bell curve represents a departure from early methods of quantifying intelligence based on absolute units, such as reaction time. Scores based on the normal curve are strictly comparative: They always show how one person performs *relative to other people*. This method has advantages, as we have seen, yet it also has one noteworthy disadvantage: It separates the measurement of intelligence from how people think and behave—the specific performances that form the substance of intelligence. We are left only with a number— an important number, granted, but one that is removed from the specific mental activities that went into it. The number tells us "how much," but says nothing much about the all-important qualities that are tucked away inside the convenient quantification of intelligence as IQ.

Can we gain any insight into the kinds of thinking that constitute intelligence? Alfred Binet was largely agnostic on the matter. He focused almost entirely on solving a practical problem: predicting children's ability to succeed in Parisian schools. Theoretical questions about whether intelligence could be dissected and possibly engineered were largely deferred. Yet Binet's practical contributions to the nascent science of intelligence were significant enough. He developed a functional technology, a test of mental capability that could predict school success. That capability was distinct from school learning and somehow more elemental. Also, and in contrast to Francis Galton, Binet shifted attention from the biological realm to the cognitive, and especially to higher-order thinking. This shift had immediate practical value to education in Paris and, later, around the world. For the emerging field of human intelligence, the consequences were even more significant. Through Alfred Binet, the groundwork was laid for an emerging new science whose focus was one of the most engaging enigmas imaginable—the nature of human intelligence.

INTELLIGENCE AND SCHOOL SUCCESS

Neither Francis Galton nor Alfred Binet was much interested in measuring intelligence for its own sake. Their measurements were in the service of predicting something else they deemed important. Galton wanted to predict social standing, and assumed that "eminence" in science, art, or leadership was the pinnacle of societal status. Binet's efforts were directed more narrowly toward predicting academic success in school settings. Besides measuring human characteristics in their own distinct ways, both men were interested in predicting variables that were proxies for success in some form. At that time and up to the present, measured human characteristics have evidenced a surprising ability to predict socially valued outcomes. IQ tests, in particular, have proven to be good predictors of success in schools and other settings. Over time, that predictive power has improved as test designs have become more sophisticated.

A key figure in this progression toward greater predictive power was the Stanford psychologist Lewis Terman. In the early 1900s, Terman published an English-language translation of Binet's test, added new test items, and established accurate age norms through extensive field testing. Terman also adopted Wilhelm Stern's handy formula for IQ as a ratio of mental age to chronological age. In practical terms, Lewis Terman was responsible for the rising popularity of intelligence testing in the United States. Terman's refinement of Binet's original intelligence test became famous, and to this day it remains one of the major commercial intelligence tests, the Stanford-Binet IQ scale.

Close cousins of intelligence tests have been applied to the prediction of academic success in the university. Known first as the "College Boards," and later as the Scholastic Aptitude Test (SAT), these instruments are still used widely in selective admissions to colleges. They tended to be modeled after IQ scales both in form and concept. In form, the tests employed easily scored test items, such as math problems or verbal analogies that could be answered in the multiple-choice format (although in recent years an essay writing component has been added to the SAT). In concept, the SAT and its precursors assumed that examinees had a latent potential—an aptitude—that is distinct from the student's actual performance on future university coursework. It was further assumed that this latent potential could be measured, and the resulting score would predict college course grades. This would justify the use of SAT scores as one factor to consider when filtering applicants during the admissions decision process.

Like IQ, scores on the SAT and its equivalent for graduate education, the Graduate Record Examination (GRE), are expressed in standard deviation units. On these tests, the mean score was initially set at 500 and the standard deviation at 100. This standardization presents a distinct advantage of comparability from year to year. Because performance is reported in terms of means and standard deviations, every new version of the SAT and GRE can be placed on a common scale, and examinees from this year can be compared with last year's and next year's examinees. A second advantage is that every point along the normal curve is translatable to percentiles. The mean translates exactly to the 50th percentile. One standard deviation above the mean translates to the 84th percentile; a score two standard deviations above average translates to the 98th percentile. The same conversion to percentiles can be carried out with precision all along the bell curve.

Tests that predict academic potential have not escaped criticism. IQ tests are easily faulted as artificial, for example. They are administered in carefully controlled settings using established procedures, and because of time constraints, IQ scores are based on a very limited sample of behavior.[16] IQ tests have also been criticized for having unfortunate effects. For example, they are sometimes used as filtering mechanisms to separate students into categories with labels that can be pejorative, limiting, and possibly self-fulfilling.[17] *Mental retardation* is one of those labels. The once technical terms, *idiot* and *imbecile*, have long been regarded as unacceptably stigmatizing and offensive. Categorization and treatment plans that are regular features of special education for low-IQ children are rightly questioned. Does the child experience an overall benefit from assessments that recognize the child as "special" and treat him as such? The answer is not always clear. Yet some commentators have argued that the use of IQ tests in diagnosing mental retardation was an overall gain for humane treatment of people whose intellectual abilities were far below normal.[18] Historically, the diagnosis of mental retardation made possible by IQ testing resulted in less frequent institutionalization. IQ tests also paved the way for programs of research showing that people with mental retardation could learn and remember information, competencies that allowed them to participate in a complex society and experience a rewarding life.

Tests of academic aptitude have other potential benefits as well, such as promoting fairness and a more equitable society. Arguably, an SAT or IQ test could provide universities with an objective means of comparing applicants. Such a test could, in theory, identify highly talented students from poor families who lacked the proper social connections or who did not enter the pipeline of prep schools that channeled its graduates to the most selective colleges. Such was the case in England in the early 20th century. Until 1939, only about 15 percent of English children attended secondary schools. At the time, some scholars argued that IQ tests could identify talented children who would ordinarily be denied access to a secondary education because of their rural locations or undistinguished social backgrounds. When such tests were later discontinued, fewer children from working class families were selected into the best secondary schools.[19] Some critics have argued that such tests as the SAT are, by effect or by design, instruments that deny access to higher education to poor or ethnically underrepresented students. Such effects are ironic when considered against the tests' original intent. As in admissions to elite secondary schools in England, entry to Harvard, Yale, and other elite colleges were once swayed by a family's social reputation and connections to alumni. The College Boards were designed to correct this bias and facilitate poorer students' access to higher education, thereby uncovering the presumed hidden intellectual talent that would otherwise be wasted.

Though both IQ tests and university admissions tests have been criticized, they continue to be widely used because to a measurable degree such tests work: They predict academic success. That prediction is far from perfect, of course. Some people earn high IQ or SAT scores yet are lackluster students in the classroom for any number of reasons—low motivation, inadequate instruction, poverty, or emotional trauma. Other students earn low scores but exceed their predicted performance levels if they compensate with self-discipline and an unstoppable drive to succeed. Thus, to say that the predictive power of IQ is imperfect is indeed true, but IQ is also not precise. For greater precision, we must quantify that predictive power. In statistics, predictive strength is most often computed through a correlation, symbolized r. Perfect prediction is indicated by a correlation value of 1, symbolized $r = 1.0$. If a test offers no predictive power at all, then $r = .0$. How good is IQ? As a rough approximation, the correlation between IQ and school success is about $r = .50$.[20] This means that IQ offers quite good prediction of academic achievement, but—as every teacher and parent knows—other factors also help determine a student's level of success.

In isolation, statistics are neither interesting nor illuminating. They require interpretation to be relevant. To interpret the correlation of IQ with school success, what's important is not the mathematical fact of prediction. The really important implication is the *relationship between* IQ scores and academic success.[21] Whatever constitutes IQ is somehow foundational to learning in schools and universities. We must interpret intelligence not as a mere number, but as set of enabling skills that deserves our attention. If intelligence is foundational to learning, and therefore to subsequent personal achievement, we need to understand it more fully. We must press for answers to the question: What human capacity is captured in an IQ score that prepares the mind for success in the academic settings and possibly other arenas?

INTELLIGENCE AND WORKPLACE SUCCESS

Soon after the pioneering work of Alfred Binet and Lewis Terman, IQ tests were discovered to be useful in settings other than schools. Just as IQ scores predicted success in the classroom, so they could predict effectiveness in the workplace. The American military was quick to capitalize on this fact. The armed forces made wide use of IQ tests and related measures of specialized abilities, such as mechanical aptitude, to assign military recruits to jobs. The Army Alpha and Army Beta tests, in particular, played a huge role in the rapid assignment of almost two million recruits to military duties during World War I.[22] Army Alpha required recruits to read the questions; the Army Beta version used pictures to minimize requirements for understanding written English.[23]

The lessons learned by military psychologists were soon picked up by psychologists who studied performance in civilian work settings.

Industrial-organizational (I/O) psychologists confirmed that IQ tests were good predictors of workplace performance in the office and on the factory floor. As in school settings, IQ tests offered moderate, though imperfect, prediction of workplace success. The correlations between IQ scores and job success were again about $r = .50$.[24] Interestingly, predictive power of IQ was somewhat higher for performance in complex jobs, about $r = .60$.[25] This heightened correlation hints of something important. Around the world the most valued forms of labor entail greater informational complexity. Intelligence is absolutely vital to the modern workplace. The amplified power of IQ to predict complex work is a strong clue that intelligence will become even *more* important in the future.

INTELLIGENCE AND LIFE SUCCESS

A century of research tells us that intelligence predicts success in schools and on the job. This is impressive enough, but we have evidence that intelligence applies even more broadly. Intelligence also predicts health and longevity: Higher IQ scores are associated with decreased susceptibility to disease as well as longer life span.[26] Intelligence also predicts success and fulfillment in life. The earliest study to investigate the lifelong influences of high IQ was led by Stanford professor Lewis Terman, the same scholar who translated and popularized Binet's original scale. Terman wondered if high IQ during childhood resulted in long-term, measurable effects later in life. He posed an intriguing question, "What sort of adult does the typical gifted child become?"[27] Starting in 1921, Terman used the Stanford-Binet Intelligence scale to identify about 1,500 children, first graders through eighth graders, whose IQs were among the top 1%. Almost all of the children had an IQ of 140 or higher. Their family backgrounds were varied, but they tended to be above average socioeconomically. For the next 70 years, Lewis Terman, along with his collaborators and successors, tracked this large group of California schoolchildren in depth. The project became the longest running longitudinal study of how psychological characteristics shape life pathways.

The lives of high-IQ children—playfully called "Terman's Termites"—were indeed distinguished from peers with average IQs. Some divergences were quite predictable. For example, a higher proportion of Terman's subjects completed college and earned advanced degrees. The "Termites" were also more likely than average to write books, make important discoveries, and to be elected to prestigious professional societies. Less predictable was the finding that childhood IQ was associated with broader outcomes, including health, longevity, quality of life, and well-being.[28] Although the high-IQ children were not immune from personal struggles, they were more likely than their peers to grow up to become successful, well-adjusted adults.[29] Other research affirms the converse truth: Low IQ is a liability. Measured low intelligence is associated with a host of poor social outcomes, including poverty, criminality, and behaviors associated with premature mortality.[30, 31]

It's not too mysterious why intelligence is a good predictor of success in the academic and job arenas, as well as in other life contexts: Intelligence is a marvelously adaptive feature of the human mind. Yet, as everyone knows, this power is not always used for good. The ability to form abstractions, manipulate symbols, and learn large bodies of knowledge can be used for evil. Indeed, throughout history, intelligence has been used to promote malevolent purposes.[32] Hitler's demagoguery is perhaps the most vivid example imaginable, yet equally disturbing is that the expansion of Nazism was not the result of one man acting alone. It took coordination among the many military and intellectual leaders who joined Hitler's cause. The lesson never to be forgotten is that human intelligence can wreak horrific destruction and generate incalculable human suffering. Reflecting upon the lessons of history, one psychologist observed that "the brilliant mind can be the most destructive force in the world."[33]

With the passage of many years, it may seem hard to believe that large numbers of people—including many whose intelligence was well above average—could be persuaded to comply with purposes so evil as those promulgated by Nazi ideology. Yet psychological experiments conducted in the United States proved that the average person is far more vulnerable to manipulation by authority figures than we might assume. In classic experiments by psychologist Stanley Milgram, everyday people displayed a startling willingness to administer electrical shocks—or what they *believed* to be electrical shocks—to other people when they were told they must do so.[34] Compliance to the demands of the "lab assistant," who in reality was only acting the role of an authority figure in Milgram's experiments, was so complete that many people continued to administer shocks even though they could hear screams and pleas for mercy coming from the adjacent room.

A backward glance at history disabuses us of any illusions that intelligence is an unmitigated good. Plainly, the human psyche is capable of extraordinary cruelty and susceptible to manipulation toward evil ends. To advance the common good, intelligence must be allied with moral understanding and commitment. Moral commitments take on different forms, including a caring regard for other human beings, a healthy self-love, and an abiding insistence on fairness and justice. Even though intelligence will not always be used to advance positive moral ends, it can be argued that without intelligence the chances of solving society's most pressing problems and challenges are slim. Because our world is complex, advancing moral good at both local and global levels requires that participants have the ability to use their minds exceptionally well. Any realistic vision of a bright future requires that the denizens of planet Earth have abundant intellectual resources.

As we redirect our focus from the larger society back to the individual, let us bear in mind what research shows so clearly: Intelligence is hugely relevant to life prospects. In the pursuit of broad life success, intelligence is an asset without peer. Intelligence is doubly important in the contexts of fast-moving, complex, and interactive cultures that define our contemporary world. In three vital contexts—school, work, and everyday life—human intelligence conveys a potent advantage.[35] It predicts achievement and, more relevant functionally, gives its possessor the intellectual tools needed for success across a wide swath of life contexts. We can generalize this way: Intelligence is the raw material for human effectiveness. Intelligence never guarantees success, but to have at one's disposal the resources of a sharp and nimble mind is an advantage without rival for every citizen of the 21st century.

THE THRESHOLD HYPOTHESIS

Even if you already believe that intelligence is a tremendous personal resource, it's fair to ask: Is more intelligence always better? Some psychologists question whether it is. A moderately high IQ is empowering, but a super-high IQ of say 150 is perhaps unnecessary. Historically, high-status jobs such as law or medicine have been largely restricted to those with at least a moderately high IQ.[36] Maybe what's important for complex work is nothing more than a moderately high IQ of about 120. We can think of this idea as the "threshold hypothesis." It implies that as long as mental acumen reaches a threshold that facilitates skill in processing abstract and complex information, then unlimited possibilities for achievement open up. Above the threshold, achievement becomes a function of personal values and commitments, such as ambition, persistence, and unrelenting commitment to hard work.[37] But below a threshold of 120 or so, a person will necessarily be limited in what he or she can achieve in a complex society.

Some evidence supports the threshold hypothesis. In the absence of moderately high levels of intelligence, lasting achievements in complex fields are rare.[38] While some data do support the threshold hypothesis, other data show that when it comes to IQ, more is better. A super-high intelligence can convey measurable benefits over a "merely" high IQ, especially in highly technical fields.[39] So, what's the answer? Is a moderately high IQ good enough, or do very high levels of intelligence help, especially as a basis for history's most remarkable and enduring achievements?

To look for answers to these questions, we can turn again to research from Lewis Terman's lab at Stanford in the 1920s. When Professor Terman was conducting his famous study of high-IQ children, his collaborator, Catherine Cox, was carrying out an independent investigation of 301 eminent achievers of Western civilization. These were luminaries who made contributions to science, art, music, politics, and philosophy from the Renaissance onward. Cox wanted to know whether these eminent men and women displayed evidence of high intelligence as children and young adults. To investigate, she and two assistants used historical and biographical information to estimate each person's IQ during childhood (from birth to age 17) and during early adulthood (from age 18 through 26). These IQ estimates were based on the ages at which the children and young adults reached developmental milestones and made significant intellectual achievements.

In 1926, Catherine Cox published a monograph of her findings, concluding that eminent men and women displayed remarkable achievements very early in life.[40] She noted, for example, that: "Voltaire wrote verses from the cradle; Coleridge at 2 could read a chapter from the bible; Mozart composed a minuet at 5. Goethe, at age 8, produced a literary work of adult superiority." Stunning precocity was in every case followed by significant and enduring achievements during adulthood. Consequently, Catherine Cox's estimates of IQ, though variable from person to person, were all far above average. Summarizing the IQ estimates for all 301 "geniuses," Cox found that the average was "not below 155 and probably as high as 165." Examples include: Jean Jacques Rousseau (125), Nicolas Copernicus (130), Rembrandt Van Rijn (135), Martin Luther (145), Charles Darwin (140), Abraham Lincoln (140), Leonardo da Vinci (150), Thomas Jefferson (150), Wolfgang Amadeus Mozart (150), Charlotte Bronte (155), Michelangelo Buonarroti (160), Galileo Galilei (165), Samuel Taylor Coleridge (165), Isaac Newton (170), John Stuart Mill (170), Gottfried Wilhelm Leibnitz (190), and Wolfgang Goethe (200). These estimates, if even approximately correct, suggest that levels of intelligence in the range of 135 to 180 are characteristic of men and women whose accomplishments leave a lasting trace on society and culture. Even in those rarefied strata, however, something like a secondary threshold can be discerned: The IQs of eminent mathematicians do not differ from the average IQ of PhDs in mathematics.[41] Apparently, intelligence functions as a necessary but not sufficient condition for achievement at high and very high IQ bands. Even in the IQ stratosphere, a capable intellect must be combined with vital personal qualities, such as vision and drive.

The cognitive resources that constitute high or super-high intelligence are desirable for anyone who wants to build academic and career success—as well as success in broader life contests. But that leaves open the key question: Must *everyone* be intelligent? One could argue that every society needs workers whose daily responsibilities do not require much by way of brainpower. Yet the case for an IQ-differentiated society is weak for several reasons. First, the unskilled labor sector, which typically requires no more than low-level intellectual skills, is shrinking rapidly. Second, because of rising expectations for efficiency, cost savings, and coordination of workflow, even semiskilled employees draw upon the ability to plan and solve problems. Third, and most important, a free society insists on opportunity for all. Even if a worker chooses work that is less intellectual by nature, then at least that person is given a choice in the matter.

If we agree that a highly capable intellect is desirable for everyone rather than a select few, another question looms: Won't every population always exhibit a range of intelligence—people who are very smart and others who are less so? Stated in those terms, the answer must be *yes*. But that simple answer omits much. We can readily acknowledge that intelligence, like every personal trait, inevitably varies from person to person. In fact, without variation the construct of intelligence is meaningless and its measurement is pointless. But even if variability is a permanent feature in human populations, this does not mean that the average level of intelligence cannot shift over time. Drawing on a crude analogy, personal computers are manufactured with a wide range of specifications at any point in time. Different models exhibit variability. But even though variation is an ongoing fact, the average level of computational power rises year after year.

A wholesale shift in a population's average level of intelligence, measured as IQ, would have tremendous consequences for any society. To understand why, let's assume that the threshold hypothesis is correct. Shifting the population IQ upward by 15 points, which is equivalent to one standard deviation, would vastly increase the numbers of adults able to work in highly technical fields, or who could apply their intellectual powers to solving tough problems in less technical domains. A few of those people would eventually make monumental contributions to society in science, art, literature, engineering, and medicine. We could anticipate benefits at the low end of the IQ scale as well. An upward shift of one standard deviation would reduce the numbers of children and adults classified as developmentally delayed. These effects would be practical: Many people, otherwise heavily dependent on societal support, would have the cognitive resources to live more self-determined, productive lives and to be less at risk for poverty, criminality, and other social ills.

WHY WE MUST BECOME MORE INTELLIGENT

Let's be realistic: If intelligence is static and unmovable, then scenarios of a brighter human race are no more than utopian fantasies—amusing, perhaps, but inconsequential. But if intelligence can be altered, the implications are powerful, perhaps even revolutionary. Can intelligence be changed? The thesis of this book is predicated on a positive answer to the question. If intelligence can be enhanced, then that one proposition becomes a conceptual anchoring point from which a multiplicity of exciting prospects follow. Among the most important is greater reason to hope for progress in addressing the world's most thorny problems—disease, terror, and the threat of ecological disaster. For any prospect of a bright and hopeful future, we need many intelligent minds to be focused and hard at work.

Any credible aspiration to raise the intelligence of the earth's population rests on more than the *possibility* of doing so. It also requires that we understand what intelligence is. To this point we have done little to probe its nature. We must dig deeper. We have already entertained the question: What is intelligence good for? Let's now ask something much more fundamental: What is intelligence?

CHAPTER 2
What Is Intelligence?

S o far, I have used the word *intelligence* without exploring its meaning in any depth. I focused instead on a much more practical question: Does the highly intelligent person have an advantage in achieving success? On this, the data clearly answer, *yes*. We know, for example, that IQ scores predict success in school. In general, children and adults who have higher IQ scores learn more efficiently and find it easier to master complex material. IQ is also a good predictor of workplace performance, especially in jobs that are complex. In today's economy, the workplace demands that people are able not only to learn, but also to think productively—to grasp complex problems and generate effective solutions. Now that we have established that intelligence is important, and increasingly so, we need to change directions. We need to confront the pressing question: What exactly is intelligence?

Let's begin with some basic distinctions. A good starting point is to recognize that IQ and intelligence are not exactly the same thing. IQ is simply the quantified summary value of intelligence. As a two- or three-digit number, IQ is reductive in the extreme. Yet the compression of intelligence into a single number has practical value for predicting future success. We would be mistaken, though, to think that IQ *is* intelligence, or that an IQ score can fully and accurately summarize the intelligence of any person. Inevitably, the reduction of intelligence to a number skims over important information. To understand why, consider other forms of numeric rating. A baseball player's batting average reveals something important, but necessarily omits much about that player's strengths, weaknesses, and style.

IQ and intelligence are not equivalent for other reasons as well. IQ tests are logically limited by our best available conceptualizations of intelligence.

Think about it: If our theories of intelligence are imperfect, which they inevitably are, then IQ tests will reflect those imperfections. Intelligence is, in many ways, deeply mysterious. Like all marvelously complex domains of nature—oceans, planets, quarks, and living ecosystems—human intelligence is an impossibly intricate puzzle that constantly awaits discovery and beckons ongoing exploration. Understanding is not achieved once and for all, but gradually and by degrees. Over the last 150 years, we have made a lot of progress in illuminating the nature of intelligence, but much more remains to be discovered. In a sense, then, an IQ score is a caricature of intelligence—a way of pinning a number on a human trait that is vast, complex, and still quite elusive.

PARADOX: UNITY OR DIVERSITY?

One way to gain a foothold in understanding intelligence is to pose a very fundamental question: Is intelligence a unified entity, or is it instead a diverse collection of intellectual capabilities? Simply stated, is intelligence one thing or many? Historically, scholars of human intelligence have been divided on the question.

Around the year 1900, the British psychologist Charles Spearman argued insistently that intelligence is a unified entity. He believed there was a general intelligence factor, which he famously called *g*. Spearman believed every intellectual act draws upon *g*, at least to some extent. On the other side of the Atlantic Ocean, the American psychologist L. L. Thurstone took the opposite position. Thurstone believed that intelligence was not a unified ability, rather it consisted of an array of separate abilities, such as memory, mathematical reasoning, and verbal comprehension.[1] He believed that each distinct ability worked in combination with the others to produce intelligent thought. If Thurstone was correct, then the term *intelligence* was a bit of a misnomer, possibly even baseless, because the work of the mind does not draw on a single unifying intelligence but rather operates through several independent forms of intelligence working in concert.

Spearman and Thurstone were not merely speculating from upholstered armchairs when they proposed their competing theories. Both were hard-nosed empiricists who subjected their theories to scientific confirmation based on objective data. To test their theories, they relied on scores from tests they administered to hundreds of people. Those tests were diverse, tapping an array of verbal, mathematical, and spatial skills, as well as various forms of reasoning, such as deduction, creativity, and problem solving. Because these tests measured such a broad span of mental activity, the correlations among the tests could, in principle, reveal patterns that illuminated the nature of intelligence—including, for example, whether it is unitary or multiple. Let's now explore how this is possible.

As we saw in the previous chapter, a correlation (symbolized r) quantifies the strength of a relationship between any two variables. We might suspect, for example, that in any population there is a positive correlation between shoe size and glove size. A correlation value can test whether or not our suspicions are true as well as quantify the extent of the association. Correlations can be used to quantify the strength of associations between other variables as well, such as height and weight, education and income, or verbal and quantitative test scores. To test their theories, Spearman and Thurstone needed a correlation value for every pair of tests. Modern software makes it very easy to compute a correlation between any pair of test variables. In Spearman's and Thurstone's day, though, correlations had to be computed by hand in a very laborious process. The correlations among tests were so vital to theory testing that the resulting data tables were worth the considerable toil.

Now here's the key: The pattern of correlations can provide evidence that favors one theory or another. One possible pattern is that high correlations appear virtually everywhere in the matrix. This tells us something: When each test is correlated with all other tests, it implies that Spearman's g is at work. A single, unified intelligence appears to be influencing performance across very different kinds of mental activity. But a second possible pattern is that test correlations are clustered—some tests correlated highly, but others weakly or not at all. That pattern supports the view that intelligence is *not* unified but is instead a collection of independent mental abilities. This is the pattern that would support Thurstone's theory of separate and distinct abilities.

Which theory wins out? The answer was unclear for several decades. Spearman's analysis came first. To test his hypothesis of unified intelligence, Spearman created a diverse array of cognitive tests of language, music, perception, mental speed, and other abilities. When he analyzed the relationships among the tests he found positive correlations spread throughout the matrix. Examinees who did well on one test were likely to do well on others, even if the content of those tests differed markedly. There seemed to be a general mental quality, which Spearman called g, on which performance depended and on which people differed. The pattern of high correlations across diverse tests of mental ability was striking. Spearman gave a name to this pattern—the positive manifold—which was primary evidence that general intelligence, Spearman's g, was real. Some theorists regard the discovery of the positive manifold as one of the most important findings in the history of psychology.[2] It meant something important: Spearman's g theory appeared to be vindicated.

The matter was not settled, however. Unlike Spearman, Thurstone did not find a uniform blanket of positive correlations across the matrix; instead, high correlations grouped together in clusters. This led Thurstone to the opposite conclusion: g does not exist. He stated this conclusion directly in 1938, declaring, "We have not found the general factor of Spearman."[3] In trying to account for why Thurstone obtained these results, it's helpful to know that he focused his research on college students. In Thurstone's day, colleges admitted only the highest achieving high school students. These students were drawn from a narrow range of IQ—that is, uniformly high. The limited variation of IQ results in what statisticians call restriction of range. Reduced variation makes it difficult to detect correlations. For example, you might believe that a family's annual income is positively associated with its overall health, but to test the hypothesis you would want to study families with a range of incomes, not only the very wealthy. Thurstone may have had difficulty detecting the correlations that compose the positive manifold precisely because the students he studied were too similar to each other intellectually.

Even though Thurstone did not detect a strong and pervasive positive manifold, he did find clusters of correlations, each of which seemed to measure a distinct dimension or factor. Those factors included numerical ability, verbal comprehension, and memory. Other scholars of intelligence later found similar patterns, namely, multiple factors instead of a unitary intelligence. Depending on the particular theory, the number of clusters, or factors, ranged widely. At the high end, the American psychologist J. P. Guilford identified a whopping 150 factors.[4] Yet even as new data and research methods became available to test theories of intelligence, the central paradox remained unresolved.

RESOLVING PARADOX ONE: THE HIERARCHICAL MODEL

The first paradox of intelligence—one or many?—was surprisingly vexing. From the start, what seemed to be a simple question did not yield a simple answer. As we have seen, Charles Spearman and L. L. Thurstone staked out the original competing theories, with each man staunchly defending his own theoretical position. Later, though, the antagonists experienced a remarkable turn of events: Each man discovered data that supported the theory of his rival.

Thurstone modified his original claim on the basis of a mathematical procedure called factor analysis. Through factor analysis it became possible to extract complex patterns in a correlation matrix that cannot be identified by simple visual inspection. As we have seen, Thurstone used factor analysis to identify six factors. By altering the assumptions of his analysis, Thurstone was able to develop an alternative solution in which the *factors themselves* were correlated. It therefore became possible to do a second factor analysis—not on the correlations between tests but on the correlations between factors. When Thurstone conducted this "second-order" factor analysis, what emerged on top was a single general factor that looked a lot like Spearman's *g*. Writing in 1941, Thurstone bravely admitted, "Our findings seem to support Spearman's claim for a general intellective factor."[5]

Like Thurstone, Charles Spearman was also willing to change his mind if the data so indicated. On the basis of further analysis, Spearman moved away from his insistence that intelligence is purely unitary. The positive manifold of correlations held true, but within that pattern some tests were more highly intercorrelated than others. In other words, Spearman's *g* factor applied across all tests—that conclusion remained unchanged—but within his matrices Spearman could also identify narrower abilities that resemble the factors Thurstone described.[6] It's a credit to both Spearman and Thurstone that each could eventually admit that his rival was correct—or at least partly so.

Now it seemed that the question of whether intelligence is "one" or "many" did not have a simple answer after all. Instead, intelligence displays qualities of both unity and diversity. Intelligence is both one *and* many. When first acknowledged by Spearman and Thurstone, this conclusion seemed deeply paradoxical. It was largely up to other brilliant theorists to put these two realities together. Eventually the paradox was resolved. The unity and diversity of intelligence were reconciled by thinking about intelligence in a new way—not as "one" or "many," but as a combination of the two. To see how this works, consider Figure 2.1.

The diagram shows Spearman's model at the top and Thurstone's at the bottom. When the two models are merged, the combined structure looks something like a pyramid. The pyramid is actually a hierarchy. Hierarchies are ubiquitous in the material world, or in the mind's way of categorizing the world, depending on your perspective. Think about sports as an example. Is the category of "sports" meaningful? Of course it is. We have sports channels, sports pages, sports magazines, and sports writers. No one is confused by the general category of "sports." But we also have particular sports—soccer, baseball, basketball, and many others. The two levels of categories fit together easily if we think of the general category, *sports*,

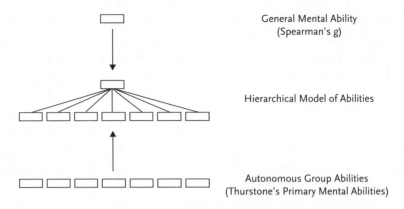

Figure 2.1
Hierarchical Model of Abilities: Combining the Theories of Spearman's g and Thurstone's Primary Mental Abilities. Reprinted with permission from Martinez, M. E. (2000). *Education as the cultivation of intelligence.* Mahwah, NJ: Erlbaum.

at the top of the pyramid and the particular varieties of sports—soccer, baseball, basketball, and so on—underneath. No doubt you can imagine hierarchical structures for other broad categories, such as animals, cars, machines, art, music, and clothing. Hierarchies are everywhere. The abstract phenomenon of intelligence, like so many other entities in human experience, can also be organized hierarchically. At the top of the pyramid is general intelligence, or Spearman's g, which extends its sweeping influence over the broad span of mental activity. Lower in the pyramid are broad abilities that resemble Thurstone's identified factors.

The hierarchical model is widely regarded as capturing something essential and enduring about intelligence: It is neither one thing nor many, but both. General intelligence is a legitimate concept, but it does not fully explain the powers of intellect. That's because intelligence also has multiple aspects or, more technically, factors, each of which expresses a particular dimension of the larger whole. To tell the whole "story" of intelligence, we needed the hierarchical model to combine its properties of unity and diversity. Reflecting on this remarkable synthesis, psychologist Raymond Cattell proclaimed that through the hierarchical structure, the ideas of Spearman and Thurstone were "reconcilable, and with mutual illumination."[7] The hierarchical model was a huge step forward. Its structure allowed for a more complex concept of intelligence, and one truer to its nature. Though established as early as 1950, the hierarchical structure of intelligence has proven to be remarkably durable. Near the end of the 20th century, prominent intelligence theorists affirmed that "the empirical evidence in favor of a hierarchical model is overwhelming."[8]

Let's be careful, though: Different theorists have proposed somewhat different hierarchical models. Which one is best? There is a very good candidate for the single best hierarchical model—the *three-stratum* model advanced by the psychometrician John Carroll.[9] John Carroll's model is compelling because it was built from a mountain of data. Instead of relying on a single data set, Carroll analyzed 460 data sets, many having historical importance reaching back decades. Carroll's three-stratum model deserves our attention. Let's have a look (Figure 2.2).

The three-stratum model has three layers, as the name suggests. At the top is general intelligence, which exerts influence over all the abilities lower in the hierarchy. In the middle layer are broad factors that bear some resemblance to Thurstone's factors. At the bottom of the pyramid are narrow factors—specialized mental abilities that are useful for particular kinds of mental performance. Procedurally, Carroll's data warranted factor extraction three times, while Thurstone required only two factor extractions to obtain a satisfactory solution. This procedural difference is what led to Carroll's model having three levels in contrast to Thurstone's model having only two.

Note one peculiarity of the three-stratum model: The pyramid is not symmetrical, but is skewed to the left. That's because connections between general intelligence at the top and the broad factors one level below are uneven. Shorter lines indicate stronger connections with general intelligence; longer lines mean that those connections are weaker. Clearly, two broad factors have especially strong connections with *g*—fluid and crystallized intelligence. These two factors further illuminate the nature of intelligence. We have already seen that intelligence is structured hierarchically, like a

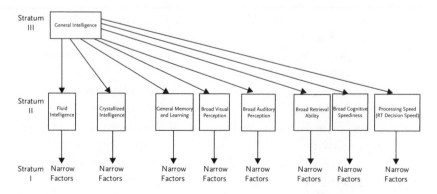

Figure 2.2
Carroll's Three-Stratum Model. Adapted with permission from Carroll, J. B. (1993). *Human cognitive abilities: A survey of factor-analytic studies.* New York: Cambridge University Press.

pyramid. Now we gain a second key insight, which is that two manifestations of intelligence—fluid and crystallized—show how a capable mind interacts with the world. Let's consider why these two aspects of intelligence are so important.

FLUID AND CRYSTALLIZED INTELLIGENCE

In everyday speech, the word *intelligence* has two distinct meanings. The most familiar meaning is the ability to think and reason. An intelligent person can manage complex information quickly and accurately, as well as generate interesting ideas, effective strategies, and warranted conclusions. A second meaning of the word *intelligence* is a body of knowledge. We see the word *intelligence* used this way when describing the missions of the Central Intelligence Agency and the British Security Service, MI-5. To a significant degree, the distinction between fluid and crystallized intelligence parallels this difference in meaning.

Fluid intelligence refers to the mind's ability to adapt to novel, complex, and challenging environments. Of these three descriptors, the word *novel* is probably the most important. Fluid intelligence is applied whenever a person must adapt to a new situation, such as an unfamiliar culture, a new job, or a perplexing problem. A person who excels in fluid intelligence has the mental resources to tackle a completely novel challenge and find a way to succeed. Crystallized intelligence, a counterpart form of intelligence, is manifest in the ability to master large bodies of information. Crystallized intelligence is also strongly associated with verbal ability, hinting that knowledge is most often learned, comprehended, and remembered in verbal form.

Fluid and crystallized intelligence complement each other beautifully. One way to think about their roles is that each represents a vital resource for the intelligent mind. Crystallized intelligence offers the invaluable resource of current knowledge—what is already known. This is more than the skillful use of memory so heavily relied on by school systems. The ability to acquire knowledge in ways that can be applied intelligently is much more complex and far-reaching. Crystallized intelligence represents the developed ability to master organized bodies of knowledge that have functional value in a complex, information-rich world. But if current knowledge is not enough, which is often the case, the gap is filled by fluid intelligence—the capacity to deal with the unknown. We draw upon both resources as we go about our lives. To think and act intelligently, knowledge is valuable and desirable, and more knowledge is almost always better. Inevitably, though, we must supplement our knowledge with the capacity to adapt flexibly to unfamiliar environments and the novel problems they present.

To some extent, the distinction between fluid and crystallized intelligence can help us understand the condition known as savant syndrome. Savants are people who are identified by low intellectual functioning except for a few particular, and often peculiar, skills in which they excel. In the movie *Rain Man*, the central character, Raymond Babbitt, played by Dustin Hoffman, could memorize a phone book and perform calculations at lightning speed. Babbitt was modeled after a real-life man named Kim Peek, who can perform numerical calculations with extreme speed; he is also a prodigious reader who is said to have memorized more than 7600 books.[10] He was born with brain abnormalities, including the absence of the corpus callosum, the nerve structure that connects the brain's left and right hemispheres. The absence of a corpus callosum may have caused Peek's brain to adapt by producing other structures that underpin his extraordinary skills.

Other savants have skills that are different, but no less striking. Some can recall sports statistics with uncanny accuracy or estimate distance precisely by sight alone. One savant named Ellen has such a highly developed sense of time that, without the aid of a clock, she can note the precise time of day to the second. These "splinter skills" are impressive, but they lack the depth and flexibility that make them broadly useful to the savant. For example, one musical savant, NP, was able to reproduce Grieg's "Melodie" on the piano after hearing it played only once. But when exposed to an unusual atonal composition, Bartok's "Whole Tone Scale," his attempts to reproduce the piece were slow and awkward. NP made errors that imposed more traditional melodic structure over the composition. Without question, NP's ability to reproduce conventional tonal music was amazing, but its operation was confined to a specific framework of performance.[11]

Kim Peek and other savants are not known for their academic success, nor for their personal effectiveness in the world. About half of all savants are autistic, and so face severe challenges in adapting to the demands of everyday life. Although Kim Peek has been employed successfully as a payroll bookkeeper, the fictional character Raymond Babbitt was institutionalized because of cognitive and behavioral limitations, despite his extraordinary abilities to calculate and memorize. The drama of *Rain Man* is closer to the lived reality of many savants. These facts lead us to an important question: How do the focused talents of savants, however extraordinary, differ from what we are calling intelligence? First, it seems clear that the ability to memorize quickly and efficiently does not adequately characterize crystallized intelligence. A person who is high in crystallized intelligence typically has no difficulty in academic settings and has a large fund of knowledge at his or her disposal. But that knowledge is not fixed like the entries in a telephone book. Rather, it is flexible and interconnected; ideas are organically related such that one can trigger another. Crystallized intelligence does not consist in sheer volume of knowledge, but rather knowledge that can be drawn upon to support intelligent behavior.

One way to understand how crystallized and fluid intelligence fit together is to map them onto "potential" and "achievement." In the investment theory of intelligence, a person high in raw intellectual ability (fluid intelligence) can "invest" that resource to develop an educated mind (crystallized intelligence).[12] The investment theory corresponds to our everyday intuitions about a child's capacity to learn. A child who has high ability, through opportunity and self-discipline, can capitalize on that resource to gain knowledge and academic success over a span of many years. When this happens, fluid intelligence is *invested* to yield an accruing dividend of crystallized intelligence. Alternatively, a child's fluid intelligence might be squandered. For any number of reasons—poor motivation, lack of discipline, inadequate resources, or simple lack of opportunity—the child who holds the resources necessary for tremendous personal achievement and contributions to the world does not develop that gift. Like a blue-ribbon seed that never germinates, uninvested fluid intelligence represents lost potential.

Among some psychologists, however, the concept of "potential" is not very popular. The reason is that "potential" hints of an imaginary entity that might or might not exist in the future. Critics argue that we can measure only what exists in the present. Yet the concept of a child's potential for future success is a very intuitive idea to most teachers, coaches, and parents. We recognize that some children display uncommon aptitudes for music, swimming, chess, mathematics, science, or art. The standout aptitude can be manifest as a keen and inquisitive mind, one that is distinguished from the crowd. Indeed, the entire field of gifted and talented education is premised on an assumption that some children are marked with an unusual aptitude—so much so that the standard curriculum is an impediment to the child's development.

Many intelligence theorists, recognizing the fluid-crystallized distinction, have designed tests to report separate scores for fluid and crystallized intelligence. Other tests, such as the Wechsler, report a similar distinction between verbal and performance (nonverbal) IQ scales, which, over time, have been interpreted as measures of crystallized and fluid intelligence. These shifts in labeling and interpretation show that the fluid-crystallized distinction has had a major influence on intelligence testing. The influence has a theoretical side as well: By studying how people solve problems, especially on tests of fluid intelligence, our understanding of intelligence has become richer and more complete.

RAVEN'S MATRICES: A CLUE TO FLUID INTELLIGENCE

Fluid intelligence can be assessed in a remarkable variety of ways. Some fluid intelligence tests use abstract shapes, while others use words or numbers. All measures, though, have this in common: Tests of fluid intelligence require a person to perceive a complex pattern and to apply that pattern to solve a problem. Another key feature is novelty. It's important that the problem or puzzle be new to the person's experience. The novelty requirement is met by a classic test of fluid intelligence, Raven's Matrices, originally developed by John Raven, a student of Charles Spearman. The task involves a 3 × 3 array of eight abstract shapes with a blank spot in the lower right corner. Figure 2.3 is an example of a Raven's-like problem.

To solve this problem, you must first examine the various elements—their shapes, orientations, number, and shading—and discover correspondences from row to row and column to column. Those rules of order dictate which pattern should fill the blank cell. A Raven's Matrices test is organized

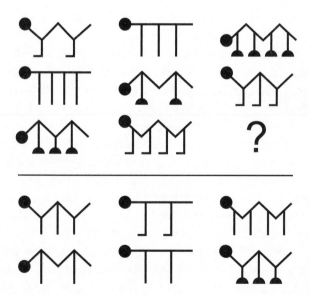

Figure 2.3
Raven's Matrices Problems. Martinez, Michael E., *Learning and Cognition: The Design of the Mind*, ©2010. Printed and Electronically reproduced by permission of Pearson Education, Inc., Upper Saddle River, New Jersey.

so that it presents relatively easy problems at the beginning and steadily progresses to more difficult problems. The most difficult problems involve multiple simultaneous transformations from top to bottom and from right to left. To solve a complex Raven's problem, a person must perceive each dimension of change in the abstract shapes, combine those dimensions mentally, and then select the ideal pattern from the options available. If any detail is overlooked, the chances of selecting the right answer are thereby reduced.

Let's probe more deeply into the kinds of thinking evoked by Raven's Matrices. The puzzles are unusual in several ways. Most important, Raven's never explains the rules that guide how the puzzle is structured. The point is precisely that the rules must be figured out based on each incomplete matrix. Those rules change from one matrix to the next. The examinee must study the specific elements of each matrix and then infer the rules that explain the pattern. In the more difficult Raven's problems, this is quite challenging: It requires careful and systematic comparison to be sure that the inferred rules are both precise and complete, enabling the prediction of the missing piece. This sequence of thought is a perfect example of inductive reasoning.

Inductive reasoning always proceeds this way: from the specific instance to a general pattern. Whenever we encounter a new situation, whether an abstract puzzle or an everyday problem, we must first understand it. That means seeing how the various parts fit together. Understanding the problem helps us to work effectively toward a solution. Inductive reasoning serves another extremely important function—it helps us to apply our understanding to a new *second* problem, then to a *third* problem, and so on indefinitely—as long as those problems are structured similarly. This portability is what allows a doctor to diagnose and treat a range of problems or a CEO to transfer effective leadership in one company to a different one.

Inductive reasoning is tremendously important. Stop to consider that scientific discovery draws heavily on inductive reasoning. Scientists work from specific data gathered in their laboratories to induce a rule, principle, or law whose validity extends beyond the specific context of discovery. It must generalize. The discovery qualifies as science precisely if it applies broadly to other laboratories and data sets, as well as across time. Inductive reasoning—finding the general pattern in specific data—is vital to the scientific enterprise. More generally, inductive reasoning is also an indispensable element of intelligent thought. It's so important, in fact, that some theorists believe inductive reasoning lies at the very heart of fluid intelligence. The most daring expression of this hypothesis was advanced by the psychometrician Jan-Eric Gustafsson, who proposed that inductive reasoning is nearly identical to fluid intelligence. He went even further to argue that fluid intelligence is, in turn, nearly identical to general intelligence.[13] Expressed compactly and without qualifiers, Gustafsson's bold hypothesis is as follows:

Inductive reasoning = Fluid intelligence = General intelligence

Even if the Gustafsson hypothesis turns out to be incorrect, its mere plausibility is instructive. Whatever the panoply of cognitive skills that compose the repertoire we call general intelligence, the place of inductive reasoning ability within that repertoire is somewhere near the very core.

A second cognitive skill used to solve Raven's Matrices is the ability to break down the larger problem into smaller problems. Rather than trying to understand the matrix in its entirety, a more flexible approach is to adopt a simpler subgoal.[14] Research shows that the most successful examinees can focus on a single aspect of the problem and progressively use the information learned from the subproblem to generate a solution that works for the problem as a whole. This very ability—to divide a cumbersome task into smaller and more manageable subproblems—is perhaps the most powerful problem-solving strategy of all. In the case of Raven's Matrices, people vary in their ability or tendency to form subgoals. Those who break down complex problems into more manageable pieces tend to have higher scores overall.

Performance on Raven's Matrices draws on yet a third cognitive skill, the ability to hold several goals in mind at once and to track progress toward those goals.[15] This is a bit like what we ordinarily call "multitasking," but applied to a single complex problem rather than to different activities that overlap in time. Careful tracking is most important in the context of information overload, and when some of that information is relevant and some merely distracting. The ability to separate relevant from irrelevant information, and to hold relevant information in mind while solving a problem, is sometimes described as executive functioning. Like a capable business executive, the mind must sift pertinent data from distractions, formulate goals and strategies, and then initiate a coordinated plan of action. Executive functioning also includes the ability to monitor progress toward goals, and to switch or modify strategies if necessary. To ensure success, no piece of essential information can be allowed to slip from active consideration. This challenging set of requirements is clearly higher-order in nature. It also ties in quite directly to the known functions of the brain's frontal lobe, the seat of higher-order thinking.

Let's take stock, then, of what we know about Raven's Matrices. First, we recognize Raven's as an important tool in the measurement of fluid intelligence. For reasons that are still somewhat mysterious, Raven's Matrices affords us a glimpse into the heart of intelligence. Because Raven's works so well, psychologists have studied what people who obtain high scores actually do. Psychologists want to know: What patterns of thinking separate high performers from low performers? Any insight we gain can help us to understand how the cognitive functions that underlie performance on Raven's Matrices might apply to non–test situations. Ultimately, the practical manifestation of intelligence is what we want to understand—the substance of real-life success, and more exactly the intellectual skill set that makes success possible.

From studying performance on Raven's, we have learned that people differ in their ability to perform three kinds of intellectual activities: (1) finding order in complex patterns, (2) breaking problems down into subproblems, and (3) managing several goals at once without being overwhelmed. When we think of these three expressions of intellect, we can easily see how they can apply broadly to the sorts of problems we face every day. First, finding order in complex patterns is vital to navigating our data-packed world. We must learn to take in the complexity that surrounds us, understand it, and then apply that understanding to make smart choices. Often those decisions are not simple. Almost always, they entail choices about how to subdivide unwieldy problems into manageable subproblems. This ability to decompose a large problem in order to make it manageable is the second skill that distinguishes high performers on Raven's. Finally, as we pursue our goals, we must do so without being overwhelmed. Our executive functions help us to keep track of our goals and pursue them in an order that makes sense, without letting any important piece of information slip from consideration.

INTELLIGENCE IN CRYSTALLIZED FORM

Crystallized intelligence is the intellectual resource that corresponds to structured knowledge, along with the learning skills that facilitate building that knowledge base over time. Knowledge is fantastically important in supporting intelligent thought and behavior. Personal experience tells us that knowledge can take many different forms. Some of what we know is like pictures in a photo album: In our mind's eye we can see familiar people, places, and objects. Some knowledge is maplike, which allows us to navigate familiar places, such as our hometown, easily and efficiently. Other forms of knowledge are mathematical in nature. We interpret our world with a sense of numerosity and make judgments about quantity in coarse terms—one or many, short or long, small or big—while knowing that quantity can also be measured precisely using the number system. The mind knows what it knows in many other ways as well. We recognize the smell of a pine forest, the taste of cheese pizza, and the texture of silk. We also know how to *do* things: walk, run, skip, shake hands, play a musical instrument, and sign our own name.

Among this vast array, one form of knowledge rises above all others in importance to the work of the mind—language. Although language has no strict monopoly on the way the mind stores knowledge, words and word meanings are so central to human cognition that some theorists treat language and thought almost as if they were two sides of the same coin. It should be no surprise, then, that what we call verbal ability has a special connection to intelligence, and in particular to crystallized intelligence. This does not mean that verbal ability and crystallized intelligence are identical. They are distinct constructs, but with significant overlap. We see a similar relationship between fluid intelligence and inductive reasoning. Fluid intelligence draws on the ability to see the order in complex problems, and to apply those inferred patterns to solve the problems.

Crystallized intelligence draws heavily on the ability to structure knowledge in verbal form, and to use language to make sense of the world. Language is important because words represent ideas and concepts that are the substance of thought. This means that language builds our understanding of the world not directly, but through the concepts that words represent. Given the connection between crystallized intelligence and language, it makes sense that the size of a person's vocabulary is a good predictor of IQ. In exploring why this is so, let's recognize two facts. First, children learn new words at a fantastically rapid rate, on average about 10 words each day.[16] Second, children vary significantly around that average— some children learn new words at a faster rate, others slower. Over time, the different rates of learning new words produce tremendous variation in the size of children's vocabulary. Adults, too, vary in the size of their vocabularies. In both children and adults, that variation correlates significantly with measured intelligence.

In the armamentarium of the human intellect, vocabulary seems to be very important—surprisingly so. This connection implies that we ought to build our functional vocabularies as much as possible. In the normal course of development, we learn new words in a variety of ways: by reading definitions in a dictionary, through instruction in school, or in the case of young children, by being taught by parents and other adults. These modes of word learning are direct and purposeful, but vocabulary growth cannot be accounted for solely by intentional teaching and learning. Word knowledge is not normally gained primarily through rote learning and memorization, but indirectly through encountering new words in the daily flow of conversation, during instruction by teachers, or through books or other media. Unfamiliar words are not usually defined outright. Instead, their meanings have to be inferred from context.

Let's also be clear about what it means to learn a new word. It's nothing like tossing a penny into a jar of coins. The mind's growing knowledge base is not a particulate array of isolated bits of knowledge. It's much more organic. Long-term memory is a massive system of interconnected concepts. We use that conceptual grid every day to interpret the elaborate world of people, things, and ideas, and to act intelligently within it. Vocabulary acquisition therefore entails much more than learning the definition of a new word. It must connect to our existing knowledge base, including other word meanings, and so becomes an element in a vast system to understand the world as well as a bridge to further learning. Language and language-based knowledge are not to be underestimated in their intellective potency. That's why knowledge in verbal form is rightly considered a powerful form of intelligence—crystallized intelligence in particular.

Together, fluid and crystallized intelligence open a window into the deep structure of intelligence. We can dismiss the simplistic notion that there exists only one form of intelligence, pure and simple. The more complex and accurate picture is that human intelligence has different manifestations, two of which are fluid and crystallized. Both are vitally important, but are they equally so? Or is one more important than the other to living intelligently in the 21st century? The answer is not obvious. Without question, crystallized intelligence is crucial. After all, structured knowledge in specialized fields is indispensable to every complex society. Think about the technical knowledge needed to design a smart phone, perform heart surgery, or draft legal documents to support the merger of two companies. Specialized knowledge matters greatly, yet a compelling argument can be made that fluid intelligence is paramount. In today's world, and pointedly in business, the best ideas—those that are most profitable and transformative—are breakthrough concepts and designs. The flashes of insight that change the way we think, act, and live are manifestations of fluid intelligence.

Crystallized and fluid intelligence are both critical. But provisions for their development in society, especially by our educational systems, are a bit lopsided. To make the point, consider which receives greater emphasis in schools. It's quite obvious that crystallized intelligence is the intelligence factor that has received the higher billing. In a way, this is understandable: It's easier to teach and test for highly structured crystallized knowledge than the capacity for adaptive thinking that constitutes fluid intelligence.[17] Yet to admit that the preponderance of educational effort is channeled to the development of crystallized intelligence is not to say that a skewed curriculum is best or should be maintained. Quite the opposite: If we believe that fluid intelligence is at least equal to crystallized in promoting the survival and success of future generations, the imbalance must be redressed. This won't be easy. Centuries of structuring curricula around traditional subject areas have established teaching practices that have formidable inertia. To build the vital intellectual capital that consists jointly of crystallized and fluid intelligence requires changes in the ways schools operate. Even more fundamentally, assumptions about the purpose of education must be challenged.

FLUID AND CRYSTALLIZED INTELLIGENCE OVER THE LIFE SPAN

To be effective, every institution—large and small, public and private— needs to cultivate a strong base of fluid and crystallized intelligence among its members. With plentiful supply of both forms of intelligence, chances are good that an organization's human capital will have both the expertise and the creative "mojo" to propel innovation in the years ahead. But how can this be accomplished? With intellectual firepower so important to modern society, and especially to a society's capacity to innovate, what can be done to equip a nation, company, or educational institution with sufficient reserves of fluid and crystallized intelligence?

To understand how to increase fluid and crystallized intelligence, we must first consider that they are not static over the course of life, but shift in predictable ways.[18] Figure 2.4 depicts the typical pattern of change through the life span.

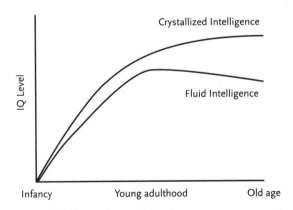

Figure 2.4
Fluid and Crystallized Intelligence Over Life Span. Martinez, Michael E., *Learning and Cognition: The Design of the Mind,* ©2010. Printed and Electronically reproduced by permission of Pearson Education, Inc., Upper Saddle River, New Jersey.

To interpret the graph, let's begin with fluid intelligence. The pattern of change over time can be stated succinctly: Starting in childhood, our capacity to adapt to challenging environments rises quickly. Through adolescence and into early adulthood, we make rapid gains in flexible thinking as applied to new problems. Unfortunately, that marvelous upward trend does not continue forever. Fluid intelligence tends to peak between the ages of 22 and 30—around the time that many young adults launch their careers or begin their most demanding periods of study in graduate or professional school.[19] It's also the age range of those who make major breakthroughs in certain technical fields, especially mathematics and physics.

For most people, learning that fluid intelligence peaks in early adulthood is no surprise. Conventional wisdom tells us that younger adults are more adaptable in thought and behavior than older adults. Other factors being equal, a young adult will display a greater degree of cognitive flexibility—the trait that we identify with fluid intelligence. It's easy to think of unflattering attributions that are commonly applied to adults in middle or advanced years: We can become "set in our ways" and find it uncommonly hard to "learn new tricks." Those clichés may contain a grain of truth.

It's not all bad, though. The picture is more assuring when we consider the counterpart trend: Over the life span, we become more knowledgeable. Crystallized intelligence typically rises until the age of 50 or so, and then is maintained indefinitely. Beyond the age of 70, crystallized intelligence may decline, but seems to do so only in response to poor health. If good health continues, crystallized intelligence might continue to rise. In this expression of intelligence, age—or rather, time—seems to be an ally. Indeed, expert status in any technical field is most often accorded to experienced adults. Years of specialized work can build technical knowledge to impressive proportions. The resulting manifestation of crystallized intelligence as expertise is a tremendous asset.

Now let's return to the trend for fluid intelligence. This is the trend that is cause for the most concern. It means that a person's ability to respond to a complex environment rises into young adulthood, but after that, through middle age and beyond, the capacity to adapt begins a long, slow decline. No one really knows why fluid intelligence tapers off as we age. Pessimistically, it may be an inevitable consequence of brain deterioration. A more optimistic explanation is that the decline is a consequence of lifestyle decisions. The first two or three decades of life are marked by rapidly shifting demands in both intellectual and social realms, and these changes demand that the young person adapt, often in very significant ways.[20] Starting in middle age, however, adults typically choose a more stable life path, one that requires less flexibility. With greater life stability we may come to rely more on routines and less on strategy shifts. The decline in fluid intelligence that accompanies aging may be a direct consequence of changes in intellectual habits.[21]

In theory, declines in intellectual flexibility could be offset by a conscious decision to resist a predictable lifestyle. This might mean taking up new areas of study, pursuing new career paths, learning a new language, or exploring the world through travel. The press to adapt, ever-present in youth and early adulthood, can be maintained through middle age and beyond with the hypothetical consequence of preserving fluid intelligence. Indeed, many older adults intuitively comprehend the connection between self-challenge and mental agility. They deliberately organize their lives to change up their daily experience, in effect forcing themselves not to rely on established routines. The hope is that this self-directed training will preserve cognitive flexibility and adaptability—the hallmarks of fluid intelligence. This hope is a reasonable expectation: Research supports the belief that engagement in an active lifestyle is associated with preservation, or even improvement, of cognitive abilities in the advanced years.[22]

THE WORKFORCE OF THE 21ST CENTURY

Perhaps in the future we will come to know the full explanation for declines in fluid intelligence with age. For now, the important fact remains that older workers tend to lack the cognitive flexibility of younger workers. By itself, this fact may be more interesting than concerning, but if a nation or company happens to have an aging workforce, then serious implications might follow. The combination of these two trends—the rising need for fluid intelligence in the 21st century and the aging workforce characteristic of many countries around the world—spells bad news. Psychologist Earl Hunt faced the dilemma squarely in his book *Will We Be Smart Enough?*[23] He pressed the question of whether aging populations pose a risk for economic viability and competitiveness. These trends might be especially worrisome for nations that are experiencing declining birthrates, such as Germany and Japan.

It's an issue for corporate workforces, too. As personal investment portfolio values declined during the recession, many workers were forced to postpone retirement. Established companies, saddled with a heavy burden of retirees' pensions, found it difficult to compete with younger companies that were less fiscally, and perhaps intellectually, encumbered. Around the world, governments must now consider whether to shift the normative retirement age upward. As the average age of workers drifts higher, organizations gain greater reserves of crystallized intelligence that derive from long years of experience. But the crucial resource of fluid intelligence—the engine of adaptability and innovation—declines on average. This downtick may well put a company or nation at a competitive disadvantage.

There is no question: Workers in every setting—businesses, universities, nonprofits, hospitals, and government agencies—benefit from the potent resource of fluid intelligence. That's why institutional leaders should consider how they can structure the experience of their workers to maintain, and possibly improve, their reserves of fluid intelligence—intelligence that helps secure a prosperous and profitable future. Yet it's a mistake to downplay crystallized intelligence in favor of fluid intelligence. Both are necessary. The combination of fluid and crystallized intelligence is what makes people—students, workers, and citizens—most effective. Fluid intelligence yields the marvelous adaptability and innovative thinking that are so highly prized and that transform the way we live. Crystallized intelligence is hugely important, too. At higher levels, it manifests as the expertise that is foundational to nearly every great achievement.

Why choose between fluid and crystallized intelligence? Is it not ideal to have generous reserves of both? And rather than worrying excessively about birthrates and average age of a workforce, wouldn't it be better to focus on raising the intelligence of everyone? If such a thing could be done, then the trend lines over the life span would retain interesting and important patterns, but would no longer suggest scenarios of doom. To enhance intelligence directly and intentionally is to gain tremendous freedom. This can become our vision for a bright and exciting future.

SIMPLE OR COMPLEX?

Psychologists tend to see intelligence as a manifestation of higher-level thinking. This was Binet's perspective: He understood intelligence as a person's ability to perceive order in a complex world, to understand that order, and to think and act adaptively within it. A person's ability to solve problems, to think critically, and to understand complex subject matter are all signs of a highly effective intellect. But is there more to intelligence? Should human intelligence be understood *only* in terms of higher-order thought?

Not necessarily. Remember that even before Alfred Binet developed his first tests of intelligence, Francis Galton collected information about people's basic perceptual acuity and reaction time. Galton believed that these lower-order biological factors underlay the manifest differences in people's success in Victorian England. Early in this chapter, we considered a fundamental paradox in understanding human intelligence: Is it one thing or many? Now we face a second paradox. If we place Binet's and Galton's theories side by side, we confront that paradox squarely: Is the essence of intelligence complex reasoning, or is it rooted firmly in differences at the level of perception and reaction time, which in turn reflect differences at the neuronal level?

This second dilemma has parallels in computer functioning. Imagine a very powerful computer. It can sift through mountains of data to find patterns, perform calculations, and formulate projections—all at lightning speed. What seems obvious is that the computer's ability to deal effectively with massive data inputs is a function of its sophisticated programming. Yet beneath this manifest performance is the computer's basic design. This architecture sets the computer's processing speed and its data storage capacity, which in turn are functions of its hardware and software parameters. To some extent, then, a computer's ability to perform rapid, complex, and perhaps even intelligent work is a function of its fundamental architecture.

Now the question is: Can we detect an equivalent to a computer's architecture in the expression of human intelligence? A fascinating body of research suggests important parallels between the two. Here, I refer to research on *elementary* cognitive processes. One of the best-known examples is an extremely basic visual task known as inspection time. In this task, a computer screen shows two parallel lines of slightly different lengths. The response is simply to indicate which one, right or left, is longer (Figure 2.5).

Respondents almost always select the correct line, and so the point of the task is not to determine whether the response is right or wrong. Instead, the parameter of interest is reaction time. How long an exposure is needed for a person to perceive a difference in the lengths of the two lines? The presentation of lines on a computer screen can be shortened to tiny fractions of a second—no more than a brief flash. If the exposure is gradually reduced, eventually it becomes so short that no viewer would be able

Figure 2.5
Inspection Time Comparison: Which Line Is Longer, Right or Left?

to detect a difference. That minimal duration varies from person to person. The briefest exposure required to answer correctly is the person's inspection time. Inspection times have surprisingly high correlations with IQ, about $r = -.50$.[24] Here, the negative sign indicates that a high IQ corresponds to a low response time. People with high IQs tend to make perceptual judgments very quickly; they need only the briefest periods of exposure to detect a difference in length between the two lines. Fast inspection times correlate especially well with high scores on tests of fluid intelligence.[25]

The most common interpretation of inspection time data is that it reveals the biological limits of information processing. For reasons that may trace to the level of neurons, people vary in the time needed to distinguish between the lengths of two lines. It's not completely clear, however, that personal limits in information processing are actually what is being measured. If the task taps some sort of fundamental limit, then we would expect inspection time to be highly stable. This turns out not to be the case. A person's inspection time can vary from minute to minute, and performance can improve significantly with practice.[26] The stable patterns that form when data are averaged are much more erratic than those averages themselves suggest. This means that the proper interpretation of inspection time research is not totally clear. Yet even if we don't know why, we must acknowledge that what seems to be a ridiculously simple cognitive performance—judging which of two lines is longer—somehow predicts a span of cognitive capabilities.

Reaction times from other elementary cognitive tasks have likewise been correlated with IQ scores. In one experiment, participants use a console of lights and buttons. At the top is a row of five lights and five buttons, one button per light. Those lights flash in a random order—such as 5, 2, 3, 4. At the bottom of the console is a single "home" button, which the participant keeps pressed until the lights stop flashing. The correct response is to move a finger from the home button to press the buttons below each light in the same sequence—5, 2, 3, 4. Though not quite as simple as the inspection time task, this task is obviously not difficult. Participants make few errors, but average reaction times do vary from person to person. On this task, also, reaction times correlate surprisingly well with IQ.[27]

What do these correlations mean? They are based on tasks that seem incredibly basic. Their correlations with IQ appear to challenge the belief that intelligence is higher-order in nature, or at least challenge the assumption that intelligence is *only* higher-order. Elementary information processing in some way composes part of the complete picture of human intelligence.[28] Certainly human intelligence includes higher-order thinking, but maybe intelligence is more truly a reflection of the nervous system—maybe it is more biological than cognitive in essence. That, at least, seems to be the standard interpretation of the data relating IQ to performance on simple tasks.[29]

These streams of research seem to link intelligence to basic brain processes. They imply that intelligence relies on the brain's ability to analyze basic sensory stimuli and to respond efficiently. Apparently, differences in basic neural architecture give rise to differences in measured IQ. However, at least two cautions are in order. First, any inference that biological factors are fully dictated by DNA is too simple. After all, genes respond to environmental variation. One person may be genetically predisposed to be tall and another to be short, but their eventual heights will be affected by nutrition. Likewise, a man who is genetically predisposed to heart disease can establish a regimen of exercise and a low cholesterol diet that counteracts the risks set by his genes. Only quite specific traits, such as eye color, are strictly controlled by genotype. So while acknowledging the shaping forces of genetics on individual differences—both physiological and intellectual—we must understand that genes rarely dictate a trait. DNA is not destiny.

A second caution applies directly to the interpretation of data on elementary cognitive processes. This caution is somewhat technical, having to do with the difference between means and standard deviations. Recall that a statistical mean is simply the average, a computation any of us can do on a calculator. The standard deviation tells us something different: It measures the spread of the data points around the average. Now let's apply this distinction—means and standard deviations—to the data on elementary cognitive tasks. It's true that people with high IQs tend to have faster reaction times compared to those with lower IQs, and this is interesting. But equally interesting is that the two groups also differ in the standard deviations. Here the focus is on personal variation—how the reaction times of a single person vary from one trial to the next. This is the most interesting part: IQ is correlated with mean reaction times, but IQ is correlated much more strongly with standard deviations.[30] Somehow, the standard deviations of reaction times are saying something important, but what?

For the explanation, consider the basic pattern: High-IQ participants tend to be *consistent* from trial to trial. Because their reaction times don't vary much, the standard deviations around their mean times are small. Lower-IQ participants show the opposite pattern. On some trials they respond quickly, but on others they are slow. Their data points scatter widely, resulting in a larger personal standard deviation. This inconsistency may explain why their average reaction times are slow. Apparently, at play in the uneven performance are lapses in attention. Such lapses directly increase the standard deviations, but they also affect the means: Slower reaction times drag down the average.

This explanation implies that at least some of the gap between high- and low-IQ people is the *inconsistency* of participants with lower IQs. In fact, it may explain the entire correlation between reaction time in IQ. It's not that high-IQ people are more capable of responding faster; rather, their more consistent responses mean that they have fewer slow responses. A similar pattern has been detected in studies of brain waves: The wave forms of high-IQ people appear to be much more consistent than those of lower-IQ subjects.[31] What explains these differences in consistency? The answer seems to involve higher-level functions of attentional control—functions that are regulated by the brain's frontal cortex, the seat of higher-level cognition.

If this line of reasoning holds, then our initial interpretation of reaction time data is now completely inverted. Reaction time, which on its face appears to be a lower-level cognitive function, involves the higher-level skills of monitoring and control. The same interpretation—that apparently simple processes might actually rely on higher-level control—may apply to other elementary tasks as well. This brings us back to the question of whether intelligence, at root, is an expression of basic biology or higher-order cognition. We have plenty of evidence to show that intelligence reflects higher-order functioning. As we have seen, one excellent test of fluid intelligence, Raven's Matrices, draws upon a person's ability to induce rules from a complex grid of patterns. Inductive reasoning, problem solving, and the management of complex goals are all known to underlie performance on IQ tests.[32] We know too much about the nature of human intelligence to believe that higher-order skills don't matter. They do. Yet even very simple perceptual tasks correlate significantly with IQ scores, so basic processes are also important. The intelligent mind relies on both lower-level and higher-level functions working in tandem.

RESOLVING PARADOXES

This chapter explored the nature of intelligence by confronting two paradoxes. Each paradox concerned two dualities—two seemingly opposite qualities. Phrased as a question, the first paradox is simply this: Is intelligence one entity, or is it many? If the answer is *many*, then the word *intelligence* may be a misnomer. Although we use the singular word *intelligence* in everyday speech, perhaps there are only "intelligences," distinct mental capabilities that coordinate to produce intelligent behavior. In a way, the question of whether intelligence is a unified whole or a diverse collection of mental abilities is the most fundamental theoretical question imaginable. To make any real progress in understanding what intelligence is, the early intelligence theorists needed an answer.

At first, the paradox of unity or diversity was only deepened by data that seemed to support both positions. The research of the British psychologist Charles Spearman confirmed the mathematical reality of general intelligence, which Spearman symbolized as g. The American researcher L. L. Thurstone arrived at the opposite conclusion: His data indicated a handful of distinct mental abilities rather than a unified general factor. Eventually the paradox was resolved—not by the vindication of either Spearman or Thurstone, but by each acknowledging that his rival was, at least to some extent, correct. Independently, each man concluded that intelligence has properties of unity and diversity.

Ultimately, the unity–diversity paradox was resolved in the hierarchical model of intelligence. At the apex of the pyramid-shaped model is general intelligence, akin to Spearman's g, and below the pinnacle is a small set of broad factors that bear some resemblance to Thurstone's primary mental abilities. Among the broad factors, two stand out as especially important—fluid intelligence and crystallized intelligence. At the base of the pyramid are narrow factors, such as perceptual speed, that identify quite specific aspects of mental proficiency. Articulated as a hierarchy, these three layers—general intelligence, broad factors, and narrow factors—present a coherent picture of intelligence.

A second paradox also emerged in the earliest days of scientific research on intelligence. It concerned whether intelligence consists essentially of elementary processes, such as reaction time and sensory acuity, or whether intelligence is at heart complex, expressed as the ability to process abstract and intricate ideas. The polarities of this paradox were identified by two pioneers in the study of human intelligence, Francis Galton and Alfred Binet. In the late 1800s, Galton poured considerable effort into testing his hypothesis that eminent achievers were biologically superior to their less remarkable peers. Galton focused on basic parameters of the senses, nerves, and motor control.

Alfred Binet's assumptions about intelligence flowed in the opposite direction. He saw intelligence as reflecting higher-order thinking, including both knowledge about the world and the ability to reason. Binet's assumptions were built into the design of the first intelligence tests and received immediate support through the ability of those tests to predict children's success in schools. Galton's assumptions, by contrast, were not immediately confirmed, but subsequent generations of researchers uncovered evidence for his ideas. Some very simple tasks, such as speed in comparing the length of two lines, correlate surprisingly well with IQ scores. These studies implied that intelligence reflects basic parameters of the nervous system, such as reaction time and nerve conduction velocity. This is not too different from the way Francis Galton thought about the sources of eminence in the mid-1800s. Alfred Binet's view, that intelligence is tied to higher-level functions, has a great deal of support and is much more popular today.

Here, then, is the resolution to the second paradox: Research supports a view of intelligence as both lower-order and higher-order. Both Galton and Binet had valid insights into the nature of intelligence. This makes sense: The mind's ability to engage in higher-level operations must in some way rest on a foundation of lower-level functions. This explanation maps nicely to a computational model of the mind. In such an interpretation, the efficiency of lower-level process such as neuron function and basic perceptual tasks are akin to a computer's underlying hardware. Higher-level reasoning and problem solving draw, in turn, on the mind's software—the accumulated content-rich knowledge acquired through experience.[33] If the comparison between the mind and a computer holds up, we see the dualities converge and reconcile. The power of any computer to do complex work rests on its elementary design parameters, such as clock speed, cache memory, and bit register size. That human intelligence might likewise depend partly on the mind's basic design parameters should not be too surprising.

We can sum up this way: Over many decades of research, progress on understanding human intelligence has entailed the exploration and eventual resolution of two fundamental paradoxes:

1. Is intelligence one or many?
2. Is intelligence simple or complex?

The history of research on intelligence reveals that the resolution of key paradoxes was not accomplished by one side winning out. Instead, the paradoxes were resolved through the emergence of new ways of thinking: Intelligence is both unified and diverse, and intelligence is both simple and complex. The answers were, in effect, more complex than the questions originally posed. This tells us something: We must understand intelligence as fantastically rich and complex, an object of inquiry that is worthy of our best efforts to illuminate it. But we should not expect simple answers. Progress will be difficult. Yet the nature of intelligence is discoverable, and its essence is still being revealed to this day. In the next chapter, we'll examine some of the more recent forays into the frontier.

CHAPTER 3
Varieties of Intelligence

From modest beginnings, Binet's and Galton's informed guesswork evolved toward improvements in methods to measure intelligence and theories to explicate its nature. Still, not everyone was satisfied. The early theories grew out of the psychometric tradition, which meant that they were based on tests and test scores. These theories were tidy and precise—perhaps excessively so. They seemed firm to a degree that could blind scholars to alternative aspects of intelligence not captured by batteries of cognitive tests.

Above all, one broad criticism loomed: Most theories of intelligence seemed excessively narrow. The charge of narrowness can be pinned down further to say that psychometric theories of intelligence were overly analytic. Even such "broad" factors as fluid intelligence and crystallized intelligence were narrow in the sense that they were collectively logical, rational, and convergent. In one way or another, every psychometric factor seemed to highlight the mind's ability to perceive the elements and rules of a problem, and to focus the intellect to produce a "correct" answer.

Important as these skills are, do they really exhaust all the ways that the human mind expresses intelligence? And if the human mind is smart in other ways, what are they? In fact, it's not too difficult to generate a short list of contenders. Creativity, for example, is obviously neglected. Also marginalized is the ability to deal effectively with other people—what is sometimes called social intelligence. By some accounts, social skills should be regarded as an important expression of intelligence. Yet another possible form of intelligence is the ability to understand oneself. After all, the person who lacks insight into his or her own preferences, hopes, dreams, and the kinds of experiences that prompt fulfillment is seriously limited.

That person's ability to think and act intelligently will to some degree be compromised.

This chapter traces scholars' explorations into areas of knowledge, insight, and skill that might potentially fall under the umbrella of *intelligence*. Their research efforts widen the scope of how the mind undergirds effective thought and action. New theories of intelligence are good for two reasons. First, any attempt to cultivate intelligence is only as good as its underlying theory, and theories are always imperfect. We never want to conclude that our current theory is a finished work, true for all time. Second, if research can deepen our understanding of any field—science, medicine, economics, or intelligence—then the application of that knowledge will ipso facto be more powerful.

However, a caution is in order. The theories described in this chapter are *emergent* rather than *modern*. That's because *modern* implies the most current and up-to-date. That's not the right way to look at these theories. Collectively, they are works in progress—interesting, provocative, and promising, but as yet proven. They are emergent pockets of theoretical exploration that might eventually lead to revisions of classic theories by supplementing, revising, or perhaps even replacing the older, established ways of thinking about intelligence. As areas of exploration, the emergent theories deserve our attention not only because they are important, but also because each is fascinating in its own right.

MULTIPLE INTELLIGENCES

Among the challenges to traditional ways of thinking about human intelligence, none has had a greater popular impact than Howard Gardner's theory of multiple intelligences. In his book *Frames of Mind*, Gardner identified seven intelligences: logical-mathematical, linguistic, spatial, musical, bodily-kinesthetic, interpersonal, and intrapersonal.[1, 2] Over the past several decades, Gardner's theory has had a sweeping influence among educators. Indeed, the term *multiple intelligences* is commonly recognizable not only to teachers, but also to the broad public.

The most distinctive feature of multiple intelligences theory is that it recognizes not a single intelligence, but rather several independent *intelligences*. The plural is significant. With the addition of a single letter, *s*, Gardner repudiated the existence of a superordinate general ability that influences every cognitive act. Instead, Gardner argued that intelligent thought and behavior are products of relatively distinct abilities. Gardner's proposed intelligences are a mix of the familiar and the innovative. Three of the intelligences—logical-mathematical, verbal, and spatial—correspond directly to factors psychometricians have recognized for many decades. As elements of Gardner's theory, they are not particularly new except in one important regard: Gardner held these expressions of intellect to be autonomous, meaning that each operates independently, untethered to a common general intelligence that binds them together.

Gardner's theory builds upon multiple strands of evidence, not just those favored by psychometricians—test scores, correlations, and factor analysis.[3] For example, Gardner took into account cultural expressions of intelligence. Some cultures prize highly skilled performances in dance, and so establish training practices to develop dancing ability to high level. Such valuation of dance within some cultures constitutes evidence (anthropological, not psychometric) of bodily-kinesthetic intelligence. Gardner also used other forms of evidence to justify his theory. He noted for example, that several candidate "intelligences" were associated with particular symbol systems. Symbol systems include written text for linguistic intelligence, numerical symbols for mathematical intelligence, and notes and scores for musical intelligence. Yet another strand of evidence comprised clinical studies of brain injuries that impaired a person's cognitive ability in a circumscribed way. For example, damage to the lower left hemisphere often results in aphasia, an inability to produce or interpret speech. Damage to counterpart regions of the right hemisphere can disrupt a person's ability to produce or interpret music. If localized brain damage results in specific cognitive impairments, Gardner took such cases as evidence that separate and distinguishable intelligences compose the human psyche.

What about the scientific validity of multiple intelligences theory? Is it proper to set aside "intelligence" and to speak instead of relatively independent "intelligences"? The simple change from single to plural is not so easily justified. In fact, the available evidence places the tenets of Gardner's theory in serious doubt. Most problematic is Gardner's central idea that the identified intelligences are relatively autonomous. This is tantamount to claiming that the common pattern of correlations known as the positive manifold does not apply to the "intelligences." Yet, as Charles Spearman and countless other investigators found over more than a century of research, Gardner's claim does not align with the psychometric evidence. Simply put, cognitive abilities are correlated.

The claim that linguistic, logical-mathematical, and spatial intelligences are relatively autonomous is easily refuted by analyses showing that these factors are significantly intercorrelated. These correlations are the mathematical basis for the top-level factor of general intelligence. On the other hand, brain-imaging studies do indicate a partial modularity: Specific brain regions can be linked to particular cognitive functions. Yet, as every neuroscientist knows, modularity is a partial truth. In every expression of higher-order thinking, distinct brain regions coordinate to accomplish complex cognitive work—writing a poem, designing a building, or composing a symphony. Also, not all brain regions are specialized: Some regions serve quite general functions that cut across diverse expressions of the intellect. The frontal lobe, for example, underlies the general function of higher-order planning; another brain structure, the hippocampus, is crucial to the formation of long-term memories. So although evidence of brain modularity may support the existence of distinct intelligence factors, the same evidence does not necessarily support a theory of multiple "intelligences" that operate relatively independently.

Despite challenges to its validity, Gardner's theory of multiple intelligences became quite popular among educators during the 1980s and 1990s. Those who became acquainted with Gardner's theory understood that traditional theories of intelligence were easy targets for criticism. The reason was simple: Those theories were not broad enough. Intelligence as classically interpreted was hyper-logical and excessively analytical. This was a problem, and Gardner knew it. Gardner himself did not reject logical and analytical thinking outright, but recognized this expression of mental capability as one of many different expressions of intelligence. It's easy to sympathize with multiple intelligences theory because it emphasizes breadth, a sensibility that motivates many other investigators in the search for a more inclusive theory.[4]

Closely related to theoretical breadth is breadth of a different sort. Multiple intelligences theory recognizes that intelligence is more liberally distributed among people than is typically assumed by those who see intelligence as those hyper-logical functions measured by IQ tests. If, instead, intelligence has diverse expressions, then it probably is expressed in diverse people. This idea, more than any other, was the likely basis for the enthusiasm generated by multiple intelligences theory. Teachers resonated with a more liberal conceptualization of intelligence because it did not order their students along a single continuum of cognitive ability. Many saw their students displaying a spectrum of intelligence in varied forms, and Gardner's theory was fully consistent with that point of view. Yet to some extent the same assumption has support within classical theories of intelligence. Although we can justifiably speak of general intelligence, person-to-person variations in cognitive profiles are common. Flat profiles, in which a person's specific factors are more or less equal, are rare. In this sense, Gardner was right: People *are* smart in different ways.

We see hints of cognitive profile differences whenever SAT and GRE tests result in quite different verbal and quantitative subscores, but such variation is also common on subtests that make up IQ batteries. Profile variation tends to be more pronounced with higher IQ scores. Uneven profiles do not negate the validity of general intelligence, but they do show that a single IQ score can hide important differences.[5] They also tell us that a highly intelligent society can be, and probably will be, an intellectually diverse society. If uneven cognitive profiles are so common, the pattern suggests untapped potential. It further implies that the purposes of education ought to be broadened to recognize talent in its diverse manifestations. Indeed, one reason Howard Gardner set forth his theory was to spur educators to question the typical school curriculum—to ask whether it was too narrow and, if so, to make corrective changes.

Of course, Gardner's theory was also intended to spur a reconsideration of intelligence theories. Traditional models of intelligence, expressed as mono-dimensional IQ scores, imply that the world's population can be ordered along a single ladder of intellectual ability. Gardner's theory of multiple intelligences presents a liberating alternative; it offers the inspiring possibility that diverse intelligences are broadly distributed in the population. Unfortunately, the theory's freeing implications rest on a foundation that is inadequate in important respects.[6] Getting our theories right is essential. We must try to understand the nature of intelligence in its truest form before we can seriously consider how to expand or increase the collective intelligence of our society. With this in mind, let us now look to other emergent theories of intelligence theory.

SUCCESSFUL INTELLIGENCE

Robert Sternberg's theory of successful intelligence is one of the major current alternatives to traditional theories.[7] The name of Sternberg's theory makes intuitive sense. In the theory of successful intelligence, we find connections to the theories of Galton and Binet in that those early theories were likewise linked to success outcomes—most often academic success. Sternberg does not challenge the fundamental basis for evaluating whether a proposed form of intelligence is legitimate. He recognizes that theories of intelligence are relevant to human activity and aspirations when they predict success in some form.[8] When success is not restricted to grade point averages but extends to real-life achievements, creative accomplishments, scientific breakthroughs, meaningful social participation, and emotional well-being, then the underlying intelligence rises further in importance.

In setting forth the theory of successful intelligence, Sternberg did not seek to replace traditional theories so much as to expand them. His theory recognizes three forms of intelligence: analytical, practical, and creative. The first, analytical intelligence, is easily understood. It equates to intelligence as construed traditionally by all of Sternberg's predecessors, namely, the ability to engage in rational, abstract, and complex reasoning. This is the form of intelligence that is particularly advantageous in academic settings.

While recognizing that analytical intelligence is important, Sternberg argued it does not make for a complete theory. It's true that analytical intelligence, the kind measured by IQ tests, is a good predictor of success in schools and on the job. But being a good predictor is not the same as being a perfect predictor. If analytical intelligence fails to measure personal qualities that factor into success outside of academic settings, what are those qualities? They potentially include a broad swath of skills and habits: the ability to prioritize, to motivate others to achieve a common goal, to persuade, to gain favor, and dozens of others. These qualities might separate students who make the Dean's list from people who go on to achieve extraordinary real-life success. Even if we cannot say exactly what those complementary skills are, we need not be deterred from placing a name on this category: practical intelligence.

In Sternberg's theory, practical intelligence is intelligence applied to real-life situations, including schools.[9] In school settings, practical intelligence can be critical to success. Schools are, after all, human institutions in which success is achieved partly by the ability to navigate the system of social relations, norms, and expectations. Practical intelligence may be particularly important in graduate school, where building loyalties and establishing reputations typically rises in value when compared to undergraduate study. Robert Sternberg noticed that some of his best graduate students did not have particularly high GRE scores, yet they were fantastically good at figuring out practical strategies to progress efficiently and to gain favor in the institution. These students were attentive to the social context of success, and particularly to the unspoken rules by which the university operated. They knew how to find the resources they needed to reach their goals. They could distinguish between the official standards of performance and the ones that really count, and knew which channels to pursue to get something done, even if those channels were unofficial.

Some research on practical intelligence investigates the specific skills that contribute to success. A business executive, for example, has to make ongoing judgments about how to handle a stream of tasks. To measure this ability, the scenario has been modeled as the "in-basket" task in which managers process a series of simulated memos, phone messages, and other work-related demands. Possible actions include delegating a task, seeking additional information, and asking for advice.[10] Performance on the in-basket task was correlated with background job knowledge, as expected. But high performance also had a creative element: Executives with higher scores were frequently able to generate a large number of related ideas.

Practical intelligence appears to be important as well as distinct from other abilities. Close in meaning to what we might call "street smarts," practical intelligence is a honed sense of how to behave smartly in particular social and work contexts. Measures of practical intelligence tend not to correlate well with IQ scores, suggesting that the ability to exercise intelligence in real-world settings is truly distinct from traditional analytical intelligence. Yet we should not be too quick to accept practical intelligence as a fully legitimate form of intelligence. For one thing, "street smarts" might be too narrowly confined to specific contexts. Practical intelligence in the domains of athletic performance, acting, entrepreneurship, comedic performance, medicine, and politics might be quite distinct ability sets with little potential for crossover benefit.

Another criterion that can be used to appraise practical intelligence is its predictive power. Traditional IQ scores display validity if they can predict academic success. Does Sternberg's construct of practical intelligence offer predictive utility for valued performance? The answer appears to be *yes*. The evidence comes from tests Sternberg designed to measure practical intelligence in specific contexts, such as a business setting. The tests presented credible scenarios, such as how to handle conflicting priorities or resolve interpersonal conflicts. Measures of practical intelligence did in fact correlate with success on the job. More important, practical intelligence had predictive power *beyond* that offered by traditional IQ tests.

Practical intelligence includes the ability to perceive unwritten rules that are conducive to success. Psychologists have a name for such unwritten rules—*tacit knowledge*. Tests devised to measure tacit knowledge have shown remarkably good power to predict success—as much as twice that of IQ—among academics and business managers. Job-related tacit knowledge predicts job performance, and the function is largely independent of that offered by traditional intelligence tests. On a technical level, measures of tacit knowledge tend to correlate across domains. This means that people who are good at detecting the unwritten rules for success in one setting are likely to be skilled at understanding a different set of rules in another context. They are quick to understand how to work with other people, what tasks are most important, and how to maximize productivity.[11]

Measures of practical intelligence have other interesting features, too, including predictable life span trends. Earlier we saw that one form of intelligence—fluid intelligence—tends to peak in early adulthood, whereas crystallized intelligence generally rises until quite late in life. Measures of practical intelligence follow trends closer to crystallized intelligence, rising through the years until about age 70. The escalating trend for practical intelligence through the life span is easily interpretable: Through extended experience, adults improve in their abilities to solve practical problems with advancing years.[12] Gains in practical intelligence also seem to parallel increases in wisdom later in life. Indeed, wisdom can be seen as a subset of practical intelligence.[13] Like practical intelligence, wisdom draws on the ability to register the tacit knowledge in a particular problem context—to understand the factors operative in a particular situation, whether tacit or explicit. Wisdom entails the ability to weigh those factors and to arrive at decisions that strike a balance between upholding individual interests and promoting the common good.

Creative intelligence is the third aspect of Sternberg's theory. Think of the world's great works of art, music, literature, architecture, and engineering. In every case, creative thinking contributed to the insights and breakthroughs that enriched society. Creativity has always figured into the advances of civilizations through the millennia, and its importance has not diminished in our own times. In the most revolutionary applications of information technologies—the Macintosh computer, the Internet, smart phones—old-fashioned analytical thinking was essential but not enough. Creativity propelled the technical breakthroughs that forever changed the way the world operated. It couldn't be more obvious: The creative mind is one very powerful force. Sternberg's theory recognizes this key expression of intellect as a fully legitimate aspect of human intelligence.

To test Sternberg's claim, let's consider again the question of predictive power. Does measured creativity predict academic success, for example? In the Rainbow Project, Sternberg pitted tests that measured creative and practical intelligence against the decidedly analytical SAT.[14] He found that when SAT scores were supplemented by tests of creative and practical intelligence, the combination was more predictive of college grades than was the SAT alone. The correct conclusion seemed to be that academic success in the university is not only a function of analytic intelligence; it also draws upon creative and practical abilities. After graduating, presumably, all three forms of intelligence continue to have value. As alumni make their way through the "real world" beyond the campus, practical and creative intelligence arguably play even more important roles in career and life success. This rationale—that analytical ability is legitimate but not fully sufficient—lies at the heart of Sternberg's theory of successful intelligence.

Besides expanding our understanding of intelligence beyond analytical ability, Sternberg's theory challenges the analytical focus of most school curricula. If diverse capabilities really do underlie success, and if the human capital of any company, community, or nation consists of diverse cognitive abilities, then our educational systems ought to recognize the fact and then cultivate those same abilities. The point is that when our assumptions about intellectual capabilities are updated, so should our ideas about the purposes and processes of education. What's at stake is not only the intellectual readiness of a population to compete in a global economy, but also the cherished democratic ideals of equity and opportunity. Powerful ideas can be springboards for positive change.

But let's not accept Sternberg's theory, or any other new theory of intelligence, too quickly. Proposing a new theory of intelligence is not the same as justifying that theory through research-based evidence. As we evaluate the credibility and utility of Sternberg's theory, we must be careful not to accept it simply because it sounds plausible; rather, we must ask whether it is supported by evidence. It's not too hard to think of challenges to Sternberg's claims. We can question, for example, whether creative ability is a broad personal trait that can be applied to many different fields, or whether it is by nature focused in particular fields, such as music or interior decorating.

Whether creativity is narrow or broad matters. When we call creative ability an *intelligence*, the implication is that it applies broadly—that creative people can employ their divergent insights to different domains. On this question, the evidence is mixed: Creativity is relatively domain-bound, but not completely. Across domains, creative expression is mildly positively correlated. Sometimes people know how to exercise their creative ability in multiple contexts. As a psychological construct, then, the coherence and predictive power of creative intelligence can be defended. The argument for creativity as a major dimension of the intellect is compelling—a fact recognized by Sternberg and many other scholars of the mind. Because this is so, we will now consider creative intelligence on its own terms and independently of Sternberg's theory.

CREATIVE INTELLIGENCE

Let's explore creativity more fully as a potential form of intelligence. We have seen that analytical intelligence is the brand of mental ability measured by most tests of intelligence and summarized in IQ scores. Those tests measure a person's ability to take in, or *consume*, information and to process that information rationally. Highly creative people, however, excel in their ability to *produce* outstanding ideas. Yet production of information is relatively neglected in most theories of intelligence. It seems hard to argue that production of information is any less important than consumption in the work of the mind. For this reason, many scholars who study giftedness regard traditional analytical intelligence as inadequate to the measurement of productive potential, especially in the creative realms.[15]

In a way, creativity has little to do with intelligence as typically conceived. The two intellectual modes might even appear to be at odds. The separation of the analytical and the creative aspects of the mind has been inspired to some extent by cases of savant syndrome. Among savants, artistic skill is sometimes correlated with actual dysfunction in the language centers of the brain.[16] The onset of dementia affecting the ability to speak can also coincide with the sudden appearance of artistic expression and other savant-like skills. Neuroscientists in Australia have applied this hypothesis experimentally to people with normal brain functioning. By pulsing magnetic fields into the language centers of the left temporal lobe, they were able to temporarily deactivate linguistic processing. During the few hours when language functions were compromised, some of the participants began to display savant-like abilities. Some subjects displayed enhanced artistic ability, while others showed improved accuracy in numerical estimation of quantity.[17] These findings suggest it is possible to "turn on" creativity and savant-like abilities by "turning off" parts of the brain responsible for other functions.

Creativity and intelligence are not necessarily antagonistic. Statistically speaking, creative thinking and intelligence are positively correlated, at least in the low to mid range of IQ. People recognized in their fields as highly creative often have at least moderately high levels of intelligence. But beyond an IQ of 120 or so, creativity and intelligence decouple such that one has little to do with the other.[18] This decoupling is consistent with the threshold theory of creativity: Its central claim is that traditional analytic intelligence is a platform on which creativity can build. A moderately high IQ seems to be all that is needed for truly outstanding creative accomplishments. But an IQ of 120 or so is a foundation, not a cutoff, and so the IQs of highly creative individuals often range much higher. In fact, the average IQ of the world's most eminent creative people extends to around 150.[19]

There is an alternative way to interpret the same data, however. It's possible that IQ and creativity are not related—at least not in any direct way.

Instead, the opportunity to be creative requires the proper certification, a degree or license for practicing a profession.[20] Such a certification typically requires prior admission to a university or professional school, which in turn requires the kinds of intelligence measured by IQ tests. If this is the true explanation of the correlation between IQ and creativity, then the supposed relationship is spurious or at least misleading. Analytical intelligence would be a bureaucratic prerequisite, nothing more.

Most scholars perceive an important relationship between analytical intelligence and creativity. They differ, however, in how they interpret that relationship. Some theorists see analytical intelligence and creative thought as organically connected—so much so that they interpret creative expression to be the "ultimate extension" of intelligence.[21] Other theorists treat intelligence and creativity as overlapping sets of cognitive abilities. Still other scholars draw firm distinctions between the two, interpreting intelligence and creativity to be quite different forms of cognitive expression. Their argument is that intelligence operates on the facts as given, whereas creativity relies much more on the particular ideas brought by the problem solver.

Creative expression may hinge on the ability to generate a large number of ideas and to select the best from among those.[22] The act of generating lots of relevant ideas or potential solutions is known as divergent production. This aspect of creativity contrasts with the requirement of convergent thinking—the generation of a single best answer or solution—demanded by many IQ and school-based tests. Divergent production entails searching broadly for relevant information and considering multiple solution paths rather than a single best response. The point is not to select the one "right" answer, but to produce many "good" answers. This criterion for evaluating ideas requires a significant shift in mindset.

Analytical and creative thinking are each distinctly valuable, but when combined they are fantastically potent. That's because these two forms of intelligence complement each other. Analytical thinking converges on a precisely correct answer, decision, or action. Creative thinking works oppositely—not through convergence but rather through divergence. The creative mind explores new possibilities, patterns, and options. It builds on what is already known but then transcends the "givens" to envision something new. The ability to think in new ways inevitably interacts with what the creative individual already knows. This raises the question of the role of knowledge in highly creative work.

Knowledge is widely believed to be double-edged.[23] On the one hand, extensive knowledge of a field is often necessary to recognize what counts as novel and creative.[24] To some extent, creative breakthroughs depend on knowing what has come before. Yet knowledge also guides thinking, and so may constrain ideation to the point that novel ideas are hard to generate or comprehend. Entrenched modes of thought might render the knowledge-able person incapable of understanding or accepting new ways of thinking. Breakthrough concepts may seem unintelligible, at least as viewed through the filter of old ideas. Highly creative people therefore face dual demands: They must be grounded in the creative field and yet have the intellectual flexibility to transcend the categories and boundaries of that field as tradi-tionally understood and practiced.

The lives of great innovators can shed light on the real-world conditions under which rarefied creativity originates. Biographies of Pablo Picasso, Igor Stravinsky, T. S. Eliot, and Martha Graham show that these luminar-ies were prepared to concentrate on their work to such an extreme degree that they isolated themselves from common pursuits and pleasures.[25] Their accomplishments required extraordinary concentration over long periods of time. To reach this supreme level of achievement seemed to require pat-terns of living that were configured to favor the creative pursuit. Other evidence suggests that highly creative people have a knack for identifying emergent ideas that are either not recognized or not respected by others, but which have high potential. Like investors who are skilled at picking underpriced stocks, innovators know how to identify undervalued ideas.

In some instances, new ideas can hold so much inherent potency that they redefine a field. Yet creative breakthroughs are sometimes powerfully resisted. To advance novel ideas, the creative individual not only needs a sense of which ideas are most promising, but also the ability to weather the countervailing opinions, including ridicule and scorn. Because new ideas may be rejected for long stretches of time, possibly through the entire life of the originator, creative people very often display extraordinary persistence.[26]

SOCIAL INTELLIGENCE

For many decades, theorists have known that intelligence can be applied to different forms of informational content, including numbers, words, and abstract symbols. In fact, we can think of classic analytical intelligence as skill in processing such abstractions. Intelligence can also be applied to abstract visual patterns or mechanical assemblages, forms of information that are not symbolic but rather are based on an understanding of spa-tial relations. Yet a third major category of information content is human behavior, both one's own behavior and the behavior of other people. The focus here is on the ability to understand and react intelligently to human behavior, the skill set sometimes known as social intelligence.

Social intelligence entails, at least in part, the ability to understand the feelings, beliefs, and intentions of other people, especially when those internal states are communicated through facial expressions, gestures, posture, or tone of voice. With some ingenuity, it's possible to test this ability. One method is to use photographs or voice recordings as stimulus materials. Examinees are asked to describe the emotions of the person depicted: Are they feeling sad, happy, afraid, guilty, tense, or bored? Such a test measures the ability to interpret behavior, but its measurement of social intelligence is passive and only partial.

Interpreting behavior and actively coping with that behavior are two independent skills, and both are manifestations of social intelligence. Social intelligence includes skill in both the passive interpretation of emotional states and the ability to interact effectively with others. This is social intelligence defined abstractly, but we can be much more specific. Skills that fall under the banner of social intelligence include interest in other people, empathy, social performance, emotional expressiveness, and sensitivity to others' lack of confidence. Potential factors that remain less explored are memory for names and faces, and the ability to produce the "right" behavior in particular settings, such as proper etiquette.

Alongside theories set forth by psychologists is research on what laypeople believe makes for a socially intelligent person. Nonpsychologists think of social intelligence as one important expression of what it means to be smart. They believe that a socially intelligent person:

- Displays curiosity
- Does not makes snap judgments
- Is sensitive to other people's needs and desires
- Understands others' thoughts, feelings, and intentions
- Is good at dealing with other people
- Has extensive knowledge of rules and norms in human relations
- Is good at taking the perspective of other people
- Adapts well in social situations
- Is on time for appointments [27]

Although social intelligence has not played a very important role in most theories of human intelligence, there are exceptions to this pattern. One is Howard Gardner's theory of multiple intelligences, described earlier. One of the "intelligences" proposed by Gardner is interpersonal intelligence, which corresponds rather closely to social intelligence. Gardner argued that clinical evidence on the effects of brain injury could help establish the legitimacy of a proposed new intelligence. He reasoned that if localized brain damage compromised one intelligence but left other intellectual abilities intact, that limited impairment constituted evidence that the particular intelligence exists and is relatively autonomous. We can apply this rule to social intelligence. Clinically, quite a bit of evidence shows that social intelligence is anatomically distinct from other cognitive abilities. The brain's frontal lobe, in particular, is crucial. This brain region allows us to interpret other people's actions and emotions, as well as exercise control over our own emotions and emotionally driven behavior.

Social intelligence entails more than the ability to label or control emotions. It also has components of knowledge stored in long-term memory. Socially relevant knowledge is of two kinds. One is factual knowledge about rules for social interaction, good manners, and so on. The other knowledge resource consists of memories of our past personal experiences. This autobiographical memory, called episodic memory by psychologists, is composed of episodes remembered from our lived experiences.[28] A large proportion of these episodes are social in nature, and this experiential memory bank is a resource we can draw upon in knowing how to interact with other people in the here and now. There is one potential complication, however: Episodic memory cannot be presumed to be accurate. Indeed, serious distortions of memory for "what actually happened" in this event or that are not only possible but common.

Let's focus now on the lingering question: Is social intelligence really a legitimate aspect of the human intellect? In some studies, social intelligence is correlated with IQ—but by itself this neither qualifies nor disqualifies social intelligence as a valid form of intelligent expression. Indeed, as a rule, different intelligence factors are positively correlated, at least moderately, and so we should not expect social intelligence to be completely independent of IQ. More problematic is that measures of social intelligence sometimes overlap with verbal ability, which is strongly associated with general intelligence. This complicates the measurement of social intelligence and throws into question its status as a legitimate, independent form of intelligence. That is because whenever social intelligence draws heavily on verbal ability, social intelligence becomes less distinguishable as an independent form of cognitive ability. Yet data also show that social intelligence holds together as a coherent factor. These mixed results indicate that, from a psychometric perspective at least, the status of social intelligence is ambiguous.

Whenever we wish to evaluate a potential new form of intelligence, we must ask whether variation in the proposed intelligence affects a person's ability to adapt. We have plenty of evidence showing that deficits in social intelligence have serious consequences. Consider that a lack of skill in relating to other people has long been recognized as a key marker of autism. Autistic people often have particular difficulty understanding that other people have thoughts that differ from their own. Nonautistic people know perfectly well that other people have independent thoughts and feelings. Those differences are, in fact, the entire basis for communication between people. Why communicate otherwise? To understand that people differ in what they think, know, and believe is to have a "theory of mind." A person who lacks this awareness is unlikely to reflect on his or her own thoughts and would find no logical reason to pursue interpersonal communication.

One reason for the semi-legitimate status of social intelligence is that it seems to be different in nature from analytic forms of intelligence. Traditional intelligence is measured on scales indicating "less" and "more" based on questions that have right and wrong answers. The personal resources that constitute social intelligence do not seem to work this way.[29] Social contexts may be too variable to submit to analyses that are reducible to right and wrong answers. Moreover, social perceptions and sensibilities that are functional in one culture may be nonfunctional in a different culture. What qualifies as intelligent social behavior might well vary from one neighborhood to another, or even from one household to another. Sensibly enough, what constitutes social intelligence must be understood in its social context as well as in the context of an individual's valued goals.

Let's conclude this way: Social intelligence has not yet been established as a fully legitimate form of human intelligence. To some extent, the problem is how to define and measure the various competencies that underlie social intelligence when we don't yet know exactly what it is or how it relates to traditional IQ. If these technical problems are eventually solved, we may find that social intelligence and traditional IQ have a complicated relationship. For example, knowing that another person's intelligence is much higher or lower than one's own can complicate how we view that person. Candidates for public office know this and may consciously try to affect the speech and demeanor of "regular folk." Such affectations are strategic. If a political candidate flaunts a very high IQ, it might be hard for rank-and-file citizens to trust the person. This may be why history's most eminent leaders seem to have moderately high, but not extraordinary, levels of intelligence. The risk of a very high IQ is that these potential leaders may talk over the heads of the general population. In two American presidential elections, for example, the highly intellectual Adlai Stevenson lost to the less brainy Dwight D. Eisenhower, possibly in part for this reason.[30]

To the degree that followers want to identify with their leaders, they may have trouble seeing a member of the intellectual elite as understanding their needs and representing their interests.

EMOTIONAL INTELLIGENCE

Without question, our emotions affect how and what we think. Anxiety and frustration can obstruct intelligent thought, whereas more positive emotions, such as interest and surprise, can direct and energize the mind.[31] One of the more studied aspects of negative emotion is test anxiety. Nearly everyone has the potential to feel anxious while taking a test, but in rare cases anxiety can be so debilitating that it nullifies a person's ability to express his or her knowledge or intellectual capabilities. Emotions can compromise rational thinking in everyday life, too. Frustration can trigger a rash decision to "let off steam" in the short term, but in the long term taking such action is counterproductive. Telling off the boss at the end of a hard day is probably imprudent, and driving a car recklessly in a fit of rage is dangerous. On the other hand, positive emotions can be powerful elements of the intellect. The capacity to become interested in ideas, insights, and discoveries—to derive satisfaction from the active use of the mind—is a sign of intellectual engagement and perhaps giftedness. Gifted children seem to have a large "capacity for high levels of interest, enthusiasm, fascination," and the ability to become deeply engrossed in an area of study.[32]

Auguste Rodin's famous sculpture *The Thinker* depicts a man in deep contemplation. His very posture exudes concentration. The Thinker's body is twisted, with his right elbow perched on his left knee and his fist placed to chin, and his torso is angled steeply forward. Rodin's sculpture communicates an incontrovertible truth about the mind: Thinking can be very hard work! Yet thinking can be highly pleasurable. Some people find the active use of their mind so rewarding that it borders on addictive. They *need* to think.[33] Just as everyday life imposes the need to consume air, food, and water, many people experience a driving appetite for ideas. Psychologists have found ways to measure a person's "typical intellectual engagement," which at the high end is expressed as interest in a wide variety topics and a persistent desire to understand the world—in short, a need to know.[34] Intellectual engagement can be deeply rewarding. The positive emotions that result from thinking can, in turn, propel the intellect to greater heights. The payoff can be tremendous: Great intellectual achievements are frequently driven by deep passions.

Almost everyone has experienced the organic connection between the active use of the mind and the pleasure that follows. Sometimes we experience that pleasure as an emotional state known as "flow."[35] Think of a time when you became completely engrossed in an activity, such as solving a difficult problem at work or pursuing a hobby that required significant concentration. If you were truly challenged—if the mental task required your full attention—then perhaps you experienced a state of consciousness called flow. The telltale sign of flow is a constriction of attention so complete that you lose a sense of time passing as well as an awareness of events around you. Hours may go by without you realizing that your attention is being dominated by the activity at hand. Yet, strangely, the experience is not at all draining. Rather, your engagement in the activity is energizing as well as highly pleasurable.

If you have experienced flow, then you know firsthand that there is an important link between emotions and intelligent thought.[36] But what exactly is that link? One theory goes by the intriguing term emotional intelligence. In contrast to theories that present intelligence as cool and calculating, emotional intelligence spotlights the ability to understand and control one's own emotions, as well as the ability to comprehend the emotions of others. The theory suggests that emotions can be powerful allies if people can channel those emotions properly. So rather than depicting emotions as contributing to irrational or erratic behavior, the theory maintains that emotions—if skillfully understood and acted upon—have tremendous potential to energize and direct intelligent thought.

Popularized by Daniel Goleman's book *Emotional Intelligence*, the concept has struck a chord with the public.[37] The theory of emotional intelligence is not a product of wild speculation, but is based on systematic programs of research carried out at Yale University and elsewhere.[38] Emotional intelligence is defined as "the ability to perceive and express emotion, assimilate emotion in thought, understand and reason with emotion, and regulate emotion in the self and others."[39] In other words, emotional intelligence involves more than simply an awareness of emotions in oneself and other people; it also includes the capacity to *use* emotions productively. Despite such an inclusive definition, theorists portray emotional intelligence in somewhat different ways. The key issue seems to be whether emotional intelligence is strictly an intellectual ability, in which emotions are the content, or whether emotional intelligence also encompasses noncognitive traits, such as personality and character.

No one doubts that both kinds of characteristics—intellectual and nonintellectual—are important. Both contribute to the full gamut of human behavior and, ultimately, to variation in success. For example, personal factors that include emotional elements are known to be good predictors of first-year college grades quite independently of SAT scores. But is it proper to call such personal qualities *intelligence*? Researchers at Yale have emphasized the intellectual aspects of emotional intelligence and segmented off emotional feelings as significant but separate from emotional intelligence and outside their realm of concern. When the definition of emotional intelligence is restricted in this way, it becomes possible to study how the intellectual aspects of emotional perception and control interact with emotional traits, such as warmth or outgoingness.[40] By excluding noncognitive traits and focusing strictly on the intellective aspects of emotional intelligence, a stronger claim might be made that the new construct really is a form of intelligence.

Yet, as we have seen, there are good reasons to be skeptical about *any* proposal to introduce a new variety of "intelligence." Any newly proposed form of intelligence must have several key qualities to be a defensible candidate. For example, to be regarded as a form of intelligence, any personal quality must be fairly stable within a person. Stability ties back to the classical notion of IQ. Whatever IQ measures, it has to be seen as stable—not to say fixed—rather than a fluctuating quality, such as mood. Variability across the population is a second important quality. Every theory of human intelligence assumes variability within the population, which in turn underlies the logic of measurement. Not just intelligence, but every important psychological construct must be variable from person to person to be meaningful. Otherwise, what is the purpose of measuring it or investigating its predictive power?

A third vital quality for any trait we call intelligence is generality across situations. When we say that a person is intelligent, we normally mean that the person expresses a high degree of intellectual skill in a variety of ways, not just narrowly, such as in card games. A card player might have a remarkable memory for previously played hands, and we may be impressed by the player's skill, but unless that impressive feat of memory is exhibited widely in other contexts and problems, its classification as a form of intelligence would not be credible. To count as intelligence, it must apply broadly. In fact, the broadest form of intelligence, general intelligence, is hypothesized to factor into *every* cognitive performance.

A fourth quality of any form of intelligence is that it has to display certain properties of measurement. In particular, when the trait is measured, the resulting scores need to show that the trait holds together as a single variable—what we call factorial coherence—rather than a collection of variables. Also, the new variable must be distinct from other constructs that have already been established. Finally, any alternative model of intelligence ought to predict human effectiveness beyond what is offered by IQ scores. Some of the initial excitement about emotional intelligence emerged from claims that emotional intelligence is a *better* predictor of success than IQ. But that claim is not true. Nor was emotional intelligence ever expected to surpass IQ in its ability to predict success. The more modest and realistic goal was to add predictive power independently of IQ scores.

So, is emotional intelligence really a form of intelligence, or not? The evidence is mixed. Tests of emotional intelligence often measure individual variation that is distinct from what IQ tests measure. At least in some contexts, emotional intelligence can predict success above and beyond IQ scores alone.[41] Also, some tests support the factorial coherence of emotional intelligence—a positive sign. Other tests, however, fail to confirm coherence as a unified factor.[42] This means that various tests of emotional intelligence measure somewhat different traits. Obviously, serious challenges remain. Someday we might conclude that emotional intelligence was actually misnamed as an intelligence. If it consists of several distinct abilities rather than a single, unified capability, it will have to be broken down into simpler and more precise constructs. The challenge facing future researchers will be to iron out these technical wrinkles by building better measures and better theories.

Emotions are clearly vital to the functioning of the intelligent mind. Perhaps emotional intelligence really is a neglected ability that ought to be developed in the population alongside traditional intelligence. One reason to recognize and value emotional intelligence is that it highlights a rare benefit of aging: Scores tend to increase over the life span. Older people often understand and regulate their emotions better than younger people do. If recognized as important, emotional intelligence could be more intentionally developed among workers for greater overall effectiveness, as well as among students to promote their own social and emotional development. A population with higher levels of emotional intelligence will almost certainly be psychologically healthier, more productive, and more capable of forming and maintaining satisfying relationships. The world might be a more pleasant and productive place if we were all more emotionally intelligent.

DISTRIBUTED INTELLIGENCE: NOT JUST IN THE MIND

Yet another theory of intelligence, still embryonic in its development, falls under the banner of distributed intelligence. The theory, introduced by Stanford professor Roy Pea, recognizes that every manifestation of human intelligence entails much more than a single mind acting in isolation. Rather, intelligence always operates in and through an array of resources defined by a culture. According to this theory, intelligence reflects the concepts and priorities of a local culture, as well as draws upon a panoply of tools, technologies, and practices offered by the culture. In Pea's words, intelligent thought and action occur in a world "thick with invented artifacts."[43]

Distributed intelligence corrects limitations of the way psychologists tend to construe intelligence—namely, as the function of individual minds and nothing more. Distributed intelligence extends the geometry of intelligence to recognize that minds interact with the "stuff" of the environment. Landing an airplane, for example, requires complex and dynamic interactions between a pilot and cockpit instrumentation, alongside coordination with air traffic controllers.[44] The pilot must be keenly aware of the plane's weight and the flap extension, and keep the airspeed within a relatively narrow band. During landing, the plane's dynamics change second by second. The intelligent thought needed to accomplish this task safely requires nuanced and highly coordinated interactions between the pilot and instrumentation—not the isolated activities of the pilot's brain.

Even simple technologies can be important aids to thought. Written information, whether on sticky notes or in treatises, can compensate for the predictable fallibility of memory. Paper plus pen plus mind, when functionally linked, are more powerful than the mind acting without external support. It is impossible to imagine the magnificent achievements of Shakespeare, Beethoven, or Galileo without the technologies available to them—quill, piano, telescope, and much more. Obviously, human capability is greatly magnified by the tools afforded by culture. Harvard psychologist David Perkins expressed the point starkly when he declared that human intelligence is "not the solo dance of a naked brain."[45]

During the last century, the powers of technology to leverage intellect grew exponentially. Digital computers are the most vivid example of technologies that have amplified the mind's capabilities. In the early days, computers eased the clerical worker's burden of tedious calculation and record keeping, but this was just the beginning. The capacity for accurate calculation and mathematical modeling, as well as long-term data storage and lightning-fast retrieval, were breakthroughs that opened possibilities that were previously inconceivable. The moon landing of *Apollo 11* in 1969 was the ultimate proof that technologies can amplify the power of intellect to unknowable proportions. Since that time, computers have extended their reach into every corner of human activity—science, the arts, music, communication, political movements, commerce, warfare, social relationships, and so on, interminably.

Other technologies, new and old, drive the point home. The invention of writing, the printing press, movable type, and word processing software catalyzed an explosion of published intellectual work and stocked the world's libraries and data servers with countless volumes of knowledge. Published knowledge, in turn, preserves knowledge for generations to come. The Internet is yet another potent example of distributed intelligence because it permits instantaneous access to the intellectual products of vast numbers of minds on all manner of topics. Those resources include shared databases, analytical tools, and visualization software—collectively known as the cyberinfrastructure—that is pushing scientific discovery into new frontiers.[46] Personal electronic devices, now ubiquitous, bring the vast and expanding electronic resources to the world's population, not only in wealthy nations but also in developing countries.

We must be careful, though: Technologies do not constitute an unmitigated good. It's all too easy to think of technologies that have brought widespread pain and misery, or that presented scenarios of destruction too terrible to contemplate. Neither do technologies inevitably make us smarter. Indeed, the invention of simple arithmetic calculators evoked deep concern among some educators that the devices would undermine students' understanding of the fundamentals of mathematics. Yet even with these caveats, the inventions of culture have undeniably expanded our cognitive powers. In aggregate, they *do* make us smarter. Arguably, nothing resembling human culture and civilization would be possible without an alliance between the mind and the mind's inventions. If this is true, then the central tenet of distributed intelligence must be valid: Intelligence is not confined to the cranium, but lives in the organic web of minds and tools that, in combination, make for a formidable intellectual force.

The tools that constitute distributed intelligence not only extend the mind's capabilities, they also affect the way the mind operates. The most profound influence in this regard is the way that written text introduced a powerful new mode of intellectual activity.[47] Gutenberg's printing press offered an unlimited capacity for replication, which meant that complex and extensive lines of reasoning captured in book form could be disseminated to a vast readership. That readership could be distributed across great spans of distance and time, removed from the original authors by thousands of years and thousands of miles. Written language, particularly in the form of books, stabilizes language and invites extended reflection and critique. During the Enlightenment and Scientific Revolution, dialogues among scholars led to rapid cycles of evolving knowledge and seismic shifts in ways of thinking about the world. In contrast to the oral discourse of myths and legends favored by the ancients, books easily conveyed ideas in expository form. These extended logical essays offered the mind a new pattern for thinking with, and about, the bodies of knowledge that constitute science, philosophy, history, and every other field of inquiry.

IS INTELLIGENCE CULTURE-BOUND?

One enduring question in intelligence theory is the role of culture in defining what intelligence means and how it can be fairly measured. It seems likely, even obvious, that what constitutes being smart in one culture cannot be precisely the same in another culture. But is the meaning of intelligence *radically* different from culture to culture? Scholars take varied positions on the matter. At one end of the spectrum are cultural psychologists who argue that intelligence is fully culture-bound, and therefore relativistic rather than absolute. This position implies that the elements of intelligent functioning in one cultural context may be distant from, or irrelevant to, that of another culture.

One anecdote memorably illustrates radical relativism with respect to culture. Working with the remote Kpelle tribe of Liberia, psychologist Joseph Glick and his collaborators presented what they thought was a straightforward categorization problem.[48] Various objects, such as a knife, hoe, potato, and orange, were placed on the ground. The Kpelle tribesman was then asked to sort the objects. The field researchers expected that the man would group the tools together into one cluster and the foods in a different cluster—a sorting method that derives from the abstract categories of *tools* and *foods*. But rather than using this scheme, the Kpelle man grouped the potato with the hoe and the orange with the knife. This arrangement was based on functional relationships, a categorization scheme that was fully sensible on its own terms, yet would be judged as unsatisfactory according to Western standards for assessing cognitive development. Was the Kpelle man intellectually stunted, or did he simply think differently from the Western scholars who presented the sorting task? Perhaps sensing bewilderment on the part of the Westerners, he justified his answer by saying that it was the way a wise man would do it. Curious, Glick asked, "How would a fool do it?"[49] In response, the man sorted the objects according the abstract categorization scheme prized by the Western intellect— foods were grouped together, tools were grouped separately, and so on.

The story of the Kpelle tribesman drives home the cogency of cultural relativism. But is the meaning and expression of intelligence fully and completely culture-bound? Some scholars take issue with this assumption, believing that what counts as intelligence does indeed vary from culture to culture, but not radically so. Instead, they propose that some cognitive capacities and skills have utility in multiple cultures, or perhaps in any culture. For example, a large memory capacity, the ability to learn quickly, and skill in the use of language would all seem to be advantageous in virtually any cultural setting. Cross-cultural psychologists want to understand precisely which aspects of the psyche are universal and which vary across cultures.[50] They seek answers not only in geographically distant cultures, but also between cultural subgroups within a common society.

Language, an intimate correlate of culture, is certain to be an important piece of the puzzle. That is because language is not simply a means of communication between people; it seems also to exert quite profound effects on thinking. A famous example is the observation that Eskimos have several distinct words that refer to snow, and that those fine distinctions allow for precision not only in communicating about snow, but also in thinking about it. The great anthropologist, Franz Boas, noted that those meanings include *falling snow*, *drifting snow*, *snow bank*, and *snow on the ground*.[51] The full number of distinct Eskimo words for snow is about a dozen, although in popular accounts that number is sometimes inflated to as many as 50.[52] Still, the hypothesis is clear: If one language has 12 words to describe variations on a concept and another language has only one, the two languages afford different levels of precision. Someone who can employ a dozen different words to distinguish various shades of meaning might well think about a concept more richly than, or at least differently from, someone whose language offers only a single word to refer to the counterpart idea.

This provocative notion—that language guides and constrains thought—is known as the Whorf hypothesis.[53] It is named for the linguist Benjamin Whorf, whose work in the 1930s included deciphering from ancient artifacts the symbols composing the written Mayan language. Whorf's conjecture has been somewhat controversial. Some linguists believe that the mind's ability to think is largely free of the effects of specific languages.[54] But the Whorf hypothesis seems to be at least partly correct. Consider, for example, the English words *river* and *stream*. Their meanings are distinguished primarily by size: Rivers are larger than streams. The rough equivalents in French are *fleuve* and *rivière*, but their meanings do not map exactly to the river and stream distinction.[55] Instead, *fleuve* refers to water that flows into the sea, and *rivière* indicates water that flows into a *fleuve*. This simple example plainly shows that the English and French words have different meanings, implying that English and French speakers, monolinguals especially, probably think about flowing water in somewhat different ways. A reasonable extrapolation is that language can guide and constrain thought. Because culture is so tightly bound to language a further inference is that thought, including intelligent thought, will have different qualities from one language and culture to another.

What can we conclude about the nexus of culture and intelligence? Minimally, this: What is regarded as intelligent thinking and behavior cannot be identical from culture to culture. That is because cultures diverge in their assumptions about the patterns of reasoning and behavior that mark the intelligent person. Those assumptions are rooted in cultural conventions—the shared values, knowledge, and modes of communication that are deemed normal and expected. The example of the Kpelle man is a perfect case in point: Western academic conceptions of intelligence readily assume that intelligence can be measured through tests that present decontextualized problems in which the measured ability (such as category formation) can be separated from the functional associations of the content (such as food and tools). The questions posed may have nothing to do with anything that is meaningful in the life of the community. Moreover, the questions are likely to be posed by a stranger who has no ongoing social connection to the examinee, which by itself might seem quite absurd.

Most problematic of all, cultures vary in how they define intellectually acute thinking, whether it goes by the name intelligence or wisdom. When abstract categories are emphasized over practical utility, then a certain view of intelligence is assumed—one that emphasizes particular aspects of intelligent thought while minimizing others. Western psychologists placed a high value on abstractions, but to the Kpelle man the detachment of category from function was foolish. Scholars may be disinclined to question their assumptions about intelligence, perhaps because their bias so easily coincides with an intellectual habit that for centuries was accorded supreme value in academe: the ability to detach oneself from context, to rise above it, and to form powerful and far-reaching generalizations.[56] If unquestioned, this classic way of thinking about the developed mind hardens into a "spurious orthodoxy"—a "right way" of thinking that pushes aside alternative ways of understanding human intelligence.[57]

The response of the Kpelle man shows that a locally legitimate expression of intelligence can clash with assumptions underlying its measurement. Other research confirms the pattern. In Kenya, Robert Sternberg and his fellow investigators found significant differences between Kenyans educated in Western-type schools and those who were not.[58] Sternberg compared the two groups on their knowledge of traditional tribal medicine and medical concepts derived from science. Kenyans who had Western-style educations did relatively well on the tests based on medical science but poorly on tests that measured knowledge of traditional medicine. Those who did not attend schools showed the opposite pattern: They performed well on tests of traditional medicine but poorly on tests that tapped knowledge of standard medical science. Clearly, different cultural contexts, Western and non-Western, called for and cultivated different forms of intellectual development. Between cultures, the only constant seems to be the adaptability of the individual to learn what is valued and useful.

Seeing intelligent thought as tied to specific contexts makes sense. In the causal chain running from ability to behavior, intelligence must eventually connect to real-world problem solving.[59] Intelligence applied to nothing is no intelligence at all. We need to be cautious, however, in drawing generalizations from limited examples. Just as we can cite examples of how intelligence is variable across cultures, we might just as easily think of cases in which certain intellectual abilities, such as the skilled use of memory, are useful across distinctly different cultures. But even when anthropologists acknowledge that some cognitive processes are probably useful across cultures, they often hold fast to a position of value neutrality—that no culture can claim to be more advanced than any another.[60] Their prime axiom is that, ultimately, each culture defines what it means to be intelligent on its own terms.

The focal dilemma here—Is intelligence culturally defined?—seems to evade an easy *yes* or *no* answer. Even if intelligence is not radically different from culture to culture, local traditions can differ markedly on the emphases placed on various aspects of intelligence. One culture might emphasize logical analysis, while another attaches particular importance to creative expression; still another might elevate social skill above all. Anthropologist Thomas Gladwin documented the unusual importance placed on spatial ability by the Puluwat people of remote Micronesia. For centuries, Puluwat men sailed between widely scattered islands without the aid of navigational technologies, such as GPS devices or premodern sextants and star charts.[61] Archipelagos in the region consist of chains of small islands separated by vast expanses of sea. Commerce and intermarriage depended on the navigators' ability to sail from island to island, yet doing so was extremely challenging by dint of sheer geometry—in Micronesia, the ratio of landmass to ocean is tiny. The perpetuation of culture and individual survival depended on sailors' ability to arrive precisely on target when sailing from one island to another.

The Puluwat people adapted to their environmental demands by recognizing a class of ocean sailors who specialized in navigation. To be admitted to the navigator guild was a prized achievement; the body of knowledge mastered by navigators was carefully guarded. Indeed, navigators constituted something of a cult group among the traditional Puluwats. Gladwin's research revealed that information utilized by navigators was multifaceted, involving knowledge of the celestial patterning of stars, and familiarity with winds and currents, as well as sea life. Navigators were apprenticed to master these convergent sources of information so that while under way they could home in on their intended destination. When integrating these various data sources, the navigators of Puluwat relied on and developed spatial reasoning to a highly pronounced degree. As we have seen, spatial ability is a recognized expression of intelligence in classic hierarchical models, but in most studies it is less sweeping in importance than fluid and crystallized intelligence. The intriguing example of the Puluwat navigators shows that in some cultures and contexts, the relative importance of intelligence factors might be ordered differently from the standard model.

Taken together, these examples converge on a crucial point: What is regarded as intelligent thinking in one culture can be very different, even opposite, from what is considered intelligent thinking in another culture. Local conceptions of intelligence can deviate sharply from Western assumptions that intelligence entails the ability to isolate problems from context. Moreover, the belief that intellectual capability is an individual trait that can be assessed independently for each person might conflict with an alternative viewpoint held by collectivist societies—that knowledge and capability are fundamentally properties of cooperative behavior.[62] An equally serious clash of beliefs may appear when examinees are asked to justify their answers to questions. Westerners are used to the idea that knowledge can be separated from the person who holds that knowledge. Other societies see knowledge and the "knower" as inextricably bound. Consequently, the expectation that a person must justify his or her beliefs may appear to be nonsensical or threatening. The assumptions inherent in modern intelligence testing—that intelligence is a property of individuals and that knowledge can be separated from the knower—appears to arise from exposure to Western-style education. In particular, the written word, which physically separates the idea from the idea generator, seems to play a crucial role in the inculcation of the Western mindset.

Knowing that intelligence testing rests on many questionable assumptions has sensitized psychologists to the relevance of culture to intelligence, and has resulted in greater caution about using published tests to judge the intelligence of non-Western people. Some psychologists have even tried to devise "culture-free" tests that present puzzles using abstract shapes and that minimize or avoid language. Yet even these tests are known to have elements that could be interpreted only with background knowledge that is grounded in culture. "Culture-free" is apparently no more than a phantom ideal. The best psychologists can hope for is to devise a test that is "culture-fair" or "culture-reduced," while bearing in mind that fairness is a matter of degree rather than an achievable absolute. This cautionary stance is commendable yet ironic: Attempts to generalize about culture—to speak about culture with detachment—are paradoxical. If we believe that culture pervades all, then there is no standing apart from culture to generalize about it. We always speak from within a culture when we speak about it. Pure objectivity is simply not possible.[63]

HABITS OF MIND

Ponder this: Does *being* intelligent guarantee consistency in *behaving* intelligently? Obviously not. Smart people do dumb things, and not infrequently. For this reason, some theories of intelligence distinguish between the ability to exercise intelligent thought and the tendency to do so. People sometimes fail to think reflectively because they lack sensitivity to occasion or do not perceive the need. For example, when faced with a dilemma in which both sides of an issue could be fruitfully explored, otherwise sensible people can jump to conclusions prematurely. They might fail to notice the opportunity to think critically or lack the inclination to consider the issue more fully. In either case, cognitive ability is not the limiting factor in the exercise of intelligent thought, but rather sensitivity and inclination are.[64] Aside from learning how to think intelligently, what's clearly important is developing the *habit* of doing so. When such inclinations are established, the intelligent person is said to exhibit positive thinking dispositions or "habits of mind."[65]

Good habits of mind can counteract mindless ways of processing information and can mitigate impulsivity. For example, ambiguous or fuzzy ideas can trigger the search for conceptual clarity. Other positive habits include forming strategic plans instead of proceeding haphazardly, and trying to be intellectually careful rather than sloppy. All these habits of mind tend to hold this in common: thinking somewhat more extensively and deeply than is our ordinary tendency.

By elevating the value of good thinking, we tacitly assume that human cognition is typically suboptimal. Is this the case? Before answering, let's think of two opposite scenarios. Depending on the occasion, we might allocate too much or too little thought in making a decision. In playing a game of checkers, for example, you might err by moving the pieces impulsively with little thought given to the consequences; alternatively, you could deliberate for an hour about the implications of a single move. Both can be seen as errors. Everyday decisions, such as choosing clothing for purchase, are likewise subject to both errors—thinking too much or too little. Is one error more common than the other? Psychologist Jonathan Baron has suggested that human cognition is biased in one direction: We tend to devote insufficient thought in forming our beliefs and decisions. If this is correct, then one way to build good habits of mind is to move the bias point of mental investment. The imperative would be to extend thought. "Think more" seems to be the most basic advice for developing good habits of mind.

As we consider how a society can teach the thinking skills that constitute intelligence, let's remember habits of mind—the tendency to apply our thinking abilities whenever we face occasions for their profitable use. Intelligence is not entirely a matter of capability; it's also about using that capability when suitable occasions arise. After all, a mechanic needs more than a well-equipped toolbox. The proper tools must be paired with a good sense of when to use each tool. When intelligence is viewed this way—as akin to an intellectual toolkit—habits of mind are clearly vital elements of our intellectual heritage. Like the knowledge and skills that compose intelligence, habits of mind must be cultivated afresh each generation. Societal institutions, schools especially, must find ways to pass on the forms of knowing, thinking, and feeling that call forth the highest and best powers of the mind.

NONHUMAN INTELLIGENCE

Our primary concern with human intelligence need not exclude considering the intelligence of other species. To gain perspective on whatever unique features the human intellect might exhibit, we may find a contrast with nonhuman species illuminating. Conceivably, the intelligences of dolphins, apes, and ravens have distinctive qualities that we could profitably emulate. With that possibility in mind, let us examine intelligence in the rest of the animal kingdom—in particular, whether the intelligence of nonhuman animals differs in degree or kind from the intelligence of human beings.

Without question, the flexible cognition offered by human intelligence is a tremendous resource for adapting to environmental demands. Nonhuman animals adapt, too, but do so primarily through genetic variation and natural selection. From a biological perspective, the defining features of any species ought to evolve over time to improve survival and reproductive success. Strangely, the reproductive advantage of human intelligence is not obvious. In human populations, the relationship between intelligence and reproductive success can even be negative—high intelligence in adults is sometimes correlated with fewer offspring.[66] What's unclear is whether human intelligence is the ultimate resource for biological fitness. Not only are many other species quite successful in biological terms with respect to *Homo sapiens*, we might entertain the possibility that human intelligence is as much a threat to survival as it is a resource.

Let's consider a marvelously adaptive resource shared by humans and other animals—vision. Perceptual judgments about classes of stimuli based on reflected light may seem too elemental to be important, but this is not the case. To classify objects and relationships in the environment is vital. Throughout the animal kingdom, the ability to parse the environment into meaningful categories is a critical component of intelligence. Moreover, the visual perception of animals can be quite flexible. For example, potential dangers must be perceived as alike even when they look very different, whether through variation in illumination or perspective. The same applies to opportunities for feeding and mating. Most of the time, animals have no problem making such adjustments instantly and accurately. Such perceptual flexibility is not trivial. The same sorts of adjustments in interpreting the visual field are notoriously difficult for computers and robots.

We know that humans can form quite abstract judgments about what they see. No one really knows whether animals think with abstractions in the wild, but in the laboratory they can be trained to perceive abstract qualities in ways that seem remarkably akin to human reasoning. Over the course of 30 years, animal psychologist Irene Pepperberg trained an African Grey Parrot named Alex to learn abstractions that we normally associate with human cognition.[67] For example, Pepperberg taught Alex to respond to the question "What color?" by vocalizing "Blue," and to "What shape?" by vocalizing "Four-corner."[68] Alex learned to make even more abstract judgments. For example, he could respond to the questions "What's same?" or "What's different" by vocalizing "Shape" or "Color," depending on which quality of the object was stable or variable. In a similar vein, chimpanzees have been trained to distinguish between pairs of objects that are the same and pairs that are different. Even more impressive, they can learn to judge relationships between unlike *pairs* of objects, perceiving (AA)(BB) as "Same" and (AA)(BC) as "Different." Such judgments are not simply about objects but also about *relationships*, which are abstractions of a higher order.

Tool use is another dimension on which we can compare humans and nonhuman species. Human intelligence is strongly identified with the use of tools, which is commonly thought to have been a huge evolutionary advantage. However, tool use among other species has been documented so extensively that it seems quite mistaken to identify tools exclusively with humans. For example, sea otters use rocks to break open shellfish and Egyptian vultures drop rocks on ostrich eggs to break them. As famously observed and described by Jane Goodall, chimpanzees use twigs for "termite fishing." Still, the use of tools by nonhuman species does not begin to approach their thorough and systematic employment by *Homo sapiens*, and so we might regard ubiquitous tool use as a major correlate of human intelligence.

Yet another criterion for judging intelligence in nonhuman species is whether animals are self-aware. One test of self-awareness is an animal's ability to recognize its own reflection in a mirror as itself rather than a different animal. The capacity to recognize a mirrored reflection as a self-image is rare, apparently restricted to chimpanzees and orangutans. Even after several days' exposure to a mirrored reflection, gorillas appear to interpret the reflection as belonging a different animal.[69] Investigators have also studied the sorts of mathematical knowledge animals possess or can learn. In one instance, a chimpanzee named Sheba was trained in the correspondence between Arabic numerals (1, 2, 3, 4…) and the number of objects in a set. When presented with a group of objects, not only could Sheba point to the corresponding numeral, she could add the number of objects at one location to the number at a different location and point to their sum. Sheba's accomplishments, achieved through painstaking teaching over a long period of time, appear to be the closest approximation of any animal to symbolic calculation.[70]

Perhaps the most controversial point of comparison is whether language is a distinctive feature of human intelligence. Language learning is so rapid and efficient in humans that, intuitively, it seems this capability could arise only through inherent brain structures that prime infants for this feat. Some scholars believe that only the human species has developed a vast system of arbitrary symbols—spoken words—that is properly called language. But even if humans are the only species to have *originated* language, this leaves open the possibility that other species can learn to *use* language. Many scholars have tried to understand the potential of nonhuman animals to learn language, along with the limits of that ability. Some experiments have involved training nonhuman primates, for example, in the use of sign language. Earlier we noted Irene Pepperberg's success in training Alex, an African Grey Parrot, to vocalize conceptual judgments about color and shape as well as more abstract qualities. Other researchers have studied dolphins, who are often presumed to be intelligent for anatomical reasons.[71] Dolphin brains are quite large, even in comparison to their total body mass, as well as highly convoluted. To make comparisons fairer across species, it's possible to compute an encephalization quotient, or EQ, which scales brain size by body mass. The average EQ across all animal species is defined to be 1.0. On this scale, humans have the highest EQ at 7.0, and dolphins are next at 4.3. Still lower on the scale are chimpanzees (2.49), dogs (1.17), and mice (0.50).[72]

Biologist Louis Herman documented that dolphins can respond to abstract concepts at a level that seems at least comparable to other non-human species. Herman trained a female bottlenose dolphin named Ake to respond to gestures that stood for nouns (such as *ball, surfboard, pool*) and verbs (such as *fetch*). She could respond correctly to commands, such as "surfboard swimmer fetch" (bring the swimmer to the surfboard) and "swimmer surfboard fetch" (bring the surfboard to the swimmer). Ake could also respond to novel gesture combinations with the appropriate behavior, showing that the gestures did not serve merely to activate previously learned routines. When commanded to perform a task that was physically impossible, Ake would merely stare at the trainer (perhaps questioning *his* intelligence). Besides responding to commands, Ake could also answer questions. By pressing paddles on the side of a pool (right paddle for *yes*; left paddle for *no*), she could respond to such questions as "Is there a ball in your pool?"

In the wild, too, dolphins are known to exhibit intelligent behavior. For example, they use a form of sonar, called echolocation, by which they emit clicking sounds that reflect or "echo" back. The reflected sounds encode information about the size, shape, and location of objects. Dolphins have been known to "eavesdrop" by listening to the echolocation information from other dolphins to determine the location of fish. Dolphins are also known for engaging in what might be seen as a quite important manifestation of intelligence—play. For no obvious reason other than enjoyment, dolphins surf on breakers and ride the bow waves of boats. Solely for their amusement, it seems, they blow "bubble rings" and watch as the beautiful donut shapes rise slowly to the ocean's surface.

In one sense, the entire enterprise of human beings trying to understand the nature and degree of nonhuman intelligence is fraught with a strong possibility of error. When humans rely on their own brand of intelligence to test the intelligence of other species, the standards applied might misrepresent or miss completely the forms of intelligence specific to the nonhuman species. Animal intelligence might have no counterpart in the human intellectual toolkit. Echolocation is a good example. Both dolphins and bats use reflected sounds to "see" their environments in dynamic three-dimensional form. Such a distinctive way of processing information hints that human conceptions of what constitutes intelligence may be terribly biased. Without an acute awareness of interspecies differences, we humans may commit serious errors in what we conclude about the intelligence of nonhumans. Errors can run in either direction: We can easily overestimate or underestimate their capabilities.

Given these caveats, two conclusions seem safe: First, features of intelligence that are often assumed to be distinctively human are not solely and exclusively qualities of the human mind after all. Human and nonhuman intelligence differ, but those differences are usually a matter of degree. Whether differences in degree—such as in use of language or tools—translate into categorical differences of kind is a matter of judgment.[73] Second, when we consider the behavior of animals trained to perform impressive, even humanlike, feats, we should not ignore the cleverness of their human trainers in eliciting displays of "intelligence." The most amazing spectacle is arguably the intelligence of trainers in devising intricate systems of reinforcement that call forth amusing behavior in dolphins, chimps, and parrots. To assign credit for "intelligent" behavior to the trained animals rather than their trainers is at least partly a judgment call.

ARTIFICIAL INTELLIGENCE (AI)

When we consider the sophisticated forms of calculation that arise from lifeless bits of silicon, plastic, and metal, we are given a glimpse into the power of human intellect to achieve something truly stunning—teaching nonintelligent pieces of matter to exhibit intelligence. Human intelligence, we have seen, is most clearly exhibited in solving problems that defy easy or straightforward solutions. So, too, with machines: The word *intelligence* is normally reserved for computational activities so complex and ill-defined that they require a human mind for their solution. Clever programming qualifies as AI only when in some credible way it rises to the level of human intelligence.

The mission of AI is to teach machines to solve complex problems. Yet, by definition, problem solving is never accomplished by the application of straightforward solutions. Rather, it entails finding a way to achieve a goal that cannot be reached through the application of known rules. When this definition of problem solving is applied to machines, any computational behavior that can be reduced to a series of rules does not qualify as AI. The challenge has been expressed this way:

> Many of the problems that AI has attempted to solve are computing problems that are computationally intractable: No algorithm, no matter how well written and efficiently executed, can hope to solve them consistently. This would seem to pose an insoluble problem for AI: How can you use a computer to solve a problem if there are no algorithms for solving it?[74]

Yet humans, even without the aid of set procedures or algorithms, solve problems all the time. We do so by applying strategies called heuristics.[75] As strategies, heuristics do not guarantee success; they simply raise the probability of finding a solution. Likewise, AI programs solve complex problems through the application of heuristics. One of the best-known heuristics, means-ends analysis, simply reduces the difference between the current problem state and the goal state. Instead of directly pursuing the top-level goal—say winning a chess match—the immediate objective is a more modest short-term goal, such as gaining a better strategic position on the chessboard. By establishing a better position, the computer (or the human chess player) moves closer to the ultimate but still uncertain goal of winning the match.

When attempting to teach computers to exhibit intelligent behavior, AI researchers face strategic choice points. One decision is whether to closely mimic human thought. Computer programs that resemble human cognition are known as "strong AI." Alternatively, AI projects intended to exhibit intelligence in any way possible, humanlike or not, are known as "weak AI." Weak AI is, by far, the more common approach. Even so, strong AI programs have a certain extra value because they serve a dual purpose. Not only do they display the potential of machines to exhibit intelligence and so advance the mission of AI, they also shine a light on the workings of human reasoning.

A second choice point concerns the information-processing logic of the computer. Traditional computers rely on programming languages that present clear and distinct commands. Those commands act upon data in symbolic form, ultimately ones and zeroes. Each bit of information has a clear and precise location in the computer's memory, and successful information processing depends fully on having an orderly and error-free program that acts on a neatly organized information base. This computational model, sometimes called the von Neumann architecture, is by far the most common way of organizing machine computation—but it is not the only way.

An alternative way of computing is the connectionist paradigm, also known as the neural networks method. This model does not rely on discrete symbols. Rather, information representing knowledge is distributed among processing units in a way that cannot be easily defined. Unlike a traditional symbol-processing computer, specific information cannot be localized to a single address in the computer's memory. Instead, stored information is spread across those computational elements and their relationships to each other. What the computer "knows" is a function of the entire system rather than one tiny corner of memory.

This connectionist computational model has the attractive feature of biological plausibility. The distribution of knowledge across a large number of entities resembles, at least superficially, the way knowledge is stored in the brain—distributed across a collection of neurons rather than assignable to a specific point location. The computational logic also bears some resemblance to the way we understand intelligence, as expressed in varied forms but having a kind of unity because of shared elements across those various expressions.[76] Additionally, it is possible to program connectionist AI models so that they vary in efficiency of learning. Models that are more adaptable progress more rapidly through stages of learning.[77] Such models not only display the "individual differences" so characteristic of human intelligence, they also show variation in learning progressions that have long been the subject of study by developmental psychologists from Jean Piaget onward.

The two forms of computation—symbolic and connectionist—have parallels in human cognition. Much of the knowledge we hold in memory is symbolic. The most obvious example is language: the individual words that stand for things in the world. Some words code for concrete objects, such as cups, cars, and cotton candy; others stand for abstract concepts, such as constitutionality and Cartesian coordinates. In addition to words, we also employ numbers, musical notes, and a wide variety of conventional signs, such as traffic lights, to understand our world. Even so, a large swath of what we know cannot be broken down into symbols without losing meaning.[78] When a wine connoisseur appraises a new vintage, for example, he or she may form a nuanced impression of the wine's quality, but that impression might not be fully expressible. To be communicated to others, what is understood in nonsymbolic form has to be translated to symbols, usually language. Like the wine connoisseur, our everyday lives present us with experiences that we understand as complex sense impressions, or perhaps feelings, that do not translate easily into words, numbers, or any other symbolic expression—at least not without losing information.

The point is that both symbolic and nonsymbolic knowledge play important roles in the human psyche. These two categories of knowledge map onto the symbolic and connectionist strategies for pursuing the mission of artificial intelligence. AI models that use symbolic representations work best when problems are well defined, such as winning a chess match. In problems where the relevant knowledge is less clear-cut, such as in speech recognition, connectionist models often work better.[79]

The field of artificial intelligence has yielded impressive, even stunning, achievements. One of the most vivid was the creation of a chess-playing computer program, called Deep Blue, which in May 1997 defeated the world's top-rated grandmaster, Gary Kasparov.[80] Previously, IBM had built a series of chess-playing programs with such oddball names as Chaos, Cray Blitz, and Chiptest. The programs played impressive chess, but were not good enough to beat the best human players. For many years no one knew whether a computer could ever defeat the world's best human players. Successive generations of chess-playing programs displayed increasing prowess, but until Deep Blue none was able to triumph.

The defeat of Kasparov in a six-game match was significant because chess had been a target domain of AI for decades.[81] Attempts to program computers to play games, such as checkers, at the level of human players had an important role in the history of artificial intelligence as early as the Second World War. By 1951, British mathematician Alan Turing had adapted a code-breaking program to play chess, but Turing's program and those that followed were no match for human opponents. Deep Blue's victory signaled a turning point because of its symbolic value: Chess is a complex game long associated with the powers of human intellect. The method of Deep Blue and most other game playing programs is to conduct "brute-force" searches of thousands of possible moves—far more than a human player would mentally simulate. The brute-force technique gives computers a definite upper hand in games such as checkers where all relevant information is openly displayed. Yet apart from the brute-force method, some game-playing AI programs have displayed truly innovative techniques. For example, when the backgammon program TD-Gammon began to defeat the best human players, some of its moves were novel and subsequently studied and imitated by players.[82] Other games, such as poker, entail hidden information, pattern matching, and the need to "read" opponents. In such games, AI has yet to match the ability of the world's best players.

The victory of Deep Blue was impressive, but it left open a crucial question: Is the program really intelligent? After all, Deep Blue was a human construction from top to bottom, fully dependent on sophisticated hardware design and software programming that ultimately traced to human intelligence. Arguably, Deep Blue merely followed instructions in accordance with the principles of physics. This line of probing raises the ultimate question underlying the entire enterprise of artificial intelligence: Can nonbiological machines truly be intelligent? In trying to answer, let's consider for a moment one branch of artificial intelligence—strong AI, the kind intended to imitate human thought. Strong AI is of interest not only to computer scientists; it has also captured the attention of philosophers. Some philosophers have claimed that strong AI is simply not possible. This is equivalent to saying that machines could never replicate intelligence as manifested by human beings.

The most famous criticism of strong AI was offered by the linguist John Searle, using a hypothetical scenario he called the Chinese Room argument. It goes like this: Imagine a man, isolated in a room, whose job is to receive messages written in Chinese and, in response, to give written replies in Chinese. The man does not know Chinese, but at his disposal is a book that maps all conceivable incoming messages with suitable replies. That man is fully adept at making those connections, and so he efficiently and dutifully replies appropriately to every incoming message. Yet the meanings of those messages are opaque to him, and so his performance is completely mechanical. To an outside observer, the messages coming from the Chinese Room imply that whoever is inside actually understands Chinese, but this is not so. Searle's Chinese Room experiment is a metaphor for interpreting all of AI: A computer's ability to match inputs and outputs according to rules are inherent to its programming and architecture. If supplied with "intelligent input" it may yield "intelligent output," but this correlation is no guarantee that the computer actually knows anything about the meaning or significance of its mediating role, however elegantly discharged.

Searle's Chinese Room experiment is completely hypothetical, but it had a close counterpart in an early AI program called ELIZA. ELIZA mimicked a psychotherapist by providing canned answers to typed input from "patients." Users were invited to tell ELIZA about themselves, including the kinds of personal information that might be expressed to a psychotherapist. ELIZA was programmed to respond to particular informational cues. For example, if a patient used the word *mother* or *mom*, ELIZA would respond, "Tell me about your mother." In response to other statements, ELIZA would simply restate the patient's comment in imitation of a therapist's active listening strategy. These responses were not sophisticated, and yet some users were completely fooled by ELIZA, convinced that they were conversing remotely with a human therapist.[83] ELIZA could not be considered to be intelligent even in the barest sense by a first-generation AI model. For those intent on challenging ELIZA, rather than playing along, ELIZA's limitations could easily be exposed.

Since the 1960s, when ELIZA was developed, AI programs designed to imitate human conversations have improved markedly. Collectively called chatterbots, the programs use words and phrases typed by the human user to generate a response that is intended to resemble an authentic conversation. If the user could be fooled into thinking that the AI program is actually another person, the chatterbot can be said to satisfy the "Turing Test." In 1950, the computational scientist Alan Turing proposed that any

AI program that could consistently fool users into thinking that the computer's written or spoken conversations were from another human being could be regarded as intelligent. The Turing Test has been, and continues to be, a litmus test for whether AI programs are intelligent. No chatterbot has ever fully satisfied the Turing Test, although some have come close. One AI scientist—an expert in chatterbots, it turns out—was lured into an online dating relationship with "Ivana" for nearly four months before realizing that his affections were directed toward a computer program.[84] In this instance, Ivana's broken English seemed perfectly understandable to a self-confessed nerd enjoying an online relationship.

In contrast to Deep Blue, ELIZA's intelligence was not a function of its computational power, but rather one of knowing how to respond in ways stereotypical of a psychotherapist. That discourse pattern, however simple, was convincing enough to win the trust of users, at least initially. A similar strategy has been used for malicious purposes by online scammers. By hacking into accounts on social media sites, such as Facebook, modern chatterbot programs can gather personal information, including the names and e-mail addresses of friends. The stolen personal information can then be reworked to send messages to the target account that appear to be from people known by the user. Like ELIZA, these simple AI programs mimic online casual conversations with just enough semblance to lure the target of the scam. The target can then be urged to download an interesting "game" or "video," which in reality is malware that raids even more detailed personal information.

The question of whether AI programs can ever exhibit true intelligence arose again recently in connection with Watson, an IBM computer program designed to act as a contestant on the television game show *Jeopardy!*[85] After the success of Deep Blue in 1997, IBM executives began searching for a new challenge that could, like Deep Blue, generate broad interest and, ideally, headlines. A suitable challenge materialized at a dinner meeting of IBM research staff when restaurant patrons ceased conversations and focused fully on the television monitors. The TV screens were showing a critical moment in the record-setting streak of Ken Jennings, the *Jeopardy!* contestant who eventually won 74 consecutive games. By 2005, IBM executives recruited David Ferrucci, an AI researcher at IBM's Semantic Analysis and Integration Department, to lead the R & D effort that resulted in Watson. Equipped with massive databases, including the entire corpus of *Wikipedia*, Watson uses key words in *Jeopardy!* clues to query multiple data sources that simultaneously generate several potential answers. Watson becomes "confident" in its response when those multiple parallel queries converge on the same answer.

Despite its sophisticated language processing algorithms and massive information databases, Watson's early performances were not impressive. In practice rounds, Watson could correctly answer only about 15% of *Jeopardy!* questions, compared to a 95% correct response rate typical of the very best *Jeopardy!* contestants. Nevertheless, IBM researchers continued to make improvements, and when its true test came on February 14, 2011, Watson was ready. During three episodes of *Jeopardy!* Watson was pitted against Ken Jennings and Brad Rutter, who held the record for the most cash winnings on the game show. At the end of the three days, Watson prevailed over both Jennings and Rutter and was awarded a prize of one million dollars.

Not everyone was awestruck, however. In particular, the philosopher John Searle argued that despite Watson's impressive performance, it was incorrect to infer that the program could actually think or understand. The reasoning behind this claim was Searle's own metaphor of the Chinese Room experiment, which illustrates that information inputs and outputs can be fully coordinated even in the absence of any understanding inside the "box." Understanding is merely simulated, not achieved. According to Searle, "Watson did not understand the questions, nor its answers, nor that some of its answers were right and some wrong, nor that it was playing a game, nor that it won—because it doesn't understand anything."[86] Searle did not downplay the technical achievements by IBM scientists in constructing Watson. His concern was the interpretation of what Watson actually does—specifically the inference that Watson has achieved anything approaching understanding or consciousness. While Watson is a remarkable achievement of computer engineering, its performances "do not show that Watson has superior intelligence, or that it's thinking, or anything of the sort."[87]

Regardless of whether Watson achieved anything approaching human cognition, the *Jeopardy!* event was the perfect follow-up to IBM's chess-playing Deep Blue, and seemed to be "a vindication for the academic field of artificial intelligence."[88] Watson's design also affirmed the vital roles of specific knowledge and processing functions in the simulation of intelligence. While Watson appeared to be equipped with both resources roughly evenly, other AI programs favor one or the other. Here we can discern yet another choice point for artificial intelligence—whether to build knowledge into the AI program (which minimizes computation at runtime) or to give the program a robust set of reasoning and problem-solving strategies (which minimizes the need for built-in knowledge). That is, AI programs can be designed to maximize either "thinking" or "knowing." This design decision parallels the fluid/crystallized distinction that is the bedrock of human intelligence theory. In any problem context, intelligent performance can draw upon a strong knowledge base (crystallized intelligence) or the ability to reason from limited information (fluid intelligence)—or, best of all, the combination of the two.

WHY WE NEED NEW THEORIES OF INTELLIGENCE

Looking back on this chapter, we have expanded the scope of our exploration to include forms of ability that challenge the confines of human intelligence, classically defined. Challenges to the classic theories—those built on the foundations established by Galton, Binet, Spearman, Terman, and Thurstone—were seen as limited in scope and limiting in application. The later emergence of the hierarchical model arose from a century of research and had plenty of grounding in data, but also had shortcomings. Most seriously, it construed intelligence as overly narrow, as too focused on analytical thinking, and too exclusive of other expressions of intellect. Such obviously important resources as creativity, the ability to interpret and channel emotional energy, and the cultural tools that amplify the work of the mind were downplayed or ignored altogether.

Collectively, the emerging theories show that a full and exhaustive understanding of human intelligence is an ongoing vision, not a completed project.[89] Efforts to build better theories of intelligence are worthwhile on their own terms, just as scholarly work in any field can deepen our knowledge even if it lacks an immediate practical application. For those who wish to promote practical outcomes, such as cultivating one's own intelligence or the collective intelligence of a school, a company, or a nation, better theories are always desirable. Any attempt to advance the intellectual powers of a human population is, essentially, an engineering project. As a practical science, engineering offers an array of options in the design of buildings, aircraft, computers, energy sources and supply, and transportation infrastructures. Inevitably, though, the practical science of engineering is constrained by the basic sciences that undergird it—physics, chemistry, and materials science. As the footing of the basic sciences extends further, its applications by engineers expand commensurably in scope, beauty, and efficiency.

Any credible attempt to raise intelligence must draw fully on what is known about intelligence. To do less is to cast aside the most promising basis for effective interventions. Knowing, for example, that fluid and crystallized intelligence are fundamental to the design of the intelligent mind, it would be foolish to ignore this vital distinction in planning efforts to engineer greater powers of the intellect. The same applies to other major discoveries about the structure of intelligence, such as the prominent roles played by working memory, executive function, inductive reasoning, spatial representation, and verbal ability. The mind's structural elements and key intellectual processes jointly represent the global trait we conveniently call intelligence, and measure as a simple IQ score.

Let's be clear: IQ and intelligence are not synonymous. In the real world, intelligence is much more than the ability to provide correct answers on vocabulary tests or analogical reasoning puzzles. Performances on intelligence tests are mere proxies for the real thing, not expressions of inherent value. IQ scores may correlate with the real-world manifestations of intelligent thought and action. Patently, however, they are not equivalent. IQ, expressed as a two or three-digit number, purports to summarize the mental resources that a person brings to the challenges and opportunities of life. By itself, an IQ score is devoid of meaning. To gain significance, it must tie into human intelligence as manifest in authentic life contexts. Intelligence gives people the capacity to engage a complex and uncertain world. Our daily lives present a deluge of potentially relevant information, shifting problems and opportunities that stretch us to our limits. In a world so profusely complex, we could not survive, let alone prosper, without the resources of intelligence.

By virtue of its predictive power, IQ is not to be disregarded. Even as an artificial construct, it exhibits remarkable utility in predicting success in academic and job environments. Equally important, the progression of research from the early days of Spearman and Thurstone to the grand hierarchical models of Carroll and others has yielded insights into the validity, structure, and working components of intelligence. IQ, though not beyond criticism as an audaciously simple artifice, has in fact opened windows into the scientific study of intelligence.

No single process defines intelligence, and neither are all constituent processes equally important. To use our knowledge of intelligence effectively, we must pay attention to the details. If we aspire to raise human intelligence, we must identify the most critical components of intelligence and test their malleability—the extent to which they can be taught and learned. Because the theory of intelligence is an unfinished project we must also be attuned to future research. Many emerging theories reveal the limitations of traditional IQ tests, yet those new theories do not currently provide a sufficient theoretical basis for making radical and permanent changes to the way intelligence is measured. Over time, the work of scholars ought to result in improvements to theory, which in turn can translate to more effective applications. This prospect is exciting, indeed. We welcome advances in any field—medicine, food science, transportation—for their benefits to society. But the possibility of raising intelligence is unique, for the human intellect is what gives rise to every other advance, whether in domains of discovery or in their applications for human betterment.

CHAPTER 4

Brain and Mind

Within a few hours of Albert Einstein's death in 1955, the great scientist's brain had been surgically removed from his skull and placed in formalin. The autopsy and the events surrounding it were shrouded in secrecy and marked by contradictory claims. The brain was extracted by a hospital pathologist named Thomas Harvey in Princeton, New Jersey, where Einstein lived during the final years of his life.[1] After the autopsy was completed, officials at Princeton University asked Harvey to turn over the brain to the university, but he refused. The pathologist claimed, but could not prove, that Einstein's family had given him permission to keep the brain indefinitely. Thomas Harvey was determined to keep Einstein's brain for himself.

For a long time, the whereabouts of Einstein's brain remained a closely guarded secret known only to a select few. To the larger public, the iconic brain seemed to have vanished, probably forever. The mystery had been nearly forgotten when, in 1978, a journalist named Steven Levy tracked down Thomas Harvey in Wichita, Kansas. Levy was determined to get some answers. After relentless questioning, Harvey "sighed deeply and pulled from a cardboard box two glass jars with sectioned pieces of Einstein's brain."[2] At long last, Einstein's brain had been recovered.

Levy subsequently published a magazine article entitled "My Search for Einstein's Brain," which put the scientific community on notice that sections of the brain might become available for research. The obvious question, intuitive to neuroscientists and laypeople alike, was whether Einstein's brain was unusual in any way. Could his prodigious intellect be correlated with any distinctive features of the brain's anatomy? The answer was not obvious. Superficially, Einstein's brain appeared to be quite average in size and structure, but more detailed analysis showed that the brain did have distinguishing features after all. One of the first scientists to receive a sample of Einstein's brain was UC Berkeley neuroscientist Marian Diamond. Diamond found that the brain sample had far more glial cells than is typical.[3] Glial cells do not directly participate in the brain's signaling, but rather provide neurons with nutritional support and maintenance. Einstein's brain cells appear to have been "well fed." Other research showed that the brain's cerebral cortex, while not particularly thick, had a high density of neurons. This finding led investigators to speculate that "an increase in neuronal density might be advantageous in decreasing inter-neuronal conduction time," thereby increasing the brain's efficiency.[4] In other words, because the neurons were tightly packed, they could presumably carry information efficiently and with exceptional speed.

Further analysis showed that Einstein's brain had an unusually large parietal lobe, a region responsible for mathematical cognition as well as mental imagery.[5] The enlarged parietal lobe seems consistent with Einstein's own accounts of how he constructed the special theory of relativity. His thought experiments included imagining how objects traveling at the speed of light would be affected. Visualization gave him insight into the problem. Einstein envisioned how a light beam would appear if he were traveling alongside the beam at the same speed.[6] Perhaps his enlarged parietal lobe helped him to integrate mental images with mathematical abstractions.

BIGGER BRAIN, HIGHER IQ?

The case of Einstein's brain illustrates the sorts of questions posed by some neuroscientists. These concern the relationship between brain structure and function. Among the most basic questions is whether a larger brain is advantageous. Evidence from the study of human evolution strongly suggests that having a larger brain helps tremendously in adapting to, and surviving in, a hostile environment. During the past three million years, the average human brain increased in size threefold, from the modest 500-gram brain of the australopithecines to the robust 1,500-gram brain of Homo sapiens.[7] However, this is a comparison between two different species—modern humans and their evolutionary ancestors. If we consider only the effects of brain size within Homo sapiens, the variation from person to person is not as clearly predictive of survival value or the ability to adapt. Einstein's brain was not particularly large, which tells us that if there is a positive correlation between brain size and intelligence, it can only be approximate.

In general, a bigger brain is a more intelligent brain. In more than 50 studies dating back to 1906, measures of head size, such as length, perimeter, and volume, are at least weakly predictive of higher IQ scores, with a correlation of about $r = .20$.[8] Many early studies, lacking brain-imaging technologies, could only approximate brain size by measuring head size. With the invention of brain-imaging technologies, such as CT and MRI scanning, it became possible to gather precise data on brain volume and compare those measurements to IQ. The more precise correlations between brain size and IQ vary quite a bit, but yield an average across research studies of $r = .38$—much higher than the correlations between head size and IQ.[9] The correlations hold with equal strength in males and females.

Changes in brain size over the life span may help explain how various forms of intelligence change with age. Recall that fluid intelligence typically declines as we get older. After early adulthood, people normally lose some of their ability to adapt to novel problems, which is the essence of fluid intelligence. On the other hand, crystallized intelligence generally continues to climb until very late in life. The connection to brain size is that total brain volume correlates positively with fluid intelligence but not with crystallized intelligence. Brain size decreases somewhat as we age, which might contribute to the decline in fluid intelligence that is common during middle age and the later years. Crystallized intelligence seems to be unaffected by the decline in total brain size, which could explain why it remains stable or increases throughout life.[10]

On a strictly structural level, the correspondence between brain size and intelligence should not be surprising. Larger brains have, in nearly direct proportion, greater numbers of neurons. More neurons mean greater computational power in the service of adaptation and survival. The intelligent brain in any species must somehow generate a model of the environment, a perceptual world, to which an animal can adapt. In reptiles, the brain constructs this internal world primarily through the sense of vision and its associated neurons.[11] The more developed brains of mammals tend to support the sensory construction of the world through hearing, as well as vision and olfaction. In primates, high visual acuity acquires special importance in representing the external world. While larger brains imply a greater ability to adapt to the environment, we should not ignore the possibility of causal influence in the reverse direction, from environment to anatomy. Certainly this is the case on an evolutionary timescale, but even at the level of individual development, it is possible that intellectually demanding events lead to a larger brain volume.[12]

The correlation between intelligence and brain size is far from perfect, as Einstein's brain vividly illustrates. Clearly, the relationship between brain size and IQ falls short of a complete account of how the brain relates to intelligence. If we want to understand how intelligence is related to the brain, we must consider factors besides sheer size. At minimum, we need to examine the basic structure of the brain and ask how that gross structure relates to function. Fortunately, we have quite a bit of research to draw upon. We know, for example, that the outer layer of the brain, the cortex, is especially important to intelligent thought. The cortex is the structural basis for complex reasoning, perception, and language—indeed, for virtually all forms of higher-order cognition. Tellingly, the cortex is especially large in the human brain. Yet the human cerebral cortex is also surprisingly thin, only about 2 to 4 millimeters thick. In three dimensions, though, the cortex achieves considerable volume because it is massively convoluted. More than two-thirds of its area is tucked away into folds. Folding allows for a large cortical volume, and a large volume gives the human brain an enhanced potential for higher-order intellective functioning.

Aside from recognizing the special importance of the cerebral cortex, anatomists have also noted the division of the brain into distinct lobes. Those lobes are shown in Figure 4.1.

Intelligence cannot be traced to a single region but is distributed through the brain.[13] All four lobes—frontal, parietal, temporal, and occipital—have important relationships to intelligence. More precisely, variation within each lobe is correlated with IQ variation.[14] Different brain regions show considerable variation from one person to another. This suggests a structural

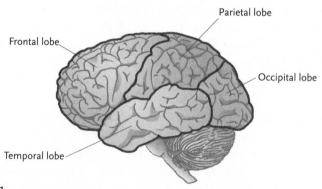

Figure 4.1
Four Lobes of the Human Brain. Martinez, Michael E., *Learning and Cognition: The Design of the Mind*, ©2010. Printed and Electronically reproduced by permission of Pearson Education, Inc., Upper Saddle River, New Jersey.

basis for different profiles of intellectual strengths and weaknesses even when overall IQ is similar.

While acknowledging that the entire brain underlies the exercise of intelligent thought, one particular lobe, the frontal lobe, has a special role: It is responsible for planning, monitoring, and problem solving. Size matters here, too. The volume of gray matter in the brain's frontal lobe is predictive of IQ, even when total brain volume is statistically held constant.[15] As its name suggests, the frontal lobe is located at the front of the brain, just behind the forehead. Neuroscientists have known about the special functions of the frontal lobe for a very long time. The earliest evidence for those functions came from clinical studies on the effects of damage to the frontal lobe. Some cases were so significant that they became historical milestones in our understanding of the brain. In the history of clinical neuroscience, one such case centers on a 25-year-old railway worker named Phineas Gage.[16]

In 1848, America was coming of age. At that time, Abraham Lincoln was a relatively unknown junior congressman from Illinois, and gold had just been discovered in the foothills of the Sierra Nevada mountains of California. Across the United States, the railroad infrastructure was expanding rapidly. Late in the afternoon of September 13, Phineas Gage and a group of his fellow workers were preparing the track bed of a new railroad in rural Vermont. Mr. Gage was packing down explosive powder into a hillside when an errant spark ignited the powder, sending a three-foot tamping bar at high speed through his left cheek, behind his left eye, and out the top of his skull, landing some distance away. Gage was knocked to the ground like a rag doll. Remarkably, he soon got up and walked away from the accident. He remained conscious throughout, and although the tamping bar had completely penetrated the frontal lobe of Gage's brain, he was able to speak.

Phineas Gage's short-term resilience was remarkable. Nevertheless, it soon became apparent that Gage's personality had been radically transformed by the accident. Previously a foreman, Gage could no longer marshal the interpersonal skills necessary to manage a crew of workers. He became easily angered and used obscene language, expressing behavior that was previously uncharacteristic and now problematic for his role as a railway worker. Within a few months of returning to work, Phineas Gage left his railroad job and joined P.T. Barnum's Museum in New York as a human curiosity. Later, he traveled to South America and drove a stagecoach in Chile before moving to San Francisco with his mother and sister. Over the years, his health and coping abilities worsened. In 1860, Gage died of seizures related to the brain injury suffered 12 years previously on the Vermont railroad.

The story of Phineas Gage spotlights the profound effects of targeted disruption of brain tissue. Gage's abilities to relate to other people and to manage his emotions were deeply compromised. By all accounts, the loss of function was directly associated with damage to his frontal lobe. For neuroscientists, the theoretical upshot was clear: Social competence, to a significant degree, seemed to have an anatomical home in the brain. The brain's frontal lobe is also deeply implicated in the executive control of information in working memory as well as in planning functions. When working memory is taxed by holding information while performing a complex task, certain areas of the frontal cortex are highly metabolically active. Overlapping regions of the frontal lobe are also active when separating relevant from irrelevant information to focus on the task at hand.[17] These associations tell us that the frontal lobe has unique importance in the exercise of intelligent thought. More than any other brain region, the volume of brain tissue in the frontal lobe is correlated with IQ scores.[18] To the degree that intelligence is an inherited trait, the genetic control of intelligence is probably exerted largely by variation in gray matter in the brain's frontal lobe.[19]

With this research in hand, we can identify with some precision the structural correspondences between brain anatomy and the two most important psychometric factors, fluid and crystallized intelligence. The brain's frontal lobe is strongly identified with the planning and control functions that are associated with fluid intelligence, whereas all other brain lobes that lie posterior to the frontal lobe—parietal, temporal, and occipital—are more closely associated with the accumulated knowledge that we call crystallized intelligence.[20] The border between the frontal lobe and the other brain lobes is marked by a large groove, the central sulcus, which runs from one side of the head to the other. This groove effectively divides the brain into two functional areas. Brain images show that the parietal lobe, situated at the top of the brain and just behind the central sulcus, is especially correlated with differences in crystallized intelligence.[21] The functional role of the parietal lobe may include the consolidation of knowledge through enhanced neuronal connectivity. The parietal lobe might also serve as a relay center connecting the brain's posterior regions with the executive planning activity that is localized in the frontal lobes.[22] Thus, the brain's central sulcus is akin to an international border, dividing the brain into the "nations" of fluid intelligence and crystallized intelligence.

The forward-most region of the frontal lobe, known as the prefrontal cortex, has special importance across the range of mental activities measured by intelligence tests. So important is the prefrontal cortex that, in some studies, it is the single brain area consistently activated by a broad array of intelligence tests.[23] If we had to name the anatomical epicenter of intelligence, it would be the prefrontal cortex. Phylogenetically, it was one of most recent evolutionary developments in humans and apes. The prefrontal cortex has distinct developmental qualities that align with its role in regulating complex thought. Its primary role is to control attention and resist distraction, both key features of working memory and absolutely vital to intelligent behavior. The prefrontal cortex develops slowly in comparison to other brain regions and shows a surprising degree of plasticity in response to experience.[24] It is one of the last areas of the brain to mature completely, with synapse formation and restructuring extending far past childhood into early adulthood. The protracted period of synaptic structuring and restructuring is use-dependent, implying that it is specially attuned to higher-order cognitive demands.

THE LEFT AND RIGHT HEMISPHERES

The case of Phineas Gage was forever instructive to neuroscientists about the functional role of the brain's frontal lobe. In 1861, a year after Gage died, a French physician named Paul Pierre Broca documented a different correspondence between localized brain injury and specific compromises to intellectual functioning. Broca found that injury to the brain's left temporal lobe, located just above the ear, produces specific and profound speech disruption, called aphasia. The localization of speech to the left hemisphere hints of a more sweeping pattern: the separation of function by the brain's left and right hemispheres.

Like two halves of an intact walnut, the brain exhibits bilateral symmetry. That structural separation, it turns out, also has counterpart functional separations: The two hemispheres exhibit somewhat different ways of processing information.[25] We noted, for example, that the left hemisphere tends to be more proficient at language processing; the right hemisphere, by contrast, specializes more directly in processing spatial and musical information. This separation of function exists not only in the temporal lobes but also in the frontal lobe. The left side of the frontal lobe is dedicated to the processing of verbal information, whereas the right side is active when spatial information is processed.[26] The bilateral separation of function must be qualified, however. It holds up well for right-handed people, but less so for left-handers: About 40% of left-handers have language centers in their right hemispheres. The brain's hemispheres also differentiate in a second way. Whereas the left hemisphere tends to process information analytically by attending to details, the right hemisphere interprets information more holistically by seeing the big picture. The two processes are, of course, complementary. Every brain needs to operate both analytically and holistically in order to interpret the environment in an intelligent way.

The brain's hemispheres display other differences of function. The most basic difference is that each hemisphere exercises muscular control over the opposite side of the body. The left hand, for example, is controlled by the right hemisphere. Partial paralysis following a stroke on one side of the brain is manifest on the opposite, or contralateral, side. Sensory information, too, is at least partly processed by the opposite hemisphere. The retina of each eye divides incoming light sensation into the right and left visual fields, and the signals from each field are shunted to the opposite brain hemisphere. Hearing is mostly contralateral, but not completely. Auditory data from each ear is sent to both hemispheres, but most of the auditory processing occurs in the hemisphere opposite to the ear that received the input.

The independent functions of the cerebral hemispheres were explored more fully in the 1960s, when in some epilepsy patients the neural bridge connecting the two hemispheres was surgically cut. The main neural structure connecting the brain's left and right hemispheres is the corpus callosum, the sheet of neurons that runs beneath the two hemispheres. In "split brain" patients, the corpus callosum was severed to alleviate symptoms of epilepsy. The surgery resulted in the functional isolation of the hemispheres, whose psychological consequences were revealed by a series of fascinating studies.[27] For example, when common objects such as scissors were presented to the right visual field, the patient had no difficulty naming the object because information was projected to the language centers in the left hemispheres. However, when objects were shown to the left visual field, the information was shunted to the brain's right hemisphere. Because the right hemisphere ordinarily has a much-reduced capacity to use language, the patient was frequently unable to name the object.

Split-brain patients sometimes displayed quite remarkable behavior showing that the left and right hemispheres could have different, and even contradictory, knowledge. Keep in mind that each brain hemisphere communicates directly only with the contralateral side of the body. Now consider what happened when conflicting instructions were presented to the brain's right and left hemispheres. Through spoken instructions to the left ear, the right hemisphere was told to pick up a paper clip; instructions to the right ear told the left hemisphere to pick up an eraser. If the left hand correctly picked up the paper clip, this action was consistent with information given to the controlling right hemisphere, but it contradicted the request given to the left hemisphere. In split-brain patients, the left hemisphere would sometimes respond by misnaming the object, calling it an eraser. The two hemispheres could even hold contradictory wishes. This was illustrated when a 15-year-old boy was asked about his ideal future job. The question was posed independently to his left and right hemispheres. The answer given by his left hemisphere was "draftsman," but his right hemisphere responded "automobile racer."[28]

Differences in function between the brain's right and left hemispheres are fascinating, but have sometimes been overextended or misapplied. For example, some people have interpreted the separation of function *within* the individual brain as a way to understand differences *between* people. That's why we sometimes hear people describe themselves or others as "left-brained" or as "right-brained." "Left-brained" people tend to process information more linearly and rationally; they are analytic, detail-oriented, and not at all averse to splitting technical hairs. By contrast, "right-brained" people prefer to consider the larger picture. Less concerned with dissecting a problem or situation, their propensity is to understand and appreciate sweeping patterns, including their aesthetic qualities.

Separating people into left-brained and right-brained is deeply problematic for two reasons. First, it fails to recognize that the separation of function in the individual brain is only partial. The relative specialization of the left side to analytical processing and the right to holistic processing is only a tendency, a partial division of labor, and certainly not a strict assignment. After all, the hemispheres are normally cross-wired by the corpus callosum, which ensures that information is communicated between the two halves of the brain. More importantly, the analytic-holistic distinction that holds up when describing the individual brain does not automatically map on to descriptions of people. For such descriptions as "left-brained" and "right-brained" to be validated, an entirely separate research track must test and verify that individuals really do differ significantly and consistently in their preferences for processing information. The binary categorization, *either* left *or* right, makes such a clean distinction unlikely. Such differences may turn out to be a continuum rather than categories, but this is speculation. Such a hypothetical dimension for understanding cognitive preferences has yet to be backed by data. These missteps and misconstruals tell us that the study of brain structure and function provides plenty of grist for speculation, but the resulting enthusiasm should be tempered with caution against errors of application.[29]

INTELLIGENCE DRAWS UPON THE ENTIRE BRAIN

As neuroanatomists continue to employ sophisticated imaging technologies to map brain anatomy to specific cognitive functions, the resulting "cartography" becomes more precise and, at the same time, less simplistic. As research continues, the emerging field of cognitive neuroscience becomes progressively more complex. Now we know that the mapping of brain function to brain anatomy does not follow a pattern of one-to-one correspondence. Instead, as a rule, every complex cognitive function is supported by several brain locations acting in a coordinated fashion. Thus, while the frontal lobe and Broca's areas have specific functions, they never work alone. Every act of intelligence requires the activation of multiple brain sites, or circuits, working in concert.[30] Reading engages its own characteristic brain circuitry;[31] mathematics activates a different circuit.[32] Brain circuits display both unity and diversity—another version of the "one and many" logic that we found describes the organization of intelligence as viewed through the lens of psychometrics.

Let's acknowledge, then, that complex cognition invokes multiple areas of the brain as coordinated circuits. This does not mean that the entire brain is activated. In fact, when neuroscientists identify multisite circuits through scans showing areas of high metabolic activity, other areas of the brain are not particularly active—at least not above baseline levels. This fact raises a question: Does the average person use all of the brain's potential capacity, or does most of that potential lie dormant? Let's ask the question in a more familiar form: Does the average person use only 10% of his or her brain's capacity? The answer is important. If the answer is *yes*, it means that the brain's potential is largely untapped, implying a lamentable waste. It also hints at something exciting—the possibility of far greater brainpower in the average person if only some of that unused 90% were put into play. If we use only 10% of our brain capacity, as is widely believed, then perhaps each of us has tremendous reserves of intellectual capacity. Is the idea valid?

To cut straight to the answer, the claim that we use no more than 10% of our brain is a myth, plain and simple. We have no evidence that 90% of the brain is held in unused reserve. How, then, did this widely believed myth arise? The claim has sometimes been attributed to Albert Einstein, though there is no evidence that he ever said anything about the topic. More likely, it traces to the great 19th-century American psychologist William James. Along with his scholarly manuscripts, Professor James wrote popular articles in which he expressed his belief that people "make use of only a small part of our mental and physical resources."[33] In 1936, this statement was paraphrased in the preface to Dale Carnegie's classic self-help book *How to Win Friends and Influence People*. The writer of the preface, journalist Lowell Thomas, attributed to James the belief that "the average man develops only ten percent of his latent mental ability."[34]

The attribution to William James gave the statement instant, but unde-served, credibility.

Other explanations for the 10% myth arise directly from the known structure and function of the brain itself. Early studies of the brain identi-fied large regions of cortex that served no identifiable function. Originally, these expanses were referred to as "silent areas," implying unused poten-tial. Later, the same regions were called "association areas," which recog-nized their function as sites of neural connections associated with learning and development. Pioneering studies by the great neuroscientist Karl Lashley further recognized the brain's remarkable plasticity of function in response to trauma or to specialized demands.[35] The brain's impressive ability to adapt may have been mistaken for untapped potential and so indirectly corroborated the 10% myth. Whatever its origin, it remains a myth—an inaccurate statement about the way brain anatomy relates to function. Though false, the 10% myth does contain a germ of truth—or perhaps more accurately, a credible hypothesis—that the mind is capable of much more than is typically realized. We have yet to understand what the human brain can achieve when developed to its full capacity.

INTELLIGENCE AT THE LEVEL OF NEURONS

The gross anatomy of the brain can take us only so far in understanding the biological basis for intelligence. To go further, we must examine the struc-ture and function of the brain at a microscopic level—at the level of special-ized cells called neurons.[36] Here we are considering a biological scale roughly 1,000 times smaller than the level of detail revealed by brain-imaging tech-nologies. At this level of detail, cells are the basic structural elements. We learned in our basic biology courses that cells are the building blocks of nearly all life forms—animals, plants, and microbes. The human body is composed of trillions of cells, including muscle cells, heart cells, and red and white blood cells. Most human cells are tiny sacs of fluid wrapped in a thin membrane. Inside the cell is its nucleus, which contains the body's genetic blueprint, coded in DNA. The genetic code gives cells their ability to replicate as well as to differentiate into their particular cell type. As liv-ing entities, cells also have the ability to metabolize food and to get rid of waste products.

Neurons are cells that carry signals in the body, much like copper wires carry signals in electrical circuits. Because neurons function something like wires, they can be very long: The longest neuron in the human body reaches from the base of the spine to the toes. We can think of neurons as serving three functions underlying intelligent behavior. First, neurons relay information from the senses. It's impossible to interact effectively with the external world unless we have some idea of what's going on outside. Our senses provide that information by carrying sensations detected by our eyes, ears, and other sense organs to the brain. In order to behave intelligently, we also need to activate muscles to control movement, whether walking, talking, or engaging in other forms of muscle control. Accordingly, a second function of neurons is to enable us to act on the environment through precisely articulated muscle activation. A third neuronal function is most relevant to our quest to understand intelligence. Although neurons are distributed through our bodies, they are concentrated in two locations, the brain and the spinal cord. In the brain especially, amassed neurons are the basis for the spectrum of information-processing activity we call "thinking." These three functions—sensory input, muscular output, and computation—are all components of intelligent behavior.

Because neurons are the anatomical basis for intelligence at the microscopic level, we need to probe more deeply into how they work. If neurons are the equivalent of wiring in a complex electrical system, say a computer, then to a first approximation a large number of neurons would seem to be advantageous. The human brain is particularly large in comparison to most other species, with about a trillion (1,000,000,000,000) neurons. For any individual, this number stays fairly constant through the life span, a fact that led some scientists to infer that adults lose the ability to generate new neurons.[37] As children, some of us were warned against reckless behavior because, it was assumed, brain cells could never be regenerated. We now know that this is not the case. Researchers have found that the adult brain can generate new neurons in the hippocampus, a brain structure that plays a key role in memory formation.[38]

One trillion neurons is such a huge number that it is nearly unfathomable. To gain some perspective, it equates to roughly 100 times the human population of the earth. That's impressive, yet it's not so much the number of *neurons* that expresses the intricacy of the human brain, but rather the number of *connections* between neurons that shows just how complex the brain is. After all, the number of neurons in the brain is irrelevant if those neurons are not connected properly. Each neuron typically connects to a thousand or so other neurons. This means that the total number of neuron-to-neuron connections in a single brain is a far greater number—approximately a quadrillion (1,000,000,000,000,000). This number is roughly equal to the number of ants living on the entire earth. The brain's dazzling intricacy has inspired some neuroscientists to claim that it is the most complex object in the universe.

The connections between neurons have a special name—synapses. A diagram showing a hypothetical neuron and close-up of a synapse connecting two neurons is shown in Figure 4.2. Notice that the synapse connecting the two neurons has a surprising feature. It is not a physical connection at all. Instead, the synapse is actually a very narrow gap separating the communicating neurons. This gap implies that the form of signaling between neurons is different from the way a signal is carried along the length of a neuron. Within a single neuron, and especially along the cable-like section called an axon, the signal is electrical. A rapidly changing voltage is propagated from one end of the neuron to the other. At the synapse, though, the signal is mediated solely through tiny messenger chemicals called neurotransmitters. In the diagram, the tiny particles shown floating across the synaptic gap from left to right symbolize this chemical signal. If enough neurotransmitters cross the gap, then the next neuron line will "fire," continuing the signal down the line to the next neuron.

The picture is starting to look complicated. Human intelligence is somehow based on wild profusions of neuronal connections, which are established through a quadrillion microscopically small connections (actually gaps) bridged by neurotransmitters. Even if we take in this complexity and assume that this picture gets even more complicated (and it does!), we can still identify a few simple ideas that give order to concepts that might otherwise seem bewildering. One idea that lends clarity is the association between learning (a mental event) and the formation of new synapses (an anatomical event). This conceptual bridge links what the mind does and how the brain reacts by restructuring itself. Because each life path is uniquely personal, our individual patterns of neuronal connections

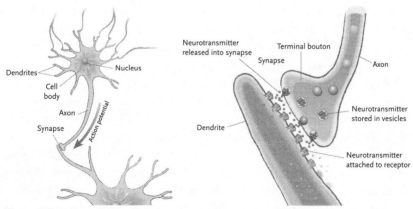

Figure 4.2
Neural Activity at the Synapse. Martinez, Michael E., *Learning and Cognition: The Design of the Mind,* ©2010. Printed and Electronically reproduced by permission of Pearson Education, Inc., Upper Saddle River, New Jersey.

are likewise uniquely constructed. Far more complex than a fingerprint, the intricate pattern of synapses makes every brain one of a kind, distinguishing even between identical twins, who share the same DNA code. The 1,000,000,000,000,000 or so neuronal connections that compose each brain's structure form its unique signature, unprecedented and unrepeatable.

The synaptic connections in the brain form our best model for learning and intelligent functioning. Whenever learning occurs, synapses change.[39] Learning can involve the formation of entirely new synapses or the modification of existing synapses. It's possible that people differ significantly in how efficiently their neurons adapt to environmental input. According to one theory, variation in IQ arises directly from how efficiently brains respond to stimulation.[40] Brains primed to respond to environmental stimulation, quite possibly through being genetically predisposed to form new connections are, for that reason, more intelligent. Less adaptable brains are not as capable of forming and maintaining new neuronal connections. This theory of brain adaptability, though somewhat speculative, has the attractive feature of merging important facts from theories of intelligence and theories of brain development.

Research on laboratory rats has provided our best understanding of how learning leads to synapse formation. In one study, rats were divided into groups and raised in one of two conditions.[41] One group was raised in cages arranged to encourage play and exploration; another group was raised in barren cages. Rats raised in the more complex environment developed healthier, more capable brains. They had larger cerebral cortices and more extensive brain vascularization. At the microscopic level, their brains also had a greater density of synapses.[42] These differences were expressed in the behavior of the animals: Rats raised in more complex environments were better at solving problems, such as how to find their way through a maze.

Applied to humans, the upshot of this research is that the connection between brain microanatomy and learning is direct. The brain's experience alters its structure. This is true not only at the level of lobes and hemispheres, but also at the microscopic and molecular levels, especially at synapses. We must therefore appreciate that the "intelligence" of a laboratory rat is not the result of a unidirectional causal force from biology to behavior. The reverse direction is also operative. Differences in behavioral experience can "echo back" to modify the organism's biological structure as manifest in modifications to its neurons.[43] The enriched environment of some cages is what produced a greater profusion of synapses and vascularization. This general responsiveness is referred to as the brain's plasticity. Neuronal structures, whether in rodents or in humans, respond to experience in ways that are sometimes surprising. In our quest to explore the potential of experience—the "nurture" term of the nature/nurture equation—the phenomenon of brain plasticity is a key discovery.[44]

In human populations, we observe clear examples of brain plasticity among professionals whose work places intense demands on focused kinds of cognition. A professional violinist, for example, relies on extraordinary finger dexterity in her left hand. Much less dexterity is required in the fingers of her right hand, which is responsible for bowing. Fine coordination between sensory inputs and muscular control is handled in the somatosensory cortex, a band of brain tissue that runs crosswise just behind the frontal cortex. Brain scans of the somatosensory cortex in violinists reveal an unusually large region devoted to the fingers of the left hand—much larger than the region that supports finger movement in the right hand.[45] The asymmetry shows that the brain has responded to the demands placed upon it. The professional violinist "needs" extraordinary finger control in the left hand, and the brain adapts by recruiting neurons to help support that function. Each finger is allocated relatively more neural "real estate" than would normally be the case. This expansion of function to adjacent neurons is beneficial—to a point. In some very experienced violinists, the recruitment of additional neurons can expand to such a degree that areas of cortex that control individual fingers begin to overlap. This results in a decline in finger dexterity, a condition known as focal dystonia. A similar pattern of degradation has been identified among Braille readers. Regions of brain tissue needed to read the elevated dots composing Braille symbols initially expand in such a way that increases sensitivity and reading efficiency. When those same brain areas expand into areas that support adjacent fingers, sensitivity and efficiency can decline.[46]

The brain's responsiveness to the cognitive demands of work has likewise been documented in a study of London taxi drivers. Unlike the grid pattern common to many capital cities, London streets run helter-skelter, often intersect at obtuse angles, and generally present drivers with a layout that is quite challenging to master. To become licensed, prospective taxi drivers must demonstrate a thorough knowledge of the London streets and traffic patterns so that they can efficiently navigate between any two points. In this study, the demands on long-term memory as well as spatial reasoning were particularly significant because the research was conducted in the 1990s, prior to widespread use of GPS navigation devices. Perhaps not too surprising, brain scans of the 16 London taxi drivers showed a particularly large posterior hippocampus, a region of the brain that supports two-dimensional spatial processing. The more intriguing finding is that, over time, the drivers' brains appeared to respond to the memory demands: The posterior hippocampus was largest in taxi drivers with more than 40 years of experience navigating the streets of London.[47]

Violinists and taxi drivers typically devote thousands of hours to their professions. Given such prolonged experience, the brain's adaptation to long-term demands may not be too surprising. Yet brain adaptation seems to accompany short-term learning and skill development as well. One study used the skill of juggling to investigate this possibility. The point was to determine whether learning to juggle would result in measurable changes to the brain. Researchers divided a group of 24 nonjugglers into two groups, asking 12 participants to independently learn how to juggle using the basic three-ball cascade routine. No new demands were placed on the other 12 participants.

After three months, all 12 in the experimental group were successful in learning to juggle for at least 60 seconds. When their brains' morphologies were compared before and after learning to juggle, the scans showed changes in regions specific to visualization in the temporal lobes. The total volume of those areas increased an average of 3%—a small but measurable difference.[48] No such structural changes were detected in the brains of the nonjuggling group. A third scan was conducted three months later. In the intervening period, none of the study participants practiced juggling. The third scan showed that the structural changes had reversed partially and now showed only a 2% structural expansion over baseline levels. The study's authors interpreted the findings as showing that the human brain's macrostructure can change in direct response to training. The specific mechanisms underlying the structural change were not completely clear—local expansion of gray matter might be the result of changes in existing neurons or, possibly, production of new neurons. Whatever the full explanation, the brains of jugglers adapted structurally, presumably in response to, at most, a few dozen hours of practice.

The research on brain adaptation tells an important story: The brain responds to the specific demands placed upon it; in particular, it exhibits structural changes as it adapts. Those changes vary in intensity and scale: Some alterations amount to no more than heightened sensitivity of the connections between neurons. A more significant form of adaptation is the formation of new synapses, which supports longer-term knowledge and skill development. The most radical structural change entails rewiring large sections of the cortex. Although we are used to thinking about learning along the timeline of minutes or hours, wholesale brain rewiring can occur over the course of many years.[49] We see manifestations of significant neurological "remodeling" in the neural organizations of professional violinists and taxi drivers. Such remodeling might even include brain enlargement.

Some scholars have advanced the intriguing hypothesis that correlations between brain size and IQ might arise, at least in part, from the behavior of individuals. Those who seek more intellectually challenging environments might experience a small but significant gain in total brain volume.[50]

The research evidence is quite clear: The human brain exhibits amazing flexibility. We saw evidence of this flexibility in the brain's adaptations to the professional demands on violinists and taxi drivers. Dramatic manifestations of functional flexibility are also apparent when large sections of the brain are injured or must be removed surgically. In some instances, trauma results in very little reduction of cognitive function; in other cases, those cognitive functions that are compromised can be substantially relearned. Sometimes this means that functions originally supported by one brain region are regained when the brain "reassigns" those functions to new areas. So while the brain's anatomy maps to specific cognitive functions, the brain can deviate from those mappings when its plasticity is what the organism needs.

INTELLIGENCE AND BRAIN WAVES

Studies of brain plasticity tell us a lot about the long-term effects of the environment on brain structure. Brain adaptations often occur over very long spans of time—years in the case of many vital forms of cognitive development, such as becoming literate, growing the capacity for abstract thought, or building the knowledge base constituent to expertise. But anyone who has been startled by a loud sound knows that the brain can also respond very rapidly to stimuli. A complete stimulus-response event can take place in mere fractions of a second. These vary rapid adaptations are surprisingly informative. They, too, can tell us quite a bit about how minds differ and why. We now shift our attention to those rapid and evanescent changes in neural activity commonly known as brain waves.

Functionally, the brain is an electrochemical organ that transmits information over biological circuits. Electrical activity in the brain can be monitored by means of electrodes attached to the scalp. This is the basis of electroencephalographic (EEG) research. As in IQ measurement, individual differences make EEG research possible as well as interesting. People differ in the patterns of brain waves that are picked up in an EEG study. One way to explore those differences is by studying so-called event-related potentials (ERPs). Here, an "event" is simply the presentation of some stimulus, such as a sound or a flash of light, and "potential" refers to voltage changes at the scalp. So, quite simply, ERP research involves studying the voltage changes on the scalp when the brain reacts to a new stimulus. Brains respond quickly to unexpected stimuli, so important voltage changes occur within the time span of a single second. This means that *changes* in wave forms are described in milliseconds (1/1000 of a second), depending on how quickly they occur after the stimulus "event."

The question we want answered is whether variations in EEG patterns relate to differences in IQ. Many decades of research have confirmed regular associations between IQ and evoked potentials. People respond differently depending on whether the stimulus is novel or familiar. Normally, we are alert to new stimuli—think of how a police siren gets our attention. We are instantly alert, but as the seconds pass we become less focused on the siren and expand our attention to the other objects and events in our immediate environment. Even though this pattern is common, it varies somewhat depending on the person. Precise measurements of brain waves show that high-IQ subjects respond with greater intensity to novel stimuli and with less intensity to familiar stimuli.[51] In other words, more intelligent brains are hyperalert to novelty, but then adjust rapidly to the new information and thereafter pay less attention to what is by now familiar. A comparable pattern has been found in infants: "Smarter" babies adapt rapidly. Infants who quickly shift attention away from familiar patterns and toward new patterns tend to have higher IQ scores years later.[52]

Other aspects of brain waves are amplitude (height) and complexity. Researchers have sometimes found associations between these wave parameters and IQ, but the associations are inconsistent. Findings from one research study are often unconfirmed in another. There is one exception, however. Among the various wave forms, one has shown consistent results—the p300. This is the positive (p) spike that occurs approximately 300 milliseconds after the stimulus. A graph showing the p300 is depicted in Figure 4.3.

To interpret the graph, note that positive voltages, or "spikes," extend downward. As its name p300 suggests, the time delay of the positive spike is typically 300 milliseconds, but it can occur as long as 600 milliseconds after the stimulus. The graph shows a p300 spike at about 400 milliseconds. Longer delays, called latencies, are associated with unfamiliar or more complex stimuli, but latencies also vary from person to person. Researchers not only measure the delay of the p300, they also measure its height, or amplitude. Both parameters—wave height (or amplitude) and time delay (latency)—correlate with IQ scores.

The p300 is the brain's signature response to recognition, revealing a sense of "I know what that is." Higher IQs are associated with higher amplitudes and shorter latencies—in everyday language, with reactions that are

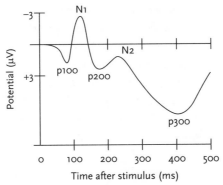

Figure 4.3
Example of an Evoked Potential Illustrating the P300 Spike.

intense and fast. The associations with IQ have been most consistent with latency. Correlations between p300 latency and IQ are in the range of $r = .30$ to $r = .50$. Shorter latencies imply that intelligence is associated with rapid recognition, which, in turn, implies efficient information processing. Even though the differences in the p300 latency are measured in fractions of a second, the marginal advantages in efficiency may accumulate over time. A small advantage can, in aggregate, lead to superiority in rendering effective decisions, learning abstract information, and solving complex problems.

INTELLIGENCE AND BRAIN METABOLISM

Another way to understand the relationship of intelligence to the brain is to explore its basis in brain metabolism. To do so, we cannot rely on measures of voltage fluctuations at the scalp. Instead, we need tools that can more directly measure brain activity internally by capitalizing on sophisticated imaging technologies, such as CT and PET scanners. CT, PET, and other imaging technologies measure somewhat different aspects of brain activity or metabolism, but all give us insight into brain activity at a greater level of precision than that afforded by clinical studies of brain damage or by external recordings of electrical activity (EEGs). To illustrate, let's consider what PET scans tell us about intelligent brains.

PET stands for positron emission tomography. PET scans require injecting a small amount of radioactive glucose into the bloodstream. Glucose serves as the basic fuel for the body's cells, so it is absorbed and metabolized throughout the body. However, glucose is absorbed fastest by the most active cells. This means that regions of the brain that are most active will absorb comparatively more of the tracer glucose. Differential uptake is important, but so is decay of the radioactive portion. An unstable fluorine atom on the glucose molecule releases a positively charged electron, called a positron. The released positrons scatter in all directions, and so the function of the PET scanner is to determine the points in the brain from which the positrons are emanating. By showing which brain areas produce relatively more positron emissions, the PET device can infer quite precisely which areas are most metabolically active. Cognitive neuroscientists extend the chain of inferences one link further: They reason that the most active brain areas mediate the cognitive functions in play while scanning occurs.

Through a chain of reasoning, PET technology can say something about the level and nature of thinking that occurs during the scan. With that as background, let's now examine more directly the connections between brain activity and intelligence. In particular, let's consider a study of how brain metabolism is associated with a classic test of intelligence, Raven's Matrices. The most basic question we can ask is whether the brain is more active when engaged in Raven's Matrices than in a less demanding task. Research confirmed that those who worked on a repetitive task consumed less glucose than those who worked on Raven's Matrices. This is exactly what we would expect: As the brain works harder, it consumes fuel faster.

The surprise came when comparing the scores on Raven's to the glucose consumption rates. Brain metabolism and Raven's scores were *negatively* correlated, indicating that those who had the highest scores had the lowest rates of glucose consumption.[53] Apparently, higher-IQ participants solved the puzzles most efficiently. Not only was their cognitive performance higher, their brains were working *less hard* to achieve a superior result. This pattern has since been replicated using a variety of IQ measures, with correlations between IQs and brain metabolisms averaging about $r = -.50$.[54] One possible explanation for the negative correlations is that higher-IQ people have relatively more gray matter in regions correlated with scores on intelligence tests. The larger volumes of gray matter would require less *average* metabolic activity in the relevant brain region.[55] Another possibility is that more intelligent brains simply operate more efficiently regardless of size or composition.

DOES THE BRAIN REMEMBER EVERYTHING?

The brain's capacity for intelligent thought is partly attributable to its ability to learn from experience. Memory is therefore one aspect of the intelligent mind, though it is far from the only, or even the most important, component of intelligence. Still, given that memory plays a role in the intellectual toolkit, we need to consider how the brain supports the formation, storage, and retrieval of memories.

Many years ago, neuroscientists thought that the brain might store complete and accurate memories from the entire life experience. If true, then every single event would be recorded in the brain, potentially available for playback if the right cue were presented to trigger that particular memory. This hypothesis was famously set forth by the great Canadian neurosurgeon Wilder Penfield based on his experiences performing brain surgery on epileptic patients. While preparing to remove brain structures to alleviate the symptoms of epilepsy, Penfield stimulated the surface of the brain to create a "map" of the patient's brain to improve surgical accuracy. The patients were awake during the procedure through conscious sedation.

When their brains were probed, some of Penfield's patients reported "hearing" sounds or "seeing" flashing lights. None of these reports were unusual; sensations of light and sound had previously been reported by patients undergoing brain surgery. But when Penfield stimulated the temporal lobes on either side of the brain, something unusual occurred: Some patients immediately described vivid personal memories, such as a familiar song or the voice of an old friend. The patients seemed to be reliving events from their past. In some cases, restimulating the same spot caused an identical memory to be reexperienced. Penfield interpreted these finding by hypothesizing that stimulation applied to the brain surface "unlocks the experience of bygone days."[56] To Penfield, these results "came as a complete surprise." He summed up his findings by saying that "there is within the brain a . . . record of past experience which preserves the individual's current perceptions in astonishing detail." The view of human memory as complete and accurate—much like a video camera—came to be widely believed. Is it true? Does the brain store a complete record of every life experience? For better or worse, the answer is *no*.

Penfield's hypothesis, though fascinating in the extreme, was incorrect. Instead of being complete and accurate, human memory is highly selective and vulnerable to distortion. As every lawyer knows, any two eyewitnesses to an accident or crime scene can remember events quite differently, even though both feel confident in the accuracy of their memories. Conflicting memories of events is in fact a recurring challenge to the practice of trial law.[57] That's precisely because memory does not function like a video camera. Instead, long-term memory is an interpretation of experience filtered through the mind's preexisting categories, values, and expectations. What we remember may have little to do with what actually occurred.

Penfield's interpretation of memory as complete and accurate was challenged in two ways. First, only about 10% of Penfield's patients reported reliving life experiences when their brains were probed. Second, and more significant, patients' recollections during surgery were never confirmed for accuracy. Electrical stimulation might well have evoked personal memories, but those could have been exactly the sort of incomplete and highly processed remembrances that we hear whenever a person tries to recount an event from the past. Dr. Penfield eventually backed down from his belief that the brain stores a memory of every life experience, but he never renounced the hypothesis completely. Despite the lack of support for Penfield's original hypothesis, the myth of complete and accurate memory storage lives on. This widely held myth proves that the workings of the human mind and its underlying brain mechanisms are not obvious, and that we can easily acquire false ideas about how they operate.

Even if we set aside Penfield's hypothesis as a poor generalization of how memory works, we know that some rare individuals do in fact have highly accurate memories. Commonly called photographic memory, the ability to remember past events—especially factual information—in great detail is known by psychologists as eidetic memory. The most celebrated "eidetiker" was the Russian journalist Solomon Shereshevskii. While working as a newspaper reporter, Shereshevskii frustrated his editor because the reporter never took notes while working on an assignment. Notes were superfluous: Shereshevskii could remember the details of any story—who, what, when, and so on—indefinitely and with perfect accuracy.

The case of the young reporter was fascinating to the Russian psychologist Alexander Luria, who studied Shereshevskii and, to preserve anonymity, gave him the code name "S." Luria confirmed that S's memory was indeed extraordinary, noting that

> his memory *had no distinct limits*... there was no limit either to the *capacity* of S's memory or to the *durability of the traces he retained*.... He had no difficulty reproducing any lengthy series of words whatever, even though these originally had been presented to him a week, a month, a year, or many years earlier.[58]

While documenting the case of S, Luria discovered many aspects of his psychology that were less than impressive and, in some cases, alarming. First, S had only average intelligence. This fact alone should prompt us to question whether having a highly accurate memory is necessarily a contributor to intelligent functioning. Of course, intelligence is manifest not only on IQ tests but also in behavior. Yet in practical ways as well, S was not the picture of a psychologically integrated human being.

According to Luria, S seemed to owe his extraordinary memory to a habit of forming profuse and unusual connections. He thought of numerals, for example, not simply as symbols but as characters with imputed personalities—7 was a man with a mustache, and 8 was a very stout woman! Normally, the ability to form connections between ideas is a functional advantage to cognition, but in S the connections were so extensive that they often resulted in confusion. S could remember details, but at the cost of forgetting context, such as whether a particular conversation took place last week or last year. Eventually, his mind came to resemble "a junk heap of impressions" more than an orderly database.[59] These drawbacks began to take a serious toll. S could no longer carry out his professional responsibilities or live a normal life. Eventually, Solomon Shereshevskii was committed to an asylum for mental pathology. The story of S lives on in the annals of psychology as a vivid reminder not to confuse an extraordinary memory with either high levels of intelligence or an effective and satisfying life.

A different variety of extraordinary memory was reported in 2006 by neuroscientists at UCLA and the University of California, Irvine.[60] The case involved a 40-year-old woman, "AJ," who had an uncanny ability to recall the events of her life over a span of several decades. Given any calendar date from 1974 forward, AJ could instantly recall the day's events. Her extraordinary memory was focused exclusively on personal information—the events of her life. In that way it differed from the heightened memory capabilities of S and, indeed, all other known cases of exceptional memory. AJ's mental habits seemed to bolster her autobiographical memories. Interviews revealed that she had an uncontrollable tendency to constantly mentally "relive" events from her past. She described her daily conscious experience as viewing two movies simultaneously—one focused on her present experience and the other a rerun of past events.

AJ's memory for autobiographical events is striking, but did not convey the advantages we normally associate with high intelligence. Indeed, AJ's measured IQ was a modest 93, within the range of normal but slightly below average, although on memory subtests she scored somewhat higher than average. Academically, AJ was not a standout student: She received mostly Cs, with a smattering of Bs and an occasional A. Although AJ earned a bachelor's degree, she admitted that learning course material was not easy. Somewhat reminiscent of the Russian mnemonist S, AJ reported suffering from recurrent anxiety and depression, which over her adult years were treated with medication and psychotherapy. What can we learn from the case of AJ, S, and lives of those rare individuals who exhibit extraordinary memory? A fair conclusion is that a photographic or eidetic memory is not necessarily the boon that most people would believe. An extraordinary memory does not lead in any predictable way to academic or career success, nor to a satisfying life.

THE COLOR OF MUSIC, THE TASTE OF SOUND

Before leaving the fascinating topic of exceptional memory, let us explore unusual modes of perception that, in some cases, may enhance a person's ability to remember information. Solomon Shereshevskii, for example, routinely forged connections between new information and the extant knowledge in his long-term memory. Those connections included interpreting digits as having personalities. Like S, the ability to see more than the stark information in everyday experience is found among people who have the capacity for synesthesia, the rare phenomenon in which sensory input in one modality is experienced in a second modality.[61] One of the most extraordinary forms of synesthesia involves the ability to see sounds as color. For such synesthetes, hearing a piece of music produces a continuously varying experience of color in addition to the normal perceptions of sound variation in pitch, tone, timbre, and rhythm. Streams of color drift through the synesthete's field of view, with hue varying by pitch and brightness increasing or decreasing in correspondence with the musical dynamics.

The most common form of synesthesia is grapheme-color synesthesia. Its defining characteristic is that letters of the alphabet are perceived as having colors. The letter "A," though printed in black ink, will commonly appear to the synesthete as red. Other letters also appear as having consistent mappings to specific colors. Neuroscientists have found objective evidence for the synesthete's subjective experience: Brain scans reveal that the perceptions of letters activate color-processing areas in the brains of grapheme-color synesthetes. Those same regions are inactive in the scans of nonsynesthetes.

A synesthete may assume that everyone else perceives the alphabet as differentiated by color, producing quite a shock when she discovers that her perceptions are unusual. One synesthete, Lynn Duffy, remembered vividly when at age 16 she realized that her perceptions were not like everyone else's. During a conversation with her father, Duffy described what happened when she changed a "P" into an "R." She said to him:

> I realized that to make an R all I had to do was first to write a P and then draw a line down from its loop. And I was so surprised that I could turn a yellow letter into an orange letter just by adding a line.[62]

Duffy's father was startled to hear Lynn's statement. He had no idea that his daughter perceived the alphabet in distinct colors.

A fascinating variety of synesthesia is the lexical-gustatory form in which the synesthete experiences sounds as distinct tastes. One synesthete reported, for example, that the sound of the letter "K" evoked the taste of an egg. Such odd cross-sensory experiences are uncommon: Only about 1 person in 200 experiences synesthesia. Though rare, the forms of synesthesia are quite varied—more than 100 varieties have been identified.

The experiential reality of synesthesia is well documented through highly consistent self-reports over time as well as through corroborating data from brain-imaging studies. Even so, the precise neurological basis of synesthesia is unclear. One quite intuitive theory postulates neurological cross-wiring. This explanation is credible given that brain regions that process written symbols and the regions that process color are anatomically quite close. In the brain of the synesthete, neurons may cross into adjacent regions that are normally neurologically distinct. A related hypothesis is that the inhibitory neurotransmitters in synesthetes may not effectively isolate neuron activity, and so excitatory signals might spill over into adjacent brain regions.

Though neurologically abnormal, synesthesia is not typically disadvantageous. Unlike S, most people who experience synesthesia are not predisposed to psychopathology, and in fact may be cognitively advantaged in some ways. Synesthetes may experience superior memory for new information because it is encoded in multiple forms, as in the case of S. Synesthetes might also be advantaged in creative pursuits as the firsthand experience of cross-modality sensation may provoke metaphors that can be expressed artistically. Subjectively, the experience of synesthesia is often reported as either neutral or pleasant.

Both eidetic memory and synesthesia are statistically very rare. Neither should be considered to be necessarily advantageous to the affected person. If a "photographic" memory or cross-sensory experiences are helpful at all, they will most likely be so in narrower pursuits. Neither has the kind of sweeping power that is normally meant by the word *intelligence*.

COGNITIVE THEORY: A POWERFUL PARADIGM

Brain-imaging technologies give us exciting insights into how neurological functioning relates to intelligence. Those technologies—PET, CT, and other methods—connect to a far older "technology" of tests and test scores. The classical approach to studying human intelligence is the psychometric paradigm, which rests firmly on correlations among test scores and the search for underlying factors. Starting with Spearman and Thurstone, research on intelligence relied on psychometric techniques, especially factor analysis, to reveal patterns among diverse tests and, ultimately, to give us insight into the nature of human intelligence.

The psychometric paradigm, though powerful, is not without limitations. One downside of the psychometric approach is that it often treats cognitive factors as "black boxes" whose inner workings remain largely mysterious. The term "black box" implies that such factors as fluid intelligence, verbal ability, and spatial ability tend to be accepted at face value, which forestalls probing their nature more analytically. Insufficient attention is paid to what forms of thinking occur when people exercise these abilities. We need to ask: How do intelligent people represent knowledge and reason through problems? Above all, we want to know: How does thinking differ between people who register high in cognitive ability and those who are less able? Understanding the thought processes that underlie cognitive factors is not really the province of psychometrics. To obtain a more detailed picture of the kinds of thinking that underlie intelligent performance, we must draw upon a different paradigm—cognitive theory.[63]

The word *cognitive* means *thinking*, so we can readily appreciate that the basic goal of cognitive theory is to understand the nature of thought. Superficially, such a quest might seem impossible. The mind's products— those varied and monumental achievements of civilizations—can be startlingly complex. How can such great achievements—writing a novel, solving a complex mathematical problem, and designing skyscrapers— be possible given the capacity limitations, distorted perceptions, and error-prone reasoning of even the world's greatest minds? Ultimately, our theories must explain not only how such marvelous feats are possible, but also why people differ so markedly in their ability to achieve them.[64] It's easy to assume that the mind must be unfathomably complex and forever opaque to scientific analysis. Fortunately, this is not so. The basic structure of the mind is surprisingly simple.

We can gain insight into the nature of human cognition by drawing on a very helpful metaphor, the digital computer. Although human minds and computers are quite different in many ways, they do evince some key similarities.[65] Both, for example, have multiple forms of memory. Whenever you purchase a new computer, you are likely to be interested in the information storage capacity for various models. Clearly, human cognition also depends quite fundamentally on memory and, like various models of computers, human beings differ in their memory capacity. Human minds and computers are also alike in that both function not simply by storing information, but also by transforming information to make it more useful. In other words, both human minds and computers are information processors. So even though we must be wary of stretching the computer metaphor too far, we can at minimum use the comparison to gain a foothold on understanding how the human mind works. With that in mind, let us explore what cognitive theory has to offer.

Consider as a starting point that the cognitive perspective recognizes two basic forms of memory—short-term and long-term memory—as well as the flow of information between those two fundamental structures.[66] Even though you may hear the term "short-term memory" in everyday conversations, it is often used incorrectly. In casual usage, short-term memory refers to memory of recent experiences, such as where you left your keys. More accurately, though, it refers the content of current thought. Whatever you are thinking about at this very moment—whether it's the ideas presented on this page or daydreams about your next vacation—*that* is the content of your short-term memory. Understood this way, the content of your short-term memory corresponds to your immediate attention and awareness. If you are thinking, then short-term memory is "where" that thinking takes place.[67]

Now let's consider long-term memory. As the name suggests, this memory holds the vast array of knowledge that each of us acquires over the course of life. Long-term memory stores the totality our knowledge of words, facts, people, life experiences, skills, and sensory perceptions. To maintain such a vast array of knowledge, long-term memory must be enormous in capacity as well as accommodating to diverse *kinds* of knowledge. Just how big is long-term memory? Unlike the capacity of your computer's hard drive, the capacity of long-term memory seems to be limitless. Indeed, the growth of knowledge over time seems to function something like a positive feedback loop in which any knowledge gained becomes the foundation for yet further learning. Layer upon layer, knowledge accumulates over a lifetime, with new knowledge always building on what is already known.

Clearly, short-term and long-term memory are quite different. Whereas long-term memory has virtually boundless capacity, the capacity of short-term memory is very restricted. You can't possibly think about 20 different ideas at once. At most, your momentary awareness consists of only a few ideas. This defining feature of cognition—the small capacity of short-term memory—is quite important to understanding how the mind works. The human mind can actively hold only a very limited amount of information—you can entertain only a small number of discrete ideas at any given moment.

To illustrate, consider what happens when you try to memorize a new phone number. Memorizing seven digits is not too difficult, but trying to memorize 10 digits might stretch your mind's ability to remember every digit in the proper order. You might well let a digit slip from memory or reverse the order of two digits. This simple difference—between seven digits and 10—tells us something important. It begins to parameterize short-term memory by pinning a number on its capacity. That number is somewhere around seven pieces of information.[68] It also implies that this processing constraint directly affects our ability to handle complexity. We often face decisions or tasks that are extremely data-rich, so much so that they can easily overwhelm our short-term memory. We simply cannot hold every bit of relevant information in conscious awareness. If we cannot fully wrap our minds around a problem, some important pieces of information may slip our memory and, subsequently, performance suffers. In this way, the restricted capacity of short-term memory places limits on our ability to think and act intelligently. This example illustrates how the design of the mind—the cognitive architecture—predicts and explains how the mind works or, in some cases, fails to work. That architecture is the structural basis for all human cognition, including intelligent thought.[69]

WORKING MEMORY: THE MIND'S INFORMATION-PROCESSING DYNAMO

Our understanding of short-term memory has evolved over time. Psychologists eventually came to appreciate that this form of memory not only *holds* information, it also *works* on that information. It's one thing to remember the numbers 10 and 11, but another to multiply them together to get 110. Because the mind actively works on information, we must recognize a related memory function—*working* memory.[70] Short-term memory and working memory are highly correlated but somewhat different in meaning and how they are measured.[71] A typical test of short-term memory is digit span. If I tell you a series of random digits—say, 5, 8, 3, 2, 9—your digit span would be the maximum number of digits you could repeat back accurately. To measure working memory, though, means that you would have to transform the information in some way, such as by saying the digits reverse order—9, 2, 3, 8, 5. This is the *backward* digit span task, a classic measure of working memory. Another working memory task is to read a series of sentences and answer comprehension questions, and to later recall the last words of each sentence.[72] Here, again, memory is combined with mental work.

Two additional facts about working memory are important. First, people vary in their ability to hold and transform information in working memory. People with larger working memory capacities have a key advantage because they can solve problems and complete tasks that are more complex. That being so, it should be no surprise that working memory capacity and IQ are highly correlated.[73] In some research that correlation is as high as 0.8 or 0.9.[74] Working memory also correlates with many other expressions of higher-order cognition, including reading comprehension, writing, following directions, reasoning, and complex learning. All these correlations make sense: As the immediate capacity for processing information increases, the mind can handle more complex information at any given moment, and this advantage ought to apply to virtually any intellectual task. Working memory preserves information even when facing potential distraction by competing or irrelevant information.[75] A person with a larger working memory capacity is better equipped to comprehend problems with many elements, think through problems without being overwhelmed, and generate complete and accurate responses. Through exercising control over attention, the mind is primed to operate intelligently. By virtue of data-linked correlations with intelligent thinking, working memory capacity is a fundamental parameter of the mind's ability to process information, akin to the basic operating parameters of an engine, such as torque or horsepower. Working memory is so important to the mind's operations that it has been called "psychology's best hope...to understand intelligence."[76]

Now consider this: What if it were possible to increase working memory capacity? For many years, the conventional wisdom among psychologists was that working memory is impervious to deliberate change. Although working memory varied from person to person, within individuals it appeared to be a stable parameter whose precise capacity was presumably an inherited function of the individual's nervous system. People whose working memory capacity was larger benefited from a superior ability to actively process more information, an advantage that translated to higher scores on cognitive tests, including tests of intelligence. But, like fingerprints, working memory capacity seemed to be dictated by genetics or other factors beyond control. The assumption of fixed capacity now appears to be false; recent research shows that working memory can in fact be expanded. How is that possible?

At one time, it was common to obtain computer memory upgrades by adding memory cards to open slots or by swapping low-capacity memory cards with high-capacity ones. In the human mind, the effect is achieved by the mental equivalent of exercise. Working memory is responsive to tasks that stretch it to its limits. In the psychology laboratory, one task that has achieved this result is the "*n*-back" procedure.[77] This is a computer-based task in which objects are presented on a computer screen. The point is to remember the position of objects in previously presented screens. The key screen might be one back from the present screen, two back, and so on. Difficulty goes up with the complexity of the information on the computer screen as well as how many screens must be kept in memory to answer correctly.

Presumably, other tasks that gradually and consistently stretch working memory to its limits can produce a similar effect. With lots of practice, for example, you may be able to increase the capacity of your backward digit span. But increasing your backward digit span is, by itself, rather pointless. After all, the point is not to increase your ability to repeat a string of digits backward, but something more significant: To increase your working memory capacity for all kinds of stimuli on a wide variety of tasks. That sort of memory augmentation would be truly advantageous. The true test of whether memory enhancement works is whether or not we find evidence of performance gains on different tasks—tasks that also challenge working memory but in ways not previously trained or tested. In the language of psychology, the question is whether apparent gains in working memory capacity *transfer* to new tasks.[78] Recent research shows that gains in working memory capacity do, in fact, transfer.[79] Working memory, a central component of the intelligent mind, can be expanded with benefits extending beyond the original training materials. For those interested in the elevation of human intelligence, this is welcome news.

OPENING THE MIND'S BLACK BOX

The concept of working memory is firmly embedded in cognitive theory. Traditionally, though, intelligence research has drawn most heavily on psychometric theory and methods, which we associate most readily with tests and patterns of test correlations. Each theory—cognitive and psychometric—has something to offer. Yet the operating logic of the mind is revealed most fully when its psychometric and cognitive aspects are explored in tandem. Psychometric research clarifies the overall structure of intellectual abilities; cognitive research opens the black boxes of psychometric factors to reveal their inner workings. Macro-level factors such as verbal ability and fluid intelligence tell us something important about the human mind, but they leave much unexplored; micro-level analyses of their underlying processes makes our understanding of the mind more complete. The macro function derives from the psychometric paradigm; the micro emerges from the cognitive paradigm.

Cognitive theory can offer remarkably clear insights into such vitally important terms as *learning*, *remembering*, and *forgetting*. Consider, for example, what it means to learn a person's name. When you meet someone new and hear that person's name for the first time, the immediate awareness of the name means that you hold it in your working memory. You might hope to remember that person's name, but doing so may not be easy. To remember the name means that you need to record it in your long-term memory. So, in cognitive terms, *learning* is defined as the movement of information from working memory to long-term memory. *Remembering* is the reverse process—the movement of information from long-term memory back into conscious awareness of working memory.[80] When this latter step fails, we call the process *forgetting*.

Cognitive theory tells us that working memory and long-term memory are linked in a very straightforward way. As a rule, the conscious awareness of working memory is the gateway to learning in long-term memory. To form any lasting memory, we must first hold that information in working memory and process that information in some productive way. Put simply: To remember, we must first think. If this is so, then we should be skeptical toward any claims that learning can occur passively, without focused attention. The possibility of passive learning is exploited by marketers who advertise products for building vocabulary or learning a foreign language during sleep. The idea is attractive for many reasons—if it works. The thought of learning effortlessly, of bypassing the requirement of active processing that we associate with working memory, sounds like an educational dream come true. Besides the ease of learning implied by passive absorption, sleep learning would allow us to capitalize on what otherwise would be nonproductive hours. Time asleep would not be time wasted.

Is sleep learning legitimate? Unfortunately, even after many decades of research, we still do not have a definitive conclusion about whether sleep learning actually works. Much of the available evidence, however, places the method in doubt. During the 1950s and 1960s, the heyday of research on sleep learning, the typical research design was to expose a person to audio recordings of word lists as they slept. Later, after waking, the person was tested for recall of those words. Typically, very little was learned. Any learning that was accomplished seemed to occur only during periods of semi-wakefulness when the participant was drifting off to sleep or waking up.[81] This timing pattern was confirmed by monitoring the participant's brain waves. Periods of semi-wakefulness were marked by slow "alpha" brain waves, which corresponded to the occasions when learning from the word lists was most likely to occur. The most obvious conclusion from this research is that learning during sleep is at best inefficient. At worst, sleep learning simply does not conform to the way the mind operates, and is no more than a myth exploited by unscrupulous marketers.

Subliminal advertising, like sleep learning, presents the possibility of passive learning and potential commercial exploitation. Decades ago, product marketers became intrigued with the notion they could influence consumers' wants and preferences, and therefore purchasing behavior, by manipulating their subconscious desires. The best-known example of using subliminal advertising to manipulate consumers traces back to 1957, when advertising researcher James Vicary was reported to have conducted a devious experiment in a New Jersey movie theater. Over a six-week period, Vicary flashed two brief messages on the movie screen:

"Hungry? Eat Popcorn"
"Drink Coca-Cola"[82]

Using a device called a tachistoscope, Vicary flashed these messages for 1/3000 of a second—too brief a period of time for the messages to register consciously in viewers. Nevertheless, according to Vicary, the flashed messages were effective. During the movie intermission, sales of Coke rose 18% over baseline levels, and popcorn sales increased 58%. Though Vicary's results were never published, the concept of subliminal advertising took hold of the public's imagination. Some people became suspicious: Perhaps marketers were manipulating consumer behavior in other ways, too. The suspicion was fueled by the publication in 1973 of the book *Subliminal Seduction* by Wilson Key. The book claimed that advertisers used sexually suggestive imagery formed by neutral objects, such as the curved shapes and shadows of ice cubes in liquor ads. Like Vicary's flashed messages, the supposed intent was to forge associations and evoke desires while bypassing the consumer's filter of consciousness.

What shall we conclude? It's quite likely that subliminal advertising is yet another myth, or at least portends a manipulative power far greater than it actually holds. The entire phenomenon of subliminal advertising is shrouded in doubt. It's unclear what evidence, if any, has ever been set forth to legitimize the concept. Vicary's movie theater experiment was never published or replicated, and Vicary himself later recanted his claims and admitted that his data were fabricated. The point is not that product marketers never manipulate consumers in order to boost sales: The effective manipulation of emotions, and eventually behavior, is much the purpose of marketing. Instead, we ought to question the specific claim that product ads can bypass the conscious awareness of the consumer that we identify with working memory. Perception without awareness is not impossible, but it is best thought of as an exception, rather than a rule about how the mind operates.[83] According to our best evidence, subliminal advertising rarely, if ever, works.[84]

Insights from cognitive theory are rich, fascinating, and deeply relevant to anyone whose work entails education in any form—teachers, certainly, but also parents, trainers, coaches, supervisors, and leaders of every stripe. Cognitive insights are also pertinent to the focused purpose of teaching intelligence, for a simple reason: It's easier to teach the specific components of intelligence than to try to teach intelligence in general. By breaking down intelligence into its components, such as verbal reasoning or strategic planning, the method of teaching intelligence becomes much clearer and, in some studies, has proven to be quite effective.[85] The challenge is thereby redefined from the vague and seemingly intractable problem of teaching a generic ability to teaching specific cognitive processes. In other words, cognitive theory can make the grand purpose of teaching intelligence practical by specifying exactly what should be taught and learned.

In the preceding paragraphs, we examined the meaning of three basic terms—learning, remembering, and forgetting. These three processes are clearly vital to the operation of the human mind, but they do not do justice to the full range of capability that defines human intelligence. What's missing are aspects of intelligence that are almost uniquely the province of the human species, the realm of higher-order thinking.[86] The term "higher-order" encompasses a wide range of cognition, all of which builds upon the foundation of the more fundamental processes that we explored earlier. Now we will shift our focus to consider three supremely important forms of higher-order thought—problem solving, metacognition, and critical thinking.

PROBLEM SOLVING

In our everyday lives, we routinely set our minds to accomplishing goals without being completely sure how to do so. This is problem solving.[87] It would not be a stretch to say that whenever we press our intellect to its full extent—whenever we do our best work—we are engaged in problem solving. The basic definition is simple: Problem solving is what we do whenever the path to a goal is uncertain.[88] This definition implies that a wide variety of human activity falls under the umbrella of problem solving. It spans from an architect's daring design for a skyscraper to a child's idea of how to build a sturdy sandcastle. Our daily lives regularly present challenges that have no easy or obvious solution: finding a way to keep a dental appointment when you've locked your keys in your car, cooking a meal when you lack key ingredients, or figuring out how to repair a damaged relationship. The span of problem solving ranges from the mundane, such as how to unclog a drain, to the profound, such as how to lead a successful life with generosity and integrity.

Sometimes problem solving is literally a matter of life and death. Such was the case onboard *Apollo 13* when during the planned mission to the moon in 1970 its crew of astronauts faced a frightening series of equipment malfunctions. Most serious was the failure of the air filtration system to remove the accumulating carbon dioxide. The stakes could not have been higher: With every exhaled breath, more CO_2 accumulated, which would eventually reach lethal levels of toxicity. Back on earth, NASA engineers knew they had to work fast. The crisis was dramatized in the 1995 movie *Apollo 13*. White-shirted NASA engineers gathered in a workroom for briefing. Their urgent task was to find a way for the astronauts to construct a replacement filter using only the materials and tools available to them onboard the spacecraft. In a spot-on depiction of problem solving, the chief engineer dumped a box of materials onto a tabletop. He then held up a functional filter and a nonmatching receptacle, declaring, "We gotta find a way to make this . . . fit into the hole for this . . . usin' nothin' but that."

By definition, problems cannot be solved by ready-made solutions. If you follow a step-by-step guide to changing a car tire, for example, you are not engaged in problem solving. Following a set recipe does not count. It's only when you venture into an unfamiliar realm or face unusual conditions that problem solving becomes your necessary method of response. But is there a contradiction here? How is it possible to reach an important goal when you don't know how to do it? Consider the paradoxical ring of another definition: Problem solving is *what you do when you don't know what you are doing*. The key to resolving the paradox is to realize that although the path to a solution may be unclear, it is not pure guesswork. Even in the absence of guaranteed solutions, we have certain strategies at our disposal.

Among the various strategies useful in problem solving, the most important one is *subgoaling*. An intricate problem is far too complicated to conceptualize as a straight-line path. A bright and ambitious high school student who aspires to be president of the United States obviously cannot face that goal as a single entity. The way ahead must be broken down into subgoals. Dividing a massive problem into manageable subgoals is a key cognitive skill employed by successful problem solvers everywhere. Strategy selection and strategy shifting are other important elements in a child's cognitive development. With practice, children learn to select and switch strategies as needed. Eventually, the most effective strategies are repeated and the least effective ones abandoned in a fashion that resembles natural selection in biological systems. The process is not perfectly efficient: Sometimes children regress to less sophisticated forms of thinking. Overall, however, the upward trajectory wins out. By putting problem-solving strategies and new ideas to the test, the child continues to progress along the continuum of development.[89]

During problem solving, the ultimate goal can almost always be reached through multiple solution paths. The various pathways might not be equal in their probability of bringing success, nor are they necessarily equally efficient. This means that problem solving entails thinking about different pathways and gauging how promising those various pathways are. One chosen route might lead to progress; another to a dead end. If you lock your keys in your car, you might call a family member who has a spare key, but if the call does not go through, then you have to try a different strategy. The intrinsic uncertainty of problem solving places value not only on the ability to formulate strategies, but also on the flexibility to shift strategies if necessary.[90] The intelligent problem solver is not someone who barrels ahead regardless, but rather someone who questions initial assumptions and modifies plans as warranted. Seen in this light, problem solving is intensely tactical—it requires the ongoing evaluation of progress. An effective problem solver must employ strategies that pay off and abandon those that lead to setbacks or stalling out. We can generalize this way—problem solving is almost always accompanied by errors, uncertainty, and setbacks. By its very nature, problem solving entails the possibility of failure.

The inevitable accompaniments of uncertainty, setbacks, and the possibility of failure bring us to a third aspect of problem solving—emotional self-regulation. Uncertainty makes most people uncomfortable. In some cases, being unsure of what to do next can lead to feelings of panic and disorientation, even decisional paralysis. The errors and false leads that mark the problem-solving pathway are real threats to the ego. Missteps, especially when committed under watchful eyes, can be intensely embarrassing. When progress toward a goal entails repeated setbacks, a problem solver can understandably feel frustrated, and repeated frustration can lead to quitting. People vary in their ability to tolerate frustration; stated more positively, people vary in their ability to persevere in the face of frustration. Some give up easily, while others bravely press on until rational analysis leads them to conclude that their chosen path is a no-go. Still other people display dogged persistence, relentlessly pursuing their goal, especially if that goal is deemed to be central to their identity or perceived purpose in life.

METACOGNITION

The human mind has a remarkable capacity to regulate itself. Intelligent thought processes do not operate by reflex, bound by the stimulus-response chains that so often dictate the behavior of animals. Rather, human cognition exhibits a fascinating duality in which the mind can supervise its own activity. It's almost as if the human mind can subdivide into two separate minds. One carries out the basic operations of perceiving, learning, remembering, and acting. The other monitors and controls these more basic actions. The latter functions—those that exert executive oversight—are collectively called *metacognition*.[91]

The category of thought called metacognition is central to human intelligence.[92] In particular, the planning and monitoring functions that are central to metacognitive control are very close to the essence of general mental ability.[93] To understand why metacognition is so important, consider what happens when you read a difficult book, one that presents ideas complex enough to challenge your comprehension. Imagine that you can understand what the author is saying, but just barely. At the cognitive level, you recognize the individual words and retrieve their meanings with no problem. But to read effectively requires much more. It entails piecing together the individual words to understand the meaning of each sentence, and then to connect the sentences so that you can follow a line of reasoning. At a higher level still, you must perceive the overall structure of the text to see how the paragraphs form an integrated whole, a coherent composition of ideas. When these multiple demands are met—when meanings build upward from low-level word recognition to comprehension of an entire chapter or book—then you truly understand.

Even the best readers, however, have less than 100% comprehension. At times you may read a page, or several pages, and then suddenly realize that although your eyes had scanned every line of print, at some point your comprehension faltered. Your failure to comprehend might have occurred because the information was too abstract or complex, or it might have resulted from a simple lapse of attention. Either way, the moment of realization puts you at a crossroads. Now you have a choice: to back up and reread the previous pages or to forge ahead hoping that you can fill in the gaps later. The two cognitive events—first realizing that comprehension was poor and then deciding what to do next—are instances of metacognition. One is a monitoring function ("I don't understand") and the other is a control function ("I will turn back a few pages and reread").

Metacognition is important to effective reading, but it is also broadly applicable to academic success.[94] The most effective students exhibit metacognitive awareness and control as they go about learning.[95] They know when they understand and when they do not, and make adaptive adjustments. They also self-regulate. Rather than depending fully on external direction from teachers or parents, they determine what they need to know and do. Greater intellectual awareness, control, and autonomy are marks of the most able students. Collectively recognized as metacognition, these qualities also typify the most intelligent thinkers. Metacognition, like other complex cognitive functions, appears to be centered in the prefrontal cortex. Neuroscientists have found that the prefrontal cortex not only mediates cognitive control, but also registers the need for deeper concentration when tasks become complex.[96]

Finally, metacognition is vital to other forms of higher-order thinking, including problem solving. It is manifestly important in problem representation: How clearly we understand the problem we are trying to solve. It's also critical when devising a plan to solve the problem and monitoring whether the plan is effective as we carry it out.[97] As we work toward a solution, we need a higher-level awareness of whether our chosen strategy is effective or not. Whenever you pursue a personal goal—getting an advanced degree, becoming more successful in your profession, or getting healthier—you need to monitor whether your strategy is honestly leading to progress. If not, then you must either change strategies or reevaluate your goal. You cannot do either without being metacognitive. That's why metacognitive monitoring and control are essential to real-world intelligence.

CRITICAL THINKING

Another vital category of higher-level cognition is critical thinking. Critical thinking describes how a person reacts to new ideas. To illustrate, imagine that while you are engaged in a conversation, a friend makes a truly astonishing claim: He is convinced that pureed asparagus cures cancer. He might try to convince you that the major pharmaceutical companies suppress this discovery because the consequences would devastate their profits. Poor critical thinking skills would lead you to simply accept your friend's claim at face value. After all, it does have a certain internal logic: Powerful corporations, in protecting their interests, have been known to suppress information. This is clearest in the history of the tobacco industry, but other examples are easy to generate. A good critical thinker, however, would not immediately accept an astonishing claim about pureed asparagus. He would ask himself, "Is this really true?" and "What evidence supports this theory?"

To think critically means to test ideas for their quality and validity. Critical thinking is truly higher-order thinking because it elevates learning above the base level of acquiring information; it rises to the higher level of questioning and critiquing that information. In the case of *Apollo 13* we saw that problem solving can have life-or-death consequences. The same applies to critical thinking. When information is evaluated inadequately or key information is ignored, the results can be devastating. Consider the case of Eastern Airlines Flight 401. In December 1972, the aircraft was flying over the Florida Everglades when an indicator light turned off on the cockpit control panel. This particular light illuminated when the landing gear was retracted. During normal flight, the light should have remained on. When the light turned off, however, it was unclear whether the landing gear had come down or whether the indicator was malfunctioning. The dilemma drew the attention of the flight crew so fully that no one noticed that the plane had started to descend. When the plane was less than 1,000 feet above the ground, air traffic controllers radioed to ask "how things were coming along," but did not receive a reply. The aircraft crashed into the Everglades, killing 100 of the 176 passengers and crew on board. The tragedy of Flight 401 can be interpreted as a breakdown in thinking about the task at hand—above all, flying the airplane—as well as a series of poor judgments about which information is relevant to making sure that task is achieved.

In statistical terms, the commercial airline industry is amazingly safe, but everyone knows that even a small misjudgment can spell disaster. Pilots and air traffic controllers are subject to distraction and fatigue that can result from insufficient rest or excessive stress. Mistakes occur. Ideally, human errors are corrected by procedural safety nets, redundancies, and backup systems. We depend on attention to safety in the design considerations of the planes we fly, as well as of the vehicles we drive and the elevators we ride. Engineering design errors can pose huge threats, especially when the vehicles and structures are subjected to earthquakes or extreme weather conditions.[98] Buildings and bridges can collapse, and supply chains of food, water, and power can break down. The result can be catastrophic loss of life and property.

Even when engineering designs are robust, poor decisions can lead to serious consequences. The ever-present possibility of human error points to the pivotal need for systematic critical thinking. Critical thinkers evaluate whether claims are true, whatever the source: friends, teachers, advertisers, or politicians. In testing truth claims, good critical thinkers apply standards of correspondence and coherence. Correspondence refers to whether claims *correspond* to the real world—whether evidence exists to support the claims. Coherence refers to whether the facts and interpretations *cohere*, or hold together, as internally consistent. In medicine, the criteria of correspondence and coherence are tremendously important. Over the past century, physicians have increasingly adhered to standards of evidence-based practice. Patient diagnosis is based on a full range of available evidence, including presented symptoms, lab analyses, and scans, if necessary. A data-based diagnosis, in turn, informs treatment choices, which also are justified on the basis of rigorous research. When life and death are on the line, we want our doctors to be good critical thinkers. We expect and appreciate that their diagnoses and prescribed treatments are evidence-based and fully consistent with the presented symptoms.

Critical thinking is clearly a force for advancing medical science and for enabling healing of billions of people. Yet the converse also holds: Human fallibility has too often resulted in tragic medical errors such as amputating the wrong foot, removing the wrong kidney, operating on the incorrect side of the brain, or conducting surgery on the wrong patient altogether. Errors have been made in administering nitrous oxide gas instead of oxygen, prescribing the incorrect medication, or giving the wrong dose of a prescribed drug. Failure to apply consistent procedures to ensure sterility has resulted in countless unnecessary infections, and therefore unnecessary morbidity and mortality. For all the wondrous curative power of the health professions, human fallibility of attention and judgment—the breakdown of critical thinking—results in such extensive collateral damage that the risks of most transportation accidents and natural disasters pale in comparison.

In the practice of law, too, critical thinking is vital. Claims about guilt or innocence are evaluated using an array of strategies for weighing evidence and drawing conclusions. In criminal law, the classic device of adversarial argument between a prosecuting attorney and a defense attorney is assumed to reveal the strongest cases both for and against guilt. The competing sides bring the most compelling evidence to light, but they stop short of pronouncing the final conclusion based on that evidence. Rendering a verdict of guilt or nonguilt is the prerogative of a judge or jury. Yet for all its integral safeguards against injustice, the legal process is clearly imperfect. DNA analysis has in some cases proven a mismatch between a convict and the genetic profile of the true perpetrator. Wrongful convictions and wrongful exonerations are realities that the legal system must try to minimize without any false hopes of eliminating them altogether.

The judicial process can be seen as an elaborate system designed to raise critical thinking to a rarefied level. This is appropriate because the cost of making a mistake is so high. Indeed, the judgments most critical to society rise to successively higher levels of judicial discrimination, culminating in the United States Supreme Court. Cases presented to the Supreme Court are deemed to be so pivotal to a just society that arguments are heard by a nine-member panel of the nation's most distinguished jurists.

In weighing legal testimony, the correspondence aspect of truth finding is critical because it checks whether claims correspond to the established facts surrounding the case. Judgments also depend heavily on the coherence aspect of critical thinking. Contradictions in evidence or testimony must be noted and, if possible, resolved. Equally important, the entire judicial process draws heavily upon precedent. Prior legal cases form an elaborate interpretive framework through which the case at hand can be properly understood. Though critical thinking applied to our everyday lives doesn't reach this level of detailed systematicity, the guiding ideals of law still hold; coming as close to the truth as possible by careful attention to evidence and to clear thinking.

THE SEEDBED OF INTELLIGENCE

This chapter started with a specific focus on the brain systems that underlie intelligent thought. We found that neuroscience, including modern imaging research, has greatly expanded our understanding of human intelligence. That work continues apace. We also found that the study of the brain must be complemented by the study of the mind—the broad array of processes that we collectively call cognition. Neuroscience and cognitive science are natural partners in the study of intelligence. In fact, their borderlands are populated by growing numbers of scholars known as cognitive neuroscientists.

For all the power of these two approaches—neuroscience and cognitive science—they do not tell us exactly how intelligence is cultivated through experience. Neuroscience illuminates the biological basis of intelligence in the structure and operation of neurons. The cognitive perspective helps us to understand the mind as an information processing mechanism—perceiving, recording, and transforming information within the schematic constraints of the cognitive architecture. Yet a crucial piece of the puzzle seems missing. Somewhat crudely, we can pose the question this way: Where does intelligence come from?

A clue to the answer is found in the writings of a once-obscure Russian psychologist named Lev Vygotsky. Vygotsky conducted his groundbreaking research nearly 100 years ago, during the period of the Russian Revolution. For many decades, Vygotsky's ideas were inaccessible to the broader world. In fact, Vygotsky's works were not translated into English until the late 20th century. To gain a sense of Vygotsky's theory, it's helpful to contrast him with another influential psychologist of the 20th century, the Swiss intellectual Jean Piaget. Both Vygotsky and Piaget were fascinated by human intelligence, and in particular how it develops in the child. Their explanations were quite different, however. Piaget saw intelligence as arising from *within* the child. He taught that intelligence unfolds as an internal quality, and that it emerges through stages of rising sophistication. An apt metaphor is a butterfly that emerges from the cocoon according to the organism's genetic program. Piaget's theory was insightful in characterizing the origins of human intelligence as a process of unfolding from within.

Vygotsky's explanation was very different. Rather than seeing the source of intelligence as emerging from within the growing child, Vygotsky proposed that its origin was *external*. By this, he meant that intelligence derives from the network of people and culture that surrounds the child. Moreover, intelligence is not a single unified mental power, but rather a collection of knowledge and skills that Vygotsky thought of as intellectual tools.[99] Such tools include imagery, cognitive processes, thinking style, and, above all, language. Intelligence, in Vygotsky's view, is fundamentally social and linked to the skilled use of language. Intelligence grows within minds only as those minds are immersed into a community that includes capable others—teachers, parents, and peers—who are, at least in some ways, further along in their intellectual development.

Vygotsky's theory is powerful because it acknowledges the roles of language and society in human intelligence. According to Vygotsky's theory, cultivating intelligence requires placing the learner in a social environment that contributes to the learner's growing knowledge and skill. The social environment matters supremely. Vygotsky's theory is practical in that it lends itself to definite teaching and learning strategies. For example, it has been used as a basis for training children to improve their metacognitive skills, the mental strategies that allow them to monitor and guide their own thinking.[100]

Intellectual development is not a magical process that will produce a bright, capable human being in a few short weeks. The timescale of deep transformation is more realistically measured in years. The most significant transformations of human intelligence and the resulting creative accomplishments can emerge only after prolonged periods of investment. Ideally, responsibility for that investment is shared between an individual and the larger society. What can emerge, eventually, are sublime examples of human achievement, works of insight and beauty that leave civilizations forever changed. We tend to think of these supreme achievements as the contributions of a select few—the geniuses of art, science, and human affairs. But intelligence is not a fixed quality in limited supply. It can be cultivated. If we assume that transformative levels of intelligence are ineluctably rare, we must change our way of thinking. The supply of sublime ideas that can enrich the entire world has no inherent limits. Nor does the number of people who can, through optimal development of their intellectual capacities, make real and lasting contributions that benefit of all humankind.

CHAPTER 5

The Nature–Nurture Dilemma

Increase human intelligence? At first mention the idea seems outlandish. The proposal that intelligence might be directly enhanced comes across as a sci-fi plot device. To take the possibility seriously is hard because of entrenched assumptions about IQ. We face conceptual barriers that make us skeptical toward the wild idea of "learnable intelligence." Among them, one barrier stands out as particularly nettlesome—a conviction, or at least a strong suspicion, that genetic factors dictate IQ scores. Genetics, manifested as a person's DNA structure, cannot be modified. If IQ is no more than a translation of DNA to structural features, like eye color, then what hope is there, really, of increasing intelligence? If we accept the deep mutual implication of genetics and intelligence, our next step is to understand more fully the connection between the two. We must understand what limits, if any, genetics imposes on intelligence. DNA is commonly perceived as a functional barrier to intelligence enhancement. We need to know whether that barrier is real or imagined.

Let's begin by conceding a fact. We can state unequivocally that genetics plays a role in setting a person's level of intelligence. This is not too surprising. In everyday language, the term "gifted" suggests that those who have high ability hold an advantage through no credit to themselves. The mythology of genius also carries an assumption of fixed intelligence. Francis Galton believed that heritable traits conveyed different levels of fitness to human beings. He wrongly focused on lower-level traits, such as reaction time, and could not verify that the British social classes were differentiated by measurable qualities of their nervous systems. Nonetheless, more sophisticated analyses in the 20th and 21st centuries placed beyond doubt the truth that genes have an important influence on intelligence. In fact, the role of genetics in intelligence can be quantified: Genetics explains almost exactly 50% of IQ variance. Researchers denote that heritability value as 0.5.

WHAT HERITABILITY MEANS

We need to be careful about how to interpret the quantification of heritability. The effect can easily be misunderstood. A key concept here is variability. Without variability, the measurement of any human trait is meaningless. Think about it: If everyone had exactly the same level of intelligence, then human intelligence would cease to have any meaning. Certainly, there would be no point in measuring it. Variation, or *variance* as statisticians call it, is critical.

Every population, say the population of a particular city, will vary quite a bit in IQ. Some people will be extremely intelligent; others less so. The same population will also vary genetically. Human beings have remarkably consistent genetic profiles—about 99% of our DNA sequence is shared with every other human being.[1] This means that genetic differences among people are confined to the roughly 1% of DNA structure that is not shared. Even so, that 1% can produce considerable variability: The human genome is estimated to have about three million discrete variations, which combine in limitless permutations. The entire human genome consists of between 30,000 and 40,000 genes, which average about 100,000 nucleotide base pairs each. This presents huge potential for compounding genetic variety.[2] That variety is expressed in body characteristics—skin color, height, and gender—as well as behavioral tendencies.

Every population therefore varies in two ways: in measurable characteristics (which geneticists call phenotype) and in DNA structure (which geneticists call genotype). Heritability connects the two. A heritability value of 0.5 quantifies how much IQ variation can be predicted from genetic variation. To determine IQ variation is easy: Give everyone an IQ test. To understand how much difference DNA can make, it's necessary to quantify the variability between people. For unrelated people you would need to conduct a sophisticated DNA analysis to determine how similar they are genetically. For blood relatives, however, this is unnecessary. Since parents and children share a known proportion of DNA variance, the computation is straightforward. Siblings also share known proportions of DNA, as do cousins, grandparents and grandchildren, uncles and nephews. Any familial comparison in which relatives are known to share a proportion of genes can contribute to the estimation of IQ heritability. Expressed most simply, heritability measures how much IQ variation in one generation (such as parents) predicts variation in another generation (such as children).

Once we know how much DNA is shared among relatives and how much variation in the personal trait—such as IQ, height, and personality—there is, we have all the essential information. Heritability is simply a ratio:

$$\text{Heritability} = \text{Trait variance/Genetic variance}$$

Behavior geneticists can compute the value of this ratio for all kinds of human traits. Over many decades of research, they have found that traits vary quite a bit in heritability. Height, for instance, is highly heritable, with a value close to 0.9. Psychological traits, such as personality and IQ, have heritability values closer to 0.5. Academic achievement, a behavioral manifestation of psychological characteristics, also appears to have a genetic basis, in part.[3] By gathering data among family members who vary in relatedness, behavior geneticists can get a good fix on the heritability value of any measurable trait.

Notice that the mathematics of heritability tells us nothing about the biology of heritability. Behavior genetics can establish the statistical fact of heritability but not the underlying molecular mechanisms. Behavior geneticists do not investigate the actual biology of gene expression and its influence on behavior. Heritability ultimately traces to DNA, of course, and DNA certainly influences the efficiency of brain structures and processes. However, a large gap separates the quantification of heritability and our understanding of how specific genes cause that variation. Learning the biological mechanisms of heritable traits is crucial, especially in extending our understanding of very low intelligence levels associated with chromosomal abnormalities.

At the end of the IQ spectrum associated with mental retardation, a large number of disorders have been linked to specific chromosomes. Genetic abnormalities can contribute strongly to very low cognitive functioning, though these abnormalities are quite varied. The most commonly known may be Down syndrome, which is caused by an extra copy of chromosome 21 in the infant's genotype. People with this syndrome have several physical manifestations, including characteristic facial features, muscle weakness, and a short neck. The manifestations on developed intelligence are profound, with average IQs of less than 50.[4] Yet Down syndrome is rare, occurring in far less than 1% of live births. Mental retardation can also arise from extra copies of genes within a particular chromosome. An example is fragile X syndrome, a genetic defect on the X chromosome, which is even less common than Down syndrome, affecting less than 0.1% of males.

Many genetic abnormalities are linked to low IQ. Yet other serious disorders are usually attributable to a single misplaced element along the DNA strand, the substitution of a single base for another. These single nucleotide polymorphisms (called SNPs, or "snips") introduce the simplest kinds of genetic variability. They often result in serious physiological abnormalities. Although these abnormalities are sometimes identified with specific chromosomes, genes, or nucleotides, the mechanisms that lead to low cognitive functioning are often poorly understood. We might assume that the mechanisms that lead to low IQ can help us to understand how intelligence varies in the normal range. This is not the case. The striking associations between genetics and mental retardation are virtually irrelevant to explaining IQ variation in nonretarded populations.[5]

Greatly complicating the search for genetic mechanisms is that most human characteristics, including intelligence, are multigenic, meaning that their underlying genes exert a combined influence to create the observed phenotype of individuals. As a rule, single genes are not responsible for variation in complex traits. Variations in complex traits are more often a function of dozens of genes, each of which exhibits structural variability. These multigenic systems, called quantitative trait loci (QTLs), operate in complex ways.[6] They also present a challenge in detection because, in QTLs, no single gene typically controls more than a small fraction of the variability in the trait of interest. The most studied gene variant, or allele, is ApoE-4, which is associated with the QTL for Alzheimer's dementia.[7] This particular gene variant is linked to inefficient repair of neurons that have been injured. People who have this particular allele are susceptible to compromised cognitive functions, including a reduced working memory capacity. Although one copy of the gene allele is a risk factor for Alzheimer's, two copies presents a much higher risk: Fifty percent of people with two copies of the gene variant eventually develop Alzheimer's disease.

Looking to the future, when we have a better understanding of which specific human genes explain the heritability of IQ in the normal range, it is certain that an enormous number of genes will be implicated. To this day, very few contributing genes have been identified. Those genes that are known to influence intelligence exert only tiny effects, typically explaining 1% or less of the variation in IQ.[8] The identified genes appear to exert effects at different junctures of brain structure and function. For example, gene variation regulates both the division of neuron cells and variations in neurotransmitter sensitivity at synapses—quite different mechanisms affecting neural plasticity. Understanding the interactions between combinations of gene variations will require complex computational analysis, such as data mining algorithms.[9]

The search for specific genes to explain human traits is the path of the future. It will signal a shift of dominant paradigms from behavioral genetics, which is statistical in nature, to molecular genetics. Many scholars see the paradigm change as necessary and welcome. One reason is that the older paradigm of behavior genetics glosses over many intricacies of how genes shape the human phenotype. As we will see later in this chapter, the separation of human variation into distinct "buckets" of genes and environment is grossly simplistic and prone to all manner of misinterpretations. To some degree, the heritability statistic has become obsolete and must now give way to research methods that trace the biology of mutual influence by specific genes and particular environments.[10] Still, heritability values have served an important purpose: They established that genetics plays an important role in human variability.

For all its limitations, the quantification of IQ heritability at 0.5 is impressive. However approximate, it pins a number on how much IQ variability can be predicted from genetic variability. Scientifically, that's progress. It's also socially relevant, for if 50% of the variation in IQ is explained by heritability, then 50% is not. Presumably, most of the nonheritable variation is a product of the environment or, more precisely, of variations in the environment. For those who appreciate a rough contrast between nature and nurture, it's fair to say that each contributes about equally to the prediction of measured intelligence. This approximation is a starting point, not a tidy conclusion, for understanding the role of genetics in the formation of intelligence.

Does a heritability value of 0.5 mean that heritable variation is preordained by gene sequences? Not at all. While appreciating the conceptual foothold that behavioral genetics provides, we need to heed the known limitations on the meaning and implications of heritability. The quantification of heritability has many such limitations—and we must explore these in order to address our central question of whether intelligence is modifiable. To begin, let's consider a single limitation of heritability: The right way to think about the heritability value of 0.5 is that it never applies to an individual, but rather to a specific group of people. It is improper for any person to say, "Half of my IQ arises from my genetics, and the other half comes from my life experiences." Such an interpretation would be convenient if the half-nature/half-nurture formula applied to individuals. But because heritability values always apply to groups, the statement is false, or perhaps nonsensical.

Because heritability applies to groups rather than to individuals, a second limitation follows: The estimate of 50% heritability applies to particular groups in particular cultures. Think about it: Heritability shows how genetic *variation* and environmental *variation* lead to IQ variation. Yet genetic variability across the globe is not uniform; some populations are more variable genetically than others. Asia, for example, has more genetic variability than Europe. Environmental variability also differs from nation to nation. In countries that have considerable gaps between the wealthy and the poor, the typical experience of a child or adult can vary radically. Other nations are more uniform in wealth or cultural practices, and in such contexts environmental variation is comparatively less. It is somewhat counterintuitive, but when living conditions improve for a population, environmental variability becomes less important and heritability can thereby increase. We have evidence, for example, that IQ heritability is higher among wealthier families than in poorer families.[11] Conversely, the heritability of IQ in low socioeconomic groups may be as low as 0.10, which points to the remarkably potent role of the environment in shaping the growth of the suite of cognitive abilities we call intelligence. For poor populations especially, the environment matters a great deal.

Genes and environments are not constant across the globe. They vary from one locale to another, as well as over time. More to the point, their *variability* varies. The upshot is that their combined prediction of IQ variation is not fixed. The heritability of IQ, estimated at 0.50, must be seen as a floating variable, not a fixed parameter of the human species. Indeed, the value of 0.50 is probably inaccurate in certain places and times. Although the average heritability of IQ is very close to 0.50, different studies have variously produced estimates ranging from 0.30 to 0.70. Any value within this range may be correct for a particular population or culture facing specific political and economic circumstances.[12] In fact, there may be a widespread downward drift of IQ heritability estimates, possibly because of changing environmental circumstances or better methods of analysis.[13] For all these reasons, some scholars object to the handy heritability estimate of 0.50. Because heritability ranges varies by location and can shift over time, they prefer to avoid the precision implied by a single, ostensibly true-for-all-time number.

RACE DIFFERENCES IN IQ

We can apply what we know about the heritability of IQ to address the hot button issue of race and intelligence. Although the term "race" is used widely to refer to such group differences as Black, Asian, and White, biologists have questioned whether the construct of race is meaningful genetically. At minimum, the genetics of race does not legitimatize drawing sharp boundaries between groups. Yet to the degree that race concepts are accepted as a basis for categorizing people, we find significant differences in the distribution of IQ, particularly in examining Black–White contrasts. Unfortunately, the heritability of IQ and the pattern of racial differences in IQ are deeply enmeshed. Suggestions that race differences in IQ might be an inescapable consequence of genetic inheritance are highly inflammatory, and understandably so. Suspicions that the genetic study of intelligence might have racist assumptions can cast the entire enterprise of behavior genetics into question.[14]

Scholars who are acquainted with the heritability of traits might be tempted to steer clear of the subject of race differences because the presumed implications are repulsive. Some scholars have suggested that to raise the issue of the heritability of IQ is often regarded as at least mildly impolite and possible incendiary, in part because it seems to undermine values of social equality.[15] Others might write off the whole business as nothing more than bigotry disguised as science.[16] Yet to set aside the question of race differences in IQ might be counterproductive. At the very least, it sidesteps a potentially important question of why race differences in IQ are recurrent. Reliable data have repeatedly shown significant differences in IQ between African-American and European-American populations. Historically, the difference in mean IQ has been about one standard deviation, which places the White average at 100 and the Black average around 85. These differences are large, even granting that they are based on averages with plenty of variation around the mean values. At this point, let us simply recognize the *existence* of those differences and withhold any judgment as to their underlying *cause*. In the pages that follow, we will address the question of what may explain those differences.

Asian Americans and European Americans have also been compared for differences in cognitive function. Their IQs are essentially identical,[17] but the predictive function of IQ is different: The academic and professional achievement of Asians is higher than their IQs would predict in European-American populations. According to one estimate, Asian Americans achieve at the level of European Americans with IQs 10 to 20 points higher.[18] This difference is believed to arise in part from stronger commitments to hard work among Asian Americans along with higher "capitalization" rates, meaning that a higher percentage of Asian Americans with at least a minimal IQ for pursuing a profession or field of study actually do so. In plainer language, Asian Americans are more likely to capitalize on opportunity.

We have evidence that cognitive ability profiles of Asians and Asian Americans differ slightly from Americans of European ancestry: Asians tend to be relatively higher in spatial ability in comparison to verbal ability. Like Asians, Native Americans display relatively greater strength in visuospatial ability compared to verbal ability. But among Native Americans, the average verbal ability is much lower—about 20 IQ points below spatial ability.[19] One possible explanation is that the similar cognitive profiles trace to the common remote ancestry of Asians and Native Americans. Yet another possibility is that depressed verbal abilities among Native Americans are partly a consequence of being prone to middle ear infections during early childhood. Chronic ear infections potentially reduce the spoken language interactions experienced by young children during a critical phase of their linguistic development.[20] Just such a connection has been established between recurrent ear infections and lower verbal IQs.[21]

Psychologists know that although IQ differences between groups can be significant, variation *within* groups is typically much larger. This makes it impossible to extrapolate from groups to individuals. There is simply too much variability within any group to generalize about any person based on race or ethnicity. To venture a prediction of IQ based on race and ethnicity, or gender for that matter, is a bad bet. This conclusion holds regardless of group membership: IQ variation within each racial-ethnic group is approximately the same as in the general population. A standard deviation of about 15 IQ points holds up within demographic groups as it does across groups.[22] To state that mean group differences in IQ are real is not to claim anything about individuals, but only about the distributions that characterize populations.

Still, group differences are puzzling and, for many, more than a little disturbing. What is the explanation? Quite separately from issues of race, we know that IQ variation has a genetic basis. Are we then to conclude that race differences must be genetically derived? Not at all. To see why, we need to understand additional restrictions on how to interpret the easily misunderstood parameter of IQ heritability, 0.5. We have been careful to say that heritability is a property not of individuals but of groups. We can be more exact about the proper application of heritability values. The heritability of IQ rightly applies to *variation within a group*, but not to *differences between groups*. The distinction seems like an obscure technicality, but it is not. Let's see why.

THE SEED CORN ANALOGY

Heritability explains variation *within* a group, not *between* groups. That statement seems quite abstract, but an illustration can make its meaning accessible. One of the best illustrations is the seed corn analogy.[23] Imagine that a farmer is interested in maximizing the quality of his seed corn. He knows that not all corn will grow to the same height or have identical yields. The quality of the planted corn depends on the specific genetics of the seed corn, which can vary even within a single batch obtained from a single supplier. Some seed will produce healthy plants and full ears of corn; other seed within the same batch will produce ears of corn that are average but not excellent. The farmer also understands that corn yield does not hinge only on the quality of the seed corn; it also depends on the soil in which it is planted.

How much does each factor—seed and soil—matter? To find out, the farmer conducts a simple experiment. The farmer tills two test plots, one rich in nutrients and the other poor in soil quality. He is careful to plant seed corn samples from the same batch, ensuring that there will be no average difference in the quality of the corn stock between the two plots. He then waters and weeds the two plots, and in all other respects treats the plots identically. Eventually the corn plants grow to maturity. At that point, the corn planted in the rich soil is visibly healthier and more productive. The poor soil produces corn stalks that are shorter; their leaves are wilted, and the ears of corn are smaller, paler, and less flavorful.

One additional pattern is apparent to the farmer. Besides the obvious differences between the rich and poor soil, there is substantial variability in the quality of plants *within* plots. Indeed, the poor soil produces quite a few healthy corn stalks. The rich soil, though advantageous, produces a number of unimpressive stalks that are unsuitable for harvesting. The farmer interprets the results in this way: The genetic variation of the seed corn is responsible for the variability of plant quality *within* plots. The variability *between* plots, however, is strictly the result of differences in soil quality. This must be the case, because the farmer was careful to plant each plot from the identical batch of corn. In other words, difference in the quality of corn plants *between* the two plots was fully a consequence of soil quality and had nothing to do with genetic factors. The farmer concluded that variation within plots is completely genetic in origin, but between plots differences in plant quality are entirely environmental. This is so even though genetics is known to influence the health and yield of corn plants. In this simple experiment, heritability is clearly irrelevant to differences in the quality of corn between the rich soil and poor soil plots.

We can apply the seed corn analogy to group IQ differences directly. When two groups are known to differ with regard to external factors, those externals can fully explain differences between groups—*even if* genetic factors are known to play a role in important traits. In the United States,

Black and White populations do not share comparable environmental conditions. On the whole, African-American populations experience much higher incidences of poverty and associated risks: Poorer standards of medical care, education, and nutrition—factors that are known to shape the cognitive development of children. As long as population groups are known to diverge in the typical quality of life experience, then heritability factors cannot be properly invoked to explain group differences in IQ or any other cognitive trait.

At this point we will leave the topic of race differences in IQ. Having barely scratched the surface of this controversial, and often inflammatory, topic, we now return to the main subject of this chapter, the role of genetics in the development of intelligence regardless of race. It might be added in closing that plenty of experiential factors are credible hypotheses for why group IQ differences are consistently found. Tellingly, when those factors are held constant, differences across groups diminish, often to zero.[24] The social implications of these statistical findings are weighty, indeed. A just and equitable society might never fully eliminate differences in the quality of experience in the general population. Such a society might, however, eliminate the correlation of such differences to group membership. One might even say that on the day this latter correlation is reduced to zero, a society will have reached a monumental milestone on the path toward justice and freedom.

MALE–FEMALE DIFFERENCES IN IQ

Let's now consider whether males and females exhibit differences in intelligence and more specific cognitive abilities. Two general patterns emerge. First, on average, males and females have virtually identical IQs. In one large-scale study, the mean IQ for males was 100.9 and the mean for females was 98.7, a negligible difference.[25] Other studies have found somewhat larger IQ differences between males and females—as large as five points or so—but neither gender is consistently favored.[26] The conclusion of "virtually identical IQs" is therefore merely an average of inconsistencies. It is also an artifact of test construction. That's because IQ tests are typically constructed to favor neither males nor females. During test construction, questions favorable to males are balanced by those favorable to females so that the resulting IQ distributions exhibit rough parity between the sexes. The upshot is that the *conclusion* of virtually identical IQ is partly a consequence of an *assumption* of no difference between males and females in cognitive ability.

Although males and females do not differ in overall IQ, the same does not hold for narrower factors. Cognitively, males and females differ. The factors on which males and females show the most significant divergence are spatial abilities. Spatial abilities refer to a family of related abilities whose common feature is that a person must actively hold a visual image in memory and process that image to extract information. You can get an idea of what this means if you imagine an orange. In your mind, peel that orange and separate the segments. Next, rotate every other segment 180 degrees (on any axis) and put the whole orange back together again. In a rough way, that mental exercise gives you a sense of what mental abilities are called upon in spatial tasks.

Compared to the example of mentally peeling an orange, most problems on tests of spatial ability are abstract. On spatial rotation tasks, for example, the examinee must hold in mind a two- or three-dimensional object and turn that object mentally to solve a problem. A familiar two-dimensional task is the game Tetris, but cognitive tests also include three-dimensional varieties of mental rotation tasks. One common item type shows two complex objects built from blocks. The question is whether the two objects are structurally identical or not. The answer is not obvious because they are shown from different perspectives. The answer, "same" or "different," requires a person to mentally rotate one of the block assemblies.[27] An example of a mental rotation task is shown in Figure 5.1.

Other forms of spatial abilities include mentally folding and unfolding imaginary paper, coordinating spatial and temporal information in a dynamic display, and generating and analyzing spatial information from memory. Across these broad forms of spatial ability, males show a consistent advantage. The gender difference is the equivalent of 7 to 10 IQ points, but the exact value differs on the specific form of spatial ability measured.[28] Male–female differences are detectable in children as early as it can be tested, at about three years of age, and extend through the life span.[29] Gender differences in spatial abilities are both intriguing and perplexing. At this point psychologists have no definitive explanation, only guesses as to their origin.

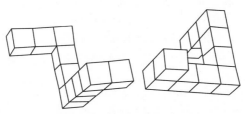

Figure 5.1
Same or Different? Two Examples of Mental Rotation Tasks.

One possible explanation is that males are socialized into sports or playing with toys that exercise spatial ability, and so have more opportunities to develop it. This, of course, is a "nurture" explanation—but there are also "nature" hypotheses claiming that evolutionary pressures over the millennia introduced differences in psychological characteristics. According to one account, males took responsibility for hunting in preagricultural societies, and were advantaged if they could employ strategies that made for effective hunting. Stalking prey and using weapons might have drawn upon the ability to plan mental simulations that involved spatial reasoning.[30] A hunter would need to coordinate the speed and trajectory of a spear with the trajectory of a moving animal. Consistent with the hypothesis of evolutionary pressure to adapt, measures of physical skills useful in hunting, such as throwing velocity, distance, and accuracy, also display large sex differences, favoring males.

Male superiority in dynamic forms of spatial ability—again, the equivalent of about 10 IQ points—is larger than other psychological differences between males and females. Males and females differ in the way they give directions, which offers another glimpse into the nature of gender differences in spatial ability. Males favor the Euclidean coordinates of north, south, east, and west; women are more likely to understand how to find locations by referring to left and right turns and landmarks.[31] Not only do males and females tend to adopt different modes for direction finding, females are now known to be superior to males, on average, in spatial location memory. These strategic differences might be linked to male–female differences in the lateralization of brain function. When males perform spatial tasks, the right hemisphere is predominantly activated; in females, the left hemisphere is comparatively more active.[32] This difference in lateralization suggests that females might employ verbal reasoning on some spatial tasks. Other gender divergences in brain structure as well as possible roles for hormones offer additional potential explanations for detectable male–female differences in cognitive profiles. One study found that females' performance varied according to cyclical fluctuations of hormones in the menstrual cycle. At mid-cycle, when levels of estrogen and progesterone were at their highest levels, performance on perceptual spatial skills declined and manual dexterity increased.[33] In other words, at least some cognitive skills that mark male–female differences appear to respond to time-linked fluctuations in hormone levels.

Smaller male–female differences have been detected in other cognitive abilities. Females typically acquire language skills at younger ages than males and develop larger vocabularies at comparable ages. Girls predictably master spoken language more readily than boys through the preschool years. These differences are unrelated to the amount of spoken interaction between mother and child. Females show a slight advantage in tests of verbal fluency, such as generating synonyms or listing words belonging to a particular category, such as animals.[34] These developed language skills become manifest in such important academic literacies as reading comprehension and writing. Also, females often display superior recall of previously learned information as well as greater facility in learning new information, including memory for life events.[35] This detectable advantage in learning ability extends throughout the life span and is consistent with the general superiority of females in earning higher grades in conventional school settings.

Females tend to outpace males in elementary school mathematics when arithmetic is emphasized. At more advanced levels of mathematics, however, males sometimes exhibit higher test scores. The far greater representation of males at the highest levels of mathematics achievement may be linked to greater facility in visuospatial strategies to understand and solve complex problems. If this is the case, then the male advantage in spatial abilities might also help us understand why males tend to dominate advanced study in mathematics and physics. Certainly other factors, including gender stereotypes, probably contribute to the imbalance, but spatial ability differences may be part of the explanation.

One final cognitive difference between males and females is especially intriguing: In general, boys exhibit greater variability. Quite often, boys are better represented at both the high and low ends of cognitive abilities, including mathematics achievement. This difference, and almost all male–female differences in psychological profiles, are small in magnitude but nonetheless consistently found. From an evolutionary perspective, sex differences in cognitive abilities should not be too surprising. On the contrary, what would be surprising is if the varied adaptive demands faced by males and females over the course of evolutionary history led them to be psychologically identical.[36]

TWO KINDS OF TWINS

Behavior geneticists study traits among relatives—parents and children, aunts and nieces, siblings, cousins, and so on. Familial comparisons allow behavior geneticists to estimate the heritability of any particular trait, such as height or happiness. Normally, nature and nurture overlap among children raised in the same family. That's because biological siblings reared in the same household share both similar genetics and environments. In theoretical terms, we can say that nature and nurture are confounded, which means it is impossible, or at least very difficult, to separate their independent effects. If two related brothers become highly accomplished scholars, entrepreneurs, or entertainers, who's to say whether common genes or common experience was more influential in directing their life paths? The confounding of genes and environment is so thorough that it can lead to the overestimation of IQ heritability.[37] Research on identical twins offers a possible way out of this bind.

Also known as monozygotic twins because they develop from one fertilized egg, identical twins present the unique case of genetically identical human beings. The implications are significant: Any measurable difference between identical twins, including IQ variation, *must* be caused by the environment. Some have called the unique case of identical twins "nature's experiment." The label is apt: Experimentation is, of course, a cornerstone of the scientific method. The purpose of experiments is to find out if X causes Y. Whenever there are many possible causes of Y, experiments are designed to hold competing factors constant except for one, the independent variable. If the scientific question at hand concerns human development, identical twins present the special opportunity to hold genetics constant while allowing the environment to vary. If the twins differ (which they inevitably will), we know that the environment is responsible.

Most twins, of course, are not identical. About two-thirds of twins are fraternal, or dizygotic, twins, because they develop from different eggs. Dizygotic twins are genetically no more alike than ordinary siblings; they just happen to coexist in their mother's womb. Yet fraternal twins present another interesting possibility for research because they normally share very similar experiences growing up. Even in utero, fraternal twins share a common environment, and they are typically raised in ways that are more alike than conditions faced by other siblings. Identical twins tend to be treated even more similarly than fraternal twins—they are more likely to dress alike, play together, have the same teacher, and sleep in the same bedroom.[38]

Twins, both identical and fraternal, are important to behavior genetics research. Identical twins, especially, provide insights into the unique effects of the environment. Although identical twins raised together in the same family are special, even more prized by researchers are identical twins raised apart. Such twins are compelling because any contrast between the twins shows most convincingly the effects of differing environments on human development. When identical twins are raised apart, usually through adoption, the arrangement presents a precious opportunity. In such rare cases "nature's experiment" (identical twins) combines with "society's experiment" (adoption). The first holds genetics constant, and the second allows the environment to vary. It's as close as behavior geneticists can get to the perfect experiment. Very limited data exist on identical twins raised apart, but the few extant studies show that IQ correlations between separated identical twins are often startlingly high—about $r = .75$.[39] The IQs of identical twins raised together are even more highly correlated, about $r = .85$. Both values are much higher than correlations between normal siblings and between parents and children (both about $r = .50$).

Exceptionally high correlations between identical twins probably overestimate the power of genetics to control IQ. The reason is simple: Even when identical twins are raised apart, it's incorrect to assume that their environments are completely unrelated. The most obvious shared environment is the prenatal environment of a common mother. In utero experience varies by the quality of available medical care, nutrition, freedom from emotional and physical trauma, and protection from exposure to toxins, such as illicit drugs and alcohol. Prenatal effects can be substantial, amounting to about 20% of the variance attributed to genetics.[40] All such prenatal factors have measurable effects on children's later cognitive development.

Not only are twins' prenatal environments correlated, so too are their postnatal environments. Even in the rare case of being raised apart, twins are not always separated immediately after being born. Adoption into different families can occur months or years after birth, during infancy or childhood, and twins may be reunited intermittently after separation. Time spent together prior to separation represents shared environments with similar experiences. Even after adoption, the twins' quality of experiences might be quite similar because adoption is not random: Placements are made with full awareness of the characteristics of adopting families. Natural and adoptive parents tend to be similar in both social class and IQ, and placements to poor families are comparatively rare.[41] Not infrequently, twins are adopted by close relatives, which further restricts the range of the child's experience to the degree that relatives have similar child-rearing practices, beliefs, and values.

We noted earlier that *differences* between identical twins must be environmental in origin. However, the converse does not hold: *Similarities* between identical twins cannot be automatically traced to shared genetics. The real-world conditions of adoption make it hard to estimate the true contribution of the environment even when identical twins are raised in different homes. By common practice, it is unlikely that identical twins would be adopted into families that are radically different in resources, values, and culture. A perfect experiment from a scientific angle would entail random placement of twins into families representing the full range of society; ethically, of course, such a manipulation is unthinkable. With the real-world limitations of twins research firmly in mind, we need to exercise care in interpreting the findings. In particular, the strikingly high heritability values found among identical twins might reflect a confluence of identical genetics and similar environments. Implied is that heritability values for identical twins may be somewhat inflated. Minimally, these considerations lead us to caution: The case of identical twins raised apart, while presenting a unique opportunity for behavior genetics, is not a perfect laboratory for separating nature and nurture.

To understand the relative power of nature and nurture, it's worthwhile to study yet another pattern of familial relations—unrelated siblings raised together. In a sense, this is the "opposite" of identical twins raised apart. The arrangement allows genetics to vary (because the siblings are genetically unrelated) but holds the environment constant (or relatively so, because experiences in the same family are similar). Any correlation presumably shows the effects of environmental similarity. Unrelated siblings raised together exhibit positive IQ correlations of about $r = .35$. This value affirms the substantial influence of being raised in the same family, but also seems to show that the environment has a weaker influence on IQ than genetics. This conclusion might not be warranted, however, for the same reason that makes us cautious in interpreting the data on identical twins raised apart: Preadoption experiences must be taken into account. Even when unrelated children are adopted into the same families, those children might have quite different preadoption experiences. Differences in maternal health care and nutrition during pregnancy, which are experiential rather than genetic, will affect development. As in the case of identical twins, the search for exemplars that show the independent effects of either nature or nurture can be approximated, but not fully achieved.

As we consider the imperfect data from which to draw conclusions on the relative roles of nature and nurture, the accumulation of research on familial relatedness and IQ shows that both genetics and environment matter. Those who hew to an extreme position—that either genetics or the environment is supreme—are incorrect. Neither position can be defended by appealing to data. Anyone who insists that intelligence is 100% nature or 100% nurture by necessity holds this extreme position not as a scientific conclusion, but rather as a personal ideology.

CONCEPTUAL LIMITATIONS OF HERITABILITY

Estimating the heritability of IQ is a tricky business. We have seen that even in the special case of identical twins raised apart, conditions that help to separate nature and nurture are imperfect. Twins reared separately tend to have similar experiences—prenatally, certainly, but also prior to and even after adoption. High correlations among twins' IQ scores may cause us to overestimate the power of genes to control intelligence. As a rule, the quantification of heritability must be interpreted cautiously. Because the limits of IQ heritability are so crucial to the possibility of learnable intelligence, we must extend our analysis still further into the nature of those limits. The purpose is not to become enamored with technical details. Instead, our goal is practical: Unless we can demystify heritability values, we are likely to interpret the phrase "learnable intelligence" with skepticism as to its legitimacy and practical utility.

To understand the power of DNA to shape intelligence and other human characteristics, we have availed ourselves of a certain conceptual convenience—the classic separation of nature and nurture. As an entry point, the binary separation is helpful. With a little probing, however, that distinction begins to look untenable. The question "nature or nurture?" presumes that it's possible to draw a clean line between the two and to understand how each contributes to the observable characteristics of people that geneticists call phenotype. One major problem with this presumption is that although genes and the environment jointly shape phenotype, they also exert mutual influences on each other.

Consider first that the environment constantly influences gene function. What this means in practice is that genes do not always work at full capacity. They can be turned on, turned off, or fine-tuned in their level of activity. In many organisms, for example, exposure to light activates genes to induce protein synthesis in the visual system.[42] The effect is not isolated: Environmental conditions commonly affect whether genes are switched on or off. Environmental influences on gene expression are crucial to human development. Indeed, in the previous chapter we saw that whenever a person learns, cognitive stimuli influence the biology of neuron function, particularly at points in the brain where neurons connect. The resulting structural changes to the brain, including the formation of new synapses, involve regulating gene expression.

Medical interventions commonly rely on external agents, especially pharmaceuticals, to alter gene expression. If a child has a genetic predisposition to a disease, the environment can powerfully intervene, either by dealing with the products of gene expression or by regulating gene action. One well-known instance is the metabolic irregularity known as phenylke-tonuria (PKU). People with PKU have a potentially fatal genetic muta-tion, which produces a nonfunctional form of the enzyme phenylalanine hydroxylase. This enzyme normally converts the amino acid phenylalanine into another amino acid, tyrosine, but in people with PKU this conversion is disabled. The resulting accumulation of phenylalanine and its derivatives in the blood wreak havoc. But since PKU pertains specifically to phenylala-nine, a very effective treatment is to restrict the diet to protein sources that do not contain the specific amino acid.

The point here is simple: Genotypes that would ordinarily exert pro-found effects on a child can be moderated by a "smart" environment. The otherwise deterministic hold of genotype on phenotype is thereby finessed. The treatment of PKU is one example of a very broad phenom-enon: Pharmaceuticals, therapies, and education itself always work with a set genetic base, the predetermined DNA sequences of people who need environmental support for positive and healthy development. When a smart environment compensates for genetic abnormalities the exact meaning of heritability estimates starts to blur. Genes no longer determine specific traits with certainty; instead, their influence is contingent on the environment—or rather a series of environments, including other genes, the cell environment, nutrition, pharmaceuticals, social conditions, and external events. The only safe claim is that heritability is a rough average, a ballpark estimate of how genes influence human variation at a given place and time.

Behavior geneticists have long acknowledged the fuzzy borderland between nature and nurture. They even have a name for it: *covariance*. Covariance means that two variables tend to go together, like height and weight. They covary. One type of covariance is *reactive covariance*.[43] Think of how parents react to their child's budding interests and talents. A child who has a strong desire to play a musical instrument can make that wish known very insistently.[44] Parents who have the means to develop the tal-ent may purchase a musical instrument and arrange for lessons. Over time and through study—that is, through purposefully arranged environmental conditions—the child may develop that initial disposition to very high lev-els of musical talent.

Now try to answer this: Is the child's developed talent an expression of nature or nurture? Here we enter the disputed borderland. The child's expressed talent is the province of neither nature nor nurture exclusively, but rather their covariance. Let's agree that the effect might be partly genetic: Constitutional predispositions might prompt a child toward a certain pursuit, and the ability to develop that interest to a high level requires at least a modicum of genetic readiness and potential. Olympian Michael Phelps is a clear example of genetic readiness to develop a specialized talent; his physical characteristics are perfectly adapted to world-class swimming competition. But for our hypothetical musical prodigy as well as for Michael Phelps, the environment has to be ready to respond to an embryonic inclination that was at least partially a product of genetic factors. When the environment reacts to interests and talents that might germinate from genetic predispositions, the environment amplifies the initial genetic tendencies. For this reason, reactive covariance does not express the independent effects of either nature or nurture, but rather their synergistic operation.

A second form of covariance is similar but recognizes the role of the individual in channeling his or her own development. *Active covariance* is the overlap of a genetic predisposition with environmental experience that is reinforced by the active choices of the individual, rather than by parents or some other authority. With greater maturity and opportunity, a person has freedom to choose experiences that have perceived value and that offer enjoyment. Genetic inclinations in one direction or another can be supported and sharpened by choices of college majors, careers, and lifestyle.

Some adolescents might be constitutionally inclined toward abstract thought, others to social gregariousness, and still others to creative expression. Each impulse can prompt specific decisions in the life path that build on preexisting qualities to make personal distinctiveness even more distinctive. In other words, the continuous sequence of life decisions can reinforce small differences that are rooted in genetics. One bit of data consistent with this principle is that the heritability of IQ tends to *increase* during adulthood.[45] Active covariance may well be responsible. If so, the influence of genes grows rather than diminishes through the active decisions a person makes in seeking and selecting particular environments.

The rising influence of heritable traits through the life span almost certainly stems from personal choices and opportunities that reinforce and amplify distinguishing qualities that trace back to genetics. This is the multiplier effect: Small initial differences can become magnified over time.[46] We become, as it were, more consistent with our genetic predispositions. But this is not the expression of genes, pure and simple. The multiplier effect also works on initial differences that might originate in the environment. Early educational advantages can lead, for example, to later opportunities for educational enrichment. Here again, nature and nurture are bundled; they covary. Anyone who insists that human development can be separated neatly into genetic and environmental effects is speaking simplistically—or is simply incorrect. Genes influence the environment both directly and indirectly, and the environment, in turn, exercises profound effects on subsequent development by building on, or occasionally counteracting, genetic tendencies. Because genetic distinctiveness can spark the oscillation of reciprocal effects, credit is typically assigned to heritability and the effects of the environment are masked.[47] Unless this mechanism is understood and appreciated, we will underestimate the power of the environment to enhance human abilities, intelligence in particular.

Behavior geneticists recognize that their most difficult task lies head: Untangling the complex ways that genes and the environment interact to give rise to human variability.[48] The phenomena of active and reactive covariance show that genes can exert their effects *through* the environment, which in turn is mediated by human agency—the choices people make with the resources available to them. Genes do not work alone; optimally, they exert effects within the medium of a favorable environment. Whether an environment is favorable or not depends significantly on society's ability to foster opportunity and the personal freedoms that contribute to talent development and well-being.

HERITABILITY DOES NOT PRECLUDE PERSONAL CHANGE

Depending on your point of view, the IQ heritability of .5 might make you either optimistic or pessimistic about the power of the environment to shape human intelligence. After all, if 50% of IQ variation is explained by genetic variation, that's quite a lot. On the other hand, if 50% of IQ variation arises from nongenetic factors, that's appreciable, too. For now, let's focus on the genetic half. I want us to question whether the heritability value of .5 is truly a barrier to the possibility of learnable intelligence. Does heritability really limit IQ change?

The quantification of heritability at .5 lends more importance to genetic factors than is warranted by implying that genes set firm limits on IQ change. Logically, such implications do not hold up. For one thing, intelligence changes very substantially during a lifetime. As proof, consider the escalating mental age of children, whose ability to reason increases steadily year after year.[49] Alfred Binet, Lewis Terman, and all who followed in their legacy understood fundamentally that the intellectual performance of an eight-year-old could not be fairly compared to that of a 12-year-old. Age norms had to be established, and those norms formed the basis for the calculation of mental age. Age norms were necessary because a child's capacity for complex and abstract thought grows prodigiously between early childhood and late adolescence. That rising capacity is expressed through school learning as well as on IQ tests. The recalibration of age norms is necessary, but has a way of concealing the dramatic escalation of intellectual powers associated with maturation. If we measured height in the same way—by using only age-based norms—we might lose sight of the fact that children actually get taller as they grow up!

In normal development, maturation leads to increased intellectual powers. Children grow in intelligence. Yet when children grow in intellectual capability, their astonishing transformations of intellect do not nullify heritability values in the least. Remember, heritability is all about predicting IQ variation from genetic variation. At any given age, children's IQ scores might be substantially predictable from the IQs of their parents, siblings, and other biological relatives. That predictive function is logically separate from the precise capabilities of children at any given age. For this reason, heritability values impose no logical limitations on escalating mental age.

Children's rising mental age is a special case of a more general pattern—intelligence varies over the course of life. Let's recall from our discussion of fluid and crystallized intelligence that these abilities are not static. They vary dramatically over the life span. As a reminder, crystallized intelligence generally follows an upward trend over six or seven decades, whereas fluid intelligence tends to peak in early adulthood and decline slowly thereafter. The trend lines for crystallized and fluid intelligence show us that IQ scores drift upward and downward in predictable patterns. In this instance as well, heritability is not challenged as long as IQ scores can be reasonably predicted from the IQs of blood relatives at any given age. Over the course of life, measured intelligence can drift up or down without any necessary challenge to the predictive function captured in the heritability value of .5.

It's clear that measured intelligence can range widely over the course of a life, but what about over narrower spans of time? Although the data on this question are not plentiful, we do know that individuals can experience significant IQ change. IQs commonly fluctuate by a few points, but larger swings up and down have been recorded. Intelligence researchers have found that significant IQ shifts are not uncommon between the ages of 3 and 17 years of age. These IQ shifts reflect uneven rates of mental growth with some periods marked by double the rate of mental maturation compared to other periods in the child's development.[50] Recent data show that IQ shifts of up to 20 points during the teenage years are not unusual. These shifts correspond to changes in brain structure. For example, changes in verbal IQ were identified with changes to gray matter in the speech centers of the brain.[51]

Rapid changes are not typical, but they do occur. But such dramatic shifts, both up and down, can be completely concealed when IQ scores are averaged over large numbers of people. Computed averages look remarkably stable when the underlying individual data are volatile. IQ shifts are responsive to changes in intellectual enrichment, as well as to modifications to life circumstances and success in coping with those circumstances.[52] As we will see, cognitive enrichment programs can also have positive implications for cognitive ability. Such varied effects point to a common conclusion: Absolute levels of intellectual ability change over time, and they are responsive to experiential circumstances.

HERITABILITY DOES NOT LIMIT INTERGENERATIONAL CHANGE

The foregoing examples tell us that intelligence can change. Optimism about altering the human intellect need not be tempered by an IQ heritability value of .50. To drive home this point, consider the issue from yet another angle: Changes in traits from generation to generation are not constrained by heritability values. To illustrate, let's consider a highly visible human trait—height. It's common knowledge that tall parents tend to have tall children. Of course, the correspondence between parents and children is imperfect, but it's close enough to generate a heritability value of about .9. This means that height is very significantly heritable—about 90% of variation in height is rooted in genetic factors.

Alongside the known heritability for height, consider a second fact: All around the world, successive generations of children have tended to be taller than their parents. For the past hundred years or so, height increased by about 3 centimeters per generation.[53] The pattern has been confirmed in Europe, North America, and Asia. How are such gains possible if height has a heritability value of .9? There is no contradiction: The two facts are perfectly compatible because heritability imposes no logical limits on inter-generational change.

To understand why, imagine that in one amazing generational shift, children grew to exactly twice the heights of their parents. This is pure fantasy, but it illustrates a point. If the freakish pattern held exactly, then the heights of children would be *perfectly* predictable from the heights of their parents—just multiply by two. Tall parents would have very tall children; short parents would have "short" children, relative to their peers. What would the effect be on heritability? In this scenario the heritability for height would be exactly 1.0. Yet consider this: Even though heritability was 100%, there was radical change from one generation to the next. The explanation is that heritability estimates are based on predictive patterns of correlation, not on the absolute values of any trait.

Heritability is silent about the magnitude of traits; it imposes no mathematical limitations to changes in the absolute value of a trait from one generation to the next. Even a very high value for heritability would not by itself limit the size of a cross-generational shift. Once this concept is grasped, it opens up a fascinating logical possibility: Regardless of the heritability of IQ, it's quite possible for the IQs of children to be much higher than those of their parents.

THE FLYNN EFFECT

A vast body of data tells us that an intergenerational shift in IQ is not a mere theoretical possibility, but rather a startling and potent reality. Starting around 1980, psychologists began to pay attention to a historical pattern in IQ data that was not completely unknown beforehand, but was certainly obscure. The object of fascination was that, around the world, IQ scores had been drifting upward for decades.[54] In some cases, the upward trend of IQ extended back more than a hundred years to the time of the Industrial Revolution.[55]

The pattern of rising IQs around the world was presented most clearly in the writings of the philosopher James Flynn. For this reason, the world-wide escalation of IQs became widely known as the Flynn effect. The pattern held in every country, approximately 20, for which long-term data were available. Moreover, the IQ gains were large. Depending on the test, IQ scores rose as much as 15 points, a full standard deviation, per generation. On every scale the Flynn effect was measured, the magnitude of IQ change over a few brief decades was so impressive that Flynn called the effect a "brute phenomenon."[56]

The trend became detectable only because IQ tests were very stable over long periods of time. As a rule, designers of IQ tests are conservative in making changes, and the resulting stability over time allows for comparisons between examinees over many decades. In 1973, for example, the Stanford-Binet was restandardized after many years but without any changes at all to the test content.[57] Yet when the new test norms were obtained, it became clear to test users that the old norms were obsolete. In particular, current children's performance was superior to that of counterparts in the 1930s and 1940s. Nine-year-old children were commonly succeeding at tasks that were previously pegged as defining a mental age of 10 years.

So profound was the upward drift in IQ scores that, at first, many psychologists doubted that the effect was real. They speculated that the intergenerational increases were spurious—artifacts, perhaps, of more widespread use of IQ tests. Or maybe the Flynn effect was no more than a statistical error based on false assumptions. In fact, psychologists advanced several possible explanations. One hypothesis—that IQ shifts resulted from changes in the genetic base of the population—was easily dismissed. Anyone who has studied high school biology knows that large shifts in the gene pool almost always occur very slowly, typically over millions of years. The timescale of the Flynn effect simply was not compatible with significant changes in population gene frequencies. Even if time were not a factor, there were reasons to doubt that the Flynn effect could arise from genetic factors. Some psychologists observed that, statistically, higher-IQ adults tended to have fewer children. This "dysgenic" pattern meant the expectable effects of reproduction would work oppositely to the Flynn effect. In any case, the hypothesis of genetic drift was easily ruled out.

Some psychologists suspected that rising IQs might simply be an artificial consequence of increasing sophistication with tests. The argument was that, over time, testing had become more common, and so rising scores reflected increases in skill and comfort with the mechanics of test taking, not changes in underlying cognitive abilities. In response, other psychologists pointed out that the frequency of IQ testing had actually declined since the early 20th century. Nowadays, it's quite possible to be educated in a modern nation without ever taking an IQ test. Moreover, the magnitude of IQ gains associated with the Flynn effect were simply too large to be explained by rising test sophistication. Practice with tests can raise scores by a few points, but nothing close to the gains of 10, 15, or 20 points that are characteristic of the Flynn effect.

The initial skepticism toward the Flynn effect is understandable. After all, the community of scientists should never be hasty to affirm every proposed new fact, law, or principle, especially if the apparent discovery has the potential to transform a field of study. The habit of caution shows the conservative side of science. It minimizes false positives—claims that a finding is valid when in fact it is not. Yet the data cited by James Flynn were so provocative that they deserved further probing. If IQ scores were truly rising around the world, explanations were needed. Those explanations had to be advanced with great care because of what the Flynn effect, if authentic, seemed to imply—that the earth's population was becoming more intelligent.

The possibility that the human population might be growing smarter over a relatively brief span of time caused quite a stir. Why so? The answer is quite clear: The Flynn effect forcefully challenged widely held assumptions that intelligence, measured as IQ, is a highly stable trait that neither changes radically within individuals nor from one generation to the next. If the empirical facts of rising IQ scores truly meant that people around the world were getting smarter, then intelligence was far more malleable than had been assumed by most psychologists and the lay pubic. The measured IQ of any particular generation could not be dictated by genetics after all. Change, including radical intergenerational shifts, was possible. And if IQ can shift between generations, then the measured IQ of any particular individual is not predetermined, but is substantially a function of the particulars of experience defined by the era in which they live and by personal circumstances.

In the search for explanations, one reasonable expectation is that IQ gains would reflect knowledge acquired though literacy and schooling. In other words, we might hypothesize that IQ gains would be most pronounced on measures of crystallized intelligence rather than fluid intelligence. If this were confirmed, then the Flynn effect would be slightly less confounding. Perhaps crystallized intelligence grew around the world as universal education took hold and as literacy rates climbed. The Flynn effect was indeed manifest on measures of crystallized intelligence. However, gains in fluid intelligence were *at least as high* as those found on crystallized intelligence.[58] If the Flynn effect were limited to gains in measurable knowledge in the form of crystallized intelligence, then widespread literacy might account for the effect. But equally large gains in fluid intelligence defeated that argument. Because the escalation of IQ is manifest in fluid intelligence as much as in crystallized, the Flynn effect can't be explained away as a mere by-product of schooling. Something much more significant had been at work: The world's population had truly become smarter.

Intergenerational shifts in IQ known as the Flynn effect *must* reflect the nurture term in the nature/nurture equation. Genes assert influence, of course, but the quantification of their influence does not dictate how smart any of us can become. Therein lies a supremely exciting possibility: Collectively, the human race can become even more intelligent in the years ahead. The Flynn effect demonstrates that this exciting vision is not a baseless fantasy. The process has already begun. To capitalize on the effect, we need to understand, in detail, its underlying causes. By the end of the 20th century, psychologists knew that the Flynn effect was large in magnitude and manifest on all major components of intelligence. The search was on for those aspects of experience that cultivate the human intellect. "Somewhere out there," wrote James Flynn, "environmental variables of enormous potency are creating IQ differences."[59]

CHAPTER 6
How Experience Cultivates Intelligence

IQs are rising all over the world and have been doing so for at least a hundred years—a phenomenon known as the Flynn effect. This fact alone is extraordinary, but what follows is a question that is equally compelling: What is the cause? Once the Flynn effect was accepted as authentic, psychologists became fascinated with possible explanations for the effect. They knew that the effect did not result from genetic shifts in the population—100 years is far too short a timeline to produce such significant genetic change. The underlying cause had to be environmental. Soon a consensus began to form: The Flynn effect was not the result of a single cause, but of multiple converging forces working together, their independent effects aggregating to produce a truly remarkable and unprecedented phenomenon.

This chapter is not strictly about the causes of the Flynn effect, but rather something much broader. We need to understand the range of environmental variables that influence IQ. Some of these are likely to be causes of the Flynn effect; others are important by virtue of their potency to predict IQ gains in small experimental studies rather than entire nations. Our ambition must be broad—to understand the scope of factors that raise cognitive functioning. We need to know how environmental factors contribute to IQ gains, but not only for the sake of our understanding of the Flynn effect. Our agenda includes the revolutionary possibility of deliberately enhancing human intelligence.

NUTRITION

Almost certainly, one cause of rising IQs is the greater global availability of nutritious foods. The world is not yet cured of hunger and malnutrition, but the typical diet even in the poorest countries is much improved over past generations. More productive varieties of food crops and improvements in agricultural methods mean that severe deficiencies in protein, vitamins, and minerals have become rarer. One manifestation of improved nutrition is the steady increase in height from one generation to the next. Another consequence is longer life spans, although improved medical care also contributes to people living longer.

The effects of good nutrition are not mysterious: Research on child development shows that nutritional factors affect brain function. Various research projects have examined the effects of nutritional enhancements on children's cognitive development. Some of those studies entailed nutritional improvements to the diets of expectant mothers. One classic experiment showed that prenatal vitamin supplementation to poor mothers boosted their children's IQ by 4 to 8 points.[1] Other studies involved making nutritional improvements to children's diets, sometimes through vitamin and mineral supplements. Among school-age children, vitamin supplementation has been associated with IQ gains on the order of 4 to 9 points.[2] Across this body of research, two conclusions seem clear. First, dietary improvements, whether to expectant mothers or to children, can have measurable effects on the cognitive ability of young children. Second, those effects are strongest among families at risk for dietary deficiencies associated with poverty. Good nutrition is important for everyone, but programmatic improvements are most effective among poor families at risk for nutritional deficiencies.[3]

One class of nutrients deserves special attention—the category of fats known as long-chain fatty acids. The best known of these fats are the omega-3s, which are commonly found in coldwater fish. These fats confer protective effects for heart disease and other chronic illnesses. The "3" in omega-3 refers to the link on the fatty acid chain that is "unsaturated," that is, not filled with hydrogen atoms. In the same general category are omega-6s and omega-9s, which also indicate the points where unsaturated links are found. The unsaturated feature is crucial, because it introduces a crook in the molecular chain, which pushes the fatty acids apart and makes them fluid rather than sticky. In fact, you can place fish oil in the freezer and it will remain fluid rather than harden because of the curved structure of the fatty acid chain. The unsaturated portion of omega-3s and similar fats conveys health benefits, but also makes the fat delicate and vulnerable to spoilage. Fish are especially vulnerable to oxidation, which can produce an unpleasant smell and, ultimately, rancidity. Nuts also contain unsaturated fats, which explains why they, too, are prone to spoilage. The health-promoting properties of unsaturated fats are related to their role as anti-inflammatory agents. Many chronic diseases, such as heart disease and arthritis, are linked to physiological inflammation.

Omega-3s and other fatty acids are significant components in the body's nervous system, including the brain. Introductory courses in brain anatomy teach that the brain is substantially composed of fat, both in the myelin sheaths that insulate neurons and in the glial cells that provide nourishment to hard-working and nutrient-demanding brain neurons. Efficient and healthy brains need fat. The brain's structural need for fat would not be an issue except for one important fact: Omega-3s and related fats are *essential* nutrients. This means both that they are required for life and that the body cannot synthesize them. Like vitamins, minerals, and essential amino acids, polyunsaturated fats must be consumed in the diet. If they are consumed in insufficient quantities, then the body will operate suboptimally. In the case of vitamins and minerals, severe deficiencies can eventually lead to disease or even death. The same is true for amino acids, the building blocks of proteins. Deficient consumption of essential fats might be manifest in poor health, but it's also possible that it can lead to suboptimal cognitive development.

EXPOSURE TO TOXINS

Nutrients are substances whose consumption promotes positive development. Toxins, by contrast, are harmful. In trying to understand the forces that affect the developing mind, we must consider both. Both nutrients and toxins and are important through the life span including prenatally. Fetuses differ significantly in their exposure both to nutritive environments and to toxins. Prenatal exposure matters greatly: Maternal effects on IQ are large, accounting for 40% of all nongenetic effects.

Cigarette smoke, drugs, alcohol, pesticides, heavy metals, and disease can all affect the developing fetus.[4] Many of these toxins are also associated with IQ deficits during childhood. For example, maternal use of the barbiturate phenobarbital has been associated with a later cognitive decrement of about 7 IQ points.[5] In high concentrations, the environmental toxins mercury and polychlorinated biphenyls (PCBs) exert harmful effects.[6] Maternal infection during pregnancy, such as with cytomegalovirus, can also interfere with an infant's later cognitive development.[7] Exposure to lead has been liked to lower IQ scores. Maternal blood lead concentrations above 10 micrograms per deciliter are predictive of suppressed cognitive development in children.[8] Evidence is accumulating that even maternal stress can have lasting negative effects on infants' later development.[9]

Among the many toxins that can disrupt a child's cognitive development, none causes more widespread destruction than alcohol. Regular and significant exposure to alcohol in utero is associated with the pattern of abnormal development known as fetal alcohol syndrome. The syndrome is identified by a child's small stature, facial abnormalities, and very significant cognitive impairment. Fetal alcohol syndrome is associated with a decrement of 35 IQ points, a horrendous penalty.[10] Through prenatal exposure to alcohol, a child who would otherwise have an average IQ of 100 would instead have an IQ of 65—well into the range of mental retardation. As devastating as these effects are objectively, another class of children—12 times as many—do not exhibit the physical traits of fetal alcohol syndrome yet suffer cognitive deficiencies that are almost as severe. The IQ decrement for a child with significant prenatal alcohol exposure, but who lacks the defining characteristics of fetal alcohol syndrome, is about 25 IQ points—still devastating and greatly worrisome because of the vast numbers of affected children.

BREASTFEEDING AND INFANT DEVELOPMENT

Nutritional factors matter a great deal in infant development. Breastfeeding is especially important for ensuring that a baby has an unrivaled source of nutrients. Breast milk is much more chemically complex than infant formula, with thousands of identifiable chemical components. These include vitamins, minerals, peptides, immunoprotective factors, and growth hormones, as well as omega-3s and other polyunsaturated fats—nutrients that are not always present in infant formula. These fats are essential to the optimal functioning of the central nervous system and are associated with superior problem-solving ability.[11] Deficiencies of essential fats, in turn, are linked to suboptimal cognitive development.[12] Consistent with the nutritional profile of breast milk, evidence has accumulated for positive associations between breastfeeding and infants' cognitive development.[13] Studies have shown that breastfeeding can confer a cognitive advantage of between 2 and 5 IQ points for full-term infants. Among low birth-weight infants, the advantage is higher still—about 8 IQ points.[14]

The cognitive benefits of breastfeeding were confirmed in a large-scale study in which 31 hospitals in Belarus were randomly assigned to one of two conditions—a program that encouraged and supported mothers to breastfeed their infants or continuation of normal hospital practices regarding breastfeeding.[15] Infants in the experimental group were breast-fed exclusively for longer periods of time. At age 6.5 years, children in the experimental group registered higher scores on an intelligence test, ranging from 2 to 6 IQ points, depending on the subscale. Additionally, teachers rated the academic performance of children in the experimental group to be higher in reading, writing, mathematics, and other subjects. The teachers' ratings were highest for those children who were breastfed exclusively for three to six months.

The role of breastfeeding in infants' cognitive development is more far reaching than we might assume. That is because the likelihood of breastfeeding is associated with social class: Middle-class women more often breastfeed their babies, while poorer mothers more often rely on infant formula.[16] As we will see in greater detail, IQ correlates significantly with social class: Average IQs are higher in the middle class than they are in working-class and poor families. Unsurprisingly, poverty is associated with decreased prospects for children's intellectual growth. It's fair to wonder whether the lower incidence of breastfeeding among poorer families is a contributing factor. In any case, parents facing a choice between breastfeeding and formula ought to consider the many nutritive advantages of breast milk, including an innumerable variety of nutrients, abundant essential fats vital to the development of the central nervous system, and immune protection against disease.

NUTRIENTS AND LEARNING

There is no question that nutrition can affect a child's IQ score, but can dietary quality also affect a child's ability to learn in school? Here, the data are thinner, but we have at least suggestive evidence that when children have access to nutritious food they become more effective learners. This was the conclusion to a dietary intervention study in New York City schools.[17] Over a period of three years, several changes were made to school meals, namely, the successive elimination of refined sugars, food colorings, and preservatives. One nutritional change was phased in each year. Test scores climbed in parallel, suggesting that the nutritional improvements were at least partly responsible.

The investigators did not believe that the rising test scores resulted directly from removing harmful additives to food. Instead, they conjectured that when processed foods were removed from the school meal menu, children were forced to choose among more healthy alternatives. Foods with fewer preservatives and with less artificial color and sugar were presumably more nutrient-rich and increased the aggregate quality of children's diets. We can't say with full certainty that dietary changes in the New York City schools were responsible for the increases in students' tests scores. The study was not a controlled experiment in which some children received dietary improvements and others did not. Pinning down a cause-and-effect relationship is therefore not possible, but we have at least correlational evidence that nutritious meals can lead to more effective learning on a large scale.

Very few parents or teachers would be surprised at research showing an association between good nutrition and effective learning. Much more surprising would be the absence of a connection. And, in fact, other research has reinforced a functional association between reliable nutrition and a child's ability to learn. At a very basic level, energy in the form of glucose—the brain's essential fuel—can help assure that cognitive processing is optimal.[18] The brain is known to consume enormous amounts of caloric energy—about 10 times the rate of the average human body cell. Although the brain accounts for just 2% of the body's total mass, it consumes roughly 20% of its metabolic energy.[19] It's no surprise, then, that simply supplying the brain with its necessary operating fuel in the form of glucose makes a difference in cognitive performance. Beyond basic calories, children are advantaged if they have dependable access to a richly nutritious diet; children who lack such access are at risk for suboptimal learning.[20]

MEDIA AND INFORMATION TECHNOLOGIES

As we continue our search for possible causes of rising IQs around the world—the Flynn effect—we must consider the rapid expansion of mass media and information technologies. During the last century, the introduction of radio into remote villages of developing nations may have had widespread effects on people's thinking and communication patterns.[21] Likewise, newspapers, magazines, and television were a source of intellectual enrichment for cultures that previously lacked access to these media. This does not mean that more informational media is always better for cognitive enrichment. Any intellectual benefit associated with mass media is really an optimization function in which an ideal mix involves moderate exposure. Excessive exposure to television reverses the correlation: Viewing television for several hours each day is associated with decreased learning.[22] This risk of overexposure does not nullify the more general pattern, however: The global spread of mass media helped to spur intellectual development around the world.

Television, radio, newspapers, and magazines are all old-style media. We also want to know whether the Internet is having effects similar to previous information technologies. It's a credible possibility: Through the Internet, users not only access mass media instantaneously, they can also query vast databases to gain specific knowledge on politics, history, science, events, and consumer products—indeed, every imaginable knowledge domain. Also, online and PC-based games are potential hothouses for specialized forms of intellectual growth. Many games stretch a user's ability to manage complex information, and so may have the unintended but positive effect of expanding cognitive powers. Greater intellectual fitness may in turn generalize to school subjects and everyday life.

To see how this is possible we must appreciate that, in order to become more proficient in computer-based games, users often must build skill in mental visualization and the ability to manipulate images in the mind. Games can stretch the game player's ability to multitask—to hold and coordinate the dynamic information needed to solve a problem. Computer-based games, sometimes feared for their possible anti-intellectual effects, may prove to be closer to mental workouts than to mind-numbing time wasters. Some research shows that computer-based games can actually enhance a player's ability to represent and transform spatial information, as well as to allocate attention on complex tasks.[23] Yet any positive effects of computer-based games will at some point yield diminishing returns—more cannot always be better—and in excess may cause a decrement in other valued forms of intellectual growth, such as the kinds of learning supported by books.

COMPLEXITY OF LIFE

Compared to previous centuries, life in modern society is vastly more complex. We live in a world far more complicated than the one inhabited by our grandparents. The rapidity of societal change is vividly displayed in the information technologies we use to communicate and network. The shelf life of a laptop computer, mobile phone, or software release is a few years at most. Soon the technology becomes unsupportable, incompatible, and obsolete. In a thousand other ways, too, we are forced to adapt to rapid change and expanding choices. Decisional complexity even applies to mundane activities. The grocery store offers aisle after aisle of bewildering food options, each potential purchase conditioned by nutritional and ethical trade-offs. Food choices are just one example. It is incumbent upon each person to keep up with innumerable options and obligations or else risk inundation in a heap of unanswered e-mails and past-due notices; likewise, "must-read" books, articles, and business advisories pile up unheeded. A lot is expected of citizens of the 21st century—arguably too much.

It's possible that the mind has upgraded its own "operating parameters" in response to rising demands. The Flynn effect might have arisen, in part, from pressures on the mind to adapt to greater complexity in the environment. In response to the need to manage the flow of information intelligently, perhaps the mind has obliged by becoming a more capable instrument. Rates of change in societies seem to link to IQ gains over time. Early accounts of the Flynn effect were largely reported in developed nations, while later gains reflected more recent modernization in other regions. Indeed, as IQ gains in developing nations advance steadily, the rise of cognitive abilities in more advanced nations, such as Denmark, seems to have leveled off.[24] The important point is that a particular society's IQ gains are apparently a function of changes within the culture, including modernization and its correlates—improvements to education, information, health care, and nutrition. Psychologist Ulric Neisser expressed the possibility this way: "Complexity of life" has produced "complexity of mind."[25]

THE WORLDWIDE EXPANSION OF EDUCATION

Another likely cause of the Flynn effect may be the most surprising of all—education. It's surprising because we normally think of education as conveying *knowledge* to young learners, but not *intelligence*. Yet rising IQs around the world may be quite directly linked to the expansion of schooling to wider populations. The expansion of schooling is a wonderful accomplishment. During the 20th century, emerging conceptions of literacy as a human right meant that, minimally, a primary school education should be made available to everyone, everywhere. Progress toward this vision, although imperfect, has been remarkable.

Alongside gains in universal education is a parallel trend toward longer periods of education. In the United States, the average number of completed grades rose substantially between 1900 and 2000. At the start of the 20th century, a high school education was a rare accomplishment, but by 1950 it had become the norm in the United States.[26] By the end of the 20th century, most young Americans had completed at least some college. In the sections that follow, we will see evidence showing that more years of schooling make a difference to students' ability to think. Stated more directly: Education has effects that go beyond teaching specific knowledge and skills—education also increases intelligence.

The relationship between education and intelligence is both enlightening and pragmatically relevant. We will see that, through education, intelligence has increased in the past. We will also see how this effect can be accomplished purposefully and intentionally in the future—schooling can systematically introduce complex and abstract information to exercise the cognitive skills that collectively define intelligence. During the 20th century, IQs increased, as did the reach of formal education in schools. Because both increased substantially over the course of a century, we can easily discern a correlation between them. But before placing too much confidence in education as a means to increase intelligence, we need firmer evidence that the connection between the two is causal, not simply correlational. Let's have a look at a few examples.

CANAL BOAT CHILDREN

Evidence that education can enhance intelligence was discovered as early as the 1920s. During that era, one important means of trade in England and northern Europe consisted of transporting goods on barges through extensive systems of canals. Nuclear families often traveled together from town to town on their barges, buying and selling. Families could make a decent living this way, and to all appearances the children raised on canal boats were healthy and well behaved. Even so, English educational authorities knew that something was wrong: The canal boat children were experiencing serious delays in their cognitive development.

The canal boat children lived very different lives from their peers who were not involved in the canal trade. One crucial difference was that the children who lived on barges rarely attended school because their families were itinerant. The British government responded by building special schools that were proximal to city ports. Even with this accommodation, the children attended school on average less than 10 days each year.[27] A second major difference between canal boat children and their geographically stable peers was that the IQ scores of the itinerant children declined steeply over time. Among five-year-olds, IQs were in the normal range, but by the age of 10 the average IQ drifted down into the 60s and 70s, a region of the IQ scale associated with mental retardation. The canal boat children's meager exposure to schooling seemed to have direct and potent negative effects on their IQ scores. With each year of schooling missed, those effects became more devastating.

The case of the canal boat children does not prove a connection between amount of schooling and measured intelligence. It does, however, offer a clue about the relationship between the two. To be convinced that education really does enhance IQ, we need more than a single historical case study. Fortunately, several other studies likewise show that IQ is correlated with the number of years of schooling, but focus less on deprivation and more on the effects of opportunity for further study. Let's now consider evidence that links changes in IQ with the extent of education experienced.

THE SWEDISH STUDIES

Research on young men recruited into the Swedish military provides a second strand of evidence that IQ is related to educational level. By the mid-20th century, several decades' worth of data showed that IQ was correlated with the number of years of schooling the men completed. Again, by itself, a positive correlation between IQ and educational achievement is unimpressive. After all, we expect bright students to have higher scores on selective admissions tests that control which students are admitted to universities, professional schools, and graduate degree programs. It's quite easy to believe that higher test scores led to more years of education rather than the other way around.

With some care in interpretation, though, it's possible to see that the reverse holds, too: More education results in higher test scores. This is clearest when the data are analyzed in a way that compares the Swedish males only with peers who received similar levels of education. The outcome variable of interest was IQ change between the age of 10, when all the males were still in school, and 20, after they had joined the military. Depending on the category of education level, the average change in IQ ranged from -1 to +11, with larger upward shifts associated with more formal education.[28] When the data were analyzed yet another way, the conclusion was essentially identical. Statistically, the children were subdivided into "blocks" with similar IQs at age 10. The analysis showed that, *within* blocks, children who had more education had higher IQ scores at age 20. In other words, when comparisons were made only among 10-year-olds with similar IQs, those who completed more years of schooling had measurably higher IQs as young adults. This pattern held even when statistical controls were used to adjust for variation in family wealth.[29] These analyses suggest that the IQ–education link is direct, not merely a function of selective admissions to advanced education.

A similar pattern was confirmed, years later, on a separate data set of Swedish youth.[30] The parameters differed slightly. This time, IQ was measured at the ages of 13 and 18. Again for this analysis, the children were blocked by their initial IQ scores. Once more, IQ changes within blocks were associated with the number of years of schooling completed.[31] Upward IQ drifts of 8 to 10 points were associated with higher levels of education. The

Swedish data begin to present a convincing case that education is *causal* in shifting IQ upward. Taken together, the data are consistent with the hypothesis that formal education does not function simply to convey more knowledge, but also to boost intelligence as measured by IQ tests.

THE AMERICAN STUDIES

In the United States, investigators obtained results similar to those found in Sweden: IQ was significantly linked to the degree of schooling completed. The American data set differed slightly. The IQ scores of American males were recorded at two age points, 14 and 34. The key predictor variable was the level of education each man achieved. The objective was to determine the pattern of connections between education level and IQ scores at the two time points.[32]

One correlation was fully expected: IQ scores taken at age 14 predicted subsequent educational achievement with a moderate correlation of $r = .36$. The correlation is unsurprising, though, because cognitive ability paves the way for educational achievement in at least two ways. One is that college admissions tests function as gatekeepers to more advanced educational levels; the second is that high IQ scores represent greater intellectual readiness to succeed in education. We can easily confirm the standard way of viewing the relationship between intelligence and education—that IQ is a good predictor of educational achievement because it represents the intellectual potential to learn effectively. What we want to know is whether the relationship works the other way: Does education affect IQ?

Because the American data included IQ at age 34, it was possible to test whether educational attainment predicted future IQ. The interesting finding here was that the men's educational attainment quite strongly predicted their IQ at age 34 with a value of $r = .68$. This value was much higher than the correlation of IQ at age 14 with later educational achievement. In fact, the effect of education on adult IQ was *more than three times* the size of the effect of child IQ on education. As with the Swedish data, the findings fall short of being definitive, but the American data add further evidence that IQ scores are affected positively by formal education. The pattern is recurrent: Education can shift IQ scores upward.

Assume for a moment that the foregoing argument is valid: Higher levels of education result in higher levels of measured intelligence. As a practical matter, does a higher IQ really make a difference? Does a change in a test score really show up in more intelligent behavior? Some evidence suggests that it does. To answer, psychologist Lloyd Humphries examined performance differences between American soldiers who served in World War I and those who served in World War II. Using data gathered by military psychologists, Humphries was able to compare how efficiently soldiers learned their jobs. This was possible because many job skills and responsibilities remained much the same between the two wars. The comparison would be telling, because between 1917 and 1942 the average IQ of military recruits rose substantially—about 15 IQ points.[33] Examining military records on job performance, Humphries concluded that the IQ shift made a real difference: World War II soldiers learned their jobs more efficiently and effectively than had their counterparts a generation earlier.[34]

World War II soldiers were advantaged by being more educated. Between World War I and World War II, the average level of schooling in the United States rose from a 9th grade education to the completion of high school at 12th grade. Three additional years of schooling may not seem very significant: Why should three years matter? Simply because those three years are particularly challenging in their demands for mastery of abstract and complex subject matter in comparison to the earlier grades. The ability to learn complex material is crucial. It seems to have made the soldiers in World War II more intelligent as well as more effective learners on the job.

WHEN SCHOOLING IS INTERRUPTED

Statistically, more extensive schooling predicts higher IQ scores. The same connection between education and IQ can be discerned from another data source—historical disruptions of schooling. When historical crises result in the suspension of formal education through school closures, the affected children suffer measurable decrements on IQ tests. One example derives from the battlefields of World War II. Between 1941 and 1944, Eindhoven, Holland, was occupied by Nazi soldiers; the town was held by Allied troops starting in 1944. Through the wartime years and for a short time afterward, schooling in Eindhoven was spotty at best. Before the war's end, many male teachers went into hiding, presumably because they were perceived as a threat to the occupying forces; children attended school irregularly, if at all.[35]

The effects of school closure on cognitive abilities can be estimated because of a convenient fact: Near Eindhoven was the Philips Academy. Philips routinely tested its applicants, and the resulting performances were readily converted into IQ scores. The scores show a definite pattern during the affected period: They first declined and then returned to baseline levels. Before 1943, the IQs of applicants averaged about 100, exactly as expected.

Between 1944 and 1948, IQs dropped approximately 5 points, arguably the result of school disruption, although emotional trauma may well have contributed to the decline. Although the war ended in 1945, average IQs did not return to prewar levels until 1949. Thus, school closures in wartime Eindhoven coincided with a dip and resurgence of IQs among school-age children.

Another historical episode presents a similar pattern—a drop in IQ that coincided with the disruption of formal education. The public schools of Prince Edward County, Virginia, were shut down from the spring of 1959 to the fall of 1963. The closure was a response to enforcement of the 1954 *Brown* decision by the Supreme Court. In the *Brown v. Board of Education* ruling, the precedent of "separate but equal" facilities for Black and White students was declared unconstitutional, making segregation illegal. The Prince Edward County School Board resisted the mandatory desegregation by taking a dramatic step: They shut down the public schools. To meet the educational needs of the county's Caucasian students, an all-White private academy was established in September 1959. In one of the most bizarre episodes of recent American history, Black students had no official provision for their education. Hastily constructed arrangements were made for some of the county's Black students to receive "compensatory education," partly through the activities of volunteers. Black students who did not receive compensatory services suffered measurably: Comparisons between the students who received compensatory education and others who did not showed a 15-point IQ advantage for those whose education continued in some form.[36]

These historical case studies are vivid, but the power of formal education to influence cognitive ability is also evident in more normal and typical events. Consider what happens to children who are almost exactly the same age, but whose exposure to formal education differs significantly. Owing to the arbitrary cutoff dates set by school boards, children can begin kindergarten or first grade with significant age variation—some school starters begin their formal education nearly a year younger than their peers. This difference carries forward such that children at any given age, say 10 years old, can differ by a whole year of formal education. Children of roughly the same age might differ considerably in exposure to more advanced material. What we want to know is whether an additional year of education affects the developing mind. Do children who start school earlier have a cognitive advantage compared to their same-age peers who are "delayed"? Alternatively, are the delayed children better off because they are neurologically more mature and therefore better prepared to learn challenging material and to experience academic success?

Not too surprisingly, researchers have found that intellectual growth is a function of both schooling and maturation. Through statistics, it is possible to separate the effect of schooling from that of biological maturation. Both effects are positive, meaning that maturation and schooling factors are each associated with intellectual growth. What may be surprising, however, is that schooling is the more powerful influence: On most tests, an additional year of schooling has twice the benefit of an additional year of maturation.[37] This means that children on the cusp of cutoff dates for grades are cognitively advantaged by going to the higher grade rather than the lower grade. The positive effects of schooling on cognitive growth are especially noticeable on tests of crystallized intelligence. Though somewhat weaker in magnitude, the same effects of schooling also show up on tests of fluid intelligence. Such information may be relevant to parents and teachers. Of course, when facing a decision about whether to place a particular child into a higher or lower grade, this research finding should not be the only factor. Nonetheless, as parents and teachers work toward a decision, the cognitive effects of education should be taken into account. Otherwise, there is a risk of regarding the child's maturation as the dominant, or even sole, consideration.

Other interesting effects can also be detected from the normal ebb and flow of schooling. For example, the typical cycle of the school year means that most children experience time away from the classroom during the summer months. We might assume that summer vacation has the same effect on all children, but research shows that this is not the case. In general, the summer experiences of middle-class children result in continuity of learning, whether through exposure to books, summer enrichment programs, or travel.[38] Poorer children are likely to have less intellectually enriching experiences—at least this seems to be the case based on patterns of cognitive change during the summer months. Differences in summer experiences have consequences: Middle-class children show continuous growth in academic achievement throughout the calendar year. During the summer months, their reading proficiency levels continue to climb, just as they do during the school year. Poorer children show a different pattern: Rather than continuity, their achievement scores display a saw-tooth pattern of climbing during the regular school year followed by a partial downward regression during the summertime.

These two patterns—steady progress versus saw-tooth—lead to a divergence of trend lines over time. In New York City, children from wealthier schools displayed reading levels two years ahead of children from poorer schools by the end of sixth grade. Half of the two-year gap could be accounted for by changes during the school year, but the other half had built up during the summer months. In other words, 50% of the achievement gap between rich and poor schools resulted from divergent summer experiences.[39] By the end of the eighth grade, the effects of summer were even more dramatic. Average achievement now differed by 2.5 years, and summers accounted for two years of that gap—a full 80%.

At this point, we must remember to acknowledge two complementary truths about how children's experience affects their development. First, schools promote intellectual growth. If it were not for schools, the intellectual trajectories of children would almost certainly be more divergent than they currently are. Seen in this light, schooling acts as a buffer to reduce differences in the slopes of achievement rates.[40] The second effect, though, is that nonschool experiences also have educational value. Much of the variation in students' academic achievement is a product of nonschool factors. We can generalize this way: *All* experiences have potential value for learning, regardless of whether those experiences occur in schools or away from the classroom.

Our span of interest concerns all forms of experience on IQ, including negative experience. That said, we note that a life of delinquency also appears to have significant effects on IQ and intelligence profiles.[41] Crime and aggression are associated with an IQ decrement of about 8 points, other factors being equal. The delinquent's profile of cognitive abilities is fairly consistent—scores on crystallized intelligence are lower than scores on tests of fluid intelligence. The reasons for the lower crystallized scores are not completely clear. The low scores could result simply from poor participation in schooling or greater impulsivity when taking school-like tests of knowledge. Some scholars have speculated that lower crystallized scores and lower IQ might be the result of brain injuries from life patterns of violence or drug abuse. Another possibility is that both lower IQ and a predisposal to delinquency are related to social factors, such as poverty.

It's a little surprising that nonschool experiences can produce such potent differences in learning outcomes, but what about school experiences? News stories often report that differences in educational quality distinguish schools in wealthy neighborhoods from those in poor communities. Not only are such differences in educational quality real, they also have effects on cognitive development, measured as IQ change. In one study, poor educational quality was associated with a decline of about 1.5 IQ points each year. This translated to the loss of a full standard deviation between the ages of 6 and 16.[42] The detrimental effects of poor educational quality held even when controlling for students' home background and were confirmed with a separate data set. IQ differences of this magnitude are consequential: They have significant effects on college admissions

tests, readiness to engage in the study of complex material, and prepared-
ness to enter intellectually challenging careers.

IS MATHEMATICS THE ENGINE?

We can speculate about which aspects of the school curriculum might hold
special importance in producing the worldwide increase in IQ scores called
the Flynn effect. In broad terms, the school curriculum introduces subject
matter and literacies that are progressively more abstract and complex. It's
reasonable to suppose that the school curriculum as a whole cultivates a
rising capacity to deal with abstract subject matter and to solve complex
problems. School subjects might differ, however, in their promotion of the
cognitive proficiencies that underlie intelligence—fluid intelligence in particular. Recall that the Flynn effect was manifest on fluid intelligence at
least equally as much as on crystallized intelligence, and in some data sets
the magnitude of the effect of rising IQs on fluid intelligence was double
that of crystallized. One domain of study might have been pivotal in the
cultivation of fluid intelligence—mathematics.

Studies of the mathematics curriculum during the span of the 20th century show a clear evolution toward increasing sophistication. The curricular
transformation ran in tandem with increasing access to formal schooling
in general. The cognitive demands of the mathematics curriculum changed
progressively to align with the cognitive characteristics of fluid intelligence.[43] In the early 1900s, mathematics was rarely offered as a subject of
study to children at the early grades. The math curriculum of the early 20th
century was fixated on basic counting skills and rote memorization; later
curricula focused much more on spurring students' ability to think mathematically. By the 1960s, a complex and articulated mathematics curriculum had been introduced through the span of grades in elementary school
education, with a rising proportion of challenging mathematics skills,
including geometry. Other problem types required students to engage in
categorization and multistep problem solving. Some of these exercises
called upon students to understand patterns, infer rules, and apply those
rules in ways that are very similar to the inductive reasoning skills characterizing fluid intelligence.

Changes to the mathematics curriculum imply that younger students
learned progressively more complex mathematics as the decades progressed.
Is this the case? A common assumption is that mathematics achievement
in the United States is declining, not rising. The data tell a different story.
National trends in achievement show that students around the world have

become more proficient in mathematics over the decades. The trend holds in other countries as well. Many teachers, particularly those in developing countries that have experienced rapid modernization, rate current students as more intelligent than students of a generation prior.[44] In between those two time points the world experienced dramatic change, including change to the typical learning experience in schools.

The mathematics curriculum appears to be a reasonable candidate for spurring the rising IQ scores that constitute the Flynn effect. Like IQ gains, the introduction of complex mathematics spread rapidly and evolved significantly over the course of a century. Mathematics may have yet another vitally important role in the school curriculum. Early mathematics achievement now appears to have surprising power to predict student academic achievement in high school—both in mathematics and in reading.[45] We do not understand fully why math seems to have such sweeping importance to the developing intellect. Research that shows this effect presents an intriguing mystery, indeed.

EDUCATION CULTIVATES INTELLIGENCE

The research we have examined challenges the way we normally think about intelligence and education. The typical way to understand their relationship is that intelligence is an input—a raw material—and an educated mind is the output. Through education, an intellectually able learner is transformed into a knowledgeable citizen and a technically skilled worker. There is nothing incorrect about this conceptualization; it is merely incomplete. The counterpart truth can be expressed this way: Intelligence is not simply a raw material for education; it is also a *product* of education. We can even quantify the impact of education on IQ: For every year of education, the counterpart gain in IQ is about ½ point.[46]

To see education as causing IQ gains can help us to interpret the purpose of education, as well as the role of teachers, in entirely new ways. Parents also play a revised role as cultivators of intelligence in their children. We know from research that parental education is a very good predictor of a child's cognitive development. The mother's level of education is particularly important in this regard. Well-educated mothers tend to interact with their children in ways that are linguistically rich. Rich language experiences, in turn, help to prepare the child for future academic success. The social and intellectual benefits of education are therefore not limited to a single generation, but can propagate across generations. Cross-generational intellectual richness is exhibited not only in the extent of parent–child interactions, but also in the tone. Well-educated, middle-class parents more often engage with their children in conversations that encourage intellectual exploration and critical thinking.

In the past, education's role in cultivating intelligence has been largely unrecognized. Now we have plentiful data showing that education has contributed to the world's supply of intelligence—but not in any planned or deliberate way. What if that role became better known and more intentional? A redefined mission of education might shift the intelligence of students even more significantly, honing their minds into more capable instruments ready to engage the problems and opportunities of the 21st century. A more intelligent population could, in turn, elevate individual and collective human effectiveness. Higher levels of intelligence would equip humanity with a greater readiness to take on the world's most pressing problems. Intelligence, combined with compassion, conscientiousness, and goodwill, could enhance our prospects for a brighter future.

THE HOME ENVIRONMENT

Among the most important environments for growing young minds is an intellectually rich and supportive home. Research tells us that a child's home life matters greatly to his or her intellectual development. The expression of every child's genetic potential relies on environmental circumstances that are information-rich and socially supportive. Impoverished or abusive home environments, by contrast, result in abnormal development. The point is proven by the extreme case of Genie, a girl who was socially isolated by her parents until she was rescued by authorities at the age of 13. Often forced to sit on a potty chair during the day and confined to a sleeping bag at night, Genie's intellectual and social skills were closer to those of a toddler than a typical teenage girl. When a medical team intervened, Genie was eager to learn. She rapidly developed an expanded vocabulary but never acquired the ability to speak in complex fluent sentences.[47]

The case of Genie demonstrates the necessity of normal social and linguistic interactions to cognitive function. One of the most potent predictors of cognitive development is the linguistic richness of the home, especially the type and amount of spoken interaction between children and caring adults. Some children grow up in homes that are language-rich, and this is a monumental advantage. Their spoken interactions with adults are frequent and entail a broad vocabulary. Other children's home experience involves much less interaction using language. As a generalization, middle-class children are exposed to richer verbal interactions than children raised in impoverished homes. Middle-class children hear, and learn to use, a much wider range of vocabulary to understand the world and communicate with others.[48]

Spoken language is crucial, but so are other aspects of home life. Children's minds are enriched by the presence of books and other media in the home environment. Material advantages such as good nutrition and health care also contribute. In the child's direct experience, the availability of toys and play materials, access to a public library, and even family vacations confer detectable benefits on the child's intellectual development. These experiences are not strictly determined by family wealth and educational background, but there is a connection. Specifically, the characteristics of home environments associated with higher IQ scores are also correlated with a child's social class, or what sociologists call socioeconomic status.

Socioeconomic status, abbreviated SES, is a complex and abstract variable, but when measured by sociologists it is rather simply calculated. SES can be measured by gathering data on parents' education, jobs, and family income. When these variables are combined, the composite number is SES. As sociologists know very well, SES is a powerful predictor of a broad range of population characteristics. Among those, SES is positively correlated with both a child's cognitive development and school learning. Perhaps the most important point here is that the home conditions that lead to healthy, normal children are not exactly the same as the conditions that lead to optimal cognitive development.[49] Except in cases of abuse or of significant poverty, the conditions for raising children with normal levels of physical, social, and cognitive development are less demanding than the array of experiences that prime children to reach toward ideal development of intellectual readiness and success in the academic and professional realms. To some extent, these differences in home conditions are what distinguish middle-class from working-class families.

Perhaps more than we would like to contemplate, social status is linked to all manner of cognitive variables, including IQ. Among adults, the correlation of SES with IQ is high, about $r = .50$. This difference is manifest as an IQ gap of 10 to 20 points between professional-technical workers and blue-collar workers.[50] Links between job status, education, and IQ are not too surprising: IQ predicts education, and education in turn opens opportunities for high-status jobs.[51] Among children, IQ and SES are correlated about $r = .30$. As a result, the average IQ gap between children from high-SES families and those from low-SES families is approximately one standard deviation, or about 15 IQ points.

Could there be a genetic explanation for these IQ differences? It's possible. Evidence for a genetic influence is derived not from the stability of social classes, but rather from social mobility data. To some extent, nuclear families are socially resifted every generation, and an important sifting element is the intelligence of children. IQ can vary substantially within families. This fact, when combined with the predictive function of adult IQ, translates into significant social mobility from one generation to the next.[52] To be specific, sons whose IQs are higher than their fathers' IQs tend to be upwardly mobile; sons whose IQs are lower than their fathers' tend to drift downward in socioeconomic status. Genetic factors are the most intuitive explanation for brothers' IQ differences because their home experiences are unlikely to vary much—at least not in comparison to the experiences of children raised in different families. Material and monetary inheritance may help preserve social standing from parents to children, but not completely. To some extent, at least, IQ seems to reassemble the composition of socioeconomic status afresh with each new generation.

SES is an abstract variable. Although it may correlate mathematically with children's intellectual growth, the abstraction of SES itself cannot be responsible. Rather, it must be other variables—patterns of parent–child interaction or the presence of books, for example—that are the proximal forces on developing IQ.[53] Indeed, children's IQ scores are more highly correlated with specific qualities of the home environment ($r = .5$) than they are with SES as an abstract variable ($r = .3$). Positive qualities of the home environment include the availability of play materials and the amount and variety of spoken language between parent and child. Such features of the home not only predict children's current IQ, they also predict future IQ levels. So-called lag correlations indicate whether qualities of the home at time 1 predict IQ at time 2, years later. Research has shown that these particular forward lag correlations are stronger than the counterpart lag correlations in which IQ at time 1 predicts home qualities at time 2.[54] Lag correlations are evidence that the home environment has a causal role in shaping the child's intellect.

Parents' attitudes are also crucial, more so than actual socioeconomic status or income. Scholars have found that parents' positive value on academic achievement, language, and the provision for children's learning inside and outside the home had a combined predictive effect of .76 on their child's IQ.[55] When we consider the potency of attitudes, we start to understand more fully that SES is only a first approximation of factors that really matter in shaping a child's intellectual development. These factors affect impoverished families greatly. We know this because data showing the heritability of IQ—roughly .50 over all populations—seems to differ markedly between middle-class and poor families. The heritability of IQ among wealthier middle-class populations is quite high, around .70, presumably because consistent environmental advantages reduce the role of nurture in shaping intelligence. The opposite is true among poorer families, where the heritability of IQ is an astonishingly low .10.[56] This tells us that environmental factors are supremely important among less wealthy families. Among the economically disadvantaged, nurture is a powerful force, overshadowing nature in its ability to influence future variation in intelligence and all its repercussive effects. With this realization comes a very significant responsibility, and opportunity, for all of society.

Among the many variables that compose family background, one has particular potency—the educational level of the mother. A mother's education correlates impressively with her child's IQ at approximately $r = .50$. Because a mother often has significant linguistic and emotional interaction with her children, the developing child is strongly affected by the extent and nature of spoken language with her. When compared to poorer or less-educated mothers, college-educated middle-class mothers not only interact with their children using a great deal more language, but also using a different style of interaction. In particular, middle-class mothers tend to use emotionally supportive tones that are nondirective and that encourage free exploration of the environment.[57] Poorer and less-educated moms instead tend to use language to warn their children not to behave in certain ways.[58] A stern tone may be understandable if the child's environment is unsafe, but the developmental effects can be detrimental if exploration is discouraged.

Patterns of linguistic interaction employed by many mothers, especially middle-class moms, include "known-answer" questions. When a mother asks her child a question such as "What does a doggie say?" the mother already knows the answer, of course. The purpose of asking the question is to help the child practice what he or she already knows. It's a teaching device. The known-answer give-and-take is a staple of school discourse: The teacher poses a question, and the student responds. Posing known-answer questions is also the discourse pattern assumed in all forms of testing. The answer to the question is not valued in itself, as it would be in everyday conversation. The ability to provide the correct answer is only a means to an end—as a way of generalizing about the person who answers. For all its artificial qualities, the known-answer discourse pattern is fundamental to the enterprise of Western education. By engaging her child in known-answer dialogue, the middle-class mother begins to prepare the young mind for successful participation in the discourse of formal education.

Parent–child interactions are not characterized simply by the amount and variety of language, but also what values are communicated. Values are important to cognitive development: Correlations between IQ and measured values and aspirations range as high as $r = .75$. Such values are communicated in parenting styles. Although limited data are available, the conclusion is consistent with common expectations or stereotypes: Middle-class parents tend to be democratic in their parenting style, whereas poorer or working-class parents gravitate toward authoritarian styles.[59] Different ways of parenting are manifest in how control is gained over children's behavior. A democratic but authoritative style lends itself to discussions and joint decisions between parents and children. Reasons are given for rules, but those rules are not necessarily ironclad; exceptions are possible when there are reasons to deviate from them. Authoritarian parenting styles, by contrast, brook no challenge: Parents' decisions are absolute and nonnegotiable.

Up to this point, we have examined patterns of correlation between SES and child's cognitive growth measured as IQ. We are left to wonder whether SES directly causes IQ change. Fortunately, a limited amount of direct evidence is available on the question. The cognitive effects of SES were examined in a rare experiment conducted in France. In this study, the influence of genes and social environment were pitted against each other in what became known as the French adoption study.[60] In a study design that was both ingenious and daring, birth families were categorized into high-SES and low-SES clusters. The adopting families, also, were categorized as either high-SES or low-SES. The study is daring in that its designers did not employ the typical practice of matching the SES of a child's birth family and adoption family. Instead, they systematically made placements on the basis of a "cross-adoption" design. This meant that half the babies born to high-SES mothers went to wealthy families and half went to poor families. The same logic applied to babies born to low-SES mothers: Half were adopted into wealthier families and half to poorer families. Through the study design, the classic developmental forces of nature and nurture were deliberately separated, with birth family SES representing genetic influences and adopting family SES representing the influence of the environment.

The findings from the adoption study were illuminating. Focusing on IQ as the main variable of interest, the layout of outcomes is shown in Figure 6.1. The standout data point is that children with the highest measured IQs were born to high-SES mothers and were adopted into high-SES families. Those "high-high" children had an average IQ of about 120. Next highest in IQ were the true cross-adoption children. These were the "high-low" children, those born to high-SES mothers and adopted into low-SES families, whose average IQ was 108. Slightly lower were the "low-high" children—those born to low-SES mothers and adopted into

	High SES Adoptive	Low SES Adoptive
High SES Biological	119.6	107.5
Low SES Biological	103.6	94.2

Figure 6.1
Neural Cross-SES Adoption Study: IQ Is Influenced by Biology and SES. Adapted with permission from Capron, C., & Duyme, M. (1989). Assessment of effects of socio-economic status on IQ in a full cross-fostering study. *Nature, 340*, p. 553.

high-SES families—whose IQ averaged about 104. Least advantaged were the children born to low-SES mothers and adopted into low-SES families. Their IQs averaged about 94.

Notice the IQ span separating the "high-high" and the "low-low" children, approximately 120 to 94, roughly a full 25 IQ points. One standard deviation on the IQ scale is 15 points, which means that the combined effects of birth SES and adopting SES are almost two standard deviations. The cross-adoption categories, "high-low" and "low-high," yielded measured IQs close to the center point of 100. This pattern shows that, in structural terms, the SES of the birth family and the SES of the adopting family both matter. We have reasons to be cautious in the interpretation of these findings, yet if one condition (birth family) can roughly be equated to nature and the other (adopting family) to nurture, we see in this experiment a parity of power to shape the young mind. Nature and nurture operate jointly. Both are important; neither is dominant by necessity, and neither is to be dismissed.

FAMILY SIZE AND BIRTH ORDER

The effects of families on IQ are manifest in yet other ways. Family size matters, for example. Children's IQ is negatively related to family size, meaning that with the addition of each child the average IQ drops. The trend is quite robust, but it is a generalization over a large number of families and never a necessary fact about any particular family. Still, interpretations for the trend are easy to generate: With the addition of each subsequent child, the amount and perhaps the quality of parent–child interaction may drop off—again not inevitably, but as an average over hundreds or thousands of families. The effect of family structure on children's cognitive development seems to generalize to school learning: A small negative effect has been found for increasing family size on mathematics and reading achievement, for example.[61]

Like family size, birth order displays a negative relationship with IQ. Firstborns are typically advantaged, with average IQ dropping slightly with each subsequent child. Several mechanisms may contribute to this effect. One example is fairly obvious: birth order and family size are not independent. To be a fourth-born child requires that one's family have at least four children. Therefore, the decline in average IQ with family size is probably related at least partly to birth order effects. With the birth of each child, the average level of intelligence in the family can be seen as decreasing in absolute terms. Spacing of children also factors in: The birth of a new sibling does not affect a teenager as much as it does a preschooler.[62]

Whatever the explanation for the decline in average IQ with birth order, the trend has a notable exception: The last child is often the beneficiary of an IQ boost. The youngest sibling may be the recipient of special attention from parents or may benefit from older siblings who may relate to the child in a quasi-parental style. Older siblings might also benefit from this quasi-parental role: Birth order effects that associate higher IQ with older siblings may result in part from their opportunities to teach younger siblings. Finally, we should note that the effects of family environment on cognitive development become weaker as children grow older. Their effects are strongest during childhood.

COGNITIVE CHANGE IN ADULTHOOD

Among adults, too, cognitive trajectories are sensitive to the quality of experience along the life path. We have seen that a more extensive education generally translates to a higher IQ score, and that this effect is detectable at all levels—elementary, secondary, and postsecondary. The effect of a university education on IQ is in the region of 5 to 15 points, an appreciable boost and not surprising given the complexity of material studied in higher education.[63] As we noted earlier in the context of family effects, the benefits associated with a college or advanced degree education extend beyond the student's immediate benefit. Education affects parenting styles, the quality of parent–child discourse, and, inevitably, the values and goals propagated to subsequent generations.

Jobs, too, have an influence on cognitive development. Their effects depend on the nature of the work performed. Jobs that require initiative, judgment, and independent thought increase a worker's ability to think flexibly. Such jobs encourage a personal value system that prizes self-direction over conformity.[64] The cognitive nature of work can, over time, shape the intellectual profiles of workers. Technical jobs that are primarily scientific or mechanical in nature enhance spatial and technical abilities; jobs that are verbally oriented enhance verbal abilities.[65] Of course, cognitive ability profiles initially predict career selection; a student who has an aptitude for spatial ability might gravitate toward engineering, for example. Yet research tells us that that the relationship between cognitive abilities and work profession is reciprocal. Cognitive abilities both *influence* and *are influenced by* subsequent experience, including experience on the job.

We know that IQ predicts job performance, and that the predictive power of IQ is somewhat higher in more complex jobs. The elevated predictive function for cognitively demanding jobs suggests that those jobs draw more heavily on the resources of intelligence. Jobs that regularly demand the application of intelligence may, in turn, nudge the trend line of IQ upward over the life span. An intellectually challenging job might generate a steady rise in crystallized intelligence—the specialized knowledge that supports highly skilled performance—as well as the flexible thinking and capacity for innovation that marks fluid intelligence. One application of this pattern is rather straightforward: Adults ought to think of their career pathway at least partly in terms of its ability to nourish and develop the intellectual resources of intelligence.

In old age, too, a person's quality of experience can shift the trajectory of cognitive growth and prevent its decline. One serious threat to cognitive performance in advanced years is degenerative disease, notably Alzheimer's. Pharmaceuticals can slow the progression of Alzheimer's disease, though at this time there is no cure. Yet even in the absence of identifiable disease, old age is statistically associated with cognitive decline. The effects of aging are most marked on fluid intelligence, which entails the capacity to think flexibly, to identify patterns in complex information, and to apply those patterns to solve new problems. Declines in fluid intelligence might be explained by decrements among older adults in processing speed as well as by reductions in working memory capacity.[66] In less technical language, older adults often cannot think as fast or cope with as much informational complexity as they did when they were younger.

No one really knows if the trend lines that associate cognitive decline with aging are inevitable. We do know, however, that individuals' life choices can affect the slopes of those trend lines. The principle "use it or lose it" inspires elderly people to stay intellectually active by reading, doing crossword puzzles, traveling, taking courses, and enjoying the company of interesting friends. There is reason to believe that intellectual activity influences brain processes in a positive way. Activity in the brain's neurons releases brain chemicals known as neurotrophins, which function to stimulate the formation of new synapses between neurons.[67] Thinking rewires the brain. Another potent stimulator of neurotrophins is physical exercise.[68] For reasons that are not entirely understood, exercise has surprisingly large effects on the formation of new brain connections. Not only that, exercise increases blood flow to the brain by promoting enhancements to the vascular system. Through both cognitive and physical exercise—and perhaps with the aid of pharmaceuticals or supplements—elderly people have powerful tools to maintain and perhaps extend their cognitive powers.

One personal trait that has enhanced potential for growth in the later years of life is wisdom. Wisdom entails the ability to make good decisions, particularly when the conditions underlying good judgment involve competing interests.[69] Superficially, wisdom and intelligence might seem to be quite independent personal traits, but it's possible to see a connection between the two. In weighing competing interests and finding solutions that balance many different considerations and project consequences of decisions, a high capacity to entertain complex information can help. The connection is implicit, in fact, in the Chinese language. The Chinese conceptualizations of intelligence and wisdom are quite close—linguistically, the two are not distinguished.[70]

A large body of research now shows that human intelligence is a function of experience. The quality of that experience varies from person to person, and the effects of experience on cognitive abilities extend through the life span. Salient factors include variation in the degree and quality of nutrition, mass media, information technology, formal education, and work. The child's family experience, including exposure to rich linguistic environments, holds special importance in setting the initial trajectories of cognitive development. In adulthood, the cognitive demands of work matter, as do engagement in physical exercise and ongoing intellectual self-challenge in the twilight years. The binding concept among these many forces for cognitive growth is that a person's level of intelligence is neither an accident nor fully determined by DNA. Instead, the potent resources that compose human intelligence are shifted up or down by specific qualities of experience.

PROGRAMS DESIGNED TO INCREASE INTELLIGENCE

Intelligence is malleable. One particularly engaging follow-up question is whether the human intellect responds favorably when experience is specifically designed to boost cognitive power. In other words, can we deliberately and intentionally enhance human intelligence? The notion that human intelligence can be *intentionally* enhanced has a strange ring. Visions of deliberate attempts to make people smarter can seem far-fetched, even audacious. Yet the conclusion from research is plain: IQ is sensitive to qualities of experience throughout the life span. Variation in experience has measurable effects on a person's cognitive profile, including measured IQ. Earlier sections of this chapter focused on aspects of the environment that varied naturally, not programmatically. In the pages that follow, we will explore the possibility that if *unplanned* variation in life experience can affect IQ, then planned interventions might also produce such effects.

Knowing that experience strongly affects intellectual change makes us aware of the potential for significant cognitive enhancement. Through deliberate attempts to raise intelligence, we can capitalize fully on that potential. In theory, it should be possible to design interventions that will improve cognitive ability markedly. If the results of such interventions are positive, then theory has translated into practice in a very consequential way. The question we must now address is whether specific programs designed to increase intelligence have been successful.

Fortunately, we have answers: Programs designed to raise intelligent functioning have been successful among participants ranging from infancy to old age. Those programs varied widely. Some programs targeted low functioning or at-risk children, while others were designed for gifted students. Some programs had financial sponsorship from national governments; others were carried out in remote corners of the world or run on shoestring budgets. In the remaining pages of this chapter, we will examine a sample of programs that were intended to improve the broad thinking capability of participants. To judge how well these programs worked, we will concentrate on IQ gains without being exclusive of other measures of intelligence. The focus on IQ is favored for quite natural reasons: For many readers, the IQ criterion lends credibility to claims that intelligence per se is enhanced. Also, IQ scores, for all their simplistic reductionism, are nonetheless an acceptable proxy for the wildly complex collection of intellectual competencies we call intelligence.

RAISING THE INTELLIGENCE OF INFANTS

In most cases, neither parents nor health professionals would consider trying to enhance the cognitive functioning of newborn babies. One exception might be newborns most at risk for suboptimal cognitive growth. Such was the case in a yearlong program designed for premature and low-birth-weight Black infants in urban Philadelphia.[71] The intervention began shortly after birth: Visual stimulation was provided by suspending "nursery bird" mobiles above the infants' cribs. Hospital nurses gave extra verbal and physical stimulation to the babies above the typical and expected standard of care in the hospital. When the babies were sent home, their families were given rattles and picture books. Mothers were also trained in how to enhance their interactions with the newborns to provide extra cognitive stimulation.

The enhanced cognitive stimulation had measurable positive effects. After just a single week of intervention, the babies displayed greater alertness compared to similar infants in a control group. At four weeks of age, infants in the experimental group exhibited superior development and weight gain. One year after birth, the children in the treatment group showed a 10-point advantage in sensorimotor IQ compared to infants in the control group. Sensorimotor IQ is much more basic than cognitive IQ manifestations among older children and adults, but it does indicate whether neurological development is proceeding along a normal and healthy pathway.

RAISING THE INTELLIGENCE OF PRESCHOOLERS

There have been many programs that have successfully raised intelligence among preschool children. One of the first programs to attempt direct cognitive enhancement was carried out in the late 1930s by psychologist Helen Dawe. Dawe met regularly with preschool children who resided in the Iowa Soldiers' Orphans' Home. Dawe's "curriculum" was not a sequence of set lessons, but rather a set of guiding principles for interacting with the children. Those interactions were language-intensive, an emphasis based on Dawe's view that "linguistic symbols [can] serve as intellectual tools."[72] She believed that as children become familiar with the forms of discourse that support asking questions, positing ideas, and presenting explanations, those children can use language to support their own growing capacity to think.

As a scholar of child development, Dawe was careful to document the effects of her program at the Orphans' Home. She matched the 11 participating children with 11 control children of comparable ages and intellectual characteristics. The IQs of both groups averaged around 80. Dawe noted that children who resided at the Orphans' Home were cognitively at risk for a simple reason: Their interactions with adults were much less frequent than in a typical family, and far below ideal. While engaged in meaningful conversations with the children, Dawe stressed the proper use of words, encouraged an attitude of curiosity, and tried to replace careless thinking with critical thinking. The entire intervention spanned a two-year period and entailed 92 days of interaction. This translated to about 50 hours of contact time with each child, either one-on-one or in groups.

Children who participated drew benefits from Dawe's program. When Dawe compared children from the treatment and control groups, she found that they differed in the quality of their spontaneous speech. Children in the treatment group asked more "intellectual" questions per hour and made analytical comments more frequently. When the two groups were compared on the Stanford-Binet Intelligence scale, children in the treatment group scored 16 points higher than did the controls. The gains of participating children were impressive; even so, Dawe did not think that they had reached their limits. Given more time, Helen Dawe believed that the children of the Iowa Soldiers' Orphans' Home would have made even greater gains.

A second program designed for preschool children was the Early Training Project, conducted in the 1960s.[73] This intervention was intended to forestall declines in cognitive ability among preschool children living in poverty. The project design assumed that such children normally have no discernible neurological abnormality, but that conditions associated with poverty can impede their intellectual development. The cumulative effects of cognitive deprivation and possible trauma may lead poor children to enter school seriously underprepared. Compared to their peers in middle-class neighborhoods, children from poor families often begin school with an intellectual disadvantage that is extremely difficult to overcome.

The Early Training Project involved poor African-American preschoolers and their families. The goal of the project was not to increase the intelligence of the children, but, more modestly, to prevent its decline. Nineteen children participated. The program (offered free of charge to families) was carried out over three summers and lasted 10 weeks during each summer. Like Helen Dawe's program, the Early Training Project focused heavily on spoken language between children and teachers. The intent was to enhance the children's use of language, as in asking thoughtful questions and forming precise verbal expressions. Self-regulatory functions were exercised by helping children to develop persistence and the ability to delay gratification. Mothers were trained in the same strategies that the teachers used so that children's exposure to the precise use of language extended to the home. The Early Training Project had measurable positive effects: Participating children gained a 9-point IQ advantage over matched controls. The 9-point IQ advantage was maintained for several years, even though the average for both groups declined over time.

These results are not uncommon. Other cognitively intensive preschool programs have likewise produced a cognitive advantage that lasted long after the program ended. More typically, though, the advantage of participating children gradually faded such that, eventually, the IQ profiles of participants were no different from those of the controls. Overall, then, program findings tended to be mixed. The most effective preschool programs showed ongoing cognitive benefits: When participating children were compared against matched controls, the IQ advantage could reach 15 to 20 points. Differences of this magnitude are remarkable and would be very consequential if they could be maintained during the school years. Yet even a very good preschool experience might not be sufficient to set a child on a permanent trajectory toward academic success. The possibility that program effects will fade is not too surprising: If the child's experience is important during the preschool years, then it will *continue* to be important once schooling begins. To repeat a theme expressed earlier, the quality of experience is relevant and consequential to intellectual development through every stage of life.

Among the best known of the small, intensive preschool programs is the Milwaukee Project. So important is the project that it has been called the "high water mark of environmentalist accomplishment."[74] The Milwaukee Project spanned the range of preschool years, from infancy to primary school entry. Poverty had left a mark on participating families: Mothers of participating children had IQs of 75 or less.[75] Like the other programs that we have considered, the Milwaukee Project focused on children's language development and concentrated on maintaining high levels of intellectual interaction between children and their teachers. In advancing children's thinking through language, teachers commonly posed open-ended questions as well as helped children to engage in problem solving and logical thinking. The main goal was not to raise the intelligence of children, but simply to prevent its decline—that is, to help children maintain pace with their more advantaged peers.

At first, the Milwaukee Project did not produce evidence of differences between treatment and control groups. After the first few years of the project, however, the cognitive trajectories of treatment and control children diverged dramatically, eventually indicating a 25-IQ point advantage for participating children.[76] Some intriguing data showed that the children enrolled in the project were not the only beneficiaries. Positive cognitive effects were also detected among siblings and neighborhood children. This finding was remarkable—somehow cognitive enrichment had spread to nonparticipants through some unidentified means, whether through peer interactions or through the mediation of parents or other adults.

The Milwaukee Project has been controversial, no doubt resulting in part from the startling gains made by participating children.[77] Some criticism was leveled against the researchers for the lack of detail provided about the research design and for the inordinate delays in providing specifics about the treatment to the research community. A more pointed critique concerned whether the treatment and control children were comparable at the start of the project. The question of comparability focused on rather arcane details about the measured body lengths of the infants at birth. What bothered some critics was not that children in the two groups differed in their average body lengths, but rather in the variability of lengths. Control children displayed somewhat greater variability, which in the opinion of some critics called into question whether the summary findings could be trusted.

Later, when Milwaukee Project children were tracked through their school years, the children continued to manifest positive effects. As a group, children who participated in the Milwaukee Project as preschoolers achieved higher scores on tests of cognitive ability during their school years. In comparison to controls, they were more academically successful even years after the program ended. Despite possible flaws in its study design, the Milwaukee Project still represents to many readers a very potent example of how an intensive cognitive intervention can have lasting effects on at-risk children. The Milwaukee Project produced such dramatic results that it attracted attention far beyond the community of academic psychologists and early childhood educators. Federal policymakers, including members of Congress, also considered the relevance of the project to government programs. Ultimately, the project prompted massive federal investment into the largest of all compensatory preschool programs, Head Start.

Head Start is a program that directs federal funds for the purpose of establishing preschool programs for children living in impoverished neighborhoods. Like the small-scale preschool interventions we have already considered, Head Start sprang from rising optimism during the 1960s that the government could combat poverty through targeted policies and programs. Head Start was a key element in President Lyndon Johnson's vision of a Great Society in which poverty was battled with the financial backing of the US government and with the intellectual resources of American scientists and citizens. Since that time, despite a somewhat mixed reputation, Head Start has reached millions of children.

Head Start was offered to preschoolers during the year just prior to school entry. The hope was that enrichment at this crucial juncture would translate to more effective learning when participating children entered school. Researchers made comparisons with matched control children and particularly monitored their comparative progress during the elementary school grades. Initially, Head Start seemed to be working extraordinarily well. Participating children showed significant cognitive growth by the end of the project year, displaying a 9-point IQ advantage over matched controls as well as a better understanding of elementary math concepts and foundational reading skills.[78] Unfortunately, the effects of Head Start faded rapidly during the first few years of school. While in first grade, Head Start children still displayed a measurable advantage over control children in their ability to learn, but by second and third grades those advantages were no longer detectable. The early gains of Head Start children had dissipated rapidly, an all-too-common pattern referred to as "fade-out."[79]

Head Start's disappointing findings of rapidly fading gains led to further analyses in which enduring boosts in cognitive functioning were documented. Field researchers found that the cognitive effects of Head Start varied somewhat by geography: Effects were comparatively large in urban communities in the southern states.[80] Even so, the overall pattern held: Initial cognitive gains were modest and tended to taper off during the first few years of elementary school. For this reason, Head Start disappointed many observers who had hoped that participants would experience long-term benefits. At its inception, Head Start presented what seemed like a marvelous possibility: If at-risk preschool children were simply provided with high-quality environments—rich in linguistic interaction, nutritious food, and medical care—they might be launched on a stable upward trajectory through the school years. Instead, Head Start children were advantaged only temporarily. Differences between participants and nonparticipants reduced to zero after only a few years. The "fade-out" phenomenon quenched what was probably unwarranted optimism that a well-funded, large-scale program could redress the cognitive effects of poverty with one masterstroke.[81] On the other hand, Head Start also taught a valuable lesson to its proponents: The preschool years are not necessarily more important than later years in the child's development.

Part of the difficulty in judging the results from Head Start is that the program was not focused solely on children's intellectual development. The goal of cognitive growth was only one of many program components. During the 1960s, other programs for preschoolers focused more directly on children's intellectual growth and produced much more impressive results. We examined a few of these in the preceding paragraphs. When compared to Head Start, these so-called boutique programs were tiny in scale and entailed extraordinary levels of effort and commitment from all project participants—children, teachers, and parents. Several such programs resulted in sizeable and durable cognitive benefits to participating children.[82]

RAISING THE INTELLIGENCE OF SCHOOL-AGE CHILDREN

The earliest programs for enhancing intellectual skills trace back to roughly 1900 and to Alfred Binet himself. When Binet was tasked by the education leaders of belle époque Paris with finding a way to measure students' intellectual capabilities, he was not deterministic: He did not believe that those capabilities were fixed, even for those children whose intellectual development was very significantly delayed. In a strong sign of faith in the plasticity of the human intellect, Binet designed a program of exercises that he called "mental orthopedics." The comparison with physical orthopedics was direct. Binet proposed that "just as physical orthopedics correct a curvature of the thoracic spine, mental orthopedics straighten, cultivate, fortify such mental abilities as attention, memory, perception, judgment, the will."[83]

Binet's program of mental orthopedics consisted of a year of training exercises that were not tied to any particular academic subject; they could be practiced in the school or at home. The exercises included a memory development activity involving a board with objects glued to the surface. After viewing the board for five seconds, children were asked to name as many objects as they could remember. Another activity was intended to develop self-regulation. When "playing statue," the teacher signaled the children to stop all activity and freeze. Periods of immobility were gradually increased from just a few seconds to one minute over the course of the training year. In addition to training memory and self-regulation, Binet's program of mental orthopedics taught children observation skills, perception, imagination, analysis, and judgment. Binet reported that his program was effective: By his own account, after one year of participation the children's school performance had advanced by two years.[84]

In recent decades, one of the most impressive intelligence-enhancing projects was a short-lived initiative called Project Intelligence.[85] Conducted in Venezuela in the early 1980s, Project Intelligence was the brainchild of the government's designated minister of intelligence, Luis Machado. Machado's energies as a cabinet minister were focused on achieving an astonishing vision—raising the intelligence of Venezuelan youth. Machado had a plan. He secured the financial support of his government along with the assistance of some of the top cognitive scientists and intelligence theorists in the world, including scholars at Harvard and the Boston-based think tank BBN.[86]

Project Intelligence was based on curriculum units designed for seventh grade students. The intervention was rather modest because its design had significant practical constraints. In particular, it had to be accommodated within the normal school agenda of ongoing instruction in reading, mathematics, and the other school subjects. The curriculum units developed for Project Intelligence were studied three times per week for a total of 56 lessons over the course of the year. The lessons emphasized thinking skills, including reasoning, the analysis of language, problem solving, decision making, hypothesis generation, and inventive thinking.

The 460 participating seventh grade students made measurable IQ gains—as much to 6 IQ points depending on the test—by the end of the school year.[87] In comparison to a control group of peers, they also demonstrated superior design and problem-solving skills. One project investigator, Richard Herrnstein, later a coauthor of *The Bell Curve*, summarized the effects of Project Intelligence by noting that "the change in behavior that resulted from this really rather modest intervention... was profound and dramatic."[88, 89] Unfortunately, Project Intelligence did not last long. A change in the Venezuelan government spelled the end of Mr. Machado's term as minister of intelligence, along with his bold plan. Nonetheless, Project Intelligence remains a vivid historical precedent: It showed that a government can take the idea of learnable intelligence seriously and can allocate its resources to mount a high quality program to pursue a unique vision for its citizens: the enhancement of intelligence.

Several other programs have been designed to boost cognitive development among school-age children. One such program is Feuerstein's Instrumental Enrichment. Conceived by Israeli psychologist Reuven Feuerstein, Instrumental Enrichment was born in the aftermath of World War II. Feuerstein, then a young psychologist working in Geneva, was recruited to test the children of Holocaust victims. The purpose was to understand the specific reasons traumatized children performed lower than expected on cognitive tests and what could be done to remediate them. When Feuerstein tested the children, he formed two powerful and lasting impressions that guided his subsequent work.[90] The first was what he called dynamic assessment. Feuerstein noted that at the beginning of testing sessions the performance of children was lackluster but that during the course of testing performance began to improve. In fact, the children's thinking seemed to become sharper while testing was under way. This implied that the object of testing, the psychological construct measured by the test, was not a static entity as traditionally assumed, but was instead a moving target that changed as assessment took place. This view of testing, which acknowledges that the child's ability can shift while testing is in progress, is what Feuerstein called dynamic assessment.

Feuerstein's second discovery while testing the Holocaust children was related to the first principle of dynamic assessment. Feuerstein knew that any learning that occurred during testing was not encouraged by the standardized testing conditions in which a child works alone in silence. Rather, dynamic gains arose most pointedly when Feuerstein interacted with the child during the testing session. Of course, Feuerstein did not tell the child the answers to the questions. The interaction was instead akin to sensitive coaching—focusing the child's attention, encouraging persistence, and providing feedback. Feuerstein called this form of interaction "mediated learning." The concept rejects learning as a strictly solo enterprise. Instead, it recognizes the powerful role of social interaction in learning, and in particular the tremendous importance of a skillful teacher in promoting the intellectual growth of a pupil. Though the idea is strongly reminiscent of Vygotsky's theory, Feuerstein maintained that he developed the principle of mediated learning independently.

These two principles—dynamic assessment and mediated learning—are the cornerstones of Feuerstein's program. Together they affirm that a child's broad cognitive ability—his or her intelligence—is not a static entity but a malleable skill set, especially in the context of skilled social interactions with a capable teacher or parent. Even when children appear not to exhibit much growth in their intellectual powers, over time they can gain the capacity for growth. In the language of Feuerstein's unmitigated optimism, even a child's *modifiability* is modifiable.

In Feuerstein's program, the full potential of cognitive modifiability cannot be realized with the use of assessments alone. The child must also be trained to develop intellectual skills, especially those skills that initially are weakest and those that pose barriers to further progress. Hence, another component of Feuerstein's program is a curriculum of cognitive exercises called Instrumental Enrichment, which is incidentally also the name of his program. The exercises utilize a series of paper-and-pencil tasks to help students sharpen specific aspects of the intellect. The activities force participants to attend to detail, focus their attention over an extended period of time, and detect patterns in abstract materials. When they face complex problems, children are taught not to attempt random or haphazard solutions, but to seek solutions through systematic exploration. The exercises, engaged under the supervision of a skilled mediator, also teach children to persist when they encounter difficulty.

Reuven Feuerstein's Instrumental Enrichment has been applied largely, though not exclusively, to students who have learning difficulties. Its primary purpose has not been to enhance intelligence in mainstream populations. Nonetheless, when applied to normative populations of teenagers and military recruits, Instrumental Enrichment has produced cognitive gains corresponding to about 9 IQ points.[91] Some data also support Feuerstein's hypothesis of divergent effects, which refers to the intriguing possibility that cognitive enhancements establish a new intellectual trajectory.[92] The idea is that a powerful intellectual experience can send the learner on a long-term track of growth over time. If the hypothesis of divergent effects is correct, a cognitive advantage actually grows in successive years such that the trend lines of participants and nonparticipants continue to diverge even after the program ends.

Unlike Instrumental Enrichment, a project carried out in Croatia focused instead on gifted students. The curriculum, devised by a high school teacher and researcher named Radivoy Kvashchev, was designed to enhance creative problem-solving skills among high-ability high school students.[93] Kvashchev found that his curriculum raised the measured intelligence of high school students the equivalent of 6 to 8 IQ points, with gains in both fluid and crystallized intelligence. The enhancements were found not only on tests; gains transferred to solving practical problems, such as how to feed a growing population.

RAISING THE INTELLIGENCE OF ADULTS

A significant body of research on enhancing the intelligence of adults has been conducted among the elderly. This population focus is quite sensible: Older people are most at risk for declines in cognitive functioning and typically have more discretionary time to devote to activities that may enhance their intellectual abilities. One such intervention was the Cognitive Training Study, a component of the Seattle Longitudinal Study of cognitive development in adulthood.[94] Investigators trained 228 participants, whose average age was 73 years, on spatial ability and inductive reasoning. The result was substantial improvement in intellectual functioning: Targeted abilities were restored to their cognitive performance levels of approximately a decade earlier.

The Cognitive Training Study produced improvements even among participants who earlier had experienced cognitive decline. The gains were long lasting, extending at least seven years out from the study period.[95] In cases where the benefits of cognitive training were later lost, follow-up training sessions showed that, even 14 years after the original training, gains could be reestablished.[96] Those retraining effects were found for both men and women, as well as in participants whose cognitive levels remained stable in the intervening years. The Training Study was subsequently replicated twice, with each replication involving close to 200 participants. The training studies showed that cognitive gains transferred to new measures of the targeted abilities—spatial ability and inductive reasoning—but not to cognitive abilities that were not trained.

DOES COGNITIVE ENHANCEMENT WORK?

A wide variety of projects designed to raise intelligence have been conceptualized and carried out, and many have obtained measurable success. Organized to promote cognitive functioning over the entire life span—from infancy to old age—these programs have produced positive effects that translated to real gains in IQ. The typical range of effects is on the order of 10 to 20 IQ points. Gains of this magnitude have significant consequences, especially at the so-called tails of a distribution. Imagine a bell-shaped curve that shifts upward one standard deviation—15 IQ points. With a shift this large, the number of people with an IQ of 120 or more would be multiplied several times. Equally significant, representation at the low end of the distribution, those with IQs of 80 or less, would also be reduced dramatically. A shift of 15 points, when applied to a large population, would greatly expand its collective capacity for complex, abstract, and creative thought. At the same time, it would reduce the numbers of people at risk for poor decision-making or inadequate coping skills that might predispose them to poverty, crime, or other unfavorable life circumstances.

The audacious and inspiring goal of raising human intelligence is not yet widely appreciated as achievable. With the exception of Head Start, cognitive enhancement programs remain obscure. Programs that demonstrate the feasibility of raising intelligence are generally known only by a small and somewhat insular community of psychologists. Because data from these programs are tucked away in technical journals and scholarly books, the imagination of the broader public has not yet been captured. For most people, the term "learnable intelligence" remains more nonsensical than inspiring—an oxymoron, a contradiction in terms. If the projects we reviewed were less obscure, a greater awareness of their successes could build momentum toward more effective interventions in the future. They could inspire a collective vision for a more intelligent society.

What are the limits to this vision? The documented effects of cognitive enhancement programs might suggest an upper bound on their power to increase intelligence. One way to interpret the results is that gains of 10 or

20 IQ points show the potential of early-stage programs. Future programs, with deeper theoretical grounding, could be more powerful. Historically, attempts to increase intelligence have been based primarily on educated guesses about the most important building blocks of intelligence. For example, many preschool programs were language-focused—a good bet for enhancing intelligent functioning. The centerpiece of the child's experience was rich and extended linguistic interaction with adults as well as with other children. Other programs, such as Instrumental Enrichment, exercised children's ability to stay focused even when tasks became difficult or confusing.

Although many programs produced sizeable cognitive gains, most were not based on a strong theory of which elements of intellectual life are both tied to measured intelligence and responsive to treatment. Programs built firmly around recent research could be much more effective than those of the past. That is because recent research has revealed more clearly the key components of intelligent cognition. Not only are the building blocks of human intelligence better understood than ever before, research has shown that many of those components can improve substantially with practice. In the language of psychologists, the components of intelligence are *trainable*.

TOWARD A VISION OF LEARNABLE INTELLIGENCE

The historical legacy of cognitive interventions is that the term "learnable intelligence" is meaningful. The human intellect can be enhanced through well-designed programs, and the resulting heightened capability applies broadly across intellectual pursuits. Intelligence truly can be upgraded, and not just within a narrow collection of skills or for the short term. The effects of interventions have sometimes extended to intellectual achievements even years after the program officially ended. Recent research adds to the legacy of successful programs by giving us even better ideas on how to raise measured intelligence. Findings include the exciting discovery that key parameters of the mind—especially working memory capacity—once presumed to be unalterable are, in fact, not. We now know, as psychologist Richard Mayer puts it, that "intellectual ability can be taught."[97]

Learnable intelligence is not a baseless fantasy. Cognitive enhancement programs constitute credible proof that the deliberate enhancement of intelligence is not just possible: It has the potential to transform society with wide-open consequences for individual well-being and collective prosperity. Where does that put us? The first systematic attempts to raise intelligence were carried out in the 1960s. Now, half a century later, we have the basis for much more powerful interventions. Given the extended record of data, theory, and experience on how to teach intelligence, we face an important choice. Will we use that base of experience to launch a sustained effort, guided by research, to raise the intelligence of the human population? Do we have the imagination and the will to pursue higher levels of intelligence in ourselves and among our fellow citizens?

CHAPTER 7

The Superstructure of Effectiveness

The skyline of Manhattan is noticeably uneven. The city's tallest skyscrapers are located at midtown, where the Empire State Building rises, as well as in lower Manhattan, home of Wall Street, Battery Park, and the site of the fallen World Trade Center. Between midtown and the south end the building heights slump significantly, creating a saddle contour between the taller structures in the north and the south. The profile of building heights on the Manhattan skyline is no accident: The maximum height of buildings on the north–south axis is a direct function of the depth of bedrock underneath. The tallest buildings are tall because they can be—they are founded on the most geologically stable sections of rock offered by Manhattan Island.

The implied rule is simple: Maximum building height is proportional to the depth of anchoring in a foundation. Applied to our lives, intelligence is a foundation. It has no great significance of its own; its value is that it provides a substructure of intellectual readiness that makes a life of achievement possible. The point of laying a foundation is to build something significant on top of it. In life, we can pursue achievements commensurate with the underlying foundation. The distinction here is between *substructure*, which is below ground, and *superstructure*, which is visible and most directly useful. When a powerful base of intellectual readiness is allied with effective character, we have a substructure that is a suitable base for building the superstructure of an effective life—one prepared to solve problems, exercise wisdom, and exhibit creativity.

Through research, we have gained many insights into the most important components of intelligence, arguably the unrivaled substructure for building an effective life. For simplicity's sake, we can think of that substructure as consisting of fluid and crystallized intelligence. We already know a lot about these two factors. Fluid intelligence is the intellectual capacity that allows us to adapt to changing circumstances; crystallized intelligence is our personal reserve of knowledge acquired over time. Fluid and crystallized intelligence are fantastically powerful resources to engage the world successfully. They must be as strong as possible.

Intelligence is a powerful resource, but it is not fully sufficient. We know that other aspects of individual style, value, and commitments also play important roles in promoting a successful life. For now, let's call that collection of personal qualities "effective character." If we believe that character combined with intelligence is a more complete picture of what it takes to be effective, we are led to a simple yet telling model. The *combination* of fluid intelligence, crystallized intelligence, and effective character is the most powerful trio of personal traits for predicting, as well as facilitating, high achievement.

AN EQUATION FOR EFFECTIVENESS

The productive teaming of intelligence and character presents a simple equation for 21st-century effectiveness:

Effectiveness = Fluid intelligence + Crystallized intelligence + Effective character

We can say quite a bit more about these three components. First, they are all important predictors of success in essential contexts—school, the workplace, and the broader life arena. Second, they are not static traits dictated by DNA. If they were, they would hold theoretical interest but little or no practical value. Fortunately, these vital traits are alterable through experience. Their pliability implies that enhancing the essential ingredients of effectiveness is within the reasonable ambitions of the individual and the collective vision of humanity. We can *choose* to become more effective people by building the personal qualities that underlie success.

Each of the three components is, to a degree, still mysterious. Research will reveal their nature more fully with time. But even if their nature remains to be explicated sometime in the future, their core essences can be expressed plainly now. That means we can explore what it takes to develop these three cornerstones of personal effectiveness.

Fluid Intelligence

Fluid intelligence is strongly associated with problem solving in new and challenging contexts. When we face situations that require us to adapt rather than to rely on learned routines, we must think fluidly. This work of fluid intelligence is deeply cognitive. It means dealing with patterns of complex information, taking in a sea of data that may be bewildering at first, and then identifying the most important patterns. Psychologists call this inductive reasoning—mentally extracting meaning and structure from complex and chaotic arrays. Once the key patterns are understood, they can be applied productively. It's not hard to see that this ability is crucial in a society that is complex and information-rich. We absolutely need to be able to make sense of our environment and to separate what is important from what is incidental.

Since the time of Spearman, inductive reasoning has been known to be very closely associated with intelligence. Later research, in turn, showed that inductive reasoning and fluid intelligence are closely aligned. To simplify greatly, think of it this way: The heart of general intelligence is fluid intelligence, and the heart of fluid intelligence is inductive reasoning. Recall that in the hierarchical model, fluid intelligence is closer to general intelligence, or *g*, than any other factor. Inductive reasoning, in turn, is fluid intelligence at its core: Understanding how new information applies to current problems, and then applying that understanding to complete the task at hand. Fluid intelligence makes us adaptive agents in the world, ready to comprehend and act positively in any situation. The theme of adaptability runs through all major theories of intelligence.[1] People who can adapt to changing circumstances avoid becoming obsolete. They can stay abreast of social and technological developments; not only can they keep up with change, they can capitalize on it.

Fluid intelligence has very practical manifestations. Among older adults, especially, the ability to succeed in everyday tasks, such as completing government forms, understanding medication dosages, and reading maps, is correlated to measures of fluid intelligence.[2] To thrive over a lifetime requires ongoing adaptation, which entails the ability to set aside anxieties while attending to new trends and learning about them with interest. As people confront change externally they are transformed internally. Adaptation occurs along the changing interface of personal qualities and environmental opportunities and demands.[3] To thrive during times of rapid change requires a willingness to explore new ideas and tools through middle age and the later years. Seen this way, fluid intelligence is what allows us to approach the world afresh through every season of life.

To cultivate fluid intelligence in the school and in the workplace means to adopt the proper attitude—that is, to regard problem solving as indispensable to each person's intellectual work. Changing the school curriculum so that it cultivates fluid intelligence will not be easy. Traditionally, schools have placed little emphasis on fluid intelligence, but instead have focused on crystallized intelligence—the intellectual resource of knowledge in structured form. The reasons for concentrating on crystallized intelligence are fairly clear. The substance of crystallized intelligence is for the most part explicit, objective, and easily tested. A student's understanding of Newton's laws or the key battles of the Civil War is relatively easy to teach and test, at least compared to the more elusive objective of teaching a student to think flexibly when facing new problems. Many educators now affirm the importance of problem solving—and this is a start—but some would be hard pressed to define problem solving, let alone teach it.

A second reason for greater emphasis on crystallized intelligence in schools is that the exact substance of fluid intelligence is maddeningly elusive. That's because what counts as a manifestation of fluid intelligence depends on the individual person. For example, knowing how to tie shoelaces would not normally be problem solving, but for a very young child it could be. Similarly, the application of Newton's laws to designing a rocket might well constitute problem solving, and therefore draw upon fluid intelligence, for a high school physics student. But for an aeronautical engineer, such problems may be so practiced that their solution is straightforward and algorithmic—more an application of crystallized intelligence than fluid intelligence. We must conclude that whether any given problem elicits fluid intelligence is strongly conditioned by the intellectual trajectory of the individual person. The limits of adaptation to innovative problems lie at the edge of competence and experience, which varies not only from person to person but also over time. Fluid intelligence is a moving target.

Fluid intelligence is difficult to teach, but fluidity is so pivotal to the prepared mind that it simply must be embraced as an essential outcome of school experience. A first step might be to incorporate an understanding of fluid intelligence into the discourse of education so that teachers, students, and principals jointly understand how vital it is to a learner's ability to think and act intelligently. As schools expand and shift their mission to include the cultivation of fluid intelligence, honest acknowledgments can be made about the difficulty of teaching and testing the ability. The process might not be 100% efficient. Even so, a change of focus is necessary from the almost exclusive concentration on teaching and testing crystallized intelligence.

Yet another impediment stands in the way of teaching fluid intelligence in schools. It has to do with the potentially threatening emotional experiences that the exercise of fluid intelligence can generate. Keep in mind that the application of fluid intelligence during problem solving always involves uncertainty. That is because the context for intelligent thought is the unfamiliar—unfamiliar conditions, rules, and solution paths. Even the intended goal of a problem can be imperfectly specified. Most threatening of all, success is uncertain. This is different from the uncertainty entailed in crystallized intelligence, which might arise from the failure to remember a rule, fact, or concept—or the failure to apply those known entities correctly. By contrast, the uncertainty that arises during problem solving is more pronounced and potentially much more disorienting.

Confusion, uncertainty, and the possibility of failure all invite anxiety and self-doubt. This is reason enough to dissuade many learners and teachers from wading into the troubled waters of fluid intelligence. Those waters are neither familiar nor emotionally safe—at least compared to the homey conceptual worlds of crystallized intelligence. It's not only that the anxieties provoked by the exercise of fluid intelligence are uncomfortable, they also bump up against the traditional values of schooling that prize confidence, efficiency, and error-free performance. None of these standards is guaranteed. In fact, all three are threatened because by its very nature problem solving does not inspire full confidence of success, nor is it efficient, and the path toward a solution is almost never without error. All this means that long-standing values of education may actually stand in the way of accepting problem solving as a legitimate form of learning activity in schools. To accept the cultivation of fluid intelligence as an important educational goal means first legitimizing the ego and emotional states that inevitably accompany problem solving.

A transformation of values and assumptions is equally needed in the workplace, if the work setting is to be a laboratory for the growth and application of fluid intelligence. Such a transformation is hardly optional. The need to innovate is now an imperative for the public and private sectors alike. Problem solving, not algorithmic thinking, is the intellectual flywheel of the world economic system. Companies face a constant requirement to think differently with emerging concepts and tools rather than yesterday's ideas or products. Success hinges on the regular application of fluid intelligence taken to a very high level. The globalization of commerce, particularly in the high-tech arena, makes the imperative to innovate urgent and pressing. That's why every community, company, and nation needs a greater supply of fluid intelligence.

Crystallized Intelligence

When considered alongside fluid intelligence, crystallized intelligence is clearly the counterpart resource. It consists of knowledge gained through study and experience, whether in schools or elsewhere. In many situations, crystallized understanding is more immediately relevant than fluid adaptivity. Through knowledge we have acquired in the past we often know exactly what to do in the present. Crystallized intelligence is the dividend of focused experience, much of it acquired during formal study in schools and universities. Crystallized knowledge is also the product of long years of immersion in a field of work. At higher levels of study and experience, crystallized intelligence evolves into expertise, the honed and polished skill set that is foundational to world-class capability.

We already know quite a bit about how to increase crystallized intelligence. Schools and universities tend to structure courses and programs as if building crystallized intelligence is the institution's primary mission. The image of education as a pipeline for the transmission of knowledge is deeply ingrained. Crystallized intelligence, the aspect of intelligence concerned with the acquisition of structured knowledge, is the mainstay of the world's educational systems. In an ideal world, schools might give equal attention to fostering fluid intelligence—and perhaps in the future they will do so. In the short term, the emphasis on crystallized intelligence—structured knowledge in verbal or other symbolic form—is almost certain to continue. This is not entirely bad; without question, crystallized intelligence is important. Although we can acknowledge that fluid intelligence lies closer to the heart of general intelligence and is essential to innovation, crystallized intelligence is a necessary and potent resource for solving real-world problems. It is impossible to imagine how doctors, architects, and engineers could do their jobs without the vast corpus of specialized knowledge that defines their professions. Fluid intelligence is important to these professions too, but competence in nearly every specialized field rests on a substantial base of crystallized intelligence.

Books and libraries are likewise aligned with the goals of developing intelligence in crystallized form, as are the vast resources of the Internet. Reading is a tremendously effective means of developing crystallized intelligence. That is because the language of books differs from the language that characterizes everyday conversation. Text is more formal, precise, and complex. It must be so because books do not present the social cues and understandings people share when speaking face-to-face. Authors write for a wider audience whose background knowledge is variable. Without the real-time cues that signal understanding, such as a nod or eye contact, the writer must strive to be complete and clear. The language of books, nonfiction especially, presents an extended discourse in which a large body of information can be conveyed in a marvelously coherent structure.[4] Such discourse patterns have almost no equivalent in everyday speech.

Something else occurs, or can occur, through exposure to text. Text is a natural springboard to critical thinking. Critical thinking, like problem solving, is one of those cognitive terms that has immediate acceptance as a desirable goal, even without a clear sense of what it actually means. Fortunately, critical thinking can be defined with the same economy as problem solving. Recall that problem solving is the pursuit of a goal when the path to that goal is uncertain. Critical thinking, a complementary process, is the evaluation of ideas for their quality, particularly in judging whether those ideas make sense. What problem solving is to fluid intelligence, critical thinking is to crystallized intelligence. Both cognitive processes make for the high-quality cognitions that express their respective forms of intelligence.

One reason critical thinking is so important to crystallized intelligence is that elaborated collections of knowledge are inevitably imperfect. Knowledge is a human construction, after all. Every instance of trying to convey truth falls short of being fully sensible, coherent, or informative. Books and lectures can present a clear and evidenced line of reasoning, but they can easily veer off course to present jumbled and unfounded claims. Critical thinking makes it possible to separate poor reasoning from a tapestry of ideas that holds together, is backed by evidence, and is insightful. By thinking critically, a reader or listener can evaluate ideas for their quality. Written language is conducive to critical thinking because it is stable and explicit. Speech, by contrast, is evanescent. Written lines of reasoning can be pondered, discussed, dissected, and critiqued so that the reader can in some sense rise above the text, judge it, and keep the very best ideas— those that pass scrutiny.

The point here is not that the formal language of books is superior to everyday conversation. Formal language and informal language serve different purposes. Indeed, discourse that is fully abstract and academic has definite drawbacks. Formal language may fail to connect to the experience of readers and so lacks interest value, or personal meaning. That's why many educators believe that the forms of discourse most conducive to learning have a conversational aspect. Even in a large lecture hall, dialogue between a professor and students can provide feedback about whether students really understand, and can inject a human element into what would otherwise be a dry monologue. But in the course of knowledge building that forms the foundation of expertise, the formal dialogue of books and lectures has a vital role to play. When combined with more interpersonal forms of discourse—discussions, conversations, or just shooting the breeze—the chances of building a powerful base of crystallized knowledge are further increased.

Of course, books and lectures alone are not sufficient to build expertise. Becoming an expert requires massive investment of time aligned with long-term focused effort. This aspect of crystallized intelligence is too often ignored in schools. At the university, however, the long-term focused experience that paves the road to expertise is built into the structure of study, particularly when upper-division undergraduate education segues into graduate and professional school. Careers in technical fields—engineering, medicine, law, and science—typically follow a sequence of structured formal education and apprenticeship.[5] Expertise is gradually achieved through such concentrated and extended study. For students who are admitted to advanced study programs, eventual world-class proficiency is a credible possibility.

One weakness of our educational system is that schools are not structured to take advantage of what we know about how capable minds develop. We saw, for example, that the value systems of schooling are often antagonistic to the development of fluid intelligence. The same applies to the cultivation of crystallized intelligence as the sort of deep understanding that leads toward expertise. If fluid and crystallized intelligence are vital to the future of the world, then we must face these disjunctures with education squarely. Institutional schooling is in deep need of reform. But reform means more than doing the same things better; it must mean doing things differently, even to the extent of rethinking the basic purposes of education. We rightly value educational programs that enhance the skills of teachers and ensure that schools are equitably resourced. Yet fundamental change means more than fine-tuning the current system. It means rebuilding the entire enterprise.

Effective Character

Fluid and crystallized intelligence are tremendous resources for anyone who wishes to live an effective life in a complex world. Among measurable human traits, both forms of intelligence are remarkably consistent predictors of success. In almost every arena of human engagement—dealing with crises, managing interpersonal conflict, planning for the future, and so on indefinitely—intelligence is an extremely useful resource. Yet for all its impressive relevance across life contexts, intelligence in its various forms has definite limitations.

IQ does not explain everything. Let's remember that the correlation between IQ and success outcomes averages roughly $r = 0.5$. This means that about half of the measurable variation in life success *cannot* be ascribed to intelligence, at least as measured by IQ tests. Perhaps some fraction of individual variation in success is random and can never be explained. Some people may be fabulously successful for reasons that are quite idiosyncratic and that will always defy explanation. Yet another possibility—the one we will now explore—is that personal qualities other than intelligence also contribute vitally to a successful life. I refer here to what is commonly called character. The importance of character seems obvious, upon reflection. Research, as well as common sense, tells us that intelligence is never enough to ensure success. To explore with any precision what is intended by the term "character," we must delve into the fascinating and profoundly important realm of personality theory.

People are complicated. Consider the huge variation in personality among your friends, family members, acquaintances, and coworkers. Personality is fantastically complex, composed of dozens of dimensions. Fortunately, the plethora of personality dimensions cluster together into five major factors. Among psychologists, these are the "Big Five" factors of personality; they provide great structural simplification.[6] The Big Five are extraversion, conscientiousness, intellectual openness, agreeableness, neuroticism. You may already be familiar with one of the five major factors, extraversion, and its polar counterpart, introversion. Extraverted people are gregarious by nature and are energized in the presence of others; introverted people tend to draw strength from solitude.

The extraversion/introversion factor can affect performance. Extraverts, for example, tend to be fast on tasks that have a speed component. Extraversion is not always an advantage, however. Extraverts may be relatively impulsive and error-prone by giving preference to speed over accuracy. They may also give up more easily on long or difficult tasks. Adding further complexity, the relationship between extraversion and IQ changes over the life span. IQ and extraversion are positively correlated until the teen years, but then the correlation changes to slightly negative. One explanation for the shift is that introverted people tend to do better on tasks that require reflection and insight. The intellectual tasks of secondary school, as well as the self-discipline required for independent studying, may be better matched to an introverted personality. In principle, however, neither extraversion nor introversion is more desirable. Personality is unlike intelligence in this way. Intelligence and all other cognitive abilities are conceptualized as unidirectional—more is assumed to be better. Personality, on the other hand, is bidirectional and assumed to be value-neutral.[7] The combination of personality "settings" that define individuals—make each person distinct, not superior or inferior to others—at least in theory.

The truth is that the presumed neutrality of personality with respect to desirability and personal success may be more an assumption than a justified conclusion. Psychologists have found that certain personality factors play strong roles in determining achievement behavior in ways that are complementary to intelligence. Intelligence alone cannot determine the track of human effectiveness apart from considering the personality characteristics that describe how individual human beings interact with the world.[8] To prove the point, consider the trait that is probably the most important in its relationship to intelligence—the personality dimension known as *conscientiousness*.[9] A conscientious person consistently upholds standards of excellence. People high in conscientiousness are achievement-oriented, pursuing their goals though organized and sustained behavior. The highly conscientious person pays attention to detail, follows through when working independently, and persists in solving difficult problems. People who are conscientiousness cannot abide shoddy work; they get the job done properly and on time. Frequently, they rise above expectations to produce work of outstanding quality.

Conscientiousness is distinctively important for this reason: It is the personality dimension that is most predictive of success. Furthermore, it is not tapped at all by IQ tests. One interesting quality of conscientiousness is that its correlation with IQ is almost exactly zero.[10] A highly intelligent person might or might not be conscientious. Your own experience probably confirms the fact. Very intelligent people may well be lazy or unreliable; less intellectually capable people may display consistent attention to the quality of their work. This disjuncture plays out mathematically: Conscientiousness and intelligence are separate dimensions. Conscientiousness does not overlap with intelligence but instead adds its predictive power to that offered by IQ.

The magnitude of prediction is impressive: Conscientiousness is approximately equal to intelligence in its ability to predict workplace effectiveness. In fact, for predicting performance on the job, conscientiousness is the only human trait that rivals measured intelligence. When combined, IQ and conscientiousness predict workplace performance at about $r = .65$, which is quite a jump from the predictive power of IQ alone, $r = .50$.[11]

Conscientiousness is a strong predictor of worker performance across a broad range of job categories.[12] It is especially good, however, at predicting worker effectiveness in jobs that require personal initiative and autonomy.[13] The combined predictive power of conscientiousness and IQ, exciting though it is to psychometricians and psychologists, confirms what organizational managers have known for a very long time: The best workers are smart *and* conscientious.

The predictive function of conscientiousness is what makes this personality dimension especially important. Just as conscientiousness predicts worker effectiveness above and beyond IQ score, so conscientiousness also predicts students' academic achievement.[14] This predictive function holds, even controlling for academic ability as measured by SAT scores. The traits that compose conscientiousness are recognized by experts to be typical of gifted students. Alongside the cognitive characteristics of high IQ, creativity, and academic achievement, gifted students often exhibit high task commitment. Signs of task commitment include "the capacity for perseverance, determination, hard work, and dedicated practice"— aspects of performance that closely correspond to the personality trait of conscientiousness.[15] A related personal trait is self-discipline, which includes the ability to delay short-term pleasure for long-term gain. In a study of eighth-grade students, self-discipline was a more effective predictor of academic achievement—including school grades—than IQ scores.[16] Not only did self-discipline predict course grades, it also predicted improvement in grades when IQ and earlier school achievement were statistically controlled.

We must regard conscientiousness as a key element of effective character. But a second personality factor in the Big Five—intellectual openness—also plays an important role. People high in this personality dimension display curiosity, artistic sensitivity, flexible behavior, and the capacity to entertain unconventional attitudes. Intellectual openness is important because it is the personality factor that is most associated with intelligence, exhibiting correlations with IQ ranging from $r = 0.33$ to 0.45.[17, 18] People high in openness typically exhibit a strong motivation to learn, tend to be fascinated by the world around them, and pursue education with enthusiasm.

The correlation between IQ and intellectual openness is particularly interesting when we think about the conceptual separation we tend to make between IQ and personality traits. In theory, intelligence and personality are distinct, yet here we see a significant correlation between the two. Why? Perhaps the emotional and behavioral dispositions that define intellectual openness are compatible with experiences that promote intellectual growth. Whereas conscientiousness works side-by-side with intelligence to maximize performance in the workplace and other arenas, intellectual openness functionally precedes intellectual growth, supplying the personal qualities that motivate a person to gain knowledge through experience. The idea is that intellectual openness drives intelligence, which, when allied with conscientiousness, drives performance.

As two of the Big Five factors, conscientiousness and intellectual openness are major personality dimensions, or "superfactors," that encompass and summarize broad spans of personality traits. Along with being major personality dimensions, both are deeply implicated in human performance either directly or indirectly. The upshot is that personality traits, though nominally neutral in value, are not to be ignored. Personality ultimately matters in the expression of intelligence. Two people with identical IQ scores but very different personality profiles will no doubt think, feel, and act very differently. As with cognitive ability profiles, personality profiles make some environments more fitting and others less so. As we understand someone's personality, we gain insight into the kinds of situations in which they are best prepared to behave intelligently. Just as plants and animals are adapted to specific ecological niches, each of us, in theory, is best prepared to thrive in some environments but not others. To the extent that we understand which environments most closely match our profiles and seek them out, we do our best to live creatively and productively in our own optimal niches.

Matching personality to the environment is important, but is that the only option? We would have more freedom, it seems, if we could also shift personalities in a manner similar to the alteration of cognitive profiles. The question is whether personality can actually change. Like cognitive abilities, personality traits exhibit stability over long spans of time. Many of us have become reacquainted with old friends after many years, even decades, and found their personality characteristics to be remarkably stable. The observed stability of personality should not be taken as evidence that an individual's personality structure does not, or cannot, change. Personalities do change over time. Over the past several decades, for example, American college students have become much more extraverted.[19] Since the 1960s, students' average levels of extraversion have risen almost a standard deviation, possibly as an adaptation to greater family mobility or the increasing value placed on cooperation and teamwork in schools and in the workplace.

Although early theories assumed personality traits were highly stable, more recent theories have regarded personality as an expression of a person's developmental history. In particular, personality is formed as a person associates meaning with particular situations. Such meanings are learned and, potentially, unlearnable. This suggests that personality, like cognitive ability, is significantly a function of experience rather than fully dictated by DNA. Just as we must regard the assumption of fixed intelligence as a myth, so we must now set aside the belief that personality is forever fixed.[20]

Personality variation is widely regarded as a very positive feature of the human condition—after all, we need different kinds of people in the world. Perhaps that's why we often assume that personality is value-neutral—that variation in personality is just one instance of multifaceted human variability in height, eye color, body type, and a thousand other characteristics. Yet a total commitment to value neutrality is probably not defensible. Extreme introversion is debilitating, for example, as is the susceptibility to emotional turbulence associated with the personality dimension of neuroticism. That is one reason why personality change is so important. To reinterpret personality as modifiable is essential when we consider the desired effects of psychotherapy. A partial restructuring of personality may be one goal in the journey toward mental health.

Intelligence and personality do not operate in isolation; indeed, a case can be made that they always operate jointly. In everyday life, intelligent behavior draws on the intellectual readiness we call intelligence, as well as on preferences and patterns of feeling and expression we call personality. The intelligence-personality coalition works in tandem to produce behavior. I have used the term "effective character" to refer to those personality aspects that promote success. Effective character is, if you will, the "smart heart." Like fluid and crystallized intelligence, the elements of effective character, like personality traits generally, may be significantly malleable.[21] Through training in a context of shared commitments to excellence, effective character can be cultivated along with fluid and crystallized intelligence. The result is an upgrade of capability—it is intelligence *plus*. If intelligence and effective character—the best predictors of human effectiveness—are both susceptible to enhancement, then exciting possibilities open for individuals, communities, and all of humanity.

PUTTING THE EQUATION TO WORK

Let's return now to the big picture. Three personal factors combine to predict effectiveness in complex and dynamic environments. We can depict these three factors as expressing the foundation for effectiveness in a simple equation:

Effectiveness = Fluid intelligence + Crystallized intelligence + Effective character

The equation is intentionally simple. As such, it does not encompass the entire span of traits that contribute to and predict success in the world. Quite a bit of research shows that beliefs about one's own ability—variously called self-concept or self-efficacy beliefs—are also important. So are personal factors that go by the name of ego resiliency, the ability to exert just the right of amount of self-control over one's own behavior. Although the model is a simplification, it is not simplistic. The equation captures much of what the decades-long body of research tells us about the basis of success in multiple arenas of life, not just in academic realms. Each of the three factors is a potent resource for navigating a complex world. Its development is a major project worthy of the best efforts of schools, families, and communities. As each success factor develops, individuals enhance their readiness to immerse themselves in the modern world, to make important contributions, and to find their work fulfilling.

The equation presents a powerful formula for effectiveness in the 21st century. What is less obvious is that the equation can inspire us to think not only about the three basic factors, but also how those factors interact. As presented, the factors appear to be simply additive; in truth, however, they may be synergistic. For example, highly motivated individuals, those who would ordinarily score high on conscientiousness, are especially primed for achievement if they are also high in fluid and crystallized intelligence.[22] Another way of expressing the interactive qualities intrinsic to the success equation is that high status on one factor is probably not adequate. The three factors must work together to produce an effective life.

We can use the equation to understand, strategically, what components of intelligence must be targeted if we expect to see gains in effectiveness. Our subject matter is the edifice of effectiveness—the entire structure of success that includes the "hidden" substructure of intelligence and effective character, along with its superstructure—the visible manifestation of intelligence expressed in the things people create and the problems they solve. We will focus attention on perhaps the most striking manifestation of intelligence, expertise.

EXPERTISE

Expertise is one of the most sublime expressions of effectiveness in the world. The word *expertise* conveys very high levels of knowledge and skill in any area of study or performance. Experts are recognized in hundreds of domains: chess, cooking, molecular biology, musical performance, coaching, entrepreneurship, teaching, wine tasting, journalism, poetry, athletic performance, architecture, and law. In any domain, the person who is called "expert" displays a significant level of proficiency that may range from highly competent to world class. As a manifestation of intelligence, expertise is highly desirable. Experts are required by a complex society, and society in turn often compensates experts with recognition and monetary rewards. As a society, we need to promote expertise as a visible expression of intelligence.[23]

One way to gain insight into the nature of expertise is a bit counterintuitive. It requires shifting focus from human intelligence to machine intelligence, in particular by considering how artificial intelligence (AI) has developed in the 20th and 21st centuries. The basic goal of AI research is to program machines—normally, digital computers—to exhibit intelligent behavior. The most distal goal of AI can be said to create machines that exhibit intelligence in every important way, equal to or surpassing that of human beings. Invoking the *Star Wars* character menagerie, researchers have expressed the vision this way: "Building C3PO, or something very similar, could be said to be the ultimate goal of AI."[24]

There is more than one route to pursue machine intelligence. AI is sometimes modeled directly on human thought processes, but it can be based on a completely different logic. Early on, AI researchers tried to formulate general strategies—ways of solving problems that were so generic that they could be applied to virtually any complex activity, whether analyzing scientific data, playing championship chess, or solving challenging puzzles.[25] To a degree this approach worked: Generic AI programs were successful in a wide variety of domains. Eventually, though, these generic methods reached a plateau. It became obvious that to perform more intelligently, AI programs needed another resource: knowledge.

This insight precipitated a strategy shift in AI research. In theoretical terms, it meant changing the dominant resource of AI programs from coded fluid intelligence (generic problem-solving methods) to crystallized intelligence (specific knowledge). When AI programs could access large databases of domain knowledge, such as medical diagnostic information, they exhibited much higher levels of intelligent functioning. Of course, those gains were necessarily domain-specific: A medical diagnostic program was no good at playing chess. Still, the trade-off resulted in a net gain in performance. Rather than mimicking the all-purpose capabilities of Renaissance men, the most impressive AI programs imitated domain specialists—chess masters, radiologists, and astronomers. In other words, the best AI programs began to exhibit expertise.

Many pioneering AI researchers were also cognitive scientists who began to formulate theories of human expertise. One of those pioneers was the Nobel laureate Herbert Simon, a polymath who won the Nobel Prize in yet another field, economics. Based on his research in both AI and cognitive science, Herbert Simon reached a pivotal conclusion that affected both fields. Simon discovered that although domain experts benefit from adaptive brainpower, their essential resource is knowledge. Without a vast array of specialized knowledge, expertise was impossible.

To Herbert Simon and other cognitive scientists, the pivotal role of knowledge was clear in the game of chess. To casual observers, chess mastery appears to be an expression of pure intelligence, yet world-class chess players have enormous funds of knowledge at their disposal. That knowledge consists of thousands of board configurations and countless strategies specific to chess. To build this massive knowledge base, chess masters study historically important chess matches, learning from the insights and errors of other great chess players. Mastering this body of knowledge requires a time investment of thousands of hours.

By studying expertise in chess and in other fields, Herbert Simon estimated the quantity of knowledge required by a domain expert. Recall that in cognitive science, the fundamental unit of knowledge is a chunk, a meaningful unit of information. Simon estimated that an expert has access to approximately 50,000 "chunks," which refers to the number of identifiable patterns that compose an expert's knowledge base in a particular field. In medicine, chunks are technical concepts, disease symptoms, pharmaceuticals, side effects, surgical techniques, and so on. 50,000 chunks constitute a vast knowledge base, which rivals in magnitude the total vocabulary of a college graduate. An expert uses knowledge of such patterns to "see" problems and opportunities in the specialized area of study, whether chess, medicine, art, or architecture. By means of a large and expanding knowledge base, the expert is prepared to push skill to progressively higher levels, and through that skill to contribute to the larger society.

EXPERTS SEE THINGS DIFFERENTLY

While progressing toward expertise, novice learners do not simply accumulate knowledge as factoids—isolated bits of information. As knowledge grows it undergoes fundamental transformations. We can think of a chunk as a single object, word, or digit. But let's appreciate a crucial insight into what a chunk really is. The individual digits in a telephone number are often independent chunks, but what happens when you encounter a phone number with a familiar area code—say 202, 415, or 949? The meaning of "chunk" changes. A chunk is no longer a single digit, but rather three digits compressed into one cluster. When we become familiar with new information, the nature of a chunk is redefined as it begins to encompass what was once several independent chunks. The more complex unit is easily remembered, probably more easily than the previously unchunked digits because it imposes less of a load on working memory. The newly formulated chunk also has flexible complexity because it can be subdivided or "unpacked" into orderly internal units. In one deft move, chunking makes knowledge both simpler and more complex depending on the momentary need.

Chunking pays tremendous cognitive dividends. It may not be terribly important in trying to remember telephone numbers, especially if pencil and paper are handy, but it is crucial in the development of expertise in every conceivable field. Let's exemplify again with chess. For beginners, a natural chunk is a single chess piece, such as a pawn, rook, or king. Unlike novices, chess masters perceive the layout of the chessboard not as individual pieces but as clusters of recognizable patterns.[26] By "chunking" the layout, the current state of play can be understood not as overwhelmingly complex, but as simple. Therein lies the payoff. The resulting cognitive simplification means that relevant information will not overload the working memory of the chess master. Some working memory must be allocated to understanding the current state of play, but the simplification allowed by chunking reduces the overall burden to memory. The unused memory capacity can be use strategically. The residual capacity of working memory can be devoted to higher-level functions—weighing options, mounting defense strategies, and launching surprise attacks. By simplifying the problem through chunking, working memory is freed up to explore those creative and strategic aspects of play that make an expert fantastically capable.

Coaches in a variety of sports apply similar principles. Basketball coaches expect their players to master the fundamentals of dribbling, passing, and shooting. In isolation, the fundamentals of play will not make for a championship team. But if those basic skills are truly mastered, they will cease to impose a burden on the player's active attention. When the fundamentals are executed automatically, working memory is freed up to perceive in precise detail the dynamic state of play, to notice an opportunity, and to carry out a complex play that requires split-second coordination with teammates, along with contingencies for recovery if the play goes wrong.

Chess masters and basketball players are not the only beneficiaries of chunking. In every profession, craft, and serious pursuit, the repackaging of complexity into simplicity through chunking is the chief mechanism that propels the human mind to higher levels of proficiency. Across fields—auto repair, medicine, interior design, computer programming, musical composition, and classroom teaching—the cognitive simplicity achieved through the perception of recurring patterns called "chunks" allows skilled performance to build steadily over long stretches of time.

Chunking is hugely important to cognitive growth. This fact alone tells us that to define *learning* as simply the accumulation of knowledge is grossly simplistic, and that the counterpart process of chunking is at least equal in importance to the acquisition of knowledge. As the brain adapts to experience, fewer demands are placed on the controlling functions of the frontal cortex. Brain activation tends to shift to the posterior portions of the brain, away from the frontal cortex, as normal processing functions become executed automatically, with less effort, and with greater efficiency.[27] In fact, higher IQ subjects typically display relatively more activation in posterior portions of the brain, suggesting more efficient and less effortful processing.[28]

We have seen that chunking applies in a straightforward way to the formation of expertise in adults, but it also operates in the cognitive growth of children. Psychologist Robbie Case proposed a theory of child development that explains a child's rapidly developing intellect as underpinned significantly by chunking.[29] Chunking is key even to the development of very elementary skills, such as grasping a moving object. An infant may be able to track a moving toy visually or grasp it if the toy is still. What may be difficult, initially, is grasping a toy while it is moving. With experience, however, a new process ensues: The two simpler skills—visual tracking and grasping—combine, which allows the infant to watch, reach, and grasp a moving object. Two skills, originally independent, now form a unified pattern, which in turn becomes the basis for still more complex psychomotor performance. Chunking is also relevant to the cognitive development of older children. With experience, they learn to perceive and interpret patterns that go unnoticed by younger children, such as when an observable event has more than one possible cause.[30] The ability to perceive such complex patterns—to chunk one's environment—may appear to be quite passive, yet it forms the basis for steady intellectual growth and progressively effective behavior all along the path of human development.

Chunking is as crucial to the development of expertise as it is to a child's intellectual progress. In the expert, knowledge transforms in other important ways as well.[31] For example, knowledge becomes better *organized* over time, forming constellations of ideas that psychologists call schemas. Chess masters have very elaborate schemas for chess; physicians have large and highly organized knowledge bases in the schemas that define their medical specialties. Schema development can also entail improvements in the *quality* of knowledge as errors are corrected and assumptions that were once held with certainty are reopened to question. As schemas grow and reorganize, knowledge becomes more organically interconnected while retaining an open quality—an intellectual raw edge that is receptive to new insights. Fundamental transformations of knowledge—or radical schema restructuring—can completely change the way a person sees the world. Occasionally, schema transformations spawn intellectual and artistic revolutions. The luminaries of science—Newton, Darwin, and Einstein—and of other domains—Aristotle, da Vinci, Mozart, and Picasso—vividly illustrate the point.

CHUNKING AND SCHOOL LEARNING

The cognitive repackaging of information that we call chunking is vitally important to school learning. This is perhaps clearest when children learn to read. Consider what reading requires at the most basic level. The most elementary units of written text are the individual letters that compose a word. A beginning reader learns to "sound out" a word, such as *cat*. The three letters in *cat* arbitrarily connect to basic sound elements of speech called phonemes. The letter "c" represents a particular sound, as do "a" and "t." The beginning reader must learn to map the alphabetic squiggles on a printed page or computer screen to simple sounds—an easy task for experienced readers but not at all easy by nature.[32] In fact, the learning disability that we call dyslexia, in which children or adults experience unusual difficulty in learning to read, often traces to problems in mastering the letter-sound correspondences called the alphabetic principle.[33]

With experience, most children learn to chunk each letter in the alphabet with its referent sound or sounds so one quickly evokes the other.[34] Reading requires that the symbol translates to the sound. In writing, the order reverses: the sound translates to the letter. But even when letter-sound mapping becomes facile and instantaneous, this is not enough; a capable reader must do much more. Rarely will a proficient reader need to "sound out" words letter by letter; good readers learn to see *cat* as a single entity rather than three. *Cat* becomes a single chunk, as do all other familiar words. For the skilled reader, chunks are individual words or word pairs, not letters.[35] As you read this page, your visual focus makes tiny jumps from word to word. With a lot of practice, your eye muscles become trained to fixate on a word for a few milliseconds, then jump to the next word and fixate again. The eye muscles eventually perform these movements precisely and effortlessly, just as your brain learns to recognize individual words as singular chunks.

Word recognition is still not enough. Once recognized, words must evoke meanings, and those meanings must connect so that each sentence can be comprehended as an integrated whole.[36] The process continues to encompass larger collections of text. The reader must link the meanings of sentences so that a paragraph can be comprehended. At higher levels, the meanings of paragraphs are mentally integrated so that entire books, such as novels, become comprehensible as unified entities. These multi-level processes all trace back to chunking at the level of letters and words. Chunking makes it possible to read words fluidly and effortlessly. Chunking also permits intelligent reading by preserving processing capacity in working memory for comprehension, making predictions, drawing implications, and critiquing the quality of the ideas. Without chunking, effective reading is simply impossible.

What about speed reading? The previous description of reading processes raises the question of whether it is possible to read large sections of text—say, an entire page—at a glance. Advertisements of speed-reading programs show images of people turning book pages continuously while wearing an uninterrupted smile of pleasure. Many of us would be enthusiastic to learn a technique that would allow us to read as fast as we can turn pages. We would be free to build knowledge on any subject rapidly and efficiently. If valid and effective, speed-reading techniques could help us to expand our understanding on virtually any topic and so increase our fund of crystallized intelligence.

Speed-reading techniques have been around for quite a while. The first programs were developed in the 1940s by the US Air Force. The technological basis of the early programs was the invention of the tachistoscope, a device that could flash information very quickly—as briefly as 1/1,000 of a second—on a display screen. The popular expansion of speed reading methods occurred in the 1950s when a schoolteacher named Evelyn Wood developed a technique in which the reader's hand or fingertips moved over the pages of a book at a steady pace, training the eyes to follow. Wood believed that many readers were hindered in their reading speed by relying on subvocalization, the small movements of muscles in the mouth that mirror the sounds of spoken words. Through practice in rapid pacing, the Wood technique aimed to break the habit of subvocalization. Evelyn Wood and other promoters of speed-reading techniques have reached many thousands of enthusiasts over the decades.

Marketers of speed-reading programs have made claims that people trained in their techniques can read as many as 1,000 words per minute with comprehension. If true, the ability would be quite astonishing. The average reading speed of a college graduate is about 300 words per minute. The fastest readers, those in the top 1% of reading efficiency, can read as many as 500 words per minute with good comprehension.[37] When probed, however, the claims of much higher efficiencies by speed readers turn out to be unsupported. Processing text at 1,000 words per minute inevitably results in skimming text with only partial or even poor comprehension. Worse still, readers who use speed reading techniques are not always aware that their comprehension is poor and may have difficulty separating important ideas from supporting details. Skimming is recognized by reading experts as an important skill, but not one to be confused with reading for high comprehension.[38] The most skillful readers know how to speed up when only a general sense of the information is needed, and they intentionally slow down to assure thorough understanding.

EXPERTS SOLVE PROBLEMS DIFFERENTLY

We know that experts' knowledge evolves over time, so it should not be surprising that the way experts *think* also evolves. This is clearest in the way that experts go about solving problems. Remember our definition of "problem": any activity in which the path to reach a goal is not immediately clear. If your car breaks down, your mechanic might not be able to diagnose the problem immediately. He or she may ask you a few questions, think about possible causes of the breakdown, and run diagnostic tests to identify the source of the malfunction. A similar process applies to the work of a doctor. A set of symptoms might not obviously indicate a specific disease. Diagnosis requires further thought and tests before treatment can ensue. In both cases, the expert has a problem to solve.

Let's concentrate on how problem solving differs between an expert and a novice—say a chief of internal medicine at a renowned hospital and a first-year medical student. One mark of expertise is that experts proceed deliberately, spending the time needed to understand the relevant facts before choosing a course of action. The expert physician does not to rush to conduct multiple diagnostic tests or to prescribe treatments that might possibly work. The implicit rule of expert action is this: *First understand, then act.* The expert thoughtfully gathers relevant information in an effort to see the big picture. That is why doctors need to understand a patient's medical history along with current symptoms. The point of being deliberate is to avoid false leads, unnecessary costs, and incorrect treatments. We have evidence that high-IQ subjects apply a very similar strategy when taking intelligence tests. They are not impetuous; instead, they devote time to understanding a problem before proceeding to solve it.[39]

Through many years of experience, experts develop a signature strategy of understanding a problem before attempting a solution. But in applying this strategy, they draw upon a tremendous resource that is also a mark of expertise—deep knowledge. Their problem solving is efficient only because of the knowledge they bring to a problem. This leads us to a second distinction between experts and novices. Not only are experts more deliberative problem solvers, they are usually more successful at seeing connections between the salient facts of a problem and the theories that underlie professional practice. An excellent physician can "see past" specific symptoms—such as a headache, rash, or lack of appetite—to possible disease processes, such as an autoimmune disorder, infection, allergic reaction, or malignancy. Although the theories taught in medical school and the presentation of clinical symptoms might not always connect for medical students, for an attending physician they often interface quite articulately. One way of expressing the connection is that the expert can perceive the *deep structure* of the problem.[40] Novices, by contrast, can be distracted by the particulars of the situation and have trouble seeing past those features to the systems that are the underlying cause. These perceptual differences between experts and novices have been found in such diverse fields as medical diagnosis,[41] computer programming, and competitive sports.

Experts display yet a third distinctive quality during problem solving. Their considerable depth of experience means that, compared to novices, they have much more opportunity to perceive recurrent patterns. An expert might say, or merely think, "This looks familiar. I think I know what to do next." When encountering familiar symptoms, whether in a patient, an automobile, or a struggling company, the expert might quickly draw from past experience to think of strategies that are promising in the current situation. The expert now has ideas about conducting further diagnostic tests, asking pointed questions, or trying possible solutions. This is not to say that the expert will always know how to solve any given problem, but through experience, the space of possible solutions is narrowed and problem solving becomes less haphazard and more streamlined.

These three qualities of expert cognition—thinking before acting, perceiving the problem's deep structure, and using familiar patterns to reduce the solution "space" to the most promising pathways—make for efficient and effective problem solving. The expert may not always bat 1,000—problem solving, after all, never guarantees success—but in general the expert proceeds with little wasted effort. Diagnostic skill, though imperfect, helps the expert to place bets on the most likely solution paths. In employing these distinctive ways of thinking, the expert relies on a knowledge base that grows, deepens, and transforms over time. Expressed in the language of intelligence theory, we can say that the expert continually and profitably draws on crystallized intelligence, particularly in the field of specialization.

THE 10-YEAR RULE

All experts rely on the vast collection of knowledge that defines their particular domain. That knowledge is chunked into meaningful patterns, profusely interconnected and coherently structured. It's also massive. Such a large fund of knowledge takes a very long time to acquire. Herbert Simon expressed the point plainly in saying that "there is no such thing as expertness without knowledge—extensive and accessible knowledge."[42] This leads us to a remarkable parameter proposed by Herbert Simon: To acquire the knowledge base constituent to expertise requires a minimum time investment of 10 years. According to Simon, "the level of world-class expert is never achieved with less than 10 years of intensive, round-the-clock effort."[43] This is the *10-year rule*: It holds for musicians, physicians, writers, and athletes—indeed, experts in every knowledge and performance domain.[44]

If you are thinking critically as you read, you might question the 10-year rule. Does it really apply in every case, or just in most? Aren't some people so brightly talented that they display extreme levels of skill with far less than 10 years' experience? What about Mozart, for example? The life of Wolfgang Amadeus Mozart is a good test case because if any great talent were identified as inborn, innate, extreme, and even a little spooky, it is Mozart's. It's true that Mozart excelled as a performer when he was little more than a toddler, and he began composing as a child. That his gift for music was unaccountably prodigious cannot be denied. What can be questioned is exactly when his gift resulted in works that were truly significant.

As a child, Mozart attracted the attention of the European aristocracy because of his precocious talent as well as calculated marketing by Mozart's father. Young Wolfgang's father was obsessed with transforming the boy into a child wonder, programming his daily routine to include several hours of practice starting at age four.[45] The strategy worked. Yet, in those early days, Wolfgang gained attention not as a first-rate composer but as a child performer. He was a child prodigy, not a world-class musician. Eventually the finest composers of Europe began to take notice of Mozart's compositions, but by then Wolfgang was in his mid-teens. It was during that time that he began to compose works that were of such high quality that they merited attention in their own right, unconditioned by youth or predictions about future promise. Sometime during adolescence, Mozart's musical accomplishments became world class. Now consider this: How long had Mozart been honing his skills as a performer and composer before being admitted to the ranks of Europe's finest musicians? If such effort began around age four and he became recognized as a serious composer around age 14, simple subtraction gives you the answer.

The childhood experience of the famous Brontë sisters provides a second example of how deep and prolonged experience is instrumental to achieving very high levels of skill.[46] As children, the three literary Brontë sisters—Charlotte, Emily, and Anne—along with their brother, Branwell, wrote stories incessantly for their own and each other's entertainment. They wrote for several hours each day, as well as read and critiqued each other's compositions. Their early works were unremarkable, just as Mozart's childhood works were undistinguished. Over a period of years, however, the siblings' writings matured, eventually attaining the quality that would lead to their reputation as literary classics. That high level of skill was not reached until the Brontës reached their late teens. As with Mozart, the Brontës did not achieve expert or world-class status before engaging in their craft intensively for at least a decade.

The 10-year rule, though nowhere carved in stone, is an amazingly powerful guide to understanding the growth trajectory of experts. The parameterization of expertise is both sobering and liberating. It's sobering because it shows that expertise never comes cheap. Any aspiring expert must be willing to invest a substantial segment of his or her life to the pursuit of excellence. Not only time, but also sweat and toil, along with inevitable frustration and setbacks, mark the road to expertise. The key role of hard work and dedication, surprising for its ordinariness, was identified long ago by Anne Roe. Studying the lives of eminent scientists, she arrived at an important conclusion: "How well you do in the field is partly a function of your capacity for that field, but even more a function of how hard you work at it."[47]

The 10-year rule of expertise is also liberating because it demystifies, at least to some extent, expert performance. It shows that expertise is not simply a function of innate and fixed talent, remote and unreachable except for a gifted few. Rather, expertise is *learned*. And because dedication is an essential ingredient, it is also *earned*. Talent is relevant, certainly, but expertise is never purely an expression of talent. Because time and fierce commitment are essential, the 10-year rule puts expertise within the reach of many who can summon the personal dedication to achieve it. Through research, expertise has been rendered less of a mystery and more the predictable consequence of prolonged investment of concentrated effort. No longer does it seem unreasonable for the common man, woman, or child to aspire to expertise.

Will an investment of 10 years *guarantee* expertise? No. A 10-year investment of time and effort falls squarely in the category of "necessary but not sufficient" conditions.[48] Other components are rather obvious: strong personal commitment and access to relevant resources and opportunities, such as books, classes, teachers, and mentors. Expertise does not emerge unaided. Like a hybrid plant that has a high potential to thrive, expertise can grow only under the right conditions and according to a reasonable timeline. The conditions of talent development are multiple, and include the regular investment of hours each day to practice. But there is something else: The novice who embarks on the road to expertise needs the support and commitment of other people. Almost always, the entire enterprise is made possible by the assent, encouragement, and even sacrifice of others. The necessary undergirding of social support is clearest in the case of extreme talent among young people.

EXTREME TALENT IN YOUTH

Children who exhibit precocious talents are fascinating. This is so not only because of their great skill, but also because their honed abilities can prompt us to wonder about the source of their talent. Is it inborn, a gift? Or, is it more accurately described as an expression of unrelenting devotion to the skill domain, allied with opportunity, access to able teachers and coaches, and supportive families?

Consider the Vietnamese chess champion Nguyen Ngoc Truong Son.[49] The earliest hints of Son's precocity in chess were exhibited when he was a mere three years old. At that time, Son liked to watch his parents play chess in their family home, a ramshackle structure in Vietnam's Mekong Delta. The family chessboard was a piece of plywood on which the 8 × 8 layout of squares was drawn with a black marking pen. By observing his parents, Son learned how to set up the chess pieces as well as the rules of the game. He became eager to play and began to pester his parents to let him join in.

Within a month, Son could easily defeat his parents. He began competing in tournaments starting at age four, and by the age of 12 Son became the youngest-ever chess champion of Vietnam.

We can learn a lot about talent development from studies of extreme talent in youth—chess prodigies, Olympic gymnasts, virtuoso musicians, and other varieties of wunderkind.[50] For one thing, children who eventually exhibit high levels of talent in a domain typically are identified early on by teachers and coaches as having unusual aptitude. This is not unexpected, but what is surprising is that giftedness is usually not noticed by parents before the teaching or coaching began. In other words, the talent that later became obvious was initially unrecognized by parents. The talent awaited discovery, but there was no guarantee that the child's tremendous inner potential would ever come to light. Had parents not made a specialized opportunity available, the child's potential for talent development may have been forever dormant, like a blue-ribbon seed kept in dry storage— never germinating or bearing fruit.

The massive investment of time that marks the path of the developing expert is just as critical to the preteen gymnast as it is to the PhD student in chemistry. Time devoted to the acquisition of extreme knowledge and skill is an indispensable ingredient of expertise development.[51] Time is not enough, however. Another element is crucial: Youth who aspire to be among the world's elite must have access to excellent instruction. Studies of talent development among musicians and athletes show a predictable pattern. The very best students—those who eventually ascend to the level of world class—are rarely taught by a single teacher or coach. The more common pattern is that the student progresses through a series of instructors who are progressively more capable. The child's first teacher is typically competent but not distinguished. This first teacher leads the young student as far as he or she is able, but there comes a point when the student must transition to a more talented teacher or coach who can take the student further. Eventually it becomes necessary to search for the very best mentors or coaches. This last step, when world-class mentors are needed, may require considerable sacrifice by the family, possibly including relocation to a different city or country.

This last point might be skipped over quickly, but it merits additional consideration. For a child to develop talent to an extreme level requires more than the child's willingness to adopt an unusual lifestyle; it almost always demands unusual effort and sacrifice from other members of the child's family.[52] Typically, parents invest large amounts of time driving the child to and from lessons. Competitions, usually located farther afield, often require substantial investments of time as well as money. Family relocation, not at all atypical, requires even greater sacrifices—possibly the disruption of careers and schooling, separation from extended family, and the need to rebuild a circle of friends. So great are the demands needed to support talent development that often families can make such sacrifices for only one child.

One additional point should be stressed about talent development in youth: The life that makes talent development possible is not a *normal* life. It cannot be called a balanced life in which an array of activities is pursued—schoolwork, hobbies, friends, movies, games, trips to the shopping mall, and sleeping in on weekends. The young person devoted to talent development forgoes many of the normal accoutrements of growing up—if not completely, then at least substantially. Some observers perceive an unhealthy and imbalanced collection of ingredients in the recipe for outstanding success. Others see the young life dedicated to defined greatness as worth every hour, dollar, and drop of sweat.

Much of what characterizes the life of the talented child also holds for the adult bound for expert status. In both cases, a life is structured around a dedicated passion. This is not a balanced life; it is eccentric. Everyone who envisions expertise as a goal possibly worth pursuing must weigh the cost of pursuit. That cost is not only one of toil; it's also the investment of thousands of hours that translates to a large segment of life. Time is a zero-sum resource: To spend time pursuing one activity means not using it for other activities. This leads to the question of opportunity cost: What other relationships, pursuits, or rewards that *might* have been experienced will never be actualized because a particular path was chosen—the road to expertise.

COMMUNITIES OF EXPERTS

Every aspiring expert needs good teachers. The typical succession of mentors and coaches, from very good to the very best, illustrates a broader set of considerations in the development of extreme skill. With precious few exceptions, the development of expertise is not a solo enterprise. The necessary investments of time and effort, expressed succinctly as the 10-year rule, are not fully sufficient. The cultivation of supreme levels of performance draws heavily upon social forces that teach, train, motivate, and in countless ways shape the novice progressively toward expert form. The aspiring expert typically becomes immersed in the social community of experts, aspiring experts, and the very best teachers, along with immersion into the performance domain—chess, music, science, sports or any field where excellence is the endpoint of development. As we appreciate the power of this social dimension, the path toward expert status begins to look less like the consumption of massive amounts of knowledge than integration into a community.[53] The social bonds and shared values of the community provide the sustaining means for growing in expertise over long periods of time. People build expertise together.

In communities devoted to high-level performance, a great deal of what is learned is knowledge of the domain—the concepts and principles denoted in courses, books, and the spoken instruction offered by mentors and coaches. But some of what is learned is never spoken aloud. This is tacit knowledge. *Tacit* means *unspoken*, but the fact of being unspoken does not mitigate the importance of such knowledge. Success in any field draws at least partly on such knowledge—the values, ethics, modes of relating to peers, supervisors, and supervisees, standards of dress, norms of work hours—in short, all manner of rules of conduct and ways of thinking that may not appear in any book, but all the same are implicit elements of expertise. In a social community, tacit aspects of expertise can be learned via the mind's remarkable ability to perceive patterns of behavior and to imitate, very possibly without an awareness of doing so.

Tacit knowledge includes skill in task performance that is not codified as rules.[54] To become successful in any field is at least partly a function of the ability to learn skilled behavior that is never taught explicitly, codified as a set of rules, or explicated in textbooks. Tacit learning ability seems to be different from the kinds of intellectual abilities that are measured by performance on intelligence tests. If that is the case, it is further evidence that IQ tests capture only a part of what's necessary for success in the world.[55] Almost by definition, tacit knowledge cannot be taught didactically in an educational curriculum. It must be learned through experience, though possibly with feedback from skilled mentors.

One example of tacit knowledge is the intuitive sense of timing used in film editing. Oscar-winning film editor Walter Murch, whose film credits include all three *Godfather* films and *The English Patient*, relies to some extent on conventions of film editing. Murch is aware, for example, that action sequences average 14 camera angles per minute, and that each frame averages 2.5 thematic elements. Such conventions can offer guidance to the film editor, but the artful craft of knowing when to cut from one angle or scene to another requires sensitivity to the unfolding story. Logical considerations alone are not sufficient. For example, it makes logical sense to cut a scene after a door closes, but a transition at precisely that point might not optimize either aesthetics or emotional impact. Murch notes that "intellectually it's right, but it doesn't feel right.' And so then I started to develop this idea of cutting on the fly."

"Cutting on the fly" means that Murch lets the film play at 24 frames per second, and at the exact moment he feels the need to cut to the next shot he hits the space bar on his editing system's keyboard, leaving a digital mark. Murch says it's like a jazz drummer knowing just when to hit the snare. It's all about timing and feeling, what he calls, the music of the scene.[56]

Murch's technique of "cutting on the fly" shows that his knowledge of the right moment is as much a matter of informed intuition as it is logical deduction.

Like Oscar-winning film editors, experts in a wide range of professions cannot rely exclusively on established rules or logical deduction, but must also draw on personal forms of knowledge that are hard to articulate.[57] Tacit knowledge, a form of understanding that is powerful yet may be difficult to express in words, must somehow be acquired by the aspiring expert through many thousands of hours of focused experience.

DELIBERATE PRACTICE

Expertise is built up over a long span of time, and this fact gives us insight into its aggregate requirements, such as the time dimension formulated in the 10-year rule. But we should also consider what day-to-day processes make growth toward expertise possible. This brings us to the topic of deliberate practice.[58] To build the cumulative experience that underlies expertise involves structuring a life so that it steadily builds the massive base of knowledge and skill that experts need. The life pattern called deliberate practice is a daily regimen of focused engagement in the domain. It includes not only engaging in the target activity, but also training in exercises specifically intended to elevate skill to higher levels. Serious golfers, for example, spend considerable time at the driving range, as well as time refining other specific strokes, such as chips and putts.

The road to expertise is a structured lifestyle that builds talent over a long period of time. A professional musician, for example, typically devotes about five hours daily to building skill. Through recurrent time investment, deliberate practice becomes a habit—part of the musician's daily routine. The investment of several hours a day provides feedback crucial to the steady advancement of skill.[59] But why not practice for eight or 10 hours a day? The reason is that deliberate practice requires tremendous concentration. By limiting engagement to briefer spans of time, the intense activity can be repeated day after day, year after year. In other words, the daily regimen of practice steadily builds to thousands of hours, but it does so in a way that is sustainable rather than exhausting. Similar patterns are common in other fields, such as writing. Periods of intense concentration are typically restricted to less than the standard eight- or nine-hour workday. This is not to say that musicians, writers, and medical students work for only five hours and then take the rest of the day off. The serious professional may engage in long work days, but beyond five or so hours of intense learning or creative performance, the remaining hours are usually devoted to activities that are less demanding, yet still relevant to the performance domain.

We know that deliberate practice is a distinguishing behavior of the aspiring expert, but further evidence of its importance comes from research that examines skill variation *within* fields. Professional musicians are not equal in skill, just as not everyone called *doctor* or *lawyer* is equivalent. Individual variation is a fact. Unquestionably, many factors contribute to variation within fields, but in the present context we will simply note that deliberate practice is one of those factors. Research has shown, for example, that in a group of professional musicians the most highly skilled had the most cumulative hours of practice.[60] This suggests that extensive engagement in any field, crudely indexed as the total numbers of hours invested, is not only a gateway into the category of *expert*, but also separates experts into those who are the very best and those who are somewhat less skilled.

THE VOLITION TO EXCEL

The path toward expertise is one of personal transformation. This, then, is the inner agenda of the expert—to establish a trajectory of indefinite growth toward excellence and to arrange the rhythms of daily life to support that project. But the expert is not merely interested in the inner agenda of becoming more capable. There is also a vital outer agenda of exercising that capability to produce great products and performances. It's one thing for a Mozart to develop the unparalleled skills necessary to produce a masterpiece and another to actually compose the *Requiem* and offer it to the world for posterity. For the world-class athlete, it's the same: As many of the world's best have known through painful firsthand experience, being primed for victory and actually winning a gold medal or championship trophy are not the same.

That one is *capable* of greatness is no guarantee of achieving it. For many reasons—some understandable, some mysterious—every great career is uneven. The world's best athletes can have dry periods, and renowned filmmakers sometimes produce duds. Even Einstein is rumored to have expressed regret that the middle and later stages of his life did not match the brilliance of his youthful contributions to physics. How do we understand the relationship between extraordinary capability and extraordinary achievement? How does tremendous talent translate to tremendous achievement?

One extremely provocative hypothesis presents a possible answer. The hypothesis is provocative because it is wildly counterintuitive. It's this: The probability of great achievement is directly proportional to the *number* of attempted contributions to a field. This is the *equal-odds hypothesis*.[61] What's *equal* is that recognized greatness, sometimes called eminence, is not a function of observed talent but instead of sheer productivity. "Equal odds" recognizes that what is regarded as a superb product or performance is rare—equally rare, in fact, for all contenders. Statistically, the chances of achieving greatness hinge on how prolific a person is: how many novels written, how many songs composed, how many competitions entered.

If true, the equal-odds hypothesis radically shifts the underpinnings of great achievement from raw talent to motivational factors, particularly to motivational factors that are volitional in nature. We usually think of motivation as desire, but volition expresses the force of will to choose and maintain a direction. To have the desire to achieve something is separate from having the will to do so. Being prolific leans heavily on volition—staying true to a prized goal for the long term through the vicissitudes of success and failure. Note a strong parallel with deliberate practice. Inner talent and external productivity both draw on a long-term vision with the counterpart ability to structure a lifestyle, a daily rhythm, dedicated to building greater skill and productivity. Both concepts—deliberate practice and the equal-odds hypothesis—shift explanations for eminence away from innate talent to factors that are under the control of the individual.

The inner status of expertise and its outer expression as great achievement both link to the power of will—that is, to volition. Those on the path toward expertise must tap into the emotional rewards, the excitement and interest sparked by their fields, to sustain their long-term commitments. Indeed, high achievers in any field are often marked by intense curiosity, passion, and unusual persistence. Can such qualities be taught? Maybe not. It may be quite difficult, even misguided, to try to teach sensitivity to the emotional rewards of intellectual activity. Perhaps the most reasonable strategy is not to attempt to teach these feelings and volitional states, but rather to establish conditions that can kindle them indirectly.[62] One possible way to do so is through exposure to the emotional expressions of teachers and fellow students.

In understanding the sources of great achievement we cannot neglect volition—the wherewithal to identify an ambitious goal and pursue it relentlessly. But where does volition figure in theories of mind? Information-processing theories tend to neglect volition altogether, probably because such theories draw heavily on the computer as a metaphor for understanding human cognition. Volition is also largely squeezed out when behavior geneticists try to account for human activity by dividing developmental influences into nature and nurture. These two shaping forces, admittedly powerful, do not recognize the volitional differences that give rise to achievement. Yet in the early days of scholarship on human intelligence, human volition was not ignored. A century ago, when Charles Spearman laid the foundations of intelligence theory, he interpreted general mental ability as consisting, at least in part, of "will power."[63] Spearman's theoretical rival, L. L. Thurstone, similarly recognized "perseverance" as essential to the nature of intelligence.[64] David Wechsler, after Terman, the most influential developer of intelligence tests, defined intelligence in part as the ability to act purposefully.[65]

At least one modern model of intelligence explicitly recognizes the key role of volition. The bioecological model of Stephen Ceci gives due recognition to innate potential abilities (nature), to environmental contexts (nurture), and to internal motivation.[66] The third factor seems essential to understand why some individuals rise to tremendous heights of achievement by force of will and self-discipline, even in the absence of favorable circumstances or obvious genetic gifts. It's not enough to be genetically primed and environmentally favored. Each person must choose. The individual who has been prepared must decide whether to capitalize on readiness by drawing upon personal reserves of imagination, planning, and grit over the long term.

Though pathways for expertise development may be built into our systems of advanced study, the underlying logic of the expert trajectory is less evident in schools. Curriculum planners who seek integration of learning objectives across grades, the vertical articulation of learning goals, know that effective education requires a multiyear time perspective. Yet students' aspirations tend to be more immediate. For college-bound high school students, building a transcript of rigorous coursework and earning a high GPA are rightly seen as critical for admission to a selective college. The temporal focus of ambitious and capable students is normally near-term and tactical, with little awareness of personal development goals that consist of more than being admitted to a selective institution.

Every student ought to learn something about the nature of expertise and how to attain it. This includes understanding the habit of deliberate practice—the road to expertise. The steady rhythm of deliberate practice is quite distinct from the bursts of study time that are expedient to getting high grades on examinations. Short-term tactical shifting from one subject to another to maximize test scores on tests is certainly rationalizable. It's a time-honored mainstay of high school and college life, and is becoming increasingly common at middle and elementary schools. But a test score, while possibly important in the short term, is distinct from the internal development that is the point of deliberate practice. This contrast—impersonal test scores and personal development—spotlights a disjuncture between the ways that schools operate and what is known about how deep competence develops in people over time. In the first case, a student's natural motivation is to *get through* the process—to complete requirements and move on. In the second case, the necessary motivation is not completion but rather continuity—not to move on, but to *stay* on.

Research on expertise is exciting. It suggests that a high level of talent, even world-class ability, is within the reach of many people. In the context of the current world economy, this is good news. The powerful engines of economic growth do not draw as heavily on physical labor and raw materials as they did in centuries past. More than ever, what propels economic prosperity are the insights and creative products generated by teams of people who are expert in their domains. Revolutions in communications technology, solar energy, and targeted cancer therapies rely on expertise applied creatively to pressing problems and budding opportunities. The world desperately needs and rewards expertise. Through research, we now know that prospective experts do not emerge from a narrow slice of the population—a genetically gifted elite—but rather from the ranks of seemingly ordinary people who have sufficient inner resources and external opportunities. Experts, those very highly skilled thinkers, workers, and performers who invent and apply the world's best ideas and products, can compose an ever-increasing segment of the population to the benefit of all.

Yet surely we are not to dismiss the obvious fact that people differ in their natural propensities to excel. It's inconceivable that we are equally predisposed to the musical achievements of Wolfgang Mozart, or to the literary breakthroughs of Charles Dickens or William Faulkner. Some fortunate people have extraordinary talent. The research on expertise does not deny talent, but shows that the natural propensity talent provides is not the only factor that predicts eventual expertise, achievement, and extraordinary success. Drive, persistence, vision, and focus—all these volitional factors enter in as well. Indeed, it's possible that these other variables are, in reality, the determining factors. After all, talent never guarantees success. The world generates countless instances of exceptional talent that never reach fruition for lack of motivation or opportunity. This ought to be a vital consideration for educators, economists, social advocates, and business leaders. Talent unrecognized and undeveloped is a deprivation for the gifted individual and, equally, a wasted resource for the common good.

Research on expertise is surprisingly practical for planning a trajectory toward high achievement in any field, but it also casts light on learnable intelligence. That's because domain expertise can be seen as focused crystallized intelligence taken to a very high level within a bounded field of knowledge. A common mechanism—the internal construction of progressively higher levels of knowledge and skill—drives both processes. As we strive to become more intelligent people, we can confidently pursue expert-like knowledge and skill. In ways that seem unlikely at first, both expertise and intelligence are not only learnable but mutually reinforcing.

CREATIVE GENIUS

Expertise is marvelous, but it is not the ultimate expression of domain proficiency. Imagine an expert who is technically proficient, but not particularly innovative—perhaps a violinist who can perform a broad repertoire flawlessly, with stunning technical proficiency. The ability to perform at such high levels of skill is one form of expertise, without a doubt. But there is another kind of expert who is equally proficient in the technical aspects of performance, but who adds something extra—a creative slant, a way of thinking that goes beyond conventional practice. We'll call the first a *technician* and the second an *innovator*.[67] The first term, *technician*, may be unfairly pejorative because this expert's skill may be so refined that he or she is rightly regarded as a virtuoso. Yet the technician lacks some sort of generative spark. The second expert, the innovator, employs all the knowledge and skill that is the province of experts but is not bound by those. When solving problems, the innovator envisions solution paths that do not occur to the technician. Through creative problem solving, the innovator stretches the boundaries of professional practice.

Every field has its superstars, those whose achievements extend far beyond the prevailing standards of practice.[68] Over the centuries, scientists, writers, artists, musicians, athletes, and architects have applied their brilliant insights to forever change their fields. In architecture, Jørn Utzon's design of the Sydney Opera House was such a turning point. The design of the Opera House and ancillary buildings on Sydney Harbor were boldly unique. Additionally, the methods for the buildings' construction had to be innovative to accommodate the distinctive shell-within-shell design. For design breakthroughs and the necessary innovations in construction techniques, Utzon won architecture's highest honor, the Pritzker Prize, in 2003. Yet to call the design and construction of the Sydney Opera House a manifestation of expertise misses something. Luminaries like Jørn Utzon *transcend* expertise. Their extraordinary ability is expressed in such dramatic fashion that it leaves a lasting mark on history and culture. The legacy of these innovators is not merely their own distinguished record; it's also shown in how subsequent generations define what they do. When we speak of these great creative minds, we shift categorical focus from expertise to something more rarefied—creative genius.

When we conceptualize *genius* as the highest expression of expertise, we define the word in a way that varies from its common use. In everyday speech, *genius* refers to someone who has a very high IQ. In our usage, though, genius is not the highest range on an IQ scale, nor is it understood primarily as an internal and personal quality. Instead, the evidence of genius is external. Genius is proven by its products: the transcendent ideas, techniques, and inventions that redefine a field.[69]

A prerequisite to creative genius is a firm mastery of the performance domain. Every genius must pass through expertise before transcending it. Stated in the language of intelligence theory, genius requires a foundation of crystallized intelligence overlaid with the flexibility of fluid intelligence. A great innovator may also require unusual personality characteristics, such as the ability to weather skepticism from doubting peers—and perhaps severe criticism, rejection, and social isolation. The innovator's dogged persistence toward a vision of something new and extraordinary may also draw upon personal qualities that are quite rare.

Tendencies toward unusual psychological profiles can sometimes reach extremes. A few researchers have discovered a propensity toward mental instability among the great innovators of history. The mythology of the world's greatest minds presents a prototype of the "mad genius"—isolated, odd, and brilliant in the extreme. Nowhere are these mythic qualities confirmed as a rule, but neither can we dismiss outright the image of the mad genius as baseless. Some data actually support a link between high levels of creativity and psychopathology. Behavioral tendencies toward social isolation, free thinking, and the ability to withstand blistering criticism might, in extreme forms, be signs of psychosis.[70] Yet true psychosis would ordinarily be too disabling for a person to make serious original contributions to a field of study.

This is not always the case, however. The book *A Beautiful Mind* by Sylvia Nasar traces the descent of the brilliant mathematician John Forbes

Nash Jr. into episodes of debilitating psychosis.[71] Nash, who was awarded the Nobel Prize in Economic Sciences in 1994, suffered regularly from paranoid schizophrenia beginning in 1959 and extending throughout his career. Those psychotic experiences included hearing voices that led Nash to weave paranoid theories of Communist plots directed at the United States, and at him personally. Nash's psychosis led to his resignation from a teaching post at MIT early in his career and to his forced admission to mental asylums for extended periods of time. Ron Howard's film adaptation of *A Beautiful Mind* shows Nash as being helped by medication, but Nash himself distrusted antipsychotic drugs. He was often noncompliant in taking his prescribed medications and entered mental hospitals only when forced to do so. Nash has expressed the belief that his delusional thinking was a way to escape the constraints of conventional thinking, noting that "to some extent, sanity is a form of conformity."[72]

While true psychosis is ordinarily so debilitating as to be incompatible with high levels of creative accomplishment, the creative genius may well exhibit traits that conform to the personality factor known as psychoticism. They may behave in ways that are arrogant, aloof, and callous—perhaps even cruel. Great creative minds might exhibit social detachment and have difficulty forming and maintaining relationships. Depression, also, has been linked repeatedly to highly creative people, particularly in writing and the arts.[73] We can easily call to mind such prototypes of tormented genius: Vincent van Gogh, Edgar Allan Poe, and Virginia Woolf. The emotional turmoil constitutional to the experience of the creative genius may be more common than is typically appreciated. The struggles of great achievers are often concealed by family members eager to protect the reputation of their eminent relative, even posthumously.

What is the role of emotional pain or dysfunction in the life and accomplishments of the highly creative person? Perhaps it is no more than an unfortunate statistical association with no real functional connection. Alternatively, psychological struggle might have a causal role in great feats of creative achievement. Personality traits that border on instability might support the unusual kinds of thinking and behavior that lead to breakthroughs. Consider that significant creative accomplishment relies on building a very deep knowledge base, which in turn requires prolonged immersion into a field of study along with potential neglect of relationships and social obligations. In addition to acquiring the extensive knowledge base that we associate with expertise, the creative genius commonly generates a profusion of ideas and idea combinations, including transformative ones. Highly divergent thinking sometimes requires the suspension of disbelief. The innovator needs the ability to tolerate harsh criticism or ridicule from mainstream thinkers and the broader public. He or she must resist the psychological mechanisms that, in most people, bend thinking and behavior back into conformity with social norms.

THE RADEX

Our exploration of creative genius might seem detached from the core aspects of intellect that we call intelligence. But that is not really the case. The work of the genius links back to intelligence theory directly. Near the end of his life, Alfred Binet, the great pioneer of intelligence theory, recognized inventiveness as a fundamental quality of the intelligent mind.[74] If we are to consider inventiveness a key quality of the intelligent mind, then we ought to reconsider how to redefine intelligence in response. Perhaps instead of thinking of intelligence as a singular entity with sharp boundaries, we can consider intelligence to be a smooth continuum that includes exceptional achievement in defined fields of study. Intelligence would then encompass a spectrum of intellectual capabilities that range from the central processes of fluid intelligence to domain-focused proficiencies that define crystallized intelligence.

To perceive this continuum visually, let's first recall John Carroll's hierarchical model, which has a pyramid shape with g at the top. Now think about this hierarchical model in a new way. Imagine the hierarchy not as a pyramid but rather as a fan in which the bottom corners sweep upward, pivoting around the apex. When the fan opens fully, the outer edge of the fan forms a complete circle. The resulting structure is no longer a hierarchical pyramid, but a series of concentric circles. It is a radex.[75]

The radex was created by Stanford professor Richard Snow and his colleagues to present the structure of intelligence in a new way. At the bull's-eye, or centroid, is Raven's Matrices, which is widely regarded to be a marker test for the purest expression of intelligence, g. It would be nice to say exactly what g consists of, but the truth is that even now, the nature of g is not perfectly understood. We know the broad array of intellectual abilities associated with g—fluid intelligence, spatial intelligence, verbal ability, and so on—but what remains unresolved is the exact contribution of g to those various expressions of intelligence.[76] What we *can* say is that tasks and tests in the middle of the radex are generally the most demanding in terms of information processing. They all require complex thinking. Viewed mathematically, the center of the radex is the aspect of intelligence, g, that applies to every single cognitive performance. All acts of intelligence involve g to some extent.

We can go some distance toward attaching meaning to *g*. We know, for example that *g* is highly related to fluid intelligence. Fluid intelligence, in turn, is highly related to inductive reasoning, the capacity to see patterns in new experiences, formulate those patterns as rules, and apply that knowledge to new problems. We also know that *g* is connected to what are called executive functions, which allocate working memory capacity as well as manage information nimbly while solving problems. Combining these two aspects, we can summarize the essence of *g* in this way: The heart of human intelligence, *g*, is the ability to perceive order in a complex environment and to apply that knowledge to solve complex problems.

The innermost ring of the radex is where we can place the major factors that lie just below *g* in the hierarchical models. In the radex, what is emphasized visually is the connection of the major factors to particular modalities—the verbal, numerical, and spatial ways of understanding and reasoning. This is a fair conversion. We know, for example, that there is a strong tie between crystallized intelligence and verbal ability. Similarly, fluid intelligence is most readily measured on tasks that entail nonverbal representation. The radex therefore makes explicit the modality qualities that are present, but de-emphasized, in the hierarchical model.

The outermost circle of the radex introduces a dimension of intelligence that is absent, or at least downplayed, in hierarchical models. The outer ring shows how achievement in various domains—mathematics, reading, and mechanical reasoning—connects to intelligence. Here we see the organic interface between cognitive *ability* and cognitive *achievement*. Remember: This is the pairing that Alfred Binet tried to establish in Parisian schools in the late 1800s—namely, that raw intellectual abilities predict the likelihood of success in learning. The radex displays the logical connections between the two: The sectors of the radex identify different *kinds* of ability interfacing with different *kinds* of achievement. Organized in this way, Snow's radex implies that people vary not only in levels of intelligence, but also in their profiles of cognitive strengths, which naturally map to the various sectors of academic learning. Some people have a propensity for mathematical reasoning, others verbal, and still others spatial.

Finally, Snow's radex of concentric circles depicts another important reality. The gradient from the center to the edge corresponds to a progression from multipurpose intellectual potential (*g*) to knowledge in specific domains. The outer edges of the radex are the knowledge foundations of the varied domains of expertise. In other words, an expanded radex could logically encompass varieties of expertise all around its perimeter. But we need not see expertise as locatable only at the edges of the radex. If intelligence is truly learnable, then the novice–expert trajectory can apply anywhere in the radex—at the edges, certainly, but also in generic cognitive factors, such as spatial ability. With a little imagination, we can entertain the possibility that intelligence is susceptible to development though the same processes—namely, extended and focused practice—that lead to expertise at the edges of the radex.

The possibility that intelligence can develop in the same manner as domain-focused expertise is not new. In a paper entitled "Abilities Are Forms of Developing Expertise," Robert Sternberg bridged theories of intelligence and theories of expertise.[77] Sometime before Sternberg published the paper, Stanford professor Richard Snow wrote directly about aptitude development as a legitimate and vital function of education—that intelligence can be learned and so should be taught. This means that the province of educational responsibility is not limited to the outer edge of the radex, as has been traditionally assumed. The span of educational concern is, rather, the *entire* radex. We now have sufficiently precise research-based theories of intelligence to guide broad-based cognitive development through education. Furthermore, we have a model of growth to help us teach intelligence: the vast body of research on the path toward expertise.

The great creative leaps of history—in the arts, technology, and science—were propelled by the productive fusion of crystallized intelligence and fluid intelligence. What if our world could have far more abundant supplies of crystallized and fluid intelligence than are available today? Such an upgrade is possible, even likely, as the conditions of modern societies nudge IQs upward. With our educational system reengineered to include the growth of intelligence as integral to its purpose, the shift toward a more intelligent society could be that much more effective and equitable. Where could this lead? If learnable intelligence were to become a driving goal of society, we might collectively witness an acceleration of creative breakthroughs—an outpouring of revolutionary ideas that could help solve the most recalcitrant problems in every human sphere. There is hardly a more exciting and hopeful view of the future.

CHAPTER 8
Ten Strategies to Enhance Intelligence

Over the course of more than a century, the field of human intelligence has evolved tremendously. Beginning with the invention of simple tests guided by little more than intuition, scholars ultimately constructed vast theories based on rigorous research. For academic researchers, these developments have been tremendous, but the accumulated research on intelligence has important messages for citizens of the 21st century. First, it affirms that intelligence is an essential quality for all people—students, workers, and everyone who hopes for an effective and satisfying life. In every worthwhile pursuit, intelligence makes a difference. Second, and equally important, intelligence is not a static quality, but is sensitive to variations in personal experience. Intelligence, the most vital resource of the human mind, can be enhanced.

The implications of these two findings are significant in the extreme. Research on human intelligence, especially its malleability, offers practical guidance to the individual who wants to pursue a more successful life. Each of us can make choices and pursue experiences that, over time, will enhance our personal reserves of fluid intelligence, crystallized intelligence, and effective character. Every person can structure a lifestyle geared toward enhancing those personal qualities by building new habits and routines. The resulting trajectories of experience will, bit by bit, yield heightened readiness to engage a complex, challenging world—a world also filled with opportunity.

Looking at human potential in this way touches upon much more than personal enhancement; it extends to the collective good. As members of communities, we can jointly design experiences that will cultivate intelligence and conscientiousness for the benefit of others and, indirectly, for ourselves. To pursue greater effectiveness through enhanced intelligence requires more than good theories. Because we face choices about how to orchestrate our personal intellectual development, we need specific strategies. For this reason, this chapter will focus on practical approaches for enhancing personal growth in intelligence.

The strategic intention to boost intelligence derives from a liberating concept: IQ is not dictated by DNA. Previous chapters show that although genetics does have an influence, intelligence is significantly a function of the quality of experience—or what we might call the *educational value* of experience. In thinking about your personal intellectual development, you might wish you could start from scratch and build an ideal stream of experience from infancy onward. For better or worse, though, we are all powerless to alter the past. Fortunately, the future presents choices. Freedom, of course, is not absolute but partial. Yet the latitude offered by choice is significant—probably more so than we would assume. And as with any pursuit, success hinges on the clarity of the vision and the strength of resolve to carry it out.

TRANSLATING THEORY INTO PRACTICE: TEN STRATEGIES

A century of research on intelligence, allied with a half-century of focused programs to enhance intelligence, have left quite a legacy. Scholars of the human mind have advanced evidenced-based theories of intelligence and designed programs to increase the powers of the human intellect. Recent research has sharpened these ideas further. Now we need to apply those theories wisely. In our highly technological era, the skillful use of the mind is more important than ever. We are primed to adopt strategic commitments that can raise intelligence, but how is this to be accomplished?

The concepts presented in the previous chapters now culminate in 10 powerful strategies that can enhance intelligence and human effectiveness. The strategies all build on ideas presented in the previous chapters, but some are speculative or conjectural in nature. For many, their value for boosting intelligence is a reasonable extrapolation from current research rather than a proven conclusion drawn from rigorous studies. It bears saying at the outset that practicing the strategies is not like swallowing a pill. A better metaphor is that they are akin to investments. A well-crafted plan for reaping profitable financial returns requires channeling limited resources in the short term to enjoy payoffs in the long run. Like long-term investments, the payoffs may be unimpressive in the initial weeks and months, but the returns begin to look truly significant in the longer timescale of years. Also, as in every thoughtful investment strategy, the portfolio is diversified—the idea is never to invest exclusively in one narrow sector, but to allocate assets wisely to different investment categories. A portfolio's ideal composition will vary depending on the goals and preferences of the investor.

What sorts of investment are we talking about? Above all, what's required is the most demanding investment of all—a change in behavior. Each strategy requires changes in how we structure our time and channel our efforts. More than that, the following strategies demand that those behavioral changes be clearly formulated and pursued with resolute dedication. To change the way we live our lives necessitates the exertion of will over whim. The costs are counted not only in sweat and toil, but also quite possibly in challenges to emotional comfort. As we make structural changes to the way we live, we may experience the sorts of ego threats that loom anytime we try something new and significant. But along with challenge comes the potential for triumph. The endgame, remember, is greater personal effectiveness by means of enhanced intelligence. What could be more motivating than that?

STRATEGY 1: SET A GOAL TO ENHANCE INTELLIGENCE

Nothing matters more to the pursuit of a new life direction than having a clear and definite goal. But a goal is empty unless it is matched with the resolve to achieve it. As you consider how to enhance your personal effectiveness by cultivating your reserves of intelligence, you must be confident that such a thing is possible. Ideally, the preceding chapters have established confidence by pointing to a monumental conclusion about human development—enhanced intelligence is a legitimate possibility, not a misplaced dream. Mountains of data attest that intelligence is sensitive to the quality of experience throughout the life span, from infancy to adulthood.

Our lives are often not as planned as we might wish or believe. Variation in experience is often an accidental pattern of seemingly random events. As adaptive organisms, we tend to go with the flow. Experience can be shaped by historical changes in culture and history, or it can shift with the vicissitudes of life circumstances in which random chance can play a role. But experiences that enhance a person's intellectual resources can also be intentional. As we have seen, intelligence can be boosted by programs designed to improve intellectual functioning. Each experience-based effect highlights the nurture term in the nature-nurture equation. Nurture is powerful, and so we must find ways to leverage it for maximal benefit. No one can claim to have pushed nurture to its limits; we don't yet know what might be achieved. It seems credible that experiential forces that boost intellectual power are potentially much more efficacious than have ever been put to the test. In this chapter, we focus on harnessing the power of imagination and will, along with the most important ideas from a century of research, to ensure that the forces that bear on intelligence are intentional, not accidental.

Unfortunately, our very assumptions about nurture may be limiting. We often interpret the word *nurture* as something that *happens to us*. We might think of how a parent nurtures a child or a teacher nurtures a student. These are fine examples of how one caring human being can help another develop his or her potential, but these cases exemplify only the passive side of nurture. If our goal is to exercise willful volition as adults in order to control the course of our lives, then we must shift the emphasis to *self*-nurturance. We must think about how to elevate the quality of our life experience through the choices we make given the options available. For those who want to pursue the enhancement of intelligence as a personal project, the daily structuring of experience to achieve those goals—self-nurturance—is the way forward.

In conventional ways of thinking, any plan to become more intelligent sounds audacious. Beyond accepting enhanced intelligence as real in concept lies the challenge of *making* it real. This means changing the way we live. Significant lifestyle changes require a disciplined existence, and especially the consistent choice of challenge over complacency. To embrace a project of newly structured experience means accepting a new pattern of living. In practice, this translates to exercising one's own volitional resources—the will to decide and follow through—to structure the outer world so that it reflects back to grow the inner mind. In the language of behavior genetics, we must understand the mutual influence of our genetic raw material and our daily experience. With self-understanding, we can structure our daily experience so that it builds from our current profile of abilities toward the constellation of personal traits that we desire. With persistence, we can become managers of our own life span intellectual development.[1] We can take hold of a vision and a plan, and with determination create a compelling future. The starting point is Strategy 1—with eyes wide open, to choose.

STRATEGY 2: BUILD FLUID INTELLIGENCE THROUGH PROBLEM SOLVING

Fluid intelligence deserves our interest and attention as the fundamental building block of cognitive enhancement. Fluid intelligence is, after all, the cognitive factor that lies closest to the heart of general intelligence. We therefore need to think intently about how we can develop this crucial intellectual ability. Recall that fluid intelligence underlies our ability to adapt. It's the cognitive resource that allows us to think and act intelligently in situations that present new challenges or that do not map comfortably to our previous experiences.

Fluid intelligence has a lot in common with problem solving, which is what we do when we face a goal without a clear path to achieve it. Based on this similarity, we can use what we know about problem solving to enhance our fluid intelligence. To state the point directly, raising fluid intelligence means that we need to build problem solving into the fabric of our daily experience. To do so, we can draw upon a handy distinction between well-structured problems and ill-structured problems. A good example of a well-structured problem is the game of chess. To solve a well-structured problem requires understanding and abiding by a clear set of rules. But the problems that arise in daily life are often ill-structured in that their goals are fuzzy and the means to obtain them unclear. They require the problem solver to be flexible and able to tolerate ambiguity. The ill-structured problems presented by our real-life experiences are often far more complex than the artificial problems that we encounter in the form of games and textbook exercises.

We all make choices regarding which goals to pursue. Many people, perhaps most, are inclined to pursue life patterns that are comfortably familiar. If this is your mode, then today's goals are likely to be repeats of yesterday's goals, and they become templates for tomorrow's. The resulting cozy lifestyle may be the equivalent of intellectual comfort food, but it's no recipe for boosting fluid intelligence. Remember, fluid intelligence peaks in early adulthood and declines thereafter. Why the decline? One credible explanation is that middle-age adults structure their lives around familiar routines rather than novel challenges. To choose a comfortable path is effectively a choice to follow the familiar rather than to attempt the new. A routine existence is the opposite of what is needed to build fluid intelligence.

We can choose differently. Lifestyle choices that involve self-challenge can help maintain the intellectual flexibility that is the hallmark of fluid intelligence. This means setting and pursuing goals that demand flexibility in thought and behavior. Without too much trouble, we can identify examples of lifestyle choices that build intellectual flexibility. In the work world, the most obvious strategy choice is a change of career. By entering a new profession, our entire work environment will impose demands that force us to adapt. Of course, the pursuit of a new career is a serious matter that requires more consideration than simply its utility for building fluid intelligence. Less radical steps are possible, such as moving in the same career line to a position that exercises a different skill set, or using previously learned skills at a higher level of cognitive demand. Each of these career choices and changes has structural demands for intellectual flexibility consistent with adaptive problem solving and fluid intelligence.

Another way to self-impose challenging intellectual demands is to travel to new cultures, perhaps for an extended period of time. International experiences, especially, may force a traveler to adapt to the new environment in a big way—not only to a new language, food, and social customs, but to an entire cultural milieu. Other pursuits that require flexible adaptation include running for political office, such as a position on the school board, studying a new language, or taking up a new hobby with serious intent. The thread running through these examples is to avoid settling on a routine, but instead committing to a long-term pursuit that will force us to think in new ways and, ideally, is intellectually and emotionally rewarding.

STRATEGY 3: BUILD CRYSTALLIZED INTELLIGENCE THROUGH BOOK READING

In the age of instant media, books may seem like relics of a pre-Internet past. Yet if the goal is to enhance intelligence, whether individually or collectively, we need to recognize the unmatched role of print—and print equivalents on electronic display devices—as a stimulus for remaking the human mind.[2] In the intellectual history of the world, books hold a very special place. Extended discourse, whether in the form of novels or expository treatises, presents the mind with a category of stimuli that can guide thinking though a long, complex, and coherent line of reasoning. Books structure ideas almost uniquely: The vocabulary and thought forms that are commonplace in book-length texts are rare in daily conversations.[3] Books present a much wider range of vocabulary, concepts, and inferences than can be found in our daily banter with friends and family members.

Anyone who wants to become more intelligent needs to develop a distinct awareness of the special qualities of text. In making this claim, I deliberately emphasize books in contrast to newspapers and magazines. Many people still read newspaper and magazine articles as part of their daily routine. Through short and easy-reading articles they can stay informed about the world around them, though sometimes superficially. Newspapers and magazines can present a richer array of ideas than we commonly experience in everyday conversations, but as a rule they do not compare to the complex tapestry of ideas found in books. Nonfiction is particularly important because the patterns of information in nonfiction are distinctive in comparison to speech. But novels can also present an interconnected web of ideas that promote cognitive enrichment in the form of crystallized intelligence.

Books of all varieties can also be a source of boundless pleasures. Unfortunately, these pleasures are untapped by many capable readers. Many adults exhibit practical "aliteracy" by letting the demands and distractions of everyday life, or more passive media such as television, squeeze out time that might otherwise be given to book reading. Let's consider the implications in the form of a question: Why not advance your fund of crystallized intelligence while you enjoy the unique pleasures of reading? You can do so by building the habit of book reading into your daily life, and holding to this commitment for the long term.

STRATEGY 4: BECOME AN EXPERT

A counterpart strategy to general book reading is the focused activity of developing extensive knowledge in a particular domain of study. This, too, builds crystallized intelligence—in particular, the form of organized understanding that is the foundation of expertise.[4] As we have seen, the expert's knowledge base is massive. It consists of a coherent assemblage of ideas and skills that number around 50,000 distinct patterns. Attaining expertise in a field is a marvelous achievement, yet it is reached by only a small percentage of people. That percentage could grow considerably. Through research on expertise, we now understand more exactly the processes by which "ordinary" people become experts, and we can use that knowledge to our advantage.

The time is right to expand the total reserves of expertise in our society and to do whatever we can to deepen our personal expertise in our chosen field of study. Our technological world demands experts and rewards them. Those who consistently deepen their knowledge and skills to become experts will position themselves favorably. But expertise comes at a cost. Reaching expert status requires a level of discipline and dedication that rises far above mere competence. Expertise conveys the right and the ability to speak with authority in a defined area; it is the quality that gets recognized among "go-to" people, those able individuals who are most likely to solve the problems that confound everyone else.

The key question is: How does one become an expert? The answer is, in a sense, rather simple. Expertise is the product of very extended experience. The simplicity of the answer should not be mistaken for ease, however.

This in turn implies an investment of thousands of hours dedicated to becoming exceptional in a focused domain. Over the centuries, the structure and social support of formal educational institutions—schools and universities—has established a framework of expectation and support for growth toward the early stages of expertise. Besides the accumulation of knowledge in defined fields of practice, a formal educational environment conveys the more general cognitive benefits of fluid and crystallized intelligence. In the quest to develop expertise and intelligence, schools and universities are natural allies.

Once past the school years, adults typically do not face the cognitive demands that characterize schooling. Generally, there is less need to use memory strategies and certain forms of abstract reasoning and critical thinking.[5] Reentry into the educational system, especially in the pursuit of an advanced degree, can deepen specialized knowledge and sharpen thinking skills. By enrolling in coursework or structured degree programs, adults in the middle and later years of life place themselves in social and intellectual environments where challenging cognitive demands are again reasserted. Self-study is another channel by which expertise can grow. Through multiple means, expertise is attainable by a broader segment of the population than ever before.

The research literature tells us that students on the road to expertise think about their fields in particular ways. For example, when novices begin study in a new area they often have very little idea about how to distinguish more important ideas from less important ones. To make this distinction, they must structure their efforts to build a foundation of domain knowledge so that deep understanding can emerge over time. In doing so, some aspiring experts become very good managers of their own intellectual development. These self-directed learners have sometimes been called "expert novices" to indicate that, although they are beginners, their structured behavior in some ways resembles that of experts. With discipline and firm commitment, they pursue ways of thinking and patterns of behavior that guide them assuredly toward expert status.[6]

STRATEGY 5: DEVELOP EFFECTIVE CHARACTER

Intelligence is a very good predictor of workplace effectiveness. Yet there is another trait, a personality factor, that rivals intelligence in its ability to predict workplace success. That trait is conscientiousness. Although conscientiousness is an *internal* trait, it is lived out through its behavioral manifestations—responsibility, follow-through, insistence on quality, and attention to detail. The behavioral expression of conscientiousness is an asset in many arenas of initiative besides the workplace. In schools, and for that matter in every context where purposeful activity is relevant, conscientiousness will facilitate success. These qualities of work are displayed to various degrees in different people, but like general intelligence, conscientiousness can be developed. There is no reason why a person who pursues greater fluid and crystallized intelligence can't also develop the attitudes and behavioral traits that define conscientiousness.

Other personality characteristics also pair nicely with intelligence to influence success outcomes. I have used the term "effective character" to refer to the mix of personality characteristics that support success in multiple life arenas. These traits include conscientiousness above all, but also extend into intellectual openness, emotional stability, and, at least in some contexts, the interpersonal affability that we associate with extraversion. The combination of intelligence and effective character presents a formidable duo that every employer or manager ought to keenly desire among workers. Applied over many months and years, conscientiousness will also support the regimen of deliberate practice that leads to expertise. The rhythm of practice for the purposes of skill development—to perfect the details of performance and to fine-tune knowledge—is essential for growing the thoroughgoing proficiency that marks expertise.

Personal effectiveness leans heavily on the intellectual resources collectively called intelligence, yet intelligence is not enough. To fully capitalize on the powerful resources intelligence offers in the pursuit of challenging and worthwhile goals, mental intellectual ability must be teamed with effective character. Because this combination of traits is unrivaled, every person, institution, and nation intent on securing a more successful future ought to have a plan for developing both.

STRATEGY 6: FIND YOUR INTELLECTUAL NICHE

In technical terms, intelligence is often defined as a unified entity. This meaning is implied when whenever we speak or read the word "intelligence." The unity of intelligence is also supported by many decades of research. Even so, we can also appreciate that intelligence has many diverse manifestations. Because people have different ability profiles, we are, it seems, "smart" in different ways. When we interpret intelligence profiles in this way—as variable from person to person—the implication is that each of us is adapted to somewhat different environments. Aptitude thereby becomes a synonym for "fit," much like a particular species of organism is adapted to fit its ecological niche.

This way of looking at intelligence—not simply as a quantity but also as a kind—has consequences. For example, it can help us to make wise choices. We can exercise intelligence not just in developing our ability profile, but also in choosing and modifying our environments so that they provide a more optimal fit with what we can do well. Such considerations matter supremely when selecting a field of study for a university degree and in choosing a career. Considerations include:

- What do I do well?
- What do I do poorly?
- What do I enjoy?

Appraising each question honestly may yield surprises. We might find, for example, that we devote considerable energy to activities we don't do particularly well. Or we may neglect our talents, failing to find opportunities for their expression or development. One key challenge for every organization it to promote the optimal match between the talents of workers and the range of responsible activity that an organization needs. Talent is a very important factor, but not the only one; another considerable dimension is enjoyment. Upon reflection, we might be surprised to realize that we devote little time to the sorts of intellectual activity that we enjoy most. The point is not to avoid work that lacks value for enjoyment. That's impractical. The recommended strategy is rather to change the mix to favor more rewarding activities, and to use the consequent positive emotion to energize activity. Again, the point is to promote fit with one's own natural ecology—to seek opportunities that draw upon our best talents and that bring us the highest and most consistent sense of fulfillment.

One mark of intellectual development in adulthood is the ability to find apt environments, or to alter existing environments so that they offer a good fit with a changing profile of strengths and weaknesses. Improving the match between personal traits and the environment is especially important among the elderly. In the later years of life, positive development is more likely if we can anticipate how our profiles might change in the months and years ahead.[7] When we exercise intelligence at this meta-level, we understand our personal intelligence profile, judge whether it matches or mismatches our present circumstances, and then do whatever we can to improve the fit.

STRATEGY 7: CULTIVATE SOCIAL INTELLIGENCE

We are used to thinking of intelligence as skill in manipulating complex symbolic information. This is not incorrect, only incomplete. Intelligence can also be applied to other forms of information, including human behavior. Everyday observations suggest that people differ radically in their ability to think and act intelligently in the social realm. Some people are tremendously skilled in social interactions—they build goodwill while achieving their own goals. They do so by working cooperatively with others, persuading, being persuaded, and forging compromises when necessary. These people are marvelously capable in the social domain. Others seem clueless. Their social interactions are awkward, and they may feel woefully misunderstood. Chances are good that they will undermine their most cherished goals because they do not know how to work with other people to achieve them.

The ability to think and act skillfully in the realm of human behavior is called social intelligence. It includes the skills needed to "read" the behavior of others in order to gain insight into their intentions and feelings. A related ability, called emotional intelligence, is manifest in understanding the emotions of other people as well as one's own emotional state. Social intelligence is the broader category that subsumes emotional intelligence, but social intelligence also includes the productive side of behavior: an ability to *act* skillfully in a shifting social landscape. Because social intelligence is a tremendously important skill set, it is one manifestation of intelligence that each person would do well to cultivate and fine-tune over time. There is no formula for doing so, only rough suggestions. Like all forms of skilled behavior, social intelligence requires practice. Though the social milieu may be off-putting, to avoid interactions with others is to compound a problem rather than to solve it.

STRATEGY 8: SEEK LIKE-MINDED FRIENDSHIPS

Intelligence can be shaped by the environment, and that environment includes other people. We can capitalize on this fact to advance our own thinking and problem-solving ability. Scholars who study the effects of the environment on intelligence note that a person's IQ is shaped in part by "the IQs of others with whom they come into contact."[8] Intelligence rises and falls in part because of a social multiplier. For better or worse, our own intelligence is significantly a function of the intellectual richness of our social environments.

We rightly stand amazed at the great minds of history. In our amazement, however, we might commit the error of extolling the brilliant insights of a few luminaries—Mozart, Michelangelo, Einstein, and their kin—forgetting that they owed much of their greatness to the achievements of other bright minds. To imagine that these geniuses acted alone is a distortion of history and misrepresents how the human intellect accomplishes great works. Isaac Newton himself declared that he stood on the shoulders of giants. He depended not only on the insights of his predecessors—Aristotle, Galileo, and Copernicus—he also needed the combative antagonism of his contemporaries, including the intellectual barbs of his rival Robert Hooke. Like Newton, each of us influences, and is influenced by, the ideas of others—sometimes by agreeing, other times by disagreeing, and often simply by being provoked to think more deeply. This mutual influence of productive minds occurs not just in the moment—our interactions with other people leave long-lasting impressions, traces of intellectual identity that become entries to our permanent store of ideas and mental habits.

The human mind is, at root, a social entity. Although we may be tempted to romanticize the rugged individual blazing the trail of discovery alone, a moment's thought will remind us that a fully isolated person is not a normal human being. The individual mind works best when it interacts freely with other minds to accomplish things, as well as to mutually influence growth and development.[9] We become smarter by the company we keep.[10] The practical application is that we do well to build relationships with the most interesting, engaged, and capable friends we can find. It's not all about IQ. Besides intelligence, of course, we want other qualities in our closest friends—mutual respect and common courtesy, among other traits—but we should consider that friends are sources of intellectual nourishment.[11]

Starting with the Russian brand of psychology advocated by Lev Vygotsky in the 1920s, psychologists began to appreciate that the individual mind acting alone wields only a tiny fraction of the intellectual power of minds working in concert. Vygotsky's theory sheds light on why this is the case. It challenges assumptions that thinking is a solitary activity. We tend to construe thought as private—as occurring inside our heads—but there is another possibility. Good thinking can also occur in the social space between people. There, thinking is rendered wonderfully explicit in the form of language, which we can learn to use as a means of expressing ideas, challenging contentions, and improving plans.

These two ways of understanding thinking—private and shared—complement each other nicely. When you and your friend take opposite sides of a debate, you contribute good ideas and so does your fellow conversant.

Both of you contribute your distinctive ways of thinking. Because those ideas are nonmaterial, they can be freely shared between people without diminishing their potency. What began as private intellectual resources and thought patterns are now communal property. Ideally, you and your friend walk away from the discussion better informed and more intellectually capable. You have made each other smarter. Educational systems and businesses take advantage of this dynamic potential in the form of graduate student seminars and design teams. In our daily lives, we take of hold of Vygotsky's theory whenever we engage others in open-minded dialogue and bring our best ideas to the table.

STRATEGY 9: SEEK OPTIMAL NUTRITION

A dynamic connection between the mind and the brain means that optimal mental performance requires ongoing access to nutrients and avoidance of toxins. Every person needs the basic components of a healthy diet along with essential nutrients that the body cannot synthesize—vitamins and minerals, as well as essential fats and amino acids.[12] Also, because brain cells require more fuel than most other body cells, regular meals and snacks can provide our brains with the energy needed to function optimally.

Poor nutrition is not uncommon: About 10% of US households do not have access to nutritionally adequate diets. When optimal nutrition cannot be guaranteed, programs that support dietary improvements can have measurable effects on cognitive development. Vitamin supplementation, for example, can boost scores on cognitive tests, especially among children living in poverty. Socioeconomic differences show up repeatedly in the incidence of breastfeeding: Middle-class mothers are more likely to breastfeed than are poor mothers. Because breast milk has health-promoting properties, including protection from infection, differences in breastfeeding rates might well contribute to social class differences in cognitive development. Children may be especially prone to the detriments of a suboptimal diet. Without minimally nutritious foods, children exhibit lower than expected academic achievement and poorer social skills—consequences that form a very weak basis for positive adjustment and achievement in the upper grades.[13]

Many adults, too, have diets that are suboptimal. Perhaps less for reasons of affordability than for access or convenience, many adults turn to processed, low-nutrient foods to satisfy their caloric requirements. We might assume that access to health-promoting foods is a baseline condition of living in a technologically advanced society—that it should be easily achieved—but this is not the case. In some locations, a high-speed Internet connection and a strong cell phone signal may be easier to access than nutritious foods. To reach and sustain our intellectual peaks, we cannot afford to think of high-quality food as a dispensable pleasure. By establishing and maintaining a high standard of nutritional quality in our daily diets, we can help ensure that the work of our well-fed brains, intelligent thought, is optimized.

STRATEGY 10: EXERCISE

Of all the strategies for raising cognitive performance, exercise may be the most counterintuitive. For reasons that are still being elucidated, exercise stimulates the brain to create new structures that are fundamental to its effective operation. Structural improvements occur in two forms—more extensive vascularization and greater numbers of the synapses that connect neurons. Both types of physical change were discovered first in laboratory rodents. When animals were coerced to exercise every day by running on treadmills, new blood vessels began to form not only in their muscles but also in their brains. As a result of exercise, the brains of mice were better nourished.[14] Similar effects of exercise on brain vascularization have also been found in monkeys.[15]

Readers of this book are presumably more interested in human intelligence than mouse or monkey intelligence. Fortunately, the effects of exercise on brain function apply to people, too. Exercise produces measurable effects on intellectual performance, presumably based on the structural changes of vascularization and synapse formation similar to those found in laboratory mice. Among the elderly, exercise regimens can be particularly effective in preserving intellectual acumen.[16] Cardiovascular fitness can reduce the typical decline of cognitive function associated with advanced years.[17] Whatever our age, however, we are well advised to establish and maintain a program of regular exercise that can span the decades of life. The benefits are multiple: It may be enough that exercise can improve our physical health—that it can make us smarter is a wonderful and somewhat unexpected bonus.

WHAT YOU CAN DO: A PERSONAL PROJECT

Any aspiration to become a more intelligent person must fit into a much larger picture of ongoing commitments and priorities. Life rarely affords us the opportunity to drop everything in order to pursue a new inter-est. The challenge is to create and maintain a life in a unified composi-tion that, like a mural, holds together with a thematic consistency. One problem is that any strategy that has a reasonable chance of enhancing intelligence calls for a significant commitment of time and energy over a protracted period of time. This cost is high—very likely too high for many people. That is why Strategy 1, presented earlier in this chapter, focused on personal choice with due regard to the price of achieving an intellectual makeover. Assuming that the cost of long-term commitment to personal intelligence enhancement is acceptable, let's consider how to move for-ward with a plan.

Lofty ideas become practical when they translate to specific actions. In constructing a plan to become more effective through enhanced intelli-gence, we can find inspiration from a popular idea in mathematical model-ing. Some years ago, the public became aware of mathematical progress in modeling complex systems, such as weather and ocean currents. Emerging models, popularized under the banner of chaos theory, showed that very complex, even chaotic, phenomena were often intelligible if examined at the right level. The idea was that chaos could often be decomposed into simpler recurrent patterns. Consider a coastline: Contours observed from satellite images have a certain random-walk look, yet photos taken closer to the earth look remarkably like the contours of a the same coastline on a larger scale. Whatever patterns define a coastline are remarkably con-sistent no matter what the scale. Repeating patterns, called fractals, also show up in ice crystals. Like coastlines, the crystal patterns hold across scales both large and small.

Human lives, too, are composed of fractals—at least metaphorically. The pattern of a single day bears similarity to the pattern of a week, a month, a year, and an entire life span. We can apply the concept of fractals in this way: Compose each day so that it looks something like the ideal long-term pat-tern, then repeat that pattern tomorrow, the next day, and so on indefinitely. The idea is to capitalize on the human propensity to repeat behavior—to form long-term routines of habit—but to carefully build habits that are self-actualizing rather than self-defeating. The near-term focus alleviates what might otherwise be an overwhelming reaction to the challenge of over-hauling a lifestyle. By concentrating on today only, it's much easier to think of specific actions and to marshal the will to carry them out.

The 10 strategies provide options. As long as they are customized to fit the realities of our lives now and in the foreseeable future, the strategies provide a menu from which to choose and adapt a few new patterns of behavior that can be "institutionalized" into our identity and that remake us in the process. That menu need not be set from day 1. There is no law against experimentation to see which ensemble works best with our logistical constraints, such as financial realities, and who we are as individuals. When a new set of behaviors is applied with daily consistency, a pattern will emerge that recurs across timescale and begins to define a new life. Subjectively, we ought to experience a greater capacity for intelligent thought along with greater authentic success—the fruit of effective thinking and behavior.

WHAT PARENTS CAN DO

This book emphasizes a dynamic connection between intelligence and education. Yet we know with certainty that schools are not the only places where education takes place. Differences in children's home experiences are crucial.[18] Indeed, the home is arguably at least equal to schools in educative importance. As we have seen, home environments vary dramatically in terms of the presence of books and other print materials, the extent of linguistic interactions between adults and children, and the emotional tone of those interactions—even typical styles of reasoning and decision making. Taken together, variations in home experience add up to tremendous differences among children in cognitive readiness when children enter school. Many children are primed for success, while others start school life lagging behind their age peers. Statistically, the less-prepared children are likely to continue on a shallower trajectory of academic learning compared to their better-prepared peers. Variation in a child's home experience continues to exert effects over the span of the formative years, including adolescence. If the broad spectrum of life experience shapes the developing intellect, then the quality of home experience is hugely important in forming the intelligence and personality factors that are the foundation of personal effectiveness.

In the home, children and adolescents learn all manner of knowledge and skills. They are exposed to attitudes toward learning, thinking, and schooling. These attitudes are pro-educational if they cultivate curiosity about the world, pleasure in learning, a love of books, and familiarity with patterns of social interaction that are common in schools. Such language patterns include known-answer questions, in which a parent points to a cat and asks, "What's that?" or "What does a dog say?" The child understands that the question is not a request for information, but a game in which the child's growing knowledge is elicited and, in the process, strengthened. Effectively, the parent and the child are "playing school."

Just as home environments can instill pro-educational attitudes or speech patterns, anti-educational ways of thinking can arise if patterns of discourse devalue learning. This can occur when a child's questions, motivated by curiosity, are treated as an annoyance. Alternatively, the nonschool hours can be anti-educational when filled with shallow forms of entertainment that offer little by way of new ideas or ways of thinking. Whether watching television is educational or anti-educational depends, of course, on the content. It is also a matter of how much time is given to the activity. An hour of TV watching daily may have an intellectual benefit, again depending on content, but a span of four or five hours in front of a television is correlated with poor academic outcome.[19] The unbalanced commitment of time to passive activities can easily squeeze out physical play and exercise. We now know that functional associations between physical fitness and mental fitness are much more robust than previously assumed. Building positive attitudes toward exercise during childhood is important because those early attitudes predict physical fitness during adulthood.[20]

Parents can do much to help their children learn the intellectual skills that will set them on a positive trajectory. Here we can draw upon the work of Sharon and Craig Ramey, who distilled positive parenting practices from dozens of studies spanning decades of research. They found that adults can encourage children to become capable thinkers by providing:

- Encouragement to explore
- Mentoring in basic cognitive skills, such as comparing and labeling
- Celebration of development advances
- Practice and extension of new skills
- Protection from negative experiences, such as unnecessary disapproval
- Rich and responsive linguistic environments[21]

Many of these practices will strike parents as common sense. They are the sorts of things that attentive parents tend to do routinely. Yet not all parents adopt such practices or foster such interactions with their children—at least not to the same degree. The ideal parenting practice is not to press these ideas to the maximum, bombarding the child in the hopes of setting him or her on a course for eventual admission to the nation's most elite colleges. A more prudent goal is to evaluate whether positive qualities of parent–child interaction are practiced in a way that is reasonable, authentic, and balanced. One final note: These parenting practices do not neatly separate cognitive from emotional goals. They are fully intertwined. This is the nature of intellectual enhancement—as cognitive and emotional beings, our growth in intellectual readiness fuses cognition and emotion from beginning to end.

WHAT TEACHERS CAN DO

For schools to embrace the cultivation of intelligence requires, above all, a change in the way society thinks about intelligence. Simply stated, intelligence must neither be dismissed as a pernicious fallacy nor assumed to be genetically determined and static for life. On the first point, we know that intelligence is no fallacy. It is an abstraction, granted, because it summarizes a broad and powerful skill set that develops over time. More than a century of research has confirmed that intelligence is not a mere curiosity or wispy phantom. It is, rather, the most potent predictor of human effectiveness. By virtue of its historical development, the quantification of intelligence as IQ was intended to predict success. IQ certainly does predict success broadly—in schools, in the workplace, and in life.

The second assumption that must change is commitment to the belief that intelligence is static. This book has documented repeatedly that this is not so. Intelligence is a dynamic quality that can rise or fall depending on the quality of personal experience over time. This causal connection with experience leads, in turn, to some very interesting implications. It is quite plausible that none of us comes close to experiencing optimal conditions for intellectual growth, which means that we universally fall short of our *potential* intelligence.

As our lives become progressively more complex, the skills that compose human intelligence are likely to rise further in importance. That skill set, whether we call it IQ, *g*, or simply intelligence, is partly shaped by heritability. Because nature and nurture apply with nearly equal force on the development of the intellect, intelligence is also shaped by life experience. People vary in the quality of that experience, which in turn is a major source of cognitive inequity in the world. One of most tragic manifestations of experiential inequity is its association with population characteristics, including race and ethnicity. The situation is far from hopeless, however. The infamous Black–White gap in educational achievement has narrowed since 1965, though in recent years the closure of the gap may have stabilized.[22] Still, knowing that the achievement gap has narrowed implies that it can close further. Ultimately, there is no reason that it cannot close completely.

Alongside commitments to equity, we deeply desire for our educational systems to be excellent. Both lofty goals—excellence and equity—are dear to the hearts of educators. If in one bright day excellence and equity were broadly achieved or even approximated, education will have met its deepest challenges and satisfied its central missions. We are miles from that goal, but there has been progress. Often, we are given the impression that the quality of education in American schools has been on a long downward spiral. But the problem is not that American schools are performing poorly compared to past decades. Averaging ups and downs over the years, academic achievement is slowly edging upward. The real challenge is that the rest of the world has made huge gains. In comparison to other countries, the United States has regressed in effectiveness. American schools may be doing somewhat better in fostering learning, but in the community of nations the relative performance of US students is sinking ever deeper.

Excellence and equity remain the ultimate goals of education as well as broad indices of societal health. Across the socioeconomic strata, access to nutritious food, medical care, educational opportunity, professional success, and political participation are not what they ought to be. Is real and lasting progress toward these two ideals truly possible? Collectively, we must believe, or at least assume, that the answer is *yes*. Progress will depend on building the intellectual capital that is the basis of effective learning, working, and living. We have seen that solving the problems of inequity and subpar academic performance will depend on society's success in building the powerful skill set we call intelligence. Ignoring the role of intelligence and its cultivation amounts to postponing a solution, and enduring another century of frustration and disappointment.

How does this translate to action? The most sensible starting point is Strategy 1: Prioritize the cultivation of intelligence as an explicit organizing goal of education. Schools and school systems ought to establish an enhancing-intelligence curriculum for every school and every student. The best current theories of intelligence are not so fully worked out as to prescribe one best approach. Rather, theories of intelligence have the dynamic quality of medicine, in which understanding of disease processes evolves alongside treatment models. Understanding grows through research, and today's standards of medical practice are open to refutation and replacement as knowledge accrues. So, too, in intelligence theory, concepts and principles are certain to evolve in the years ahead. Nonetheless, we know enough at this point to put knowledge into action. One impediment to applying what we already know is that the study of intelligence remains largely an academic enterprise, sealed off from the world of praxis. Ideally, that imbalance will shift during this century so that false beliefs about intelligence can be replaced by a more accurate account of intelligence as malleable.

Education must change, but how? The agents and contexts of education are quite varied. Alongside schools, families, peers, and even self-study are credible candidates for the primary role in advancing the mind's proficiency set. Nonetheless, the steady rhythm and structure of schools makes them vital institutions for teaching literacy, numeracy, and subject matter knowledge. Schools are also crucial for cultivating intelligence. Historically, schools have evolved into institutions finely geared to the development of crystallized intelligence. This leaves fluid intelligence sorely neglected. This omission can be addressed through the serious pursuit of Strategy 2: Build fluid intelligence through problem solving. Although fluid intelligence is not part of the professional vocabulary of practicing teachers, problem solving is. Over the past several decades, educators have recognized problem solving as an important educational goal. Problem solving has been integrated, at least to some extent, into curriculum materials and summative assessments. Cultivating fluid intelligence in schools will require greatly bolstering the emphasis on problem solving, with a concentration on flexible and adaptive thinking.

Yet another way for schools to enhance intelligence is to build greater vertical integration of the curriculum over the years spanning elementary and secondary education. Logically, it makes sense to align the learning goals of any school year with the learning goals of prior years and the years that follow. The standards movement has contributed to greater vertical alignment of the curriculum. Yet something else is needed here, which is the counterpart development of the learner's ability to deliberately pursue the development of cumulative knowledge and skill over many years. This connects to Strategy 4, "Become an expert," in the sense that the vision and volition of the aspiring expert can be developed in young learners as part of their school experience. Then, when the time comes for learners to seriously pursue expertise, they will have the requisite resolve and persistence to turn their dreams into reality.

School leaders ought to consider other strategies, such as supporting effective nutrition and regular exercise as life habits. We now know that exercise and nutrition are essential not only for promoting health, but also for building optimal brain vasculature and synaptic connectivity. Yet, specific strategies are debatable. The important point is to place the cultivation of intelligence centrally in the mission of school and to let the specific implications fit the particulars of the community. Again, awareness must be the first step. Finding a place for intelligence development in the school curriculum alongside the essentials of reading, mathematics, science, and history presumes that the notion of *learnable intelligence* has entered the lexicon of teachers, principals, school board members, and parents. For schools to take on this exciting new role, there must be a much broader awareness that intelligence development is not only possible, but also a legitimate mission of schooling. That conceptual shift is radical: Education must be redefined to include the enhancement of intelligence as a core function.

Is there a contradiction in this line of reasoning? Haven't we already seen that schooling is strongly correlated with IQ gains? Indeed, one consequence of formal education is the development of the intelligence repertoire. In earlier chapters we saw evidence that the extent of formal education predicts adult IQs even when initial IQ is held constant. Schools, therefore, are *already* hothouses of intelligence development. Even now, teachers are cultivators of intelligence, gardeners who plant and water the seeds of intellect, though they may not always see themselves in such terms. More likely, they view their roles quite differently, namely as teachers of academic content and skills. Yet in addition to fostering students' ostensible achievements in reading, math, and the standard school subjects, teachers nourish the deeper roots of intelligence. As teachers teach, students become smarter.

The unwitting development of intelligence in schools is a bit of a problem precisely *because* it is unplanned and accidental. If intelligence is a mere by-product of education rather than an intentional outcome, then its conveyance to students is likely to be less than fully efficient and equitable. In other words, the accidental consequence of rising IQ fails to satisfy, or even approach, the ideals of excellence and equity. To expand on the equity issue, some students will readily pick up powerful modes of thinking but others will not. That's because intelligent cognition is not taught directly but rather is buried in the curriculum; it is tacit rather than explicit. To perceive and to internalize ways of thinking that underlie intelligence entails "code breaking" on the part of students. The entire process of intellectual growth could be more powerful, and fairer, if the most basic elements of intelligence were brought to light.

The components of intelligence could be taught directly through coherent curricula to present those components and tests specially designed to assess whether or not students learn them.[23] The most common interpretation of "test" is large-scale standardized testing used for school and teacher accountability. This meaning may be legitimate, but the most powerful forms of testing provide feedback functions to teachers and students. Students advance at finely differentiated rates as they develop the core competencies of intelligence, and progress will likely be measurable in small increments. For these reasons, the ideal metacurriculum of intelligence will have a strong component of individualized learning with feedback. Some elements of the intelligence metacurriculum may be unusually challenging. Expanding students' working memory capacity, for example, may require a great deal of concentration over a long period of time. Unlike progress in mastering a standard curriculum unit, such as knowledge of the Cold War, progress on the intelligence metacurriculum may seem quite gradual and incremental. Continuous feedback to students will help them to see that they are making progress over time. All this assumes that, as a society, we are able to see the purpose of education in a fresh light—in particular, as redefined to place the enhancement of intelligence as a central goal. Stanford professor Richard Snow, the eminent scholar of human intelligence, expressed the concept this way: Intelligence is "education's most important product, as well as its most important raw material."[24]

A reformulated metacurriculum would elevate learnable intelligence to the status of literacy and numeracy, whose curricular importance is justified because these competencies transfer broadly to many other areas of study. The power of reading and mathematics is manifest in how they open broad vistas of intellectual development, both in making information accessible as well as in structuring powerful modes of thinking. The ability to read with comprehension opens a window to the riches of intellectual history as well as to current thought in social, political, consumer, and scientific spheres. As a metacurricular subject, mathematics prepares students for advanced study and careers in science, technology, and medicine. Equally important, mathematics introduces a way of thinking about the world—an ability to see complexity not as hopelessly chaotic, but as amenable to precise comprehension. Recurring patterns can be discerned as constructs that can be defined, symbolized, measured, and mapped to other constructs. To comprehend order is to achieve greater predictability and, ultimately, a greater degree of control.

Literacy and numeracy compose a distinct metacurriculum whose intellectual benefits apply to diverse areas of study. Both have an ancillary effect of structuring the way the mind perceives and orders the world. Together, they are the curricular precedents for understanding how the cultivation of intelligence can have a place in the canon of formal education.

WHAT INSTITUTIONAL LEADERS CAN DO

Psychologists learned long ago that IQ scores are good for much more than predicting academic success. Measured intelligence is also a very good predictor of worker productivity. Of course, this is just another way of saying something that every employer knows without having to read an academic paper to prove the point. When hiring a new employee, every employer looks for a nimble mind that learns quickly. A deep grounding in the relevant field is vital. Many professions require a well-ordered knowledge base that characterizes expertise. That's all crystallized intelligence. But something else is necessary, especially in today's fast-moving world. More and more, employers seek workers who can apprehend novel problems and solve them, often through innovative thinking. That's fluid intelligence. But employers know that these two—grounded expertise and pure intellectual firepower—are not enough. The employee also needs a third quality that reflects not so much intellect but personal dedication to excellence, follow-through, prioritization, and attention to detail—all backed by a thoroughgoing commitment to hard work. We have called this third quality effective character. Like fluid and crystallized intelligence, effective character is not a personality profile fixed for life, but can be modulated by experience, situational norms, feedback, and personal volition.

These three personal qualities—crystallized intelligence, fluid intelligence, and effective character—are the golden trio of success. Are they fully sufficient? Certainly not. Other traits are important, too. Loyalty, ethics, social skills, and a sense of humor are valued by employers and fellow employees alike. For the sake of conceptual simplicity, however, the personal traits that underlie intelligence can be boiled down to the three named factors. As these factors undergird workplace effectiveness, they are potential guides for recruiting and selecting new workers. Because they remain important after an employee has been hired, the golden trio is a worthwhile target for ongoing worker development. If all three key factors can be developed, then the workplace is an educational institution alongside the schools and universities that grant diplomas and degrees.

The thesis of this book is that intelligence is not a static quality, but rather a consequential trait that can change as a function of experience. When understood as a modifiable personal quality, intelligence takes on heightened importance as intellectual capital. Not only is worker intelligence an unrivaled resource to draw upon, it is also a source of inventive potential that can grow over time. In one way at least, the stakes are higher for business and nonprofit organizations than they are for schools. Schools exist first for the benefit of students and secondarily for the good of the broader society. In business and other organizations, the priorities are reversed: The paramount goal is the viability of the organization. In a competitive environment, the intellectual capital of an organization is essential to its survival and prosperity. Schools should do all they can to advance knowledge and skill as a matter of principle and public trust. Businesses *must* do so as a matter of survival.

In the business realm, leaders who understand the power of fluid intelligence, crystallized intelligence, and effective character can diligently recruit employees who excel in these areas. More important, business leaders can structure the ongoing experience of their workers to develop the building blocks of effectiveness among employees. This might mean asking supervisors and supervisees to jointly set annual performance goals targeting crystallized intelligence, fluid intelligence, and effective character. The overarching purpose would be to build a company's capacity to innovate, to press workers toward higher levels of expertise, and to foster commitment to standards of excellence. The goal should not be generic effectiveness, but effectiveness defined in ways that conform to the mission of an organization. In specific economic sectors, the qualities of fluid and crystallized intelligence, as well as effective character, are best defined with reference to a company's identity and vision. Understood this way, the formula for human effectiveness should always be tailored to each institution's mission—its reason for existence.

WHAT WORLD LEADERS CAN DO

At the founding of America and other democracies, there arose a counterpart need to raise the overall intellectual wherewithal of the citizenry. In the past, as now, there was a broad public "conviction that for children to have more, rather than less, intelligence was a good thing, worthy of social investment."[25] This agenda was advanced through the public school movement in which education was offered freely to all. Such was the vision of Horace Mann, Thomas Jefferson, and John Dewey. Each understood profoundly the necessity of education to a viable democracy.

The establishment of free and universal public education became the first major public policy related to intelligence. Because our world experienced deep social and technological transformations at the dawn of the 21st century, we now face a new set of societal conditions just as radical as emergent democracy. The functionality of today's society, with its freedoms, protections, and potential, relies on intelligence as never before. What passed for sufficient intelligence to guide civic choices for a functional democracy is no longer adequate in a world in which the armature of participation and prosperity is the highly proficient use of the mind. As never before, intelligence must be democratized.

As a global society, we understand that the resources of crystallized intelligence, fluid intelligence, and effective character need not be armaments for competition. To address the world's most pressing problems, intelligent cooperation is necessary. The effectiveness formula is therefore germane to the long-term viability of the planet. The world's grand conundrums—political, economic, social, and environmental—appear as tangled masses of interlocking data and interpretations, claims and counterclaims, often suffused with hot emotions. The resources of intelligence can help us progress toward solutions. For this reason, too, learnable intelligence is not a luxury. It is as necessary as oxygen.

Of course, the world requires more than intelligence. Wisdom is called for—wisdom that collectively allows us to understand complex and difficult circumstances and to achieve goals that advance the common good, recognizing that the way forward cannot possibly please every stakeholder. Wisdom means finding solutions that minimize collective harm or that spread sacrifice equitably rather than asking one person or group to bear the costs that inevitably accompany hard times. Wise decisions promote comparatively good and fair outcomes, not perfect solutions. They require understanding one's own interests and the interests of others.[26] These interests are not strictly economic, but entail emotional factors as well as more abstract commitments to law, ethics, and morality. The exercise of wisdom can never be reduced to a formula—to a single correct solution. Seen this way, wisdom has a creative aspect in that wise solutions to changing circumstances necessarily involve fresh ways of thinking. That is why wisdom can never be taught as an established body of knowledge. The best we can do is to teach the tools of wisdom, partly by precept but mostly by example, and hope that they will be exercised skillfully in context when the need arises.

How can we possibly make progress toward the vaunted goals implied by every vision of a better world—fairness, freedom, discovery, opportunity, health, beauty, and prosperity? In the abstract, each is worthy of investment. To some degree, all draw from the intellectual readiness that is assured by abundant reserves of intelligence in society. Is it really possible to advance learnable intelligence not simply in theory, but as an experienced reality? I have argued that learnable intelligence will take root on a grand scale only by changing long-held assumptions. Ever since Alfred Binet invented the first IQ test more than a century ago, we have tended to think of intelligence in counterproductive ways. One error is to deny altogether that intelligence is a psychological quality of enormous importance. Another mistake is to assume that intelligence is fully determined by genetics and therefore impervious to attempts to change it. Both beliefs reflect outmoded thinking.

The old assumptions are not merely wrong, they undermine our potential to survive and thrive. In the history of ideas that define human identity and potential, we must jettison the assumption of fixed intelligence and take hold of a new way of thinking. Intelligence is a crucial personal quality, a gift of unrivaled importance. Intelligence is also, thankfully, a malleable product of high-quality experience. Already, intelligence has been developed, albeit inefficiently, by educational institutions and through other life contexts. We now collectively face an imperative to change the way we think about intelligence so that we can proceed to cultivate it more directly, effectively, and equitably. Perhaps all we need now is a modest shift of beliefs and commitments, the beginnings of real momentum. The social multiplier effect recognizes that a positive environmental change can spark an upward spiral of enrichment. Gains of intelligence among some have the potential to enrich the environment for many more.[27] There is nothing wrong with starting small as long as our commitments are clear. We must choose to become more intelligent people and to reach toward greater effectiveness in our world—a world whose fate is perilously uncertain, yet whose future is also poised for possibilities of unimaginable beauty and good.

NOTES

CHAPTER 1

1. Reich, R. (1992). *The work of nations: Preparing ourselves for 21st-century capitalism.* New York: Vintage.
2. Reich, R. (2005). *Reason: Why liberals will win the battle for America.* New York: Vintage.
3. Levy, F., & Murnane, R. J. (2004). *The new division of labor: How computers are creating the next job market.* New York: Russell Sage Foundation.
4. Mackintosh, N. J. (1998). *IQ and human intelligence.* New York: Oxford University Press.
5. Levy, F., & Murnane, R. J. (2004). *The new division of labor: How computers are creating the next job market.* New York: Russell Sage Foundation.
6. Reich, R. (1992). *The work of nations: Preparing ourselves for 21st century capitalism.* New York: Vintage. Stewart, T. A. (1997). *Intellectual capital: The new wealth of organizations.* New York: Doubleday/Currency.
7. Galton, F. (1869). *Hereditary genius: An inquiry into its laws and consequences.* London: Macmillan, p. 12. Cited in Mackintosh, N. J. (1998). *IQ and human intelligence.* New York: Oxford University Press, p. 8.
8. Cianciolo, A. T., & Sternberg, R. J. (2004). *Intelligence: A brief history.* Malden, MA: Blackwell. Galton is credited also with being the first to identify the nature versus nurture antithesis in accounting for human variation.
9. Brody, N. (2000). History of theories and measurements of intelligence. In R. J. Sternberg (Ed.), *Handbook of intelligence* (pp. 16–33). New York: Cambridge University Press.
10. Deary, I. (2000). Simple information processing and intelligence. In R. J. Sternberg (Ed.), *Handbook of intelligence* (pp. 267–284). New York: Cambridge University Press.
11. Jensen, A. R. (1982). Reaction time and psychometric *g*. In H. J. Eysenck (Ed.), *A model for intelligence* (pp. 93–132). New York: Springer-Verlag.
12. This did not settle the matter forever. In the years that followed, some researchers confirmed Galton's result (Wissler, 1901), but others eventually found connections between higher-order intelligence and basic measures of reaction time and sensory discrimination. This research stream that was taken up with renewed interest in the 1980s and 1990s, and remains a small but important branch of research on intelligence to this day (Deary, 2000; see note 10). Wissler, C. (1901). The correlation of mental and physical tests. *Psychological Review Monograph Supplements, 3*(6).

13. Brody, N. (2000). History of theories and measurements of intelligence. In R. J. Sternberg (Ed.), *Handbook of intelligence* (pp. 16–33). New York: Cambridge University Press.

14. Stern, W. L. (1912). *Psychologischen Methoden der Intlligenz-Prüfung*. Leipzig: Barth.

15. Ramey, C. T., & Ramey, S. L. (2000). Intellectual and public policy. In R. J. Sternberg (Ed.), *Handbook of intelligence* (pp. 534–548). New York: Cambridge University Press.

16. Kaufman, A. S. (2000). Tests of intelligence. In R. J. Sternberg (Ed.), *Handbook of intelligence* (pp. 445–476). New York: Cambridge University Press.

17. Rosenthal, R., & Jacobsen, L. (1968). *Pygmalion in the classroom: Teacher expectation and pupils' intellectual development*. New York: Holt, Rinehart, & Winston.See also Wineburg, S. (1987). Does research count in the lives of behavioral scientists? *Educational Researcher, 16*(9), 42–44.

18. Detterman, D. K., Gabriel, L. T., & Ruthsatz, J. M. (2000). Intelligence and mental retardation. In R. J. Sternberg (Ed.), *Handbook of intelligence* (pp. 141–158). New York: Cambridge University Press.

19. Mackintosh, N. J. (1998). *IQ and human intelligence*. New York: Oxford University Press.

20. Disattenuated correlations range between .40 and .70, averaging about .50.Mackintosh, N. J. (1998). *IQ and human intelligence*. New York: Oxford University Press.Neisser, U., Boodoo, G., Bouchard, T. J., Boykin, A. W., Brody, N., Ceci, S. J., Halpern, D. F., Loehlin, J. C, Perloff, R., Sternberg, R. J., & Urbina, S. (1996). Intelligence: Knowns and unknowns. *American Psychologist, 51*(2), 77–101.

21. Mayer, R. E. (2011). Intelligence and achievement. In R. J. Sternberg & S. B. Kaufman (Eds.), *The Cambridge handbook of intelligence* (pp. 738–747). New York: Cambridge University Press.

22. Kaufman, A. S. (2000). Tests of intelligence. In R. J. Sternberg (Ed.), *Handbook of intelligence* (pp. 445–476). New York: Cambridge University Press.

23. Cianciolo, A. T., & Sternberg, R. J. (2004). *Intelligence: A brief history*. Malden, MA: Blackwell.

24. Mackintosh, N. J. (1998). *IQ and human intelligence*. New York: Oxford University Press.

25. Schmidt, F. L., & Hunter, J. E. (1998). The validity and utility of selection methods in personnel psychology: Practical and theoretical implications of 85 years of research findings. *Psychological Bulletin, 124*, 262–274.

26. Deary, I. J., & Batty, G. D. (2011). Intelligence as a predictor of health, illness, and death. In R. J. Sternberg & S. B. Kaufman (Eds.), *The Cambridge handbook of intelligence* (pp. 683–707). New York: Cambridge University Press.

27. Terman, L. M., & Oden, M. H. (1947). *Genetic studies of genius, Volume IV: The gifted child grows up*. Stanford, CA: Stanford University Press.Terman, L. M., & Oden, M. H. (1959). *Genetic studies of genius, Volume V: The gifted child at mid-life*. Stanford, CA: Stanford University Press.

28. Holahan, C. K., & Sears, R. R. (1995). *The gifted child in later maturity*. Stanford, CA: Stanford University Press.

29. Schoon, I. (2000). A life span approach to talent development. In K. A. Heller, F. J. Mönks, R. J. Sternberg, & R. F. Sternberg (Eds.), *International handbook of giftedness and talent* (2nd ed., pp. 213–225). New York: Elsevier.

30. Herrnstein, R. J., & Murray C. (1994). *The bell curve: Intelligence and class structure in American life.* New York: Free Press.
31. Deary, I. J., & Batty, G. D. (2011). Intelligence as a predictor of health, illness, and death. In R. J. Sternberg & S. B. Kaufman (Eds.), *The Cambridge handbook of intelligence.* New York: Cambridge University Press.
32. McLaren, R. B. (1993). The dark side of creativity. *Creativity Research Journal, 6*(1&2), 137–144.
33. Tannenbaum, A. J. (1996). Giftedness: The ultimate instrument for good or evil. In C. P. Benbow & D. Lubinski (Eds.), *Intellectual talent: Psychometric and social issues* (pp. 447–465). Baltimore, MD: Johns Hopkins University Press, p. 447.
34. Milgram, S. (1974). *Obedience to authority: An experimental view.* New York: Harper & Row.
35. Neisser, U., Boodoo, G., Bouchard, T. J., Boykin, A. W., Brody, N., Ceci, S. J., Halpern, D. F., Loehlin, J. C, Perloff, R., Sternberg, R. J. & Urbina, S. (1996). Intelligence: Knowns and unknowns. *American Psychologist, 51*(2), 77–101.
36. Mackintosh, N. J. (1998). *IQ and human intelligence.* New York: Oxford University Press.
37. Ochse, R. (1990). *Before the gates of excellence: The determinants of creative genius.* Cambridge, UK: Cambridge University Press.
38. Simonton, D. K. (2000). Genius or giftedness: Same or different? In K. A. Heller, F. J. Mönks, R. J. Sternberg, & R. F. Subotnik (Eds.), *International handbook of giftedness and talent* (2nd ed., pp. 111–121). New York: Elsevier.
39. Lubinski, D., Benbow, C. P., Webb, R. M., & Bleske-Rechek, A. (2006). Tracking exceptional human capital over two decades. *Psychological Science, 17*(3), 194–199.
40. Cox, C. M. (1926/1992). The early mental traits of 300 geniuses. In L. M. Terman (Ed.), *Genetic studies of genius.* Stanford, CA: Stanford University Press.
41. Simonton, D. K. (1988). *Scientific genius: A psychology of science.* Cambridge, UK: Cambridge University Press.

CHAPTER 2

1. Embretson, S. E., & Schmidt McCollam, K. M. (2000). Psychometric approaches to understanding and measuring intelligence. In R. J. Sternberg (Ed.), *Handbook of intelligence* (pp. 423–444). New York: Cambridge University Press.
2. Jensen, A. R. (1998). *The g factor: The science of mental ability.* Westport, CT: Praeger.
3. Thurstone, L. L. (1938). Primary mental abilities. *Psychological Monographs, 1,* p. vii.
4. Guilford, J. P. (1988). Some changes in the structure-of-intellect model. *Educational and Psychological Measurement, 48,* 1–4.
5. Thurstone, L. L, & Thurstone, T. G. (1942). *Factorial studies of intelligence.* Chicago: University of Chicago Press, p. 3.
6. Carroll, J. B. (1996). A three-stratum model of intelligence. Spearman's contribution. In I. Dennis & P. Tapsfield (Eds.), *Human abilities: Their nature and measurement* (pp. 1–17). Mahwah, NJ: Erlbaum.Spearman, C., & Wynn Jones, L. (1950). *Human ability: A continuation of "The abilities of man."* London: Macmillan.
7. Cattell, R. B. (1987). *Intelligence: Its structure, growth, and action.* New York: North-Holland.

8. Gustafsson, J.-E., & Undheim, J. O. (1996). Individual differences in cognitive functions. In. D. C. Berliner & R. C. Calfee (Eds.), *Handbook of educational psychology* (pp. 186–310). New York: Macmillan, p. 204.

9. Carroll, J. B. (1993). *Human cognitive abilities: A survey of factor-analytic studies.* New York: Cambridge University Press.

10. Treffert, D. A., & Wallace, G. L. (2007). Islands of genius. *Scientific American Mind Special Report.*

11. Sloboda, J. A., Hermelin, B., & O'Connor, N. (1985). An exceptional musical memory. *Musical Perception, 3,* 155–170.

12. Cattell, R. B. (1987). *Intelligence: Its structure, growth, and action.* New York: North-Holland.

13. Gustafsson, J.-E. (1999). Measuring and understanding G: Experimental and correlational approaches. In P. L. Ackerman, P. C. Kyllonen, & R. D. Roberts (Eds.), *Learning and individual differences: Process, trait, and content determinants* (pp. 275–289). Washington, DC: American Psychological Association.

14. Lohman, D. F. (2000). Complex information processing and intelligence. In R. J. Sternberg (Ed.), *Handbook of intelligence* (pp. 285–340). New York: Cambridge University Press.

15. Carpenter, P. A., Just, M. A., & Shell, P. (1990). What one intelligence test measures: A theoretical account of the processing in the Raven Progressive Matrices Test. *Psychological Review, 97,* 404–431.

16. Ellis, N. (1994). Vocabulary acquisition: The implicit ins and outs of explicit cognitive mediation. In N. C. Ellis (Ed.), *Implicit and explicit learning of languages* (pp. 211–282). London: Academic Press.

17. Lohman, D. F. (1993). Teaching and testing to develop fluid abilities. *Educational Researcher, 22*(7), 12–23.

18. Kaufman, A. S. (2000). Tests of intelligence. In R. J. Sternberg (Ed.), *Handbook of intelligence* (pp. 445–476). New York: Cambridge University Press. Predictable cognitive changes over the course of life has led to age norms not only for children but for adults as well.

19. Schaie, K. W. (1996). *Intellectual development in adulthood: The Seattle Longitudinal Study.* New York: Cambridge University Press.

20. Yet another possibility is that declines in fluid intelligence over the life span are at least partly artifactual. Data that document such changes are primarily cross-sectional, relying on different age cohorts for estimating distributions of cognitive abilities at each point along the life span, rather than tracking changes among individuals over time.

21. Scheidt, R. J., & Schaie, K. W. (1978). A situational taxonomy for the elderly: Generating situational criteria. *Journal of Gerontology, 33,* 348–357.

22. Schaie, K. W. (1996). *Intellectual development in adulthood: The Seattle Longitudinal Study.* New York: Cambridge University Press.

23. Hunt, E. B. (1995). *Will we be smart enough? A cognitive analysis of upcoming workforce.* New York: Russell Sage Foundation.

24. Nettlebeck, T. (2011). Basic processes of intelligence. In R. J. Sternberg & S. B. Kaufman (Eds.), *The Cambridge handbook of intelligence* (pp. 371–393). New York: Cambridge University Press.

25. Nettleback, T. (1987) Inspection time and intelligence. In P. A. Vernon (Ed.), *Speed of information processing and intelligence* (pp. 295–346). Norwood, NJ: Ablex.

26. Deary, I. (2000). Simple information processing and intelligence. In R. J. Sternberg (Ed.), *Handbook of intelligence* (pp. 267–284). New York: Cambridge University Press.

27. Jensen, A. R. (1992). Understanding *g* in terms of information processing. *Educational Psychology Review, 4*, 271–308.

28. Deary, I. (2000). Simple information processing and intelligence. In R. J. Sternberg (Ed.), *Handbook of intelligence* (pp. 267–284). New York: Cambridge University Press.

29. Deary, I. J., & Stough, C. (1997). Looking down on intelligence. *American Psychologist, 52*, 1148–1150.

30. Larson, G. E., & Saccuzzo, D. P. (1989). Cognitive correlates of general intelligence: Toward a process theory of *g. Intelligence, 13*, 5–31.

31. Mackintosh, N. J. (1998). *IQ and human intelligence*. New York: Oxford University Press.

32. Lohman, D. F., & Lakin, J. M. (2011). Intelligence and reasoning. In R. J. Sternberg & S. B. Kaufman (Eds.), *The Cambridge handbook of intelligence* (pp. 419–441). New York: Cambridge University Press.

33. Baltes, P. B., Lindenberger, U., & Staudinger, U. M. (1998). Life-span theory in developmental psychology. In W. Damon (Editor-in Chief) & R. M. Lerner (Vol. Ed.), *Handbook of child psychology, Vol. 1: Theoretical models of human development* (pp. 1029–1144). New York: Wiley.

CHAPTER 3

1. Gardner, H. (1983). *Frames of mind*. New York: Basic Books.

2. Gardner, H. (Winter 1998). A multiplicity of intelligences. *Scientific American Presents, 9*(4), 36–41.Gardner later added naturalistic and existential intelligences to his theory. Gardner, H. (1999). *Intelligence reframed: Multiple intelligences for the 21st century*. New York: Basic Books.

3. The Cattell/Horn hierarchical model, which first distinguished fluid and crystallized intelligence, was eventually expanded on the basis of evidence that was not strictly psychometric: Horn, J. L. (1986). Intellectual ability concepts. In R. J. Sternberg (Ed.), *Advances in the psychology of human intelligence* (Vol. 3, pp. 33–77). Hillsdale, NJ: Erlbaum.

4. Kyllonen, P. C., Roberts, R. D., & Stankov, L. (2007). *Extending intelligence: Enhancement and new constructs*. New York: Erlbaum.

5. Daniel, M. H. (2000). Interpretation of intelligence test scores. In R. J. Sternberg (Ed.), *Handbook of intelligence* (pp. 477–491). New York: Cambridge University Press.

6. Callahan, C. M., Tomlinson, C. A., Moon, T. R., Tomchin, E. M., & Plucker, J. (1995). *Project START: Using a multiple intelligences model in identifying and promoting talent in high-school students* [Research Monograph 95136]. Storrs: University of Connecticut, National Research Center on the Gifted and Talented.

7. Sternberg, R. J. (2011). The theory of successful intelligence. In R. J. Sternberg & S. B. Kaufman (Eds.), *The Cambridge handbook of intelligence* (pp. 504–527). New York: Cambridge University Press.

8. Sternberg, R. J. (1996). *Successful intelligence*. New York: Simon & Schuster.

9. Sternberg, R. J., Nokes, K., Geissler, P. W., Prince, R., Okatcha, F., Bundy, D. A., & Grigorenko, E. L. (2001). The relationship between academic and practical intelligence: A case study in Kenya. *Intelligence, 29*, 401–418.

10. Wagner, R. K. (2000). Practical intelligence. In R. J. Sternberg & S. B. Kaufman (Eds.), *The Cambridge handbook of intelligence* (pp. 550–563). New York: Cambridge University Press.

11. Wagner, R. K. (2000). Practical intelligence. In R. J. Sternberg (Ed.), *Handbook of intelligence* (pp. 380–395). New York: Cambridge University Press.

12. King, P M., & Kitchener, K. S. (2004). Reflective judgment: Theory and research on the development of epistemic assumptions through adulthood. *Educational Psychologist, 39*(1), 5–18.

13. Sternberg, R. J. (2000). Intelligence and wisdom. In R. J. Sternberg (Ed.), *Handbook of intelligence* (pp. 631–649). New York: Cambridge University Press.

14. Sternberg, R. J. (2006). The Rainbow Project: Enhancing the SAT through assessments of analytical, practical, and creative skills. *Intelligence, 43*, 321–350.

15. Callahan, C. M. (2000). Intelligence and giftedness. In R. J. Sternberg (Ed.), *Handbook of intelligence* (pp. 159–175). New York: Cambridge University Press.

16. Miller, B. L., Cummings, J., Mishkin, F., Boone, K., Prince, F., Ponton, M., & Cotman, C. (1998). Emergence of artistic talent in frontotemporal dementia. *Neurology, 51*(4), 978–982.

17. Young, R. L., Ridding, M. C., & Morrell, T. L. (2004). Switching skills on by turning off part of the brain. *Neurocase, 10*(3), 213–222.Snyder, A., Bahramali, H., Hawker, T., & Mitchell, D. J. (2006). Savant-like numerosity skills revealed in normal people by magnetic pulses. *Perception, 35*, 837–845.

18. Callahan, C. M. (2000). Intelligence and giftedness. In R. J. Sternberg (Ed.), *Handbook of intelligence* (pp. 159–175). New York: Cambridge University Press.Barron, R. (1963). *Creativity and psychological health.* Princeton, NJ: D. Van Nostrand.

19. Sternberg, R. J., & O'Hara, L. A. (2000). Intelligence and creativity. In R. J. Sternberg (Ed.), *Handbook of intelligence* (pp. 611–630). New York: Cambridge University Press.

20. Hayes, J. R. (2010). Cognitive processes in creativity. In J. A. Glover, R. R. Ronning, & C. R. Reynolds (Eds.), *Handbook of creativity: Perspectives on individual differences.* (pp. 135–145). New York: Springer.

21. Haensly, P. A., & Reynolds, C. R. (2010). Creativity and intelligence. In J. A. Glover, R. R. Ronning, & C. R. Reynolds (Eds.), *Handbook of creativity: Perspectives on individual differences* (pp. 111–134). New York: Springer, p. 114.

22. Lubart, T. I. (1994). Creativity. In R. J. Sternberg (Ed.), *Thinking and problem solving* (pp. 289–332). San Diego, CA: Academic Press.

23. Sternberg, R. J., & O'Hara, L. A. (2000). Intelligence and creativity. In R. J. Sternberg (Ed.), *Handbook of intelligence* (pp. 611–630). New York: Cambridge University Press.

24. Nickerson, R. S. (1999). Enhancing creativity. In R. S. Sternberg (Ed.), *Handbook of creativity* (pp. 392–430). New York: Cambridge University Press.

25. Gardner, H. (1993). *Creating minds: An anatomy of creativity as seen through the lives of Freud, Einstein, Picasso, Stravinsky, Eliot, Graham, and Gandhi.* New York: Basic Books.

26. Cox, C. M. (1926/1992). The early mental traits of 300 geniuses. Reprinted in L. M. Terman (Ed.), *Genetic studies of genius.* Stanford, CA: Stanford University Press.

27. Sternberg, R. J., Conway, B. E., Ketron, J. L., & Bernstein, M. (1981). People's conceptions of intelligence. *Journal of Personality and Social Psychology, 41*,

37–55.Kosmitzki, C., & John, O. P. (1993). The implicit use of explicit conceptions of social intelligence. *Personality & Individual Differences, 15,* 11–23.

28. Tulving, E. (2002). Episodic memory: From mind to brain. *Annual Review of Psychology, 53,* 1–25.

29. Kihlstrom, J. F., & Cantor, N. (2011). Social intelligence. In R. J. Sternberg & S. B. Kaufman (Eds.), *The Cambridge handbook of intelligence* (pp. 564–591). New York: Cambridge University Press.

30. Simonton, D. K. (1984). *Genius, creativity and leadership: Historiometric inquiries.* Cambridge: Harvard University Press.

31. Lohman, D. F. (2000). Complex information processing and intelligence. In R. J. Sternberg (Ed.), *Handbook of intelligence* (pp. 285–340). New York: Cambridge University Press.

32. Renzulli, J. S. (1986). The three-ring conception of giftedness: A developmental model of creative productivity. In R. J. Sternberg & J. E. Davidson (Eds.), *Conceptions of giftedness* (pp. 53–92). New York: Cambridge University Press, p. 75.

33. Cacioppo, J. T., Petty, R. E., Feinstein, J. A., & Jarvis, W. B. G. (1996). Dispositional differences in cognitive motivation: The life and times of individuals varying in need for cognition. *Psychological Bulletin, 119*(2), 197–253.

34. Goff, M., & Ackerman, P. L. (1992). Personality-intelligence relations: Assessment of typical intellectual engagement. *Journal of Educational Psychology, 84*(4), 537–552.

35. Csikszentmihalyi, M. (1975). *Beyond boredom and anxiety.* Hoboken, NJ: Jossey-Bass.

36. Bower, G. H., & Forgas, J. P. (2001). Mood and social memory. In J. P. Forgas (Ed.), *Handbook of affect and social cognition* (pp. 95–120). Mahwah, NJ: Erlbaum.

37. Goleman, D. (1995). *Emotional intelligence.* New York: Bantam.

38. Salovey, P., & Mayer, J. D. (1989–90). Emotional intelligence. *Imagination, Cognition and Personality, 9,* 185–211.

39. Mayer, J. D., & Salovey, P. (1997). What is emotional intelligence? In P. Salovey & D. Shayer (Eds.), *Emotional development and emotional intelligence: Implications for educators* (pp. 3–31). New York: Basic Books, p. 5.

40. Mayer, J. D., Salovey, P., & Caruso, D. (2000). Models of emotional intelligence. In R. J. Sternberg (Ed.), *Handbook of intelligence* (pp. 396–420). New York: Cambridge University Press.

41. Mayer, J. D., Salovey, P., & Caruso, D. (2000). Models of emotional intelligence. In R. J. Sternberg (Ed.), *Handbook of intelligence* (pp. 396–420). New York: Cambridge University Press.

42. Matthews, G., Roberts, R. D., & Zeidner, M. (2004). Seven myths about emotional intelligence. *Psychological Inquiry, 15*(3), 179–196.

43. Pea, R. D. (1993). Practices of distributed intelligence and designs for education. In G. Salomon (Ed.), *Distributed cognitions* (pp. 47–87). New York: Cambridge University Press, p. 48.

44. Hutchins, E. (1995). How a cockpit remembers its speeds. *Cognitive Science, 19,* 265–288.

45. Perkins, D. N. (1995). *Outsmarting IQ: The emerging science of learnable intelligence.* New York: Free Press, p. 323.

46. Martinez, M. E., & Peters Burton, E. E. (2011). Cognitive affordances of the cyberinfrastructure for science and math learning. *Educational Media International, 48*(1) 17–26.

47. Olson, D. R. (1976). Culture, technology, and intellect. In. L. R. Resnick (Ed.), *The nature of intelligence* (pp. 189–202). Hillsdale, NJ: Erlbaum.

48. Cole, M., Gay, J., Glick, J. A., & Sharp, D. W. (1971). *The cultural context of learning and thinking: An exploration in experimental anthropology.* New York: Basic Books.

49. Glick, J. (1975). Cognitive development in cross-cultural perspective. In D. Horowitz (Ed.), *Review of child development research* (Vol. 4, pp. 595–654). Chicago: University of Chicago Press, p. 636.

50. Greenfield, P. M. (1997). You can't take it with you: Why ability assessments don't cross cultures. *American Psychologist, 52*(10), 1115–1124.

51. Boas, F. (1911). Introduction to *The handbook of North American Indians, Vol. 1, Bureau of American Ethnology Bulletin* 40, Part 1. Washington, DC: Smithsonian Institution. Reprinted by Georgetown University Press (1963) and by University of Nebraska Press (1966).

52. Pullum, G. K. (1991). *The great Eskimo vocabulary hoax and other irreverent essays on the study of language.* Chicago: University of Chicago Press.

53. Whorf, B. L. (1956). *Language, thought, and reality: Selected writings of Benjamin Lee Whorf.* (J. B. Carroll, Ed.). Cambridge, MA: MIT Press.

54. Pinker, S. (1995). *The language instinct.* New York: Perennial.

55. Culler, J. (1986). *Ferdinand de Saussure.* Ithaca, NY: Cornell University Press.

56. Serpell, R. (2000). Intelligence and culture. In R. J. Sternberg (Ed.), *Handbook of intelligence* (pp. 549–577). New York: Cambridge University Press.

57. Serpell, R. (2000). Intelligence and culture. In R. J. Sternberg (Ed.), *Handbook of intelligence* (pp. 549–577). New York: Cambridge University Press.

58. Sternberg, R. J., Nokes, K., Geissler, P. W., Prince, R., Okatcha, F., Bundy, D. A., Grigorenko, E. L. (2001). The relationship between academic and practical intelligence: A case study in Kenya. *Intelligence, 29*, 401–418.

59. Davidson, J. E., & Downing, C. L. (2000). Contemporary models of intelligence. History of theories and measurements of intelligence. In R. J. Sternberg (Ed.), *Handbook of intelligence* (pp. 34–49). New York: Cambridge University Press.

60. Berry, J. W. (2004). An ecocultural perspective on the development of competence. In R. J. Sternberg & E. L. Grigorenko (Eds.), *Culture and competence.* Washington, DC: American Psychological Association.

61. Gladwin, T. (1970). *East is a big bird: Navigation and logic on Puluwat Atoll.* Cambridge, MA: Harvard University Press.

62. Greenfield, P. M. (1997). You can't take it with you: Why ability assessments don't cross cultures. *American Psychologist, 52*(10), 1115–1124.

63. Greenfield, P. M. (1997). You can't take it with you: Why ability assessments don't cross cultures. *American Psychologist, 52*(10), 1115–1124.

64. Grotzer, T. A., & Perkins, D. N. (2000). Teaching intelligence: A performance conception. In R. J. Sternberg (Ed.), *Handbook of intelligence* (pp. 492–515). New York: Cambridge University Press.

65. Perkins, D. N., Jay, E., & Tishman, S. (1993). Beyond abilities: A dispositional theory of thinking. *Merrill-Palmer Quarterly, 39*(1), 1–21.

66. Zentall, T. R. (2000). Animal intelligence. In R. J. Sternberg (Ed.), *Handbook of intelligence* (pp. 197–215). New York: Cambridge University Press.

67. Pepperberg, I. M. (2006). Intelligence and rationality in parrots. In S. Hurley & M. Nudds (Eds.), *Rational animals?* (pp. 469–488). Oxford: Oxford University Press.

68. Zentall, T. R. (2000). Animal intelligence. In R. J. Sternberg (Ed.), *Handbook of intelligence* (pp. 197–215). New York: Cambridge University Press.

69. Gallup, G. G. (1998). Self-awareness and the evolution of intelligence. *Behavioural Processes, 42*, 239–247.

70. Deheane, S. (2011). *The number sense: How the mind creates mathematics* (Revised and expanded edition). New York: Oxford University Press.

71. Lilly, J. C. (1967). *The mind of the dolphin: A nonhuman intelligence*. Garden City, NY: Doubleday & Company.

72. Herman, L. M. (2006). Intelligence and rational behaviour in the bottlenose dolphin. In S. Hurley & M. Nudds (Eds.), *Rational animals?* (pp. 439–467). Oxford: Oxford University Press.

73. Zentall, T. R. (2011). Animal intelligence. In R. J. Sternberg & S. B. Kaufman (Eds.), *The Cambridge handbook of intelligence* (pp. 309–327). New York: Cambridge University Press.

74. Schank, R. C., & Towle, B. (2000). Artificial intelligence. In R. J. Sternberg (Ed.), *Handbook of intelligence* (pp. 341–356). New York: Cambridge University Press.

75. Polya, G. (1957). *How to solve it: A new aspect of mathematical method* (2nd ed.). Princeton, NJ: Princeton University Press.

76. Mackintosh, N. J. (1998). *IQ and human intelligence*. New York: Oxford University Press.

77. Garlick, D. (2002). Understanding the nature of the general factor of intelligence: The role of individual differences in neural plasticity as an explanatory mechanism. *Psychological Review, 109*, 116–136.

78. Bereiter, C. (2002). *Education and mind in the knowledge age*. Mahwah, NJ: Erlbaum.

79. Schank, R. C., & Towle, B. (2000). Artificial intelligence. In R. J. Sternberg (Ed.), *Handbook of intelligence* (pp. 341–356). New York: Cambridge University Press.

80. Newborn, M. (1997). *Kasparov versus Deep Blue: Computer chess comes of age*. New York: Springer.

81. Ginsberg, M. L. (1998). Computers, games, and the real world. *Scientific American, 9*(4), 84–89.

82. Tesauro, G. (2002). Programming backgammon using self-teaching neural nets. *Artificial Intelligence, 132*, 181–199.

83. Schank, R. C., & Towle, B. (2000). Artificial intelligence. In R. J. Sternberg (Ed.), *Handbook of intelligence* (pp. 341–356). New York: Cambridge University Press.

84. Epstein, R. (2007, October/November). From Russia, with love: How I got fooled (and somewhat humiliated) by a computer. *Scientific American Mind*.

85. Markoff, J. (2011, February 16). Computer wins on "*Jeopardy!*": Trivial it's not. *The New York Times*. Retrieved from http://www.nytimes.com

86. Searle, J. (2011, February 23). Watson doesn't know it won on "Jeopardy!" *The Wall Street Journal*. Retrieved from http://online.wsj.com

87. Searle, J. (2011, February 23). Watson doesn't know it won on "Jeopardy!" *The Wall Street Journal*. Retrieved from http://online.wsj.com

88. Markoff, J. (2011, February 16). Computer wins on "*Jeopardy!*": Trivial it's not. *The New York Times*. Retrieved from http://www.nytimes.com

89. Kyllonen, P. C., Roberts, R. D., & Stankov, L. (2007). *Extending intelligence: Enhancement and new constructs*. New York: Erlbaum.

CHAPTER 4

1. Abraham, C. (2001). *Possessing genius: The bizarre odyssey of Einstein's brain.* New York: St. Martin's Press.

2. Levy, S. (1978, August). My search for Einstein's brain. *The New Jersey Monthly*, p. 43.

3. Diamond, M. C., Scheibel, A. B., Murphy, G. M., & Harvey, T. (1985). On the brain of a scientist: Albert Einstein. *Experimental Neurology, 88*, 198–204.Einstein's brain was compared to the brains of 11 other deceased males. The comparison subjects were significantly younger on average at the time of death.For a critique of the Diamond study, see Hines, T. (1998). Further on Einstein's brain. *Experimental Neurology, 150*, 343–344.

4. Anderson, B., & Harvey, T. (1996). Alterations in the cortical thickness and neuronal density in the frontal cortex of Albert Einstein. *Neuroscience Letters, 210*, 161–165.

5. Levy, S. (1999, June 28). The roots of genius: The odd history of a famous old brain. *Newsweek*, p. 32.

6. Einstein, A. (1979). *Autobiographical notes.* LaSalle, IL: Open Court.

7. Mackintosh, N. J. (1998). *IQ and human intelligence.* New York: Oxford University Press.

8. Vernon, P. A., Wickett, J. C., Bazana, G., & Stelmack, R. M. (2000). The neuropsychology and psychophysiology of human intelligence. In R. J. Sternberg (Ed.), *Handbook of intelligence* (pp. 245–264). New York: Cambridge University Press.

9. Mackintosh, N. J. (1998). *IQ and human intelligence.* New York: Oxford University Press.

10. Vernon, P. A., Wickett, J. C., Bazana, G., & Stelmack, R. M. (2000). The neuropsychology and psychophysiology of human intelligence. In R. J. Sternberg (Ed.), *Handbook of intelligence* (pp. 245–264). New York: Cambridge University Press.

11. Jerison, H. J. (2000). The evolution of intelligence. In R. J. Sternberg (Ed.), *Handbook of intelligence* (pp. 216–244). New York: Cambridge University Press.

12. Garlick, D. (2002). Understanding the nature of the general factor of intelligence: The role of individual differences in neural plasticity as an explanatory mechanism. *Psychological Review, 109*(1), 116–136.

13. Haier, R. J. (2011). Biological basis of intelligence. In R. J. Sternberg & S. B. Kaufman (Eds.), *The Cambridge handbook of intelligence* (pp. 351–361). New York: Cambridge University Press.

14. Haier, R. J., Jung, R. E., Yeo, R. A., Head, K., & Alkire, M. T. (2004). Structural brain variation and general intelligence. *NeuroImage, 23*, 425–433.

15. Gray, J. R., & Thompson, P. M. (2004). Neurobiology of intelligence: Science and ethics. *Nature Reviews: Neuroscience, 5*, 471–482.

16. Macmillan, M. B. (1986). A wonderful journey through skull and brains: The travels of Mr. Gage's tamping iron. *Brain and Cognition, 5*, 67–107.

17. Bunge, S. A., Ochsner, K. N., Desmond, J. E., Glover, G. H., & Gabrieli, J. D. E. (2001). Prefrontal regions involved in keeping information in and out of mind. *Brain, 124*, 2074–2084.

18. Haier, R. J., Jung, R. E., Yeo, R. A., Head, K., & Alkire, M. T. (2004). Structural brain variation and general intelligence. *NeuroImage, 23*, 425–433.

19. Haier, R. J., Jung, R. E., Yeo, R. A., Head, K., & Alkire, M. T. (2004). Structural brain variation and general intelligence. *NeuroImage, 23*, 425–433.

20. Gray, J. R., & Thompson, P. M. (2004). Neurobiology of intelligence: Science and ethics. *Nature Reviews: Neuroscience, 5*, 471–482.

21. Gray, J. R., & Thompson, P. M. (2004). Neurobiology of intelligence: Science and ethics. *Nature Reviews: Neuroscience, 5*, 471–482.

22. Haier, R. J., Jung, R. E., Yeo, R. A., Head, K., & Alkire, M. T. (2004). Structural brain variation and general intelligence. *NeuroImage, 23*, 425–433.

23. Gray, J. R., & Thompson, P. M. (2004). Neurobiology of intelligence: Science and ethics. *Nature Reviews: Neuroscience, 5*, 471–482.

24. Blair, C., Gamson, D., Thorne, S., & Baker, D. (2005). Rising mean IQ: Cognitive demand of mathematics education for young children, population exposure to formal schooling, and the neurobiology of the prefrontal cortex. *Intelligence, 33*, 93–106.

25. Reuter-Lorenz, P. A., & Miller, A. C. (1998). The cognitive neuroscience of human laterality: Lessons from the bisected brain. *Current Directions in Psychological Science, 7*(1), 15–20.

26. Prabhakaran, V., Narayanan, K., Zhao, Z., & Gabrieli, J. D. E. (2000). Integration of diverse information in working memory within the frontal lobe. *Nature Neuroscience, 3*(1), 85–90.

27. Milner, B., Taylor, L., & Sperry, R. W. (1968). Lateralized suppression of dichotically presented digits after commissural section in man. *Science, 161*, 184–186.

28. Gazzaniga, M. S. (1980). *Psychology*. San Francisco: Harper & Row.

29. Fischer, K. W., Daniel, D. B., Immordino-Yang, M. H., Stern, E., Battro, A., & Koizumi, H. (2007). Why mind, brain, and education? Why now? *Mind, Brain, & Education, 1*(1), 31–43.

30. Dehaene, S. (1997). *The number sense: How the mind creates mathematics*. New York: Oxford University Press.

31. Posner, M. I., Peterson, S. E., Fox, P. T., & Raichle, M. E. (1988). Localization of cognitive operations in the human brain. *Science, 240*, 1627–1631.

32. Dehaene, S. Spelke, E., Pinel, P., Stanescu, S., & Tviskin, S. (1999). Sources of mathematical thinking: Behavioral and brain-imaging evidence. *Science, 284*, 970–974.

33. Beyerstein, B. L. (1999). Whence cometh the myth that we only use 10% of our brains? In S. Della Sala (Ed.), *Mind myths: Exploring popular assumptions about the mind and brain* (pp. 3–24). New York: John Wiley & Sons.

34. Carnegie, D. (1936). *How to win friends and influence people*. New York: Simon & Schuster, p. 11.

35. Lashley, K. (1929). In search of the engram. In physiological mechanisms and animal behavior. *Symposium of the Society for Experimental Biology*, no. 4. New York: Academic Press.

36. Society for Neuroscience. (2002). *Brain facts: A primer on the brain and nervous system*. Washington, DC: Author.

37. Terry, R. D., DeTeresa, R., & Hansen, L. (1987). Neocortical cell counts in normal human adult aging. *Annals of Neurobiology, 21*, 530–537.

38. Eriksson, P. S., Perfilieva, E., Björk-Eriksson, T., Alborn, A.-M., Nordberg, C., Peterson, D. A., & Gage, F. H. (1998). Neurogenesis in the adult human hippocampus. *Nature Medicine, 4*, 1313–1317.

39. Kandel, E. R. (2006). Learning to find your way. *Natural History, 115*(2), 32–38.

40. Garlick, D. (2003). Integrating brain science with intelligence research. *Current Directions in Psychological Science, 12*(5), 185–189.

41. Greenough, W. T. (1976). Enduring brain effects of differential experience and training. In M. R. Rosenzweig & E. L. Bennett (Eds.), *Neural mechanisms of learning and memory* (pp. 255–278). Cambridge, MA: MIT Press.

42. Turner, A. M., & Greenough, W. (1985). Differential rearing effects on rat visual cortex synapses. I. Synaptic and neuronal density and synapses per neuron. *Brain Research, 329,* 195–203.

43. Kandel, E. R. (2006). *In search of memory: The emergence of a new science of mind.* New York: W. W. Norton.

44. Nelson, C. A. (1999). Neural plasticity and human development. *Current Directions in Psychological Science, 8,* 42–45.

45. Elbert, T., Pantev, C., Wienbruch, C., Hoke, M., Rockstoh, B., & Taub, E. (1995). Increased use of the left hand in string players associated with increased cortical representation of the fingers. *Science, 220,* 21–23.

46. Hamilton, R. H., & Pascual-Leone, A. (1998). Cortical plasticity associated with Braille reading. *Trends in Cognitive Sciences, 2*(5), 165–174.Sterr, A., Müller, M. M., Elbert, T., Rockstroh, B., Pantev, C., & Taub, E. (1998). Perceptual correlates of changes in cortical representations of fingers in blind multifinger Braille readers. *The Journal of Neuroscience, 18*(11), 4417–4423.

47. Maguire, E. A., Gadian, D. G., Johnsrude, I. S., Good, C. D., Ashburner, J., Frackowiak, R. S. J., & Frith, C. D. (2000). Navigation-related structural change in the hippocampi of taxi drivers. *Proceedings of the National Academy of Sciences, 97*(8), 398–403.

48. Draganski, B., Gaser, C., Busch, V. Schuierer, G., Bogdahn, U., & May, A. (2004). Changes in gray matter induced by training. *Nature, 427,* 311–312.

49. Squire, L. R., & Kandel, E. R. (1999). *Memory: From mind to molecules.* New York: Scientific American Library.

50. Gray, J. R., & Thompson, P. M. (2004). Neurobiology of intelligence: Science and ethics. *Nature Reviews: Neuroscience, 5,* 471–482.

51. Davidson, J. E., & Downing, C. L. (2000). Contemporary models of intelligence. History of theories and measurements of intelligence. In R. J. Sternberg (Ed.), *Handbook of intelligence* (pp. 34–49). New York: Cambridge University Press.

52. Chen, Z., & Siegler, R. S. (2000). Intellectual development in childhood. In R. J. Sternberg (Ed.), *Handbook of intelligence* (pp. 92–116). New York: Cambridge University Press.

53. Haier, R. J., Siegel, B. V., Nuechterlein, K. H., Hazlett, E., Wu, J. C., Paek, J., Browning, H. L., & Buchsbaum, M. S. (1988). Cortical glucose metabolic rate correlates of abstract reasoning and attention studies with positron emission tomography. *Intelligence, 12,* 199–217.

54. Vernon, P. A., Wickett, J. C., Bazana, G., & Stelmack, R. M. (2000). The neuropsychology and psychophysiology of human intelligence. In R. J. Sternberg (Ed.), *Handbook of intelligence* (pp. 245–264). New York: Cambridge University Press.

55. Haier, R. J., Jung, R. E., Yeo, R. A., Head, K., & Alkire, M. T. (2004). Structural brain variation and general intelligence. *NeuroImage, 23,* 425–433.

56. Penfield, W. (1958). *The excitable cortex in conscious man.* Springfield, IL: Charles C. Thomas, pp. 34, 20, and 34–35.

57. Loftus, E. (1996). *Eyewitness testimony.* Cambridge, MA: Harvard University Press.

58. Luria, A. L. (1968). *The mind of a mnemonist.* New York: Basic Books, pp. 11–12, emphasis in original.

59. Bruner, J. S. (1968). Foreword. In A. R. Luria, *The mind of a mnemonist*. New York: Basic Books, p. viiii.

60. Parker, E. S., Cahill, L., & McGaugh, J. L. (2006). A case of unusual autobiographical remembering. *Neurocase, 12*, 35–49.

61. Ramachandran, V. S., & Hubbard, E. M. (2003). Hearing colors, tasting shapes. *Scientific American, 288*(5), 52–59.

62. Duffy, P. L. (2001). *Blue cats and chartreuse kittens*. New York: W. H. Freeman.

63. Martinez, M. E. (2010). *Learning and cognition: The design of the mind*. Upper Saddle River, NJ: Merrill.

64. Lohman, D. F. (2000). Complex information processing and intelligence. In R. J. Sternberg (Ed.), *Handbook of intelligence* (pp. 285–340). New York: Cambridge University Press.

65. Anderson, J. R. (1996). A simple theory of complex cognition. *American Psychologist, 51*(4), 355–365.

66. Ericsson, K. A., & Kintsch, W. (1995). Long-term working memory. *Psychological Review, 102*(2), 211–245.

67. This is a bit of a conceptual shortcut. Short-term memory is the site of active cognitive work, but thinking always draws to some extent on knowledge stored in long-term memory.

68. Miller, G. A. (1956). The magical number seven, plus or minus two. *Psychological Review, 63*, 81–97.

69. Simon, H. A., & Kaplan, C. A. (1989). Foundations of cognitive science. In M. I. Posner (Ed.), *Foundations of cognitive science* (pp. 1–48). Cambridge, MA: MIT Press.

70. Baddeley, A. (1986). *Working memory*. Oxford, UK: Clarendon.

71. Engle, R. W., Tuholski, S. W., Laughlin, J. E., & Conway, A. R. A. (1999). Working memory, short-term memory, and general fluid intelligence: A latent-variable approach. *Journal of Experimental Psychology: General, 128*(3) 309–331.

72. Daneman, M., & Carpenter, P. A. (1980). Individual differences in working memory and reading. *Journal of Verbal Learning and Verbal Behavior, 19*, 450–466.

73. Kyllonen, P. C., & Christal, R. E. (1990). Reasoning ability is (little more than) working-memory capacity?! *Intelligence, 14*, 130–143.

74. Lohman, D. F. (2000). Complex information processing and intelligence. In R. J. Sternberg (Ed.), *Handbook of intelligence* (pp. 285–340). New York: Cambridge University Press.

75. Engle, R. W., Tuholski, S. W., Laughlin, J. E., & Conway, A. R. A. (1999). Working memory, short-term memory, and general fluid intelligence: A latent-variable approach. *Journal of Experimental Psychology: General, 128*(3) 309–331.

76. Oberauer, K., Schulze, R., Wilhelm, O., & Süß, H. M. (2005). Working memory and intelligence—their correlations and their relation: A comment on Ackerman, Beier, and Boyle (2005). *Psychological Bulletin, 131*, 61–65.Cited in Conway, A. R. A., Getz, S. J., Macnamara, B., & Engel de Abreu, P. M. J. (2011). Working memory and intelligence. In R. J. Sternberg & S. B. Kaufman (Eds.), *The Cambridge handbook of intelligence* (pp. 394–418). New York: Cambridge University Press.

77. Jaeggi, S. M., Buschkuehl, M., Jonides, J., & Perrig, W. J. (2008). Improving fluid intelligence with training on working memory. *Proceedings of the National Academy of Sciences* (PNAS Early Edition). www.pnas.org/cgi/doi/10.1073/pnas.0801268105.Verhaeghen, P., Cerella, J. & Basak, C. (2004). A working

memory workout: How to expand the focus of serial attention from one to four items in 10 hours or less. *Journal of Experimental Psychology: Learning, Memory and Cognition, 30*(6), 1322–1337.

78. Bransford, J. D., & Schwartz, D. (1999). Rethinking transfer: A simple proposal with multiple implications. *Review of Research in Education, 24*, 61–100.

79. Jaeggi, S. M., Studer-Luethi, B., Buschkuehl, M., Su, Y.-F., Jonides, J., & Perrig, W. J. (2010). The relationship between n-back performance and matrix reasoning—implications for training and transfer. *Intelligence, 38*, 625–635.

80. The terms "move" and "movement" are metaphorical. They describe information flow in the abstract schematic of the cognitive architecture that includes working memory and long-term memory as vital components.

81. Eich, E. (1988). Learning during sleep. In *Enhancing Human Performance: Background Papers*. Washington, DC: National Academies Press.

82. Moore, T. E. (1982). Subliminal advertising: What you see is what you get. *Journal of Marketing, 46*(2), 38–47.

83. Merikle, P. M., Smilek, D., & Eastwood, J. D. (2001). Perception without awareness: Perspectives from cognitive psychology. *Cognition, 79*, 115–134.

84. Moore, T. E. (1988). The case against subliminal manipulation. *Psychology & Marketing, 5*(4), 297–316.

85. Mayer, R. E. (2000). Intelligence and education. In R. J. Sternberg (Ed.), *Handbook of intelligence* (pp. 519–533). New York: Cambridge University Press.

86. Anderson, L. W., & Krathwohl, D. R. (Eds.). (2001). *A taxonomy of learning, teaching, and assessment: A revision of Bloom's taxonomy of educational objectives.* New York: Longman.

87. Mayer, R. E., & Wittrock, M. C. (2006). Problem solving. In P. A. Alexander & P. H. Winne (Eds.), *Handbook of educational psychology* (2nd ed., pp. 287–303). Mahwah, NJ: Erlbaum.

88. Martinez, M. E. (1998). What is problem solving? *Phi Delta Kappan, 79*, 605–609.

89. Chen, Z., & Siegler, R. S. (2000). Intellectual development in childhood. In R. J. Sternberg (Ed.), *Handbook of intelligence* (pp. 92–116). New York: Cambridge University Press.

90. Flexible strategy shifting is a recognized component of high performance on intelligence tests.Lohman, D. F. (2000). Complex information processing and intelligence. In R. J. Sternberg (Ed.), *Handbook of intelligence* (pp. 285–340). New York: Cambridge University Press.

91. Brown, A. L. (1978). Knowing when, where, and how to remember: A problem of metacognition. In R. Glaser (Ed.), *Advances in instructional psychology* (Vol. 1, pp. 77–165). Hillsdale, NJ: Erlbaum.Flavell, J. H. (1979). Metacognition and cognitive monitoring: A new area of cognitive-developmental inquiry. *American Psychologist, 34*, 906–911.

92. Grotzer, T. A., & Perkins, D. N. (2000). Teaching intelligence: A performance conception. In R. J. Sternberg (Ed.), *Handbook of intelligence* (pp. 492–515). New York: Cambridge University Press.

93. Mackintosh, N. J. (1998). *IQ and human intelligence.* New York: Oxford University Press.

94. Tobias, S., & Everson, H. T. (1996). *Assessing metacognitive knowledge monitoring.* College Board Report No. 96–1. New York: College Board.

95. Langer, E. J. (1997). *The power of mindful learning.* Reading, MA: Addison-Wesley.

96. Bunge, S. A., Ochsner, K. N., Desmond, J. E., Glover, G. H., & Gabrieli, J. D. E. (2001). Prefrontal regions involved in keeping information in and out of mind. *Brain, 124*, 2074–2084.

97. Zeidner, M., & Matthews, G. (2000). Intelligence and personality. In R. J. Sternberg (Ed.), *Handbook of intelligence* (pp. 581–610). New York: Cambridge University Press.

98. Chiles, J. R. (2001). *Inviting disaster.* New York: HarperBusiness.

99. Cianciolo, A. T., & Sternberg, R. J. (2004). *Intelligence: A brief history.* Malden, MA: Blackwell.

100. Brown, A. L., & Palincsar, A. S. (1989). Guided, cooperative learning and individual knowledge acquisition. In L. B. Resnick (Ed.), *Knowing, learning, and instruction: Essays in honor of Robert Glaser* (pp. 393–451). Hillsdale, NJ: Erlbaum.

CHAPTER 5

1. Cianciolo, A. T., & Sternberg, R. J. (2004). *Intelligence: A brief history.* Malden, MA: Blackwell.

2. Plomin, R. (2002). Individual differences research in the postgenomic era. *Personality and Individual Differences, 33*, 909–920.

3. Mackintosh, N. J. (1998). *IQ and human intelligence.* New York: Oxford University Press.

4. Cianciolo, A. T., & Sternberg, R. J. (2004). *Intelligence: A brief history.* Malden, MA: Blackwell.

5. Grigorenko, E. L. (2000). Heritability and intelligence. In R. J. Sternberg (Ed.), *Handbook of intelligence* (pp. 53–91). New York: Cambridge University Press.

6. Plomin, R. (2002). Individual differences research in a postgenomic era. *Personality and Individual Differences, 33*, 909–920.

7. Espeseth, T., Greenwood, P. M., Reinvang, I., Fjell, A. M., Walhovd, K. B., Westlye, L. T., Wehling, E., Lundervold, A., Rootwelt, H., & Parasuraman, R. (2006). Interactive effects of APOE and CHRNA4 on attention and white matter volume in healthy middle-age and older adults. *Cognitive, Affective, & Behavioral Neuroscience, 6*(1), 31–43.

8. Espeseth, T., Greenwood, P. M., Reinvang, I., Fjell, A. M., Walhovd, K. B., Westlye, L. T., Wehling, E., Lundervold, A., Rootwelt, H., & Parasuraman, R. (2006). Interactive effects of APOE and CHRNA4 on attention and white matter volume in healthy middle-age and older adults. *Cognitive, Affective, & Behavioral Neuroscience, 6*(1), 31–43.

9. Gray, J. R., & Thompson, P. M. (2004). Neurobiology of intelligence: Science and ethics. *Nature Reviews: Neuroscience, 5*, 471–482.

10. Grigorenko, E. L. (2000). Heritability and intelligence. In R. J. Sternberg (Ed.), *Handbook of intelligence* (pp. 53–91). New York: Cambridge University Press.

11. Turkheimer, E., Haley, A., Waldron, M., D'Onofrio, B., & Gottesman, I. I. (2003). Socioeconomic status modifies heritability of IQ in young children. *Psychological Science, 14*(6), 623–628.

12. Mackintosh, N. J. (1998). *IQ and human intelligence.* New York: Oxford University Press.

13. Grigorenko, E. L. (2000). Heritability and intelligence. In R. J. Sternberg (Ed.), *Handbook of intelligence* (pp. 53–91). New York: Cambridge University Press.

14. Gould, S. J. (1981). *The mismeasure of man.* New York: Norton.

15. Gray, J. R., & Thompson, P. M. (2004). Neurobiology of intelligence: Science and ethics. *Nature Reviews: Neuroscience, 5,* 471–482.

16. Gould, S. J. (1981). *The mismeasure of man.* New York: Norton.

17. Cianciolo, A. T., & Sternberg, R. J. (2004). *Intelligence: A brief history.* Malden, MA: Blackwell. Cited studies are inconsistent, some showing slightly higher IQs for White populations, others showing a slight IQ advantage for Asians.

18. Flynn, J. R. (1991). *Asian Americans: Achievement beyond IQ.* Hillsdale, NJ: Erlbaum.

19. Loehlin, J. C. (2000). Group differences in intelligence. In R. J. Sternberg (Ed.), *Handbook of intelligence* (pp. 176–193). New York: Cambridge University Press.

20. McShane, D., & Mitchell, J. (1979). Middle ear disease, hearing loss and educational problems of American Indian children. *Journal of American Indian Education, 19,* 7–11.

21. McShane, D., & Berry, J. W. (1988). Native North Americans: Indian and Inuit abilities. In S. H. Irvine & J. W. Berry (Eds.), *Human abilities in cultural context* (pp. 385–426). New York: Cambridge University Press.

22. Loehlin, J. C. (2000). Group differences in intelligence. In R. J. Sternberg (Ed.), *Handbook of intelligence* (pp. 176–193). New York: Cambridge University Press.

23. Tavris, C. (1995). A place in the sun. *Skeptic, 3,* 62–63.

24. Martinez, M. E. (2000). *Educational as the cultivation of intelligence.* Mahwah, NJ: Erlbaum.

25. Reynolds, C. R., Chastain, R. L., Kaufman, A. S., & McLean, J. E. (1987). Demographic characteristics and IQ among adults: Analysis of the WAIS-R standardization sample as a function of stratification variables. *Journal of School Psychology, 25,* 323–342. The comparison on full-scale IQ was based on a stratified, nationally representative sample of 940 male and 940 females.

26. Mackintosh, N. J. (1998). *IQ and human intelligence.* New York: Oxford University Press.

27. It's also possible to solve rotation talks without imagery by analyzing objects feature by feature.

28. Weiss, E. M., Kemmler, G., Deisenhammer, E. A., Fleischhacker, W. W., & Delazer, M. (2003). Sex differences in cognitive functions. *Personality and Individual Differences, 35,* 863–875.

29. Halpern, D. F., & LaMay, M. L. (2000). The smarter sex: A critical review of sex differences in intelligence. *Educational Psychology Review, 12*(2), 229–246.

30. Buss, D. (1995). Psychological sex differences: Origins through sexual selection. *American Psychologist, 50*(3), 164–168.

31. Dabbs, J. M., Jr., Chang, E.-L., Strong, R. A., & Milun, R. (1998). Spatial ability, navigation strategy, and geographic knowledge among men and women. *Evolution and Human Behavior, 19,* 89–98.

32. Mackintosh, N. J. (1998). *IQ and human intelligence.* New York: Oxford University Press.

33. Hampson, E., & Kimura, D. (1988). Reciprocal effects of hormonal fluctuations on human motor and perceptual-spatial skills. *Behavioral Neuroscience, 107*(2), 456–459.

34. Weiss, E. M., Kemmler, G., Deisenhammer, E. A., Fleischhacker, W. W., & Delazer, M. (2003). Sex differences in cognitive functions. *Personality and Individual Differences, 35,* 863–875.

35. Halpern, D. F., & LaMay, M. L. (2002). The smarter sex: A critical review of sex differences in intelligence. *Educational Psychology Review, 12*(2), 229–246.

36. Buss, D. (1995). Psychological sex differences: Origins through sexual selection. *American Psychologist, 50*(3), 164–168.
37. Grigorenko, E. L. (2000). Heritability and intelligence. In R. J. Sternberg (Ed.), *Handbook of intelligence* (pp. 53–91). New York: Cambridge University Press.
38. Cianciolo, A. T., & Sternberg, R. J. (2004). *Intelligence: A brief history*. Malden, MA: Blackwell.
39. Bouchard, T. J., & McGue, M. (1981). Familial studies of intelligence: A review. *Science, 212*, 1055–1059.Scarr, S. (1997). Behavior-genetic and socialization theories of intelligence: Truth and reconciliation. In R. J. Sternberg & E. L. Grigorenko (Eds.), *Intelligence, heredity, and environment* (pp. 3–41). New York: Cambridge University Press.
40. Devlin, B., Daniels, M., & Roeder, K. (1997). The heritability of IQ. *Nature, 388*, 468–478.
41. Scarr, S., & Weinberg, R. A. (1983). The Minnesota adoption studies: Genetic differences and malleability. *Child Development, 54*, 260–267.
42. Greenough, W. T., & Black, J. E. (1992). Induction of brain structure by experience: Substrates for cognitive development. In M. R. Gunnar & C. A. Nelson (Eds.), *Developmental behavioral neuroscience: The Minnesota symposia on child psychology* (pp. 155–200). Hillsdale, NJ: Erlbaum.
43. Wachs, T. D. (1996). Environment and intelligence: Present status, future directions. In D. K. Detterman (Ed.), *Current topics in human intelligence, Vol. 5: The environment* (pp. 31–44). Norwood, NJ: Ablex.
44. Winner, E. (1996). The rage to master: The decisive role of talent in the visual arts. In K. A. Ericsson (Ed.), *The road to excellence: The acquisition of expert performance in the arts and sciences, sports, and games* (pp. 271–301). Mahwah, NJ: Erlbaum.
45. Pederson, N. L., Plomin, R., Nesselroade, J. R., & McClearne, G. E. (1992). A quantitative genetic analysis of cognitive abilities during the second half of the life span. *Psychological Science, 3*, 346–353.
46. Dickens, W. T., & Flynn, J. R. (2001). Heritability estimates versus large environmental effects: The IQ paradox resolved. *Psychological Review, 108*(2), 346–369.
47. Dickens, W. T., & Flynn, J. R. (2001). Heritability estimates versus large environmental effects: The IQ paradox resolved. *Psychological Review, 108*(2), 346–369.
48. Grigorenko, E. L. (2000). Heritability and intelligence. In R. J. Sternberg (Ed.), *Handbook of intelligence* (pp. 53–91). New York: Cambridge University Press.
49. Garlick, D. (2003). Integrating brain science with intelligence research. *Current Directions in Psychological Science, 12*(5), 185–189.
50. McCall, R. B., Meyers, E. D., Jr., Hartman, J., & Roche, A. F. (1983). Developmental changes in head circumference and mental performance growth rates: A test of Epstein's phrenoblysis hypothesis. *Developmental Psychobiology, 16*, 457–468.
51. Ramsden, S., Richardson, F. M., Josse, G., Thomas, M. S. C., Ellis, C., Shakeshaft, C., Seghier, M. L., & Price, C. (2011, October 19). Verbal and non-verbal changes in the teenage brain. *Nature, 479*(7371), 113–116. http://www.nature.com/nature/journal/v479/n7371/full/nature10514.html
52. Haan, N. (1977). *Coping and defending: Processes of self-environment organization*. New York: Academic Press.

53. Bock, R. D., & Moore, E. G. J. (1986). *Advantage and disadvantage: A profile of American youth*. Hillsdale, NJ: Erlbaum.

54. Flynn, J. R. (1987). Massive IQ gains in 14 nations: What IQ tests really measure. *Psychological Bulletin, 101*(2), 171–191.

55. Flynn, J. R. (1998). IQ gains over time: Toward finding the causes. In U. Neisser (Ed.), *The rising curve: Long-term gains in IQ and related measures* (pp. 25–66). Washington, DC: American Psychological Association.

56. Flynn, J. R. (1998). IQ gains over time: Toward finding the causes. In U. Neisser (Ed.), *The rising curve: Long-term gains in IQ and related measures* (pp. 25–66). Washington, DC: American Psychological Association, p. 25.

57. Kaufman, A. S. (2000). Tests of intelligence. In R. J. Sternberg (Ed.), *Handbook of intelligence* (pp. 445–476). New York: Cambridge University Press.

58. Neisser, U. (1997). Rising scores on intelligence tests. *American Scientist, 85,* 440–447.

59. Flynn, J. R. (1998). IQ gains over time: Toward finding the causes. In U. Neisser (Ed.), *The rising curve: Long-term gains in IQ and related measures* (pp. 25–66). Washington, DC: American Psychological Association, p. 53.

CHAPTER 6

1. Harrell, R. F., Woodyard, E., & Gates, A. I. (1955). *The effect of mothers' diets on the intelligence of offspring*. New York: Teachers College, Columbia University.

2. Schoenthaler, S. J., Amos, S. P., Eysenck, H. J., Peritz, E., & Yudkin, J. (1991). Controlled trial of vitamin-mineral supplementation: Effects on intelligence and performance. *Personality and Individual Differences, 12,* 351–362. Benton, D., & Roberts, G. (1988). Effect of vitamin and mineral supplementation on intelligence of a sample of schoolchildren. *The Lancet, 1,* 140–143.

3. Eysenck, H. J., & Schoenthaler, S. J. (1997). Raising IQ level by vitamin and mineral supplementation. In R. J. Sternberg & E. L. Grigorenko (Eds.), *Intelligence, heredity, and environment* (pp. 363–392). New York: Cambridge University Press.

4. Martinez, M. E. (2000). *Education as the cultivation of intelligence*. Mahwah, NJ: Erlbaum.

5. Reinisch, J. M., Sanders, S. A., Mortensen, E. L., & Rubin, D. B. (1995). In utero exposure to phenobarbital and intelligence in adult men. *JAMA: The Journal of the American Medical Association, 274*(19), 1518–1525.

6. Jacobson, J. L., & Jacobson, S. W. (1996). Intellectual impairment in children exposed to polychlorinated biphenyls in utero. *The New England Journal of Medicine, 335*(11), 783–789.Marsh, D. O., Clarkson, T. W., Myers, G. J., Davidson, P. W., Cox, C., Cernichiari, E., Tanner, M. A., Lednar, W., Shamlaye, C., Choisy, O., Hoarneau, C., & Berlin, M. (1995). The Seychelles study of fetal methylmercury exposure and child development: Introduction. *NeuroToxicology, 16*(4), 583–596.

7. Breitmeyer, B. J., & Ramey, C. T. (1986). Biological nonoptimality and quality of postnatal environment as codeterminants of intellectual development. *Child Development, 57,* 1151–1165.

8. Harris, P., Clark, M., & Karp, R. J. (1993). Prevention and treatment of lead poisoning. In R. J. Karp (Ed.), *Malnourished children in the United States: Caught in the cycle of poverty* (pp. 91–100). New York: Springer.

9. Lou, H. C., Hansen, D., Nordentoft, M., Pryds, O., Flemming, J., Nim, J., & Hemmingsen, R. (1994). Prenatal stressors of human life affect fetal brain development. *Developmental Medicine and Child Neurology*, *36*, 826–832.

10. Mattson, S. N., Riley, E. P., Gramling, L., Delis, D. C., & Jones, K. L. (1997). Heavy prenatal alcohol exposure with or without physical features of fetal alcohol syndrome leads to IQ deficits. *The Journal of Pediatrics*, *131*, 718–721.

11. Willatts, P., Forsyth, J. S., DiModugno, M. K., Varma, S., & Colvin, M. (1998). Effects of long-chain polyunsaturated fatty acids in infant formula on problem solving at 10 months of age. *The Lancet*, *352*, 688–691.

12. Makrides, M., Neumann, M., Simmer, K., Pater, J., & Gibson, R. (1995). Are long-chain polyunsaturated fatty acids essential nutrients in infancy? *The Lancet*, *345*, 1463–68.

13. Horwood, L. J., & Fergusson, D. M. (1998). Breastfeeding and later cognitive and academic outcomes. *Pediatrics*, *101*(1), 1–7.

14. Drane, D. L., & Logemann, J. E. (2000). A critical evaluation of the evidence of the association between type of infant feeding and cognitive development. *Paediatric and Perinatal Epidemiology*, *14*, 349–356.

15. Kramer, M. S., Aboud, F., Mironova, E., Vanilovich, I., Platt, R. W., Matusch, L., Igumnov, S., Fombonne, E., Bogdanovich, N., Ducruet, T., Colet, J.-P., Chalmers, B., Hodnett, E., Davidovsky, S., Skugarevsky, O., Trofimovich, O., Kozlova, L., Shapiro, S., & PROBIT Study Group. (2008). Breastfeeding and child cognitive development: New evidence from a large randomized trial. *Archive of General Psychiatry*, *65*(5), 578–584.

16. Kauffman, M. (1999, June 7). Fight over formula additive heats up. *Los Angeles Times*, pp. S4–S5.

17. Schoenthaler, S. J., Doraz, W. E., & Wakefield, J. A. (1986). The impact of low food additive and sucrose diet on academic performance in 803 New York City public schools. *International Journal of Biosocial Research*, *8*(2), 185–195.

18. Donohoe, R. T., & Benton, D. (2000). Glucose tolerance predicts memory and cognition. *Physiology and Behavior*, *71*, 395–401.

19. Mackintosh, N. J. (1998). *IQ and human intelligence*. New York: Oxford University Press.

20. Pollitt, E., & Matthews, R. (1998) Breakfast and cognition: An integrative summary. *American Journal of Clinical Nutrition*, *68*, 804S–813S.

21. Martinez, M. E. (2000). *Education as the cultivation of intelligence*. Mahwah, NJ: Erlbaum.

22. Huston, A. C., & Wright, J. C. (1998). Mass media and children's development. In I. E. Sigel & K. A. Renninger (Eds.), *Handbook of child psychology, Vol. 4: Child psychology in practice* (5th ed., pp. 999–1058). New York: Wiley.

23. Subrahmanyam, K., Greenfield, P., Kraut, R., & Gross, E. (2001). The impact of computer use on children's and adolescents' development. *Applied Developmental Psychology*, *22*, 7–30.

24. Teasdale, T. W., & Owen, D. R. (2008). Secular declines in cognitive test scores: A reversal of the Flynn effect. *Intelligence*, *36*, 121–126.

25. Neisser, U., Boodoo, G., Bouchard, T. J., Boykin, A. W., Brody, N., Ceci, S. J., Halpern, D. F., Loehlin, J. C, Perloff, R., Sternberg, R. J. & Urbina, S. (1996). Intelligence: Knowns and unknowns. *American Psychologist*, *51*(2), 77–101, p. 90.

26. Blair, C., Gamson, D., Thorne, S., & Baker, D. (2005). Rising mean IQ: Cognitive demand of mathematics education for young children, population exposure to

formal schooling, and the neurobiology of the prefrontal cortex. *Intelligence*, *33*, 93–106.

27. Gordon, G. (1970/1923). The intelligence of English canal boat children. In I. Al-Issa & W. Dennis (Eds.), *Cross-cultural studies of behavior* (pp. 111–119). New York: Holt, Rinehart, & Winston.

28. Husén, T. (1951). The influence of schooling on IQ. *Theoria*, *17*, 61–88.

29. Husén, T., & Tuijnman, A. (1991). The contribution of formal schooling to the increase in intellectual capital. *Educational Researcher 20*(7), 17–25.

30. Balke-Aurell, G. (1982). *Changes in ability structure as related to educational and occupational experience.* Goteborg, Sweden: Acta Universitatis Gothoburgensis.

31. Harnqvist, K. (1968). Relative changes in intelligence from 13 to 18. *Scandinavian Journal of Psychology*, *9*, 50–64 (Part I) & 65–82 (Part II).

32. Lorge, I. (1945). Schooling makes a difference. *Teachers College Record*, *46*, 483–492.

33. Tuddenham, R. D. (1948). Soldier intelligence in World Wars I and II. *American Psychologist*, *3*, 54–56.

34. Humphreys, L. G. (1989). Intelligence: Three kinds of instability and their consequences for policy. In R. L. Linn (Ed.), *Intelligence: Measurement, theory, and public policy* (pp. 193–216). Urbana: University of Illinois Press.

35. deGroot, A. D. (1948). The effects of war upon the intelligence of youth. *Journal of Abnormal Social Psychology*, *43*, 311–317.deGroot, A. D. (1951). War and the intelligence of youth. *Journal of Abnormal Social Psychology*, *46*, 596–597.

36. Green, R. L., Hofmann, L. J., Morse, R. J., Hayes, M. E., & Morgan, R. F. (1964). *The educational status of children in a district without public schools* (Cooperative Research Project No. 2321). East Lansing: Michigan State University College of Education.

37. Cahan, S., & Cohen, N. (1989). Age versus schooling effects on intelligence development. *Child Development*, *60*, 1239–1249.

38. Heyns, B. (1978). *Summer learning and the effects of schooling.* New York: Academic Press.

39. Hayes, D. P., & Grether, J. (1983). The school year and vacations: When do students learn? *Cornell Journal of Social Relations*, *17*(1), 56–71.

40. Heyns, B. (1978). *Summer learning and the effects of schooling.* New York: Academic Press.

41. Zeidner, M., & Matthews, G. (2000). Intelligence and personality. In R. J. Sternberg (Ed.), *Handbook of intelligence* (pp. 581–610). New York: Cambridge University Press.

42. Jensen, A. R. (1977). Cumulative deficit in IQ of Blacks in the rural South. *Developmental Psychology*, *13*, 184–191

43. Blair, C., Gamson, D., Thorne, S., & Baker, D. (2005). Rising mean IQ: Cognitive demand of mathematics education for young children, population exposure to formal schooling, and the neurobiology of the prefrontal cortex. *Intelligence*, *33*, 93–106.

44. Cocodia, E. A., Kim, J.-S., Shin, H.-S., Kim, J.-W., Ee, J., Wee, M. S. W., Howard, R. W. (2003). Evidence that rising population intelligence is impacting in formal education. *Personality and Individual Differences*, *35*, 797–810.

45. Duncan, G. J., Claessens, A., Huston, A. C., Pagani, L. S., Engel, M., Sexton, H., Dowsett, C. J., Magnuson, K., Klebanov, P., Feinstein, L., Brooks-Gunn, J., Duckworth, K., & Japel, C. (2007). School readiness and later achievement. *Developmental Psychology*, *43*(6), 1428–1446.

46. Blair, C., Gamson, D., Thorne, S., & Baker, D. (2005). Rising mean IQ: Cognitive demand of mathematics education for young children, population exposure to formal schooling, and the neurobiology of the prefrontal cortex. *Intelligence, 33*, 93–106.

47. Davis, K. (1947). Final note on a case of extreme isolation. *American Journal of Sociology, 52*(3), 432–437.

48. Hart, B., & Risley, T. R. (1995). *Meaningful differences in the everyday experiences of young American children*. Baltimore: Brookes.

49. Wachs, T. D. (2000). *Necessary but not sufficient: The respective roles of single and multiple influences on individual development*. Washington, DC: American Psychological Association.

50. Loehlin, J. C. (2000). Group differences in intelligence. In R. J. Sternberg (Ed.), *Handbook of intelligence* (pp. 176–193). New York: Cambridge University Press.

51. Mackintosh, N. J. (1998). *IQ and human intelligence*. New York: Oxford University Press.

52. Mackintosh, N. J. (1998). *IQ and human intelligence*. New York: Oxford University Press.

53. Bradley, R. H., Caldwell, B. M., Rock, S. L., Ramey, C. T., Barnard, K. E., Gray, C., Hammond, M., A., Mitchell, S., Gottfried, A. W., Siegel, L., & Johnson, D. L. (1989). Home environment and cognitive development in the first 3 years of life: A collaborative study involving six sites and three ethnic groups in North America. *Developmental Psychology, 25*, 217–235.

54. Bradley, R. H., Caldwell, B. M., Rock, S. L., Ramey, C. T., Barnard, K. E., Gray, C., Hammond, M., A., Mitchell, S., Gottfried, A. W., Siegel, L., & Johnson, D. L. (1989). Home environment and cognitive development in the first 3 years of life: A collaborative study involving six sites and three ethnic groups in North America. *Developmental Psychology, 25*, 217–235.

55. Mackintosh, N. J. (1998). *IQ and human intelligence*. New York: Oxford University Press.

56. Turkheimer, E., Haley, A., Waldron, M., D'Onofrio, B., & Gottesman, I. I. (2003). Socioeconomic status modifies heritability of IQ in young children. *Psychological Science, 14*(6), 623–628.

57. Hart, B., & Risley, T. R. (1995). *Meaningful differences in the everyday experiences of young American children*. Baltimore: Brookes.

58. Jennings, K. D., & Connors, R. E. (1989). Mothers' interactional style and children's competence at 3 years. *International Journal of Behavioral Development, 12*, 155–175.

59. Ogilvy, C. M. (1990). Family type and children's cognition in two ethnic groups. *Journal of Cross-Cultural Psychology, 21*, 319–334.

60. Capron, C., & Duyme, M. (1989). Assessments of effect of socio-economic status on IQ in a full cross-fostering study. *Nature, 340*, 552–554.

61. Grissmer, D. W., Williamson, S., Kirby, S. N., & Berends, M. (1998). Exploring the rapid rise in Black achievement scores in the United States (1970–1990). In U. Neisser (Ed.), *The rising curve: Long-term gains in IQ and related measures* (pp. 251–285). Washington, DC: American Psychological Association.

62. Zajonc, R. B., & Bargh, J. (1980). The confluence model: Parameter estimation for six divergent data sets on family factors and intelligence. *Intelligence, 4*, 349–361.

63. Pascarella, E. T., & Terenzini, P. T. (1991). *How college affects students: Findings and insights from twenty years of research*. San Francisco: Jossey-Bass.

64. Schooler, C. (1998). Psychological effects of complex environments during the life span: A review and theory. *Intelligence, 8,* 259–281.

65. Balke-Aurell, G. (1982). *Changes in ability structure as related to educational and occupational experience.* Goteborg, Sweden: Acta Universitatis Gothoburgensis.

66. Berg, C. A. (2000). Intellectual development in adulthood. In R. J. Sternberg (Ed.), *Handbook of intelligence* (pp. 117–137). New York: Cambridge University Press.

67. Cotman, C. W., & Neeper, S. (1996). Activity-dependent plasticity and the aging brain. In E. L. Schneider & J. W. Rowe (Eds.), *Handbook of the biology of aging* (4th ed., pp. 283–299). San Diego, CA: Academic Press.

68. Colcombe, S. J., Erickson, K. I., Raz, N., Webb, A. G., Cohen, N. J., McAuley, E., & Kramer, A. F. (2003). Aerobic fitness reduces brain tissue loss in aging humans. *Journal of Gerontology, 58A*(2), 176–180.

69. Staudinger, U. M., & Glück, J. (2011). Intelligence and wisdom. In R. J. Sternberg & S. B. Kaufman (Eds.), *The Cambridge handbook of intelligence* (pp. 827–846). New York: Cambridge University Press

70. Yang, S., & Sternberg, R. J. (1997). Conceptions of intelligence in ancient Chinese philosophy. *Journal of Theoretical and Philosophical Psychology, 17,* 101–119.Yang, S. & Sternberg, R. J. (1997). Taiwanese Chinese people's conceptions of intelligence. *Intelligence, 25,* 21–36.

71. Scarr-Salapatek, S., & Williams, M. L. (1973). The effects of early stimulation on low-birth-weight infants. *Child Development, 44,* 94–101.

72. Dawe, H. C. (1942). A study of the effect of an educational program upon language development and related mental functions in young children. *Journal of Experimental Education, 11,* p. 208.

73. Klaus, R. A., & Gray, S. W. (1968). The Early Training Project for disadvantaged children: A report after five years. *Monographs for the Society for Research in Child Development, 33*(4).

74. Page, E. B., & Grandon, G. M. (1981). Massive intervention and child intelligence: The Milwaukee Project in critical perspective. *The Journal of Special Education, 15,* p. 240.

75. Garber, H., & Heber, R. (1982). Modification of predicted cognitive development in high-risk children through early intervention. In D. K. Detterman & R. J. Sternberg (Eds.), *How and how much can intelligence be increased* (pp. 121–137). Norwood, NJ: Ablex.

76. Garber, H. L. (1988). *The Milwaukee Project: Preventing mental retardation in children at risk.* Washington, DC: American Association on Mental Retardation.

77. Page, E. B. (1972). Physical miracle in Milwaukee? *Educational Researcher, 2,* 2, 4.

78. Zigler, E., Styfco, S. J., & Gilman, E. (1993). The national Head Start program for disadvantaged preschoolers. In E. Zigler & S. J. Styfco (Eds.), *Head Start and beyond: A national plan for extended childhood intervention* (pp. 1–41). New Haven, CT: Yale University Press.

79. Datta, L. (1976). The impact of the Westinghouse/Ohio evaluation of the development of Project Head Start. In C. C. Abt (Ed.), *The evaluation of social programs* (pp. 129–190). Beverly Hills, CA: Sage.

80. Smith, M. S., & Bissell, J. S. (1970). Report analysis: The impact of Head Start. *Harvard Educational Review, 40,* 51–104.

81. Haskins, R. (1989). Beyond metaphor: The efficacy of early childhood education. *American Psychologist, 44,* 274–282.

82. Ramey, C. T., MacPhee, D., & Yeates, K. O. (1982). Preventing developmental retardation: A general systems model. In D. K. Detterman & R. J. Sternberg (Eds.), *How and how much can intelligence be increased* (pp. 67–119). Norwood, NJ: Ablex.

83. Binet, A. (1911). *Les idees modernes sur les enfants*. Paris: Flammarion, p. 111. Cited in Cianciolo, A. T., & Sternberg, R. J. (2004). *Intelligence: A brief history*. Malden, MA: Blackwell.

84. Cianciolo, A. T., & Sternberg, R. J. (2004). *Intelligence: A brief history*. Malden, MA: Blackwell.

85. Nickerson, R. S. (1986). Project Intelligence: An account and some reflections. *Special Services in the Schools, 3*(1–2), 83–102.

86. Harvard University. (1983, October). *Project Intelligence Overview: The development of procedures to enhance thinking skills*. Final Report, submitted to the Minister for the Development of Human Intelligence, Republic of Venezuela.

87. Herrnstein, R. J., Nickerson, R. S., de Sanchez, M. & Swets, J. A. (1986). Teaching thinking skills. *American Psychologist, 41*(11), 1283.

88. Herrnstein, R. J., & Murray, C. (1994). *The bell curve: Intelligence and class structure in American life*. New York: Free Press.

89. Herrnstein, R. J. (1987). Introduction, and the Venezuelan experiment. In D. N. Perkins, J. Lochhead, & J. Bishop (Eds.), *Thinking: The second international conference* (pp. 51–53). Hillsdale, NJ: Erlbaum, p. 53.

90. Feuerstein, R., Hoffman, M. B., Rand, Y., Jensen, M., Tzuriel, D., & Hoffman, D. B. (1986). Learning to learn: Mediated learning experiences and instrumental enrichment. *Special Services in the Schools, 39*(1–2), 49–82.

91. Rand, Y., Mintzker, Y., Miller, R., Hoffman, M. B., & Friedlender, Y. (1981). The instrumental enrichment program: Immediate and long-term effects. In P. Mittler (Ed.), *Frontiers of knowledge in mental retardation, Vol. 1: Proceedings of the fifth congress of IASSMDI—Social, educational and behavioral aspects* (pp. 141–152). Baltimore: University Park Press.

92. Feuerstein, R., Rand, Y., Hoffman, M., & Miller, R. (1980). *Instrumental enrichment: An intervention program for cognitive modifiability*. Baltimore: University Park Press.

93. Stankov, L. (1986). Kvashchev's experiment: Can we boost intelligence? *Intelligence, 10*, 209–230.

94. Schaie, K. W. (2005). *Developmental influences on adult intelligence: The Seattle Longitudinal Study*. New York: Oxford University Press.

95. Willis, S. L., & Nesselroade, C. S. (1990) Long-term effects of fluid ability training in old-old age. *Developmental Psychology, 26*(6), 905–910.

96. Willis, S. L., & Schaie, K. W. (1986). Training the elderly on the ability factors of spatial orientation and inductive reasoning. *Psychology and Aging, 1*(3), 239–247.

97. Mayer, R. E. (2000). Intelligence and education. In R. J. Sternberg (Ed.), *Handbook of intelligence* (pp. 519–533). New York: Cambridge University Press, p. 530.

CHAPTER 7

1. Davidson, J. E., & Downing, C. L. (2000). Contemporary models of intelligence. History of theories and measurements of intelligence. In R. J. Sternberg (Ed.), *Handbook of intelligence* (pp. 34–49). New York: Cambridge University Press.

2. Berg, C. A. (2000). Intellectual development in adulthood. In R. J. Sternberg (Ed.), *Handbook of intelligence* (pp. 117–137). New York: Cambridge University Press.

3. Berg, C. A. (2000). Intellectual development in adulthood. In R. J. Sternberg (Ed.), *Handbook of intelligence* (pp. 117–137). New York: Cambridge University Press.

4. Olson, D. R. (1976). Culture, technology, and intellect. In L. R. Resnick (Ed.), *The nature of intelligence* (pp. 189–202). Hillsdale, NJ: Erlbaum.

5. Rogoff, B. (1990). *Apprenticeship in thinking: Cognitive development in social context*. New York: Oxford University Press.

6. The "Big Five" personality superfactors are extraversion, neuroticism, conscientiousness, agreeableness, and openness (Bouchard, 1994). These factors have been referred to by various names in the personality research literature.Bouchard, T. J. (1994). Genes, environment, and personality. *Science, 264*, 1700–1701.

7. Zeidner, M., & Matthews, G. (2000). Intelligence and personality. In R. J. Sternberg (Ed.), *Handbook of intelligence* (pp. 581–610). New York: Cambridge University Press.

8. Goff, M., & Ackerman, P. L. (1992). Personality-intelligence relations: Assessment of typical intellectual engagement. *Journal of Educational Psychology, 84*(4), 537–552.

9. Landy, F. J., Shankster, L. J., & Kohler, S. S. (1994). Personnel selection and placement. *Annual Review of Psychology, 45*, 261–296.

10. The correlation of IQ with conscientiousness is about $r = .02$.Zeidner, M., & Matthews, G. (2000). Intelligence and personality. In R. J. Sternberg (Ed.), *Handbook of intelligence* (pp. 581–610). New York: Cambridge University Press.

11. Schmidt, F. L., & Hunter, J. E. (1998). The validity and utility of selection methods in personnel psychology: Practical and theoretical implications of 85 years of research findings. *Psychological Bulletin, 124*, 262–274.

12. Barrick, M. R., Mount, M. K., & Judge, T. A. (2001). Personality and performance at the beginning of the new millennium: What do we know and where do we go next? *International Journal of Selection and Assessment, 9*, 9–30.

13. Barrick, M. R., & Mount, M. (1993). Autonomy as a moderator of the relationships between the big five personality dimensions and job performance. *Journal of Applied Psychology, 78*, 111–118.

14. Conard, M. A. (2006). Aptitude is not enough: How personality and behavior predict academic performance. *Journal of Research in Personality, 40*, 339–346.

15. Renzulli, J. S. (1986). The three-ring conception of giftedness: A developmental model of creative productivity. In R. J. Sternberg & J. E. Davidson (Eds.), *Conceptions of giftedness* (pp. 53–92). New York: Cambridge University Press, p. 75.

16. Duckworth, A. L., & Seligman, M. E. P. (2005). Self-discipline outdoes IQ in predicting academic performance of adolescents. *Psychological Science, 16*, 939–944. Note: Self-discipline can be considered a separate personality dimension than conscientiousness, but because they share overlapping qualities, and for the sake of simplicity, both are treated here under the banner of conscientiousness.

17. Ackerman, P. J., & Heggestad, E. D. (1997). Intelligence, personality, and interests: Evidence for overlapping traits. *Psychological Bulletin, 121*, 219–245. Graham, J. D. (2011). *Elements of human effectiveness: Intelligences, traits, and*

abilities that lead to success and fulfillment in life. (Unpublished doctoral dissertation). University of California, Irvine.

18. Kyllonen, P. (1997). Smart testing. In R. Dillon (Ed.), *Handbook on testing* (pp. 347–369). Westport, CT: Greenwood.

19. Twenge, J. M. (2001). Birth cohort changes in extraversion: A cross-temporal meta-analysis, 1966–1993. *Personality and Individual Differences, 30,* 735–748.

20. Mischel, W. (1973). Toward a cognitive social learning reconceptualization of personality. *Psychological Review, 80,* 252–283.

21. Twenge, J. M. (2001). Birth cohort changes in extraversion: A cross-temporal meta-analysis, 1966–1993. *Personality and Individual Differences, 30,* 735–748.

22. Zeidner, M., & Matthews, G. (2000). Intelligence and personality. In R. J. Sternberg (Ed.), *Handbook of intelligence* (pp. 581–610). New York: Cambridge University Press.

23. Ackerman, P. L. (2011). Intelligence and expertise. In R. J. Sternberg & S. B. Kaufman (Eds.), *The Cambridge handbook of intelligence* (pp. 847–860). New York: Cambridge University Press.

24. Schank, R. C., & Towle, B. (2000). Artificial intelligence. In R. J. Sternberg (Ed.), *Handbook of intelligence* (pp. 341–356). New York: Cambridge University Press, p. 354.

25. Newell, A., & Simon, H. A. (1972). *Human problem solving.* Englewood Cliffs, NJ: Prentice-Hall.

26. de Groot, A. (1965). *Thought and choice in chess.* The Hague: Mouton.

27. Rivera, S. M., Reiss A. L., Eckert, M. A., & Menon, V. (2005). Developmental changes in mental arithmetic: Evidenced for increased functional specialization in the left inferior parietal cortex. *Cerebral Cortex, 15,* 1779–1790.

28. Haier, R. J., Jung, R. E., Yeo, R. A., Head, K., & Alkire, M. T. (2004). Structural brain variation and general intelligence. *NeuroImage, 23,* 425–433.

29. Case, R. (1991). *The mind's staircase: Exploring the conceptual underpinnings of children's thought and knowledge.* Hillsdale, NJ: Erlbaum.

30. Chen, Z., & Siegler, R. S. (2000). Intellectual development in childhood. In R. J. Sternberg (Ed.), *Handbook of intelligence* (pp. 92–116). New York: Cambridge University Press.

31. Murphy, P. K., & Mason, L. (2006). Changing knowledge and beliefs. In P. A. Alexander & P. H. Winne (Eds.), *Handbook of educational psychology* (2nd ed., pp. 305–324). Mahwah, NJ: Erlbaum.

32. Snow, C. E., Burns, M. S., & Griffin, P. (1998). *Preventing reading difficulties in young children.* Washington, DC: National Academy Press.

33. Paris, S. G., Morrison, F. J., & Miller, K. F. (2006). Academic pathways from preschool through elementary school. In P. A. Alexander & P. H. Winne (Eds.), *Handbook of educational psychology* (2nd ed., pp. 61–85). Mahwah, NJ: Erlbaum.

34. Rayner, K., Foorman, B. R., Perfetti, C., Pesetsky, D., & Seidenberg, M. S. (2002, March). How should reading be taught? *Scientific American, 286,* 84–91.

35. Just, M. A., & Carpenter, P. A. (1980). A theory of reading: From eye fixations to comprehension. *Psychological Review, 87,* 329–354.

36. Pressley, M. (2002). *Reading instruction that works: The case for balanced teaching* (2nd ed.). New York: Guilford Press.

37. Carver, R. P. (1990). *Reading rate: A review of research and theory.* San Diego, CA: Academic Press.

38. Cunningham, A. E., & Stanovich, K. E., Wilson, M. R. (1990). Cognitive variation in adult students differing in reading ability. In T. H. Carr & B. A. Levy

(Eds.), *Reading and its development: Component skills approaches* (pp. 129–159). New York: Academic Press.

39. Lohman, D. F. (2000). Complex information processing and intelligence. In R. J. Sternberg (Ed.), *Handbook of intelligence* (pp. 285–340). New York: Cambridge University Press.

40. Chi, M. T. H., Feltovich, P. J., & Glaser, R. (1981). Categorization and representation of physics problems by experts and novices. *Cognitive Science, 5,* 121–152.

41. Coughlin, L. D., & Patel, V. L. (1987). Processing of critical information by physicians and medical students. *Journal of Medical Education, 62,* 818–828.

42. Simon, H. A. (1980). Problem solving and education. In D. T. Tuma & F. Reif (Eds.), *Problem solving and education: Issues in teaching and research* (pp. 81–96). Hillsdale, NJ: Erlbaum, p. 82.

43. Simon, H. A. (1991, Fall). The cat that curiosity couldn't kill. *Carnegie Mellon Magazine, 10*(1), 35–36, p. 36.

44. Ross, P. E. (2006). The expert mind. *Scientific American, 295*(2), 64–71.

45. Howe, M. J. A. (1999). *Genius explained.* New York: Cambridge University Press.

46. Howe, M. J. A. (1999). *Genius explained.* New York: Cambridge University Press.

47. Roe, A. (1953). *The making of a scientist.* New York: Dodd, Mead, p. 170.

48. Ackerman, P. L. (2011). Intelligence and expertise. In R. J. Sternberg & S. B. Kaufman (Eds.), *The Cambridge handbook of intelligence* (pp. 847–860). New York: Cambridge University Press.

49. Marshall, A. (2003, February 17). Small wonders. *Time (Asia). 161*(7). http://www.time.com/time/magazine/article/0,9171,421085,00.html.

50. Bloom, B. S. (1985). Generalizations about talent development. In B. S. Bloom (Ed.), *Developing talent in young people* (pp. 507–549). New York: Ballantine.

51. Sosniak, L. A. (1985). A long-term commitment to learning. In B. S. Bloom (Ed.), *Developing talent in young people* (pp. 477–506). New York: Ballantine.

52. Sloane, K. D. (1985). Home influences in talent development. In B. S. Bloom (Ed.), Developing talent in young people (pp. 439–476). New York: Ballantine.

53. Rogoff, B. (1990). *Apprenticeship in thinking: Cognitive development in social context.* New York: Oxford University Press.

54. Tacit knowledge that takes the form of skilled behavior is sometimes called implicit knowledge, a product of implicit learning.

55. Mackintosh, N. J. (1998). *IQ and human intelligence.* New York: Oxford University Press.

56. Block, M. (2005, November 8). Behind the scenes with film editor Walter Murch. In Michele Norris (Producer), *All Things Considered.* Washington, DC: NPR.

57. Polanyi, M. (1958). *Personal knowledge: Towards a post-critical philosophy.* Chicago: University of Chicago Press.

58. Ericsson, K. A. (1996). The acquisition of expert performance: An introduction to some of the issues. In K. A. Ericsson (Ed.), *The road to excellence: The acquisition of expert performance in the arts and sciences, sports, and games* (pp. 1–50). Mahwah, NJ: Erlbaum.

59. Schraw, G. (2006). Knowledge: Structures and processes. In P. A. Alexander & P. H. Winne (Eds.), *Handbook of educational psychology* (2nd ed., pp. 245–263). Mahwah, NJ: Erlbaum.

60. Ericsson, K. A., Krampe, R. T., & Tesch-Römer, C. (1993). The role of deliberate practice in the acquisition of expert performance. *Psychological Review, 100,* 363–406.

61. Simonton, D. K. (1996). Creative expertise: A life-span developmental perspective. In K. A. Ericsson (Ed.), *The road to excellence: The acquisition of expert performance in the arts and sciences, sports, and games* (pp. 227–253). Mahwah, NJ: Erlbaum.

62. Grotzer, T. A. & Perkins, D. N. (2000). Teaching intelligence: A performance conception. In R. J. Sternberg (Ed.), *Handbook of intelligence* (pp. 492–515). New York: Cambridge University Press.

63. Spearman, C. (1927). *The abilities of man.* New York: Macmillan.

64. Embretson, S. E., & Schmidt McCollam, K. M. (2000). Psychometric approaches to understanding and measuring intelligence. In R. J. Sternberg (Ed.), *Handbook of intelligence* (pp. 423–444). New York: Cambridge University Press.

65. Daniel, M. H. (2000). Interpretation of intelligence test scores. In R. J. Sternberg (Ed.), *Handbook of intelligence* (pp. 477–491). New York: Cambridge University Press.

66. Ceci, S. J. (1996). *On intelligence: A bioecological treatise on intellectual development* (Expanded edition). Cambridge, MA: Harvard University Press.

67. Bereiter, C., & Scardamalia, M. (1993). *Surpassing ourselves.* Peru, IL: Open Court.

68. Ericsson, K. A., & Charness, N. (1994). Expert performance: Its structure and acquisition. *American Psychologist, 49,* 725–747.

69. Feldman, D. H. (1986). Giftedness as a developmentalist sees it. In R. J. Sternberg & J. E. Davidson (Eds.), *Conceptions of giftedness* (pp. 285–305). New York: Cambridge University Press.

70. Jensen, A. R. (1996). Giftedness and genius: Crucial differences. In C. P. Benbow & D. Lubinski (Eds.), *Intellectual talent: Psychometric and social issues* (pp. 393–411). Baltimore, MD: Johns Hopkins University Press.

71. Nasar, S. (2001). *A beautiful mind: The life of mathematical genius and Nobel laureate John Nash.* New York: Touchstone.

72. http://www.pbs.org/wgbh/amex/nash/sfeature/sf_nash.html

73. Eysenck, H. J. (1998). *Intelligence: A new look.* New Brunswick, NJ: Transaction.

74. Binet, A. (1911). *Les idees modernes sur les enfants.* Paris: Flammarion.

75. Snow, R. E., & Lohman, D. F. (1989). Implications of cognitive psychology for educational measurement. In R. L. Linn (Ed.), *Educational measurement* (3rd ed.), pp. 263–331. New York: Macmillan.

76. Gray, J. R., & Thompson, P. M. (2004). Neurobiology of intelligence: Science and ethics. *Nature Reviews: Neuroscience, 5,* 471–482. The ambiguity is a consequence of how the mathematical analysis of psychometric data is interpreted.

77. Sternberg, R. J. (1998). Abilities are forms of developing expertise. *Educational Researcher, 27,* 11–20.

CHAPTER 8

1. Brandtstadter, J., & Greve, W. (1994). The aging self: Stability and protective processes. *Developmental Review, 14,* 52–80.

2. Olson, D. R. (1976) Culture, technology, and intellect. In L. R. Resnick (Ed.), *The nature of intelligence* (pp. 189–202). Hillsdale, NJ: Erlbaum.

3. Cunningham, A. E., & Stanovich, K. E. (1998). *What reading does for the mind.* American Educator, 22(1&2), 8–15.

4. Ackerman, P. L. (2011). Intelligence and expertise. In R. J. Sternberg & S. B. Kaufman (Eds.), *The Cambridge handbook of intelligence* (pp. 847–860). New York: Cambridge University Press.

5. Berg, C. A. (2000). Intellectual development in adulthood. In R. J. Sternberg (Ed.), *Handbook of intelligence* (pp. 117–137). New York: Cambridge University Press.

6. Grotzer, T. A. & Perkins, D. N. (2000). Teaching intelligence: A performance conception. In R. J. Sternberg (Ed.), *Handbook of intelligence* (pp. 492–515). New York: Cambridge University Press.

7. Berg, C. A. (2000). Intellectual development in adulthood. In R. J. Sternberg (Ed.), *Handbook of intelligence* (pp. 117–137). New York: Cambridge University Press.

8. Dickens, W. T., & Flynn, J. R. (2001). Heritability estimates versus large environmental effects: The IQ paradox resolved. *Psychological Review, 108*(2), 346–369, p. 347.

9. Rogoff, B. (1990). *Apprenticeship in thinking: Cognitive development in social context.* New York: Oxford University Press.

10. Baltes, P. B., & Staudinger, U. M. (Eds.). *Interactive minds: Life-span perspectives on the social foundations of cognition.* New York: Cambridge University Press.

11. Harris, J. R. (1995). Where is the child's environment? A group socialization theory of development. *Psychological Review, 102*(3), 458–489.

12. Kretchmer, N., Beard, J. L., & Carlson, S. (1996). The role of nutrition in the development of normal cognition. *American Journal of Clinical Nutrition, 63,* 997S–1001S.

13. Iyoti, D. F., Frongillo, E. A., & Jones, S. J. (2005). Food insecurity affects children's academic performance, weight gain, and social skills. *The Journal of Nutrition, 135,* 2831–2839.

14. Isaacs, K. R., Anderson, B. J., Alcantara, A. A., Black, J. E., & Greenough, W. T. (1992). Exercise and the brain: Angiogenesis in the adult rat cerebellum after vigorous physical activity in motor skill learning. *Journal of Cerebral Blood Flow & Metabolism, 12,* 110–119.

15. Rhyu, I. J., Boklewski, J., Ferguson, B., Lee, K., Lange, H. Bytheway, J., Lamb, J., McCormick, K., Williams, N., Cameron, J., & Greenough, W. T. (2003). Exercise training associated with increased cortical vascularization in adult female cynomolgus monkeys. *Society for Neuroscience Abstracts, 29,* 920–921.

16. Kramer, A. F., Bherer, B., Colcombe, S. J., Dong, W., & Greenough, W. T. (2004). Environmental influences on cognitive and brain plasticity during aging. *Journal of Gerontology, 59A*(9), 940–957.

17. Hillman, C. H., Weiss, E. P., Hagberg, J. M., & Hatfield, B. D. (2002). The relationship of age and cardiovascular fitness to cognitive and motor processes. *Psychophysiology, 39,* 303–312.

18. Hart, B., & Risley, T. R. (1995). *Meaningful differences in the everyday experiences of young American children.* Baltimore: Brookes.

19. Martinez, M. E., & Lahart, C. (1990). *Profile: Student background characteristics from the 1986 and 1988 NAEP assessments.* Research Report No. RR-90-20. Princeton, NJ: Educational Testing Service.

20. Thompson, A. M., Humbert, M. L., & Mirwald, R. L. (2003). A longitudinal study of the impact of childhood and adolescent physical activity experiences on adult physical activity perceptions and behaviors. *Qualitative Health Research, 13*(3), 358–377.

21. Ramey, S. L., & Ramey, C. T. (1992). Early education intervention with disadvantaged children—To what effect? *Applied and Preventive Psychology, 1*, 131–140, p. 136.
22. Hedges, L. V., & Nowell, A. (1998). Black-White test score convergence since 1965. In C. Jencks & M. Phillips (Eds.), *The Black-White test score gap* (pp. 149–181). Washington, DC: Brookings Institution.
23. Lin, X., Schwarz, D. L., & Hatano, G. (2005). Toward teachers' adaptive metacognition. *Educational Psychologist, 40*(4), 245–255.
24. Snow, R. E. (with Yalow, E.). (1982). Education and intelligence. In R. J. Sternberg (Ed.), *Handbook of human intelligence* (pp. 493–585). New York: Cambridge University Press.
25. Ramey, C. T., & Ramey, S. L. (2000). Intellectual and public policy. In R. J. Sternberg (Ed.), *Handbook of intelligence* (pp. 534–548). New York: Cambridge University Press.
26. Sternberg, R. J. (2000). Intelligence and wisdom. In R. J. Sternberg (Ed.), *Handbook of intelligence* (pp. 631–649). New York: Cambridge University Press.
27. Dickens, W. T., & Flynn, J. R. (2001). Heritability estimates versus large environmental effects: The IQ paradox resolved. *Psychological Review, 108*(2), 346–369.

INDEX

bilateral symmetry in brain, 93
Binet, Alfred
    complex reasoning *vs.* perception
        and reaction time, 41
    human intelligence studies, 10, 13,
        45–46, 85, 148
    intellectual abilities *vs.* success, 232
    intellectual enhancement program,
        187
    intelligence tests and, 6–7, 9, 11
    inventiveness and, 231
    IQ tests and, 259
    successful intelligence connection
        to, 51
birth order and IQ, 177–178
"black box" in psychometrics, 112
Boaz, Franz, 69
bodily-kinesthetic intelligence, 48, 49
book reading and crystallized
        intelligence, 240–241
Braille reader studies, 101
brain functioning. *See also* frontal lobe;
        memory; neurons
    adaptation, 102
    brain waves, 103–105, 105*f*, 117
    cerebral cortex in, 88, 90
    cognitive theory, 111–114
    critical thinking, 123–126
    of Einstein, Albert, 87–88
    four lobe structure and, 90–91, 90*f*
    frontal cortex, 92, 101, 212
    hormones and, 140
    intelligence and, 95–97, 126–128
    left and right hemispheres, 93–95
    metabolism, 105–106
    metacognition, 122–123
    modes of perception, 110–111
    neurotrophins and, 180
    nutrition impact on, 156
    overview, 87–88
    plasticity and, 93, 100–101
    prefrontal cortex, 92–93, 123
    problem solving and, 119–121, 123
    size and IQ, 88–89, 100, 103
    somatosensory cortex, 101
    structure and IQ, 90–93, 90*f*
    10% myth, 96–97
brain-imaging technologies, 49–50, 89,
        95–96
brain injury studies, 49, 60, 169

brain plasticity. *See* plasticity in brain
brain waves, 103–105, 105*f*, 117
breastfeeding and infant development,
        158–159, 247
British Security Service, 28
Broca, Paul Pierre, 93, 96
Brontë, Branwell, 218
Brontë, Charlotte, Emily, Anne, 17, 218
Brown v. Board of Education (1954), 167
brute-force technique of artificial
        intelligence, 81
Buonarroti, Michelangelo, 17, 246

canal boat children, 163–164
Carnegie, Dale, 96–97
Carroll, John, 27, 86, 231
Case, Robbie, 212
Cattell, Raymond, 26
Central Intelligence Agency (CIA), 28
central sulcus in brain, 92
cerebral cortex in brain, 88, 90
cerebral hemispheres. *See* left
        hemisphere; right hemisphere
Chaos (chess-playing computer
        program), 81
chatterbots (human conversation
        imitation program), 82–83
chess playing
    aptitude for, 30
    chunking in, 211–213
    computer programs for, 79, 80–81, 84
    experts in, 209, 210, 221
    intelligence and, 239
    talent for, 219–220
children/child development
    after exposure to trauma, 188–189
    at-risk children and IQ, 181
    canal boat children, 163–164
    chronological age studies, 7–8
    chunking in, 212
    cognitive ability in, 189
    education of mother, 171, 175
    high-IQs in, 14–15, 17
    increasing intelligence in, 187–190
    intelligence in adulthood *vs.*, 14
    linguistic interaction and IQ, 175, 180
    low-IQs, 12, 15
    parental role in, 171–172, 174–176
    talent development in, 219–221
    toxin exposure, 157–158

trauma exposure and, 188–189
vitamin supplementation and, 156
chimpanzee studies, 75–76
Chinese Room experiment, 82, 84
Chiptest (chess-playing computer program), 81
chronological age studies in children, 7–8
chunks/chunking in learning, 211–215
cognitive ability
    brain injuries and, 49
    in children, 189
    cognitive achievement *vs.*, 232
    educational achievement, 165, 167
    enrichment programs for, 150
    gender differences in, 138–139
    improvements to, 181, 185
    intelligent thought and, 73, 112
    multiple intelligences theory, 50
    nutrition impact on, 156
    personality profiles and, 206–207
    racial differences in, 135–136
    social intelligence, 60
cognitive decline, 179, 190
cognitive development
    adulthood IQ changes, 178–180
    breastfeeding and, 158–159
    of canal boat children, 163–164
    factors affecting, 138
    job impact on, 178–179
    socioeconomic status (SES) and, 173–174, 176–177, 177f
cognitive flexibility, 38–29
cognitive modifiability, 189
cognitive theory of brain functioning, 111–114
Cognitive Training Study, 190–191
Coleridge, Samuel Taylor, 17
complex cognition, 50, 96, 123
complexity of life, 161–162
computation. *See* thinking skills
computer technology
    as cognitive process comparison, 112–113
    gaming and, 161
    to leverage intellect, 66
connectionist computational model, 79–80
conscientiousness, 204–206, 242–243
constitutional predispositions of talent, 146–147

conversation imitation programs, 82–83
Copernicus, Nicolas, 17
corpus callosum of brain, 94
covariance in genetics, 146–148
Cox, Catherine, 17
Cray Blitz (chess-playing computer program), 81
creative genius, 228–231
creative intelligence, 52, 54–58
critical thinking
    increase in, 183
    memory strategies, 242
    overview, 123–126
    parental role, 172
    text exposure and, 201
Croatia, 190
crystallized intelligence
    in AI programs, 84–85, 209
    book reading and, 240–241
    brain size and, 89
    brain structure and, 92
    effectiveness and, 196, 200–202, 208
    genius and, 229
    importance of, 85
    increases in, 153
    intellectually challenging job and, 179
    IQ and, 149, 170
    narrowness of, 47
    over life span, 37f
    overview, 28–31, 34–39
    schools and, 254
    teaching and testing of, 199
    through book reading, 240–241
    verbal ability, 28, 232
CT scans, 89, 105, 111
culture and intelligence, 68–73
"culture-free" tests, 72–73
cyberinfrastructure, 67

Darwin, Charles, 5, 6, 17, 213
da Vinci, Leonardo, 17, 213
Dawe, Helen, 182–183
decisional complexity, 161–162
Deep Blue (chess-playing computer program), 80–81, 83, 84
deliberate practice concept, 223–224
delinquency and IQ, 169
dementia, 56, 132
democratic parenting style, 175, 176
developing nations, IQ gains, 162

intellectual openness, 205–206
intelligence. *See also* g factor; nature *vs.*
  nurture; Raven's Matrices; social
  intelligence; spatial intelligence;
  success and intelligence
  benefit of, 19, 86
  biological basis of, 97–103, 99*f*
  brain and, 95–97
  brain waves and, 103–105, 105*f*
  broad quality of, 64, 86
  capitalizing on, 3
  in childhood *vs.* adulthood, 14
  computational activities and, 78
  diverse expressions in, 50
  education and, 162–163, 171–172
  environmental influences on, 155,
    175
  higher-order intellective functioning,
    90
  importance of, xviii, 126–128
  internal *vs.* external, 127
  IQ *vs.*, 86, 205
  job/workplace and, 13–14, 52–53,
    242
  measurement quality of, 64
  metabolism and, 105–106
  as modifiable, xiv, 128
  morality of, 15–16
  paradoxes of, 44–46
  parental role in intelligence,
    171–172, 174–176, 250–252
  practical intelligence, 52–54
  reproductive success and, 74–75
  school success, 10–13, 52
  self-challenge and, 39, 180, 239
  "street smarts," 53
  theories of, 48, 50, 85–86, 100, 229
  wage premiums and, 1–2
  wisdom and, 180
intelligence, defined
  crystallized intelligence, 28–31,
    34–39, 37*f*
  fluid intelligence, 28–31, 36, 37–39,
    37*f*
  genetics and, xviii, 5, 180
  hierarchical model of abilities,
    24–28, 26*f*
  overview, 21–22
  Raven's Matrices, 31–34, 31*f*, 44
  resolving paradoxes, 44–46

unity or diversity paradox, 22–24
  workforce of the 21st century, 39–40
intelligence, increasing. *See also*
  enhancing intelligence
  of adults, 190–191
  crystallized intelligence, 153
  fluid intelligence, 153
  Flynn effect and, 151–153, 155
  heritability of IQ and, 147
  of infants, 181–182
  knowledge of, 85
  learnable intelligence, 129, 192–193,
    233
  of preschoolers, 182–187, 192
  programs for, 180–181
  of school-age children, 187–190
  success of, 191–192
  in working memory, 115–116
intelligence, varieties. *See also* artificial
    intelligence
  analytical intelligence, 52, 55–57
  creative intelligence, 52, 54–58
  as culture bound, 68–73
  distributed intelligence, 65–68
  emotional intelligence, 62–65
  habits of mind, 73–74
  multiple intelligences, 48–51
  nonhuman intelligence, 74–78
  overview, 47–48
  social intelligence, 47–48, 58–62
  successful intelligence, 51–55
  theories of, 85–86
intelligence quotient (IQ). *See also*
    African-Americans and IQ;
    high-IQs; intelligence; low-IQs
  after college degree, 2
  bell curve computations of, 8–9
  brain metabolism, 105–106
  brain size and, 88–89, 100, 103
  brain structure and, 90–93, 90*f*, 92
  creativity and, 56–57
  in developing nations, 162
  EEG patterns and, 104
  fluxuation of, xviii–xiv, 18, 150–151
  genetics influence on, 129
  genius and, 229
  intelligence *vs.*, 86, 205
  like-minded relationships and, 245
  measurement of, 43
  popularity of, 11

intelligence quotient (IQ) (*cont.*)
  predictive power of, 13, 14
  as predictors of success, 21, 210
  quotient defined, 7–8
  synapses in brain and, 100
  tests for, 6–10, 151
  threshold hypothesis, 16–18
  unfortunate effects of, 11–12
  in workplace, 13–14, 256–257
intelligence quotient (IQ), and experience
  adulthood changes in, 178–180
  American military studies on,
    165–166
  breastfeeding and infant
    development, 158–159
  of canal boat children, 163–164
  complexity of life, 161–162
  education and, 162–163
  family size and birth order, 177–178
  home environment, 172–177, 177*f*
  mathematics curriculum studies,
    170–171
  media and information technologies,
    160–161
  nutrition and, 155–157, 159–160
  overview, 155
  programs to increase, 180–181
  schooling interruption and, 166–170
  socioeconomic status (SES) and,
    173–174, 176–177, 177*f*
  Swedish military studies on, 164–165
  toxin exposure, 157–158
intergenerational change in IQ,
  150–151, 153
International Health Exhibition
  (1884), 5
the Internet, 160–161
interpersonal intelligence, 48, 59
intrapersonal intelligence, 48
introverted personality, 203–204
Iowa Soldiers' Orphans' Home, 182–183
IQ heritability. *See* heritability of IQ

James, William, 96–97
Jefferson, Thomas, 17, 258
Jennings, Ken, 83–84
Jeopardy! (TV show), 83–84
job/workplace
  cognitive development and, 178–179
  fluid intelligence, 198

intelligence, defined, 39–40
  intelligence and, 13–14, 52–53, 242
  IQ and, 13–14, 256–257
Johnson, Lyndon, 185
judicial process thinking, 125–126
juggling studies, 102

Kasparov, Gary, 81
Kenyan educational differences, 70–71
Key, Wilson, 118
knowledge
  education and, 162
  of experts, 210
  findings on, 57–58
  published knowledge, 67
  schema development in, 213
  "street smarts," 53
  tacit knowledge, 53–54, 222–223
known-answer give-and-take discourse,
  175
Kpelle man, 68, 70
Kvashchev, Radivoy, 190

lag correlations and IQ, 174
language
  in animals, 76
  in artificial intelligence, 80
  of books, 200–202
  culture and, 69
  defined, 212
  dysfunction and artistic skill, 56
  experiences and education, 171–172
  of intelligence theory, 229
  male-female differences in, 140–141
  processing in brain, 93
  role in human intelligence, 127
  written language, 67, 201
Lashley, Karl, 96–97
learnable intelligence, 129, 192–193,
  233, 254
learning
  chunks/chunking in, 211–212
  defined, 117
  differences in social classes, 168–169
  from experience, 105–106
  maturation in, 149, 168
  mediated learning principle, 189
  novice learners, 209
  nutrition and, 159–160
  self-directed learners, 39, 178, 242

socioeconomic status (SES) and IQ, 173–174, 176–177, 177*f*
somatosensory cortex, 101
Son, Nguyen Ngoc Truong, 219–220
spatial intelligence
    "black box" in psychometrics, 112
    brain functioning and, 93, 101
    cognitive ability and, 136
    defined, 48–49
    importance of, 71–72, 85–86
    increases in, 190–191
    in job/workforce, 179
    male-female differences in, 139–141
    mental rotation tasks, 139*f*
    the radex and, 231
spatial location memory, 140
Spearman, Charles, 49
    g factor, 22–26, 26*f*, 45
    human intelligence studies, 86, 112
    inductive reasoning and, 197
    perseverance and, 226
speed reading, 214–215
split brain patients, 94–95
standard deviation units, 9, 43
Stanford-Binet IQ scale, 9, 11, 14
Stern, Wilhelm, 7–8, 11
Sternberg, Robert, 51–55, 70, 233
stimulus materials, 59, 240
stimulus-response event, 103–104, 105*f*, 122
strategy in problem solving, 120–121
"street smarts," 53
strong AI (artificial intelligence), 79, 81–82
subgoals in problem solving, 33, 120–121
subliminal advertising, 118–119
Subliminal Seduction (Key), 118
success and intelligence
    conscientiousness and, 204
    first intelligence tests, 6–10
    IQ as predictor of, 21, 210
    life and, 14–16
    measuring the mind, 4–6
    metacognition and, 122–123
    overview, 1–4
    schools and, 10–13
    threshold hypothesis, 16–19
    workplace and, 13–14

successful intelligence theory, 51–55
summer vacation and learning, 168
Swedish military studies on IQ, 164–165
symbol-processing computer, 79
symbol systems, 49, 80
synapses (neuronal connections), 99–100, 99*f*, 102
synesthesia, 110–111

tacit knowledge, 53–54, 222–223
talent
    expertise and, 218–219, 228
    extreme talent in youth, 219–221
    giftedness, 5, 30, 181
    importance of, 244
    nature *vs.* nurture in, 146–147
TD-Gammon (backgammon program), 81
teacher role in enhancing intelligence, 252–256
technician expert, 228
teenage intelligence variability, 149
television exposure, 160–161, 251
temporal lobe in brain, 56, 90, 90*f*, 93, 102, 107
10% myth of brain, 96–97
10-year rule in expertise, 217–219
Terman, Lewis
    high-IQ children study, 17
    human intelligence studies, 85, 148, 226
    IQ tests and, 10–11, 13, 14
test anxiety, 62
theories of intelligence, 48, 50, 85–86, 100, 229
theory of evolution, 5
"theory of mind," 61
The Thinker sculpture, 62
thinking skills. *See also* critical thinking; higher-order thinking
    algorithmic thinking, 199
    cognitive ability and, 73, 112
    coherence in, 125
    flexible thinking, 179–180, 229
    increasing in preschoolers, 184
    judicial process thinking, 125–126
    neurons and, 98
    value of, 73–74

THE TAKING

WITHDRAWN
FOR SALE

3 8002 02242 349 7

Also by Kimberly Derting

THE BODY FINDER
DESIRES OF THE DEAD
THE LAST ECHO
DEAD SILENCE

THE REPLACED